THE COMPLETE FAMILY ALBUM

GUIDING LIGHT

The Complete Family Album

BY JULIE POLL

WITH CAELIE M. HAINES

General Publishing Group Los Angeles

Publisher: W. Quay Hays
Editorial Director: Peter L. Hoffman
Art Directors: Chitra Sekhar, Maritta Tapanainen
Production Director: Trudihope Schlomowitz
Color and Pre-Press Manager: Bill Castillo
Production Assistants: Tom Archibeque, Lisa Barnes, David Chadderdon, Gus Dawson,
Russel Lockwood, Phillis Stacy
Copy Editors: Amy Spitalnick, Dianne Woo

For information:
General Publishing Group, Inc.
2701 Ocean Park Boulevard, Suite 140
Santa Monica, CA 90405

Library of Congress Cataloging-in-Publication Data

Poll, Julie
    Guiding light : the complete family album / by Julie Poll with
Caelie M. Haines.
        p.   cm.
    ISBN 1-57544-006-7
    1. Guiding light (Television program)   I. Haines. Caelie M.
II. Title.
PN1992.77.G83P66   1997
791.45'72—dc21   97-10865
                                                                        CIP

Printed in the USA by RR Donnelley & Sons Company
10 9 8 7 6 5 4 3 2 1

GENERAL PUBLISHING GROUP

Los Angeles

TABLE OF CONTENTS

INTRODUCTION

"I created 'Guiding Light' with one fundamental theme in mind: the brotherhood of man." So wrote the show's creator, Irna Phillips, in 1937. Who could've imagined that that breathtakingly simple intention, written at the beginning of FDR's second term as president, would carry the show to its 60th anniversary in 1997? In a business so transient that more and more often it seems to measure its merit and fame in 15-minute increments, "Guiding Light's" six decades of broadcasting—roughly 16,000 episodes— is all the more remarkable. The show's longevity outstrips anything ever done in theatrical history.

"Guiding Light's" 60-year milestone, however, is not just a broadcasting benchmark but a story-telling asset to its audience. Its achievement allows the show to thrive in a self-created artistic atmosphere unique in all of storytelling. Today the show continues not only to reflect life but also to parallel it in real time. Birth, childhood, maturity, courtship, marriage, regeneration, old age, death and all the rituals that accompany them resonate to the clockwork of real months and years, adding a depth and poignancy that other art forms can only simulate.

As Ross Marler, a third-generation character, I have been featured on the show for nearly 20 years and, like my castmates, I'm honored to help continue telling a tale whose seed was planted by preceding generations of actors. I'm also both mystified and grateful that a television show can affect so many people so forcefully for so long.

Over the years I've discussed the show with thousands of fans not only from the United States but also from Canada, Great Britain, Italy, Germany, the Caribbean nations and elsewhere. While talking with them, it often occurs to me that Irna Phillips was quite correct when she had the show's very first character, the Rev. Ruthledge, preach, "There is a destiny that makes us all family, one family, God's family."

To remember the past and create a legacy for the future, families cherish keepsakes, mementos, scrapbooks and that most treasured possession, the family album. Here is our family album.

Jerry ver Dorn

ACKNOWLEDGMENTS

The challenge of writing a book commemorating the longest running daytime drama in broadcast history is awesome, exciting and indeed, an honor. Many people gave generously of their time and their energy to see that "Guiding Light" was properly celebrated in this special anniversary book. First to CBS and Procter & Gamble Productions for bringing us this exceptional program for a landmark 60 years, with special thanks to Lucy Johnson, Senior VP Daytime/Children's Programming and Special Projects, CBS, and Wendy Fishman, Director of Daytime Programs New York, and Mary Alice Dwyer-Dobbin, Executive in Charge of Production, Procter & Gamble, for their enthusiastic support. I also wish to thank the publicity department of DMB&B, who made reams of information available and contributed their knowledge and expertise: Janet Storm, Liz Susman Karp, Susan Savage, Maria Ferrari and their staffs and to Cindy Marshall and Jennifer Maloney for their cheerful and willing assistance.

My special thanks to executive producer Paul Rauch for opening the doors of the "Guiding Light" studios and allowing me all important access, and for his insights into the heartbeat and soul of the show.

This mammoth task could not have been completed without the extraordinary contributions of Fritz Brekeller and John Kelly Genovese. To Fritz, who put together enormous amounts of material with care and sensitivity, organized researchers, scheduled hard-to-get interviews, used his invaluable production skills to guide us through our day "Behind the Scenes," and his work on a cast list that harks back to the '30s, many, many thanks. Writer/researcher John Kelly Genovese helped to form the 60-year story of "Guiding Light" with insight and talent and great care. For his contributions to the chronology, the cast list and much more, thank you John!

To the actors, producers, writers, directors and crew of "Guiding Light" past and present, who gave so graciously of their time and shared their invaluable insights. A special thank you to Lisa Randolph who sought out pictures, props, tapes and scripts; worked on the chronology; spent weekends organizing stacks of research materials; and was constantly checking in to see if I needed something, which I always did. To "Guiding Light" writer's assistant Jill Lorie Hurst for her expert help and hospitality, and production coordinators Wally White, David Kreizman and

Natasha Katzive, who also doubled as photographer when needed.

To John Brehens at the CBS Archives, John Filo at the CBS Photo Department and Robert Christie of the National Academy of Television Arts and Sciences for their time and their help and to Ed Rider, head of Procter & Gamble archives in Cincinnati for making his resources readily available. A very special thank you to Jennifer Dakroub who traveled to Wisconsin to scour Irna Phillips' scripts and summarize her wonderful stories, for her fine work and her dedication to this project. To Jennifer Mader, who took over in a pinch, as did the Bernstein sisters, Laura and Jill. My thanks to the people who helped put together the chronology: Danielle Page, Chip Capelli, Alexandra Verner Roalsvig, David Ryan, Tamra Pica, Kristen Powers, Diane Brounstein, Travis Kinsey, and Joe Gallicchio. With a special thanks to Melanie Haseltine, Jessica Mandoki, Jimmy Bohr, Tom Alberg, Brett Hellman, and Lamont Craig for their help on the cast list. To my transcriber and friend Donna Hornak, who translated hundreds of hours of tape into readable interviews, organized the cast list, sought out articles and clippings and reminded me to eat. To photographers E.J. Carr for access to his amazing "Guiding Light" collection, and the expertise and talent that made our day "Behind the Scenes" so special, and Victoria Arlak for making her wonderful photographs graciously available.

Much of the material for the chronology came from *Soap Opera Digest* and *Soap Opera Weekly*. My thanks to Lynn Leahey, Editor-in-Chief of *Soap Opera Digest* and Mimi Torchin, Editor-in-Chief of *Soap Opera Weekly* for making their materials available, with special thanks to Jody Reines and Tammy Cain of *Soap Opera Digest* for their assistance.

Much thanks to General Publishing Group, Inc. To Quay Hays who had the foresight to do a book on this incredible show, to Peter Hoffman, editor extraordinaire for his unfailing support, and Sharon Hays, Trudihope Schlomowitz, Harlan Boll, Chitra Sekhar, Maritta Tapanainen, Gus Dawson and Susan Anson. To my agent, Ricki Olshan of Don Buchwald & Associates for her guidance. To authors Gary Warner and Marnie Winston-MacCauley for sharing their knowledge, and my friends who accepted the fact that I disappeared for months to write this book and stood by me anyway. A special thank you to my daughter Amy Poll who came on board and gave her precious free time to lend her considerable organizational and archival skills to this project, and my daughter Melissa Poll for her loving support.

1937-1946

The Rev. Dr. John Ruthledge was a liberal, nonsectarian clergyman in the little Chicago suburb of Five Points. Week after week, parishioners from all faiths came to the Little Church of Five Points to hear Dr. Ruthledge speak out against the insidiousness of racial prejudice, the horror of war and the injustice of poverty.

But Dr. Ruthledge's influence on the townspeople extended far beyond his weekly sermons. In the window of his study, his reading lamp—known fondly as the Friendship Lamp—always burned brightly, a signal to those in need who would seek his counsel. This lamp was as constant and as comforting a presence as Dr. Ruthledge himself and was known to all in Five Points as "The Guiding Light."

Dr. Ruthledge's wife died early in their marriage, leaving him to raise their daughter, Mary, alone. Shortly thereafter, a troubled young woman named Frances Holden left her eight-year-old son, Ned, in the minister's care. Frances was on the run after being implicated in a robbery committed by her slick and abusive husband, con man Paul Holden. Mary and Ned were raised as sister and brother, but as they grew older they realized that they were very much in love.

After Ned had become a successful author, he

bought a brooch for Mary from a charming but mysterious woman named Frederika Lang. Little did Ned know that Frederika was actually his estranged mother, Frances Holden! Her on-again, off-again marriage to the errant Paul reached a tragic climax when Paul followed her to Five Points. Paul told Frances of his plan to reveal to Ned that they were his parents, in hopes that they could then live off Ned's substantial book royalties. This bombshell sent Frances completely over the edge, and she shot and killed the contemptible Paul. Dr. Ruthledge saved Frances from the electric chair by convincing the governor to give her a reprieve. Ned was sickened to discover that "Frederika" was the mother who had abandoned him, and he bitterly wrote her off. Shaken to the core, Ned sought solace with a showgirl named Torchy Reynolds and impulsively married her. But Torchy soon realized that Ned still loved Mary, and she generously granted him a divorce.

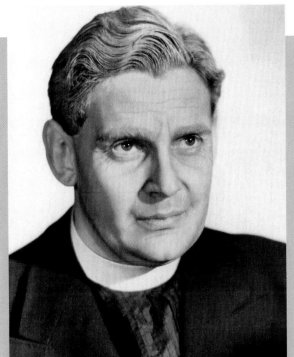

Memorable Moments

In the 1930s and 1940s, when listeners tuned in to "The Guiding Light," the first words they heard were the Rev. Ruthledge's simple philosophy, spoken by the announcer of the day: "There is a destiny that makes us brothers / None goes his way alone. / All that we send into the lives of others / Comes back into our own."

The cast of "The Guiding Light," circa 1937, gathers around the microphones and waits for the announcer to say, "And now, The Guiding Light.... As we listen in, we hear..."

Ned forgave his mother and married Mary, with Dr. Ruthledge proudly officiating the ceremony.

Mary's closest friend was Rose Kransky, an Orthodox Jew whose parents owned a secondhand store near Dr. Ruthledge's church. Rose worked in the store with her brother, Jacob, but felt hemmed in by her conservative father, Abe, who constantly pressured her to marry and raise a family. Against Abe's wishes, Dr. Ruthledge loaned Rose the money to attend secretarial school, and in time she became executive secretary to a handsome publisher named Charles Cunningham. Soon Rose and Charles began an affair, which was duly discovered by his shrewish wife, Celeste. A messy divorce ensued, in which a weak Charles denied his involvement with Rose. To add to Rose's troubles, her father died of influenza...and she found herself pregnant by Charles! Rose gave birth to a son, whom she named Johnny.

When Ned Holden discovered his mother's true identity, he went into a tailspin and impulsively married Torchy Reynolds, a showgirl he'd met in San Francisco.

Enter Ellis Smith, a longtime friend of Rose's. Ellis was the antithesis of Dr. Ruthledge, with whom he had many a debate about the human condition. A born cynic, Ellis believed that the basic nature of man was selfish and hypocritical. To Dr. Ruthledge and others in Five Points, Ellis appeared to have no emotional or familial ties, earning him the nickname "Mr. Nobody from Nowhere." In actuality, Ellis was the scion of a wealthy family who vehemently opposed his dream of becoming an artist. Disgusted by his family's extravagance and superior airs, Ellis swore them off and became a drifter. His reunion with the valiant and self-sufficient Rose inspired Ellis to put down roots in Five Points. Rose gave Ellis the courage and creative verve to paint again, and he nobly offered to marry her and be a father to little Johnny. Charles, however, begged Rose for another chance. Rose succumbed to his charms once more and they planned to marry. Then tragedy struck. One of Jacob Kransky's friends accidentally left the front gate open, and Johnny wandered out into the street, where he was hit by a car and killed. Rose broke off her engagement to Charles.

After the tragedy, Ellis and Rose remained close friends and their lives took some fascinating turns. Ellis was blinded in a fire. Later, an art student named Nancy Stewart moved to Five Points. Ellis knew—though Nancy did not—that she was his daughter from a brief and disastrous marriage to a Chicago debutante. Ellis struck up a friendship with Nancy, but she reacted badly once she learned he was her father. Ellis also befriended the showgirl Torchy, who was as worldly but more optimistic than he, along with an enigmatic woman named Iris Marsh, who shared his tastes and his persistent cynicism about humanity. Torchy became extremely jealous of Iris and briefly dated Martin Kane, with whom she organized a campaign to train seeing-eye dogs to help blind war veterans. Eventually, Ellis and Torchy ended up together, Ellis' blindness was cured by surgery and he reconciled with Nancy.

Shattered by little Johnny's death, Rose tried to work through her grief by becoming a governess for wealthy Edward and Norma Greenman. Edward was quite taken with Rose when he saw her give his two children the love and nurturing that Norma seemed incapable of. This time, Rose elected not to repeat her history with Charles and kept her friendship with Edward platonic. But Norma was neurotically jealous until she learned the reason for her irrationality—she had a brain tumor. Taking responsibility for her own life, Norma underwent brain surgery and later opened a nursery school so she could learn how to be better with children. One day, she saw one of her little charges fall through the ice on a frozen lake, and she jumped in to rescue the child. She succeeded but died the next day of pneumonia. Knowing of the attraction between Rose and Edward, Edward's teenage daughter, Joan, accused him of orchestrating Norma's death so he could be with Rose. But in time Joan realized otherwise, and with Dr. Ruthledge as her guide, she apologized to her father. Now free to acknowledge their mutual feelings, Rose and Edward were happily married.

With World War II now raging, Dr. Ruthledge decided he was needed for the war effort and left to serve as a chaplain in Europe. He was replaced at the Little Church by the Rev. Dr. Richard Gaylord, who later was replaced by the Rev. Frank Tuttle. Both new ministers became caught up in the life of young Claire Marshall, who had married pilot Tim Lawrence and adopted a little boy, Ricky. Claire was shocked to learn that Ricky was, in fact, Tim's natural son by his first wife, Nina! Claire and Tim were trying to come to grips with this revelation when Tim was killed in an airplane crash. After a period of grieving, Claire married Dr. Jonathan McNeill, and the two moved to Los Angeles. The newlyweds were happy to discover that "The Guiding Light" had followed them to their new home.

The years 1947 to 1951 marked a major transition for "Guiding Light" and Dr. Ruthledge's cherished Friendship Lamp. The beloved minister died, but not before he entrusted his son-in-law, Ned Holden, with his final wish: to deliver the lamp to his dearest friend from his years at the seminary, the Rev. Dr. Charles Matthews. Dr. Matthews was the pastor of the Church of the Good Samaritan in a rough Los Angeles neighborhood known as Selby Flats, where he lived with his sister, Winifred "Winnie" Hale, and Winnie's daughter, Pamela. Deeply moved upon receiving the lamp, Dr. Matthews addressed the inmates at the nearby state prison, working his sermon around the "Guiding Light" theme. He summarized his homily with the sobering but calming words that had been the Rev. Ruthledge's touchstone:

There is a destiny that makes us brothers
None goes his way alone.
All that we send into the lives of others
Comes back into our own.

One prisoner, however, took exception to these words of wisdom. A few days following Dr. Matthews' sermon, Roger Barton was released from jail after serving fifteen years for embezzlement, a crime he didn't commit. Changing his name to Ray Brandon in hopes of wiping out the past, the embittered ex-con went to Dr. Matthews, threw the Friendship Lamp on the floor and told him how unmoved he was by his message. The lamp itself was only slightly damaged; Dr. Matthews could see that Ray was the one whose life had been shattered.

Eventually, Ray began to confide in Dr. Matthews as well as in Charlotte Wilson, an attractive but somewhat world-weary young woman who lived in his apartment building. Ray had left behind a wife, Julie, and a son, Roger Jr. A shallow, self-involved woman, Julie had divorced her convict husband to marry the successful Frank Collins, who had adopted Roger Jr. as his own. Now that Roger Sr. was back in Los Angeles as Ray Brandon, Julie forbade him from making contact with his son, having told young Roger that his father was dead. But Ray and Charlotte sneaked in to see Roger speak at his high school graduation, and from a distance Ray beamed upon seeing the son who had grown into such a fine young man.

But Ray still could not fully enjoy his return to civilian life because he was consumed with the idea of killing Martin McClain, the man who had framed him. Now a wealthy corporate vice president, the snide and dispassionate Martin was a cold father to his motherless daughter, Susan. Ironically, Susan and Roger were attending the same college and soon became quite smitten

The Bauers—Charita, Meta, Papa and Bill—directed by Ted Corday and accompanied by organist Rosa Rio, appeared on the scene in 1947–48 and remain a prominent "Guiding Light" family today.

LAW AND ORDER

It was a broadcasting first in 1951 when Irna Phillips let listeners decide the guilt or innocence of Meta White (second from right). Announcer: "This is Bud Collyer (right), ladies and gentlemen, speaking from the courtroom where the trial of The People vs. Meta White has reached its highest point of interest. The defendant herself is on the witness stand. As you know, through the medium of radio, these court sessions have been followed day by day from one end of the nation to the other. I wish to remind you at this time that the final verdict of guilty or not guilty that will be pronounced on Meta White will be delivered by the listening audience—the audience who each day has heard the testimony, weighed the evidence and who will deliver the final verdict. You the listener will, within a few days, determine the future of Meta White…. You know, of course, that for the past few hours the defense counsel, Ray Brandon, has been questioning Meta as to her past—her childhood and her girlhood. The defendant showed little evidence of emotion until Ray Brandon questioned her about a baby—a baby and Ted White."

with each other, not knowing, of course, the truth behind their fathers' enmity. But Julie knew, and she tried to put a stop to the romance without telling Roger the reason for her disapproval. Frank railed at his wife for manipulating Roger, believing that the boy should get to know his real father without her interference.

At this time, a major catalyst surfaced in the form of

Larry Lawrence, a fortune-hunting cad who had once been involved with Charlotte. Larry began to charm Claire McNeill, who had been married to his late brother, Tim, in hopes that she would divorce her successful doctor husband, Jonathan, and marry him. But Claire and Jonathan's marriage proved too strong for him to penetrate, and Larry soon found a better opportunity in Julie after Frank was paralyzed in a car accident in which their children, Betty and Michael, were tragically killed. When Roger discovered the affair, he was horrified by Julie's callous neglect of Frank, the man he knew and loved as his father. One rainy night, Frank's wheelchair skidded on the muddy pavement, sending the helpless man over a rocky cliff to his death. Consumed with guilt, Julie hysterically confessed that she had killed Frank, but the crime was later ruled an accident.

Meanwhile, Ray was trying hard to get on with his life. When he confronted Martin with a gun, Ray couldn't bring himself to pull the trigger. Afterward, he ran to the Church of the Good Samaritan and made amends with the God he had once mocked and disavowed. Julie finally allowed Ray to have a relationship with Roger, but as father and son bonded, both realized Julie had only done it in the vain hope of reconciling with Ray. Soon after, Roger and Susan married and had a daughter named Betty Ann. Much to Susan's annoyance, Julie was an interfering mother-in-law, but when Julie saved little Betty Ann from a fire, all was forgiven. Roger and Susan left Los Angeles, and a terminally ill Martin confessed his embezzling crime to Dr. Matthews on his deathbed, exonerating Ray at last.

Ray and Charlotte married as well, and the marriage was immediately put to the test. Ray completed the law degree he had begun studying for before his prison term and became a successful, hardworking attorney. Feeling neglected, Charlotte caught the show business bug and became a radio star, thanks to an adroit and fast-talking manager named Sid Harper. But it was slick, wealthy British advertising executive Ted White who would ultimately call the shots in Charlotte's career. Charlotte's friend and neighbor at the Towers apartments in Los Angeles was an ambitious model named Jan Carter, who also had dreams of show business glamour and began pursuing Ted for his prestigious connections. Jan's roommate, Dr. Mary Leland, was a dedicated surgeon who was constantly encountering prejudice because she was a woman doctor. There was one patient, however, who trusted Mary implicitly: a warm, down-to-earth German immigrant known simply as Mama Bauer. Mama and her husband, Friedrich (Papa) Bauer, had three children: Meta, Bill and Gertrude (Trudy). Six years earlier, Meta had fled the family home because Papa was an Old World tyrant who refused to allow her the freedoms enjoyed by typical American girls. Papa had since destroyed all pictures of Meta and forbade the family to ever mention her name. But now Mama had cancer, and she longed to see Meta again. Bill was a drugstore clerk in his mid-20s and engaged to his childhood sweetheart, Bertha (Bert) Miller, a spunky and outspoken young woman with an annoying penchant for social climbing. Trudy, the youngest, was a plain Jane who'd always lived in the shadow of Meta's striking beauty. But Trudy felt attractive around Dr. Ross Boling, the new doctor who rented the Bauers' upstairs apartment.

Pained to see how much his sick wife missed Meta, Papa told his family that he regretted driving his eldest child away. It was now his fondest wish to find Meta and bring her home before Mama died. What the Bauer family didn't realize, though, was that Meta was already back in Los Angeles. Jan Carter, Dr. Leland's roommate, was really Meta! Meta kept this secret until she found herself in a sad predicament—she was pregnant by Ted White, a man she had used but did not love. Meta confided in Dr. Matthews and sought refuge at a convent in New York, where she gave birth to a baby boy whom Dr. Matthews and Dr. Leland arranged to be adopted—by Charlotte and Ray! Unaware of the identities of their child's parents, the Brandons named their son Charles (Chuckie), after Dr. Matthews, and looked forward to a happy life. But the new family was doomed from the start. Meta tearfully returned to the family fold on Mama and Papa's silver wedding anniversary and eventually told them her painful story. She also told Ted in hopes that they would marry and get Chuckie back. Ted had no use for Meta, so Meta and Ted each filed separate custody suits against the Brandons. During Meta's court case, Ray was appalled when Charlotte spoke sympathetically about her! Identifying with Meta, Charlotte came to believe that Chuckie would be better off with his natural mother. The court awarded the boy to Meta, leaving Ted to formulate a secret plan: He would marry Meta, prove her to be an unfit mother and get the boy all to himself. At this time, however, Meta and Ross Boling were beginning to have feelings for one another, leaving Trudy to bitterly resent her sister's return. But Meta succumbed to family pressure to marry for Chuckie's sake, and she and Ted tied the knot in Las Vegas.

Ray blamed Charlotte for the loss of Chuckie. Dis-

traught, Charlotte began purchasing illegal drugs from Larry Lawrence and soon became a crazed, strung-out addict. Eventually, Larry was arrested and Charlotte conquered her addiction, but she was now uncertain about her future with Ray. Sid Harper had developed feelings for Charlotte and considered Ray partly responsible for her addiction. Ray had to admit that Sid was right and worked hard to convince Charlotte of his love for her.

Dr. Matthews decided to move on from Selby Flats, but before he did, he gave a considerable sum of money to be used for the construction of Cedars Hospital. Both Mary Leland and Ross Boling joined the hospital staff. The Rev. Dr. Paul Keeler replaced Dr. Matthews at the Church of the Good Samaritan, and inherited "The Guiding Light."

Meta fell in love with Joe Roberts, the reporter who believed in her innocence and made her plight known. The two eventually married, but Joe's daughter, Kathy, never accepted Meta as her stepmother and caused much heartache for the couple in the years to come.

ON CALL AT CEDARS

When son Joey Roberts came down with rheumatic fever, Joe hired nurse Peggy Regan from Cedars Hospital to care for him. Peggy was an instant hit with the Roberts children, who hoped their dad would marry her instead of Meta.

Meta's objections, Ted hired a strict governess for the sensitive boy and forbade any mention of religion in their home. Unable to stand Ted's tyranny, Meta left him and initiated a custody battle for Chuckie. Thanks to Ray's adept legal representation, Meta won primary custody, and Ted had the boy on weekends.

Ted continued to influence Chuckie, insisting he take boxing lessons so that he could learn to "be a man." Chuckie was only of kindergarten age at the time. One day, when Ted and little Chuckie were practicing in a boxing ring, Chuckie fell over the ropes and hit his head. The boy lay in a coma for weeks before he tragically died. Overcome by grief and hatred, Meta went to Ted's home and shot him dead. As Meta endured the consequences of imprisonment and a gut-wrenching court trial, the story of the pretty murderess who avenged the death of her illegitimate child made headlines in all the Los Angeles newspapers. Some of those articles were penned by Joe Roberts, a hard-nosed reporter from the *City Times* who had seen it all and done it all during his years as a war correspondent. Joe was soon to lose his job when his hard angle softened after he personally interviewed Meta. He was touched by Meta's love for her child, for he, too, was a parent. A widower, Joe was dedicated to his teenage children, Kathy and Joey. Through Joe's compassionate articles, readers grew to sympathize with Meta, and public opinion won out—Meta was acquitted.

By now, it was obvious to Meta and Joe that they had strong feelings for one another. This did not sit well with Joe's daughter, Kathy. A precocious and manipulative teenager, Kathy intercepted and hid a letter that Meta had sent to Joe. When Joey cornered her into admitting what she'd done, Joe came down hard on his daughter and decided to seize his chance to be happy. He and Meta eloped to Malibu but kept the marriage a secret in hopes that Kathy would eventually accept Meta. The couple split their time between Los Angeles and a rented Malibu beach cottage, using the cover story that Joe was frequently "on assignment." But when Joey came down with rheumatic fever, Joe rushed to the bedside of the son who'd always loved and supported him. To care for Joey during his convalescence, Joe hired a friendly and dedicated young nurse from Cedars Hospital named Peggy Regan. Peggy was an immediate hit with the Roberts children, who hoped that Joe would marry Peggy instead of Meta. Peggy was, indeed, developing a crush on Joe, but she knew she had no future with the older reporter and later left Cedars.

Amid all this turmoil, the Bauers found a reason to celebrate—on Dec. 9, 1949, Bill and Bert were married. However, the marriage was troubled from day one because Bert proved to be a nagging, shrewish wife who pressured Bill to become successful so she could have a big house and fancy clothes. On their honeymoon, they were having the first of what would be many arguments over money when they received the sad news that Mama Bauer had died. After they returned, Bill and Bert moved in with Bert's snobbish parents, who wanted little contact with the middle-class Bauers. But Bert had bigger ideas. She pressured Ted White into giving Bill a plum job with his advertising agency and promptly financed a trendy new house in the Hollywood Hills! Bill felt completely out of place among Ted's college-educated cronies and was living beyond his means in a house that didn't feel like home. It wasn't long before Bill sought refuge in alcohol.

As strained as it was, Bill and Bert's marriage was a fairy-tale romance compared with Meta and Ted's. Ted raised Chuckie like a little adult, stoic and unemotional, just as Ted had been raised by his divorced father. Over

At this time, Trudy's future looked bright because there was an exciting new man in her life. After Ross Boling left Los Angeles, Trudy went on vacation to Jamaica alone. There she met Clyde Palmer, a charming, well-to-do young bachelor from New York City. A whirlwind courtship ensued, and the two lovers continued to write to each other after they both returned home. Before long, they were married. Trudy and Clyde set up house in New York, and Meta stayed with them for a while during Joey's illness. Meta was now feeling like a fifth wheel in Joe's life. Their marriage was still a secret, and she was questioning their decision to elope. While in New York, Meta met Clyde's friend, a successful doctor named Bruce Banning. Tired of living a lie with Joe, Meta began to wonder if her future lay with Bruce rather than with a husband who was still tied exclusively to his grown children.

By contrast, the marriage of Ray and Charlotte Brandon was growing stronger. The Brandons adopted a motherless nine-month-old girl named Penny, and her problematic fourteen-year-old brother, Jimmy. Charlotte soon regretted adopting Jimmy, who was sullen and belligerent, and wanted to send him off to military school. But Ray won the boy over, and in time the Brandons moved to New York, where Ray pursued an exciting new legal position.

As for the Bauers, Bill lost his job and was forced to sell the house in the Hollywood Hills. While Bert nagged and complained, Bill went through a succession of menial jobs, drowning his sorrows at the local cocktail lounge. It was there that he met Gloria LaRue, a beautiful blond singer with whom he had a brief affair. Herself a recovered alcoholic, Gloria convinced Bill to get off the bottle and urged him to make a go of his marriage, even though she was secretly falling in love with him. But life with Bert was becoming intolerable, and one day Bill blurted out that there was another woman in his life and that he wanted a divorce. Despite all her faults, though, Bert was steadfast in her love for Bill and refused to let him go. When she discovered she was pregnant, Bill agreed to try to save their marriage. Gloria briefly fell off the wagon as a result, and Sid Harper restored her confidence by launching her in a promising new radio and television career, of which Bill, who was now back in advertising, was a part. Before long, Gloria and Sid were married, and the Bauers, with a baby on the way, were a family once again.

Between 1952 and 1956, the actors continued to entrance radio audiences....

...then raced over to another studio, where they performed the same script in front of cameras for a new medium known as television.

1952-1956

The years 1952 to 1956 were filled with secrets, class conflicts and the tortures of young love. Central to all three of these issues was a wealthy new family who had some surprising ties to Los Angeles.

Kathy Roberts was amazed and happy to discover that Richard Grant Jr., a handsome medical student she met while visiting San Francisco, was Peggy Regan's first cousin. Peggy's mother, Margaret, had long lamented the fact that her sister, Laura, wanted little to do with her after marrying a wealthy civil engineer named Richard Grant. While Richard Sr. was a warm, supportive father with a solid sense of values, Laura was a shallow, mean-spirited woman who tried to impose her nouveau riche affectations on her children, Karen and Richard Jr., known respectively as Bunny and Dick. Laura was not

at all happy to see Dick become interested in Kathy, whose stepmother, Meta, was notorious for having killed Ted White.

Back in Los Angeles, Kathy's euphoria proved short-lived when Meta and Joe finally revealed that they were married. It had been Kathy and Joey's wish for Joe to marry Peggy, and now their hopes were dashed forever. Joey was at least civil to Meta, but Kathy was nasty, belligerent and rebellious toward her father and stepmother. Kathy feared that if Meta killed once, she could

In the premiere TV episode (6/30/52), Kathy was the rebellious daughter of Joe Roberts, Meta's second husband, and she hated her stepmother from day one. In an effort to help his sister, Bill intervened in a family squabble.

Unlike his sister, Kathy, Joey Roberts was uncomplicated, a good kid who embraced Meta wholeheartedly as his new mother.

she didn't want to stay married to him. Bob became angry and began driving wildly. The car crashed, Bob was killed instantly and a bewildered Kathy fled the scene. Afterward, she unwisely confided everything about the tragedy to Alice and swore her roommate to secrecy.

Meanwhile, Laura was chagrined when Richard, having landed a new government project, announced that they were moving to Los Angeles. Laura Grant was a pillar of San Francisco society and would have to leave all that behind. Once they were settled in L.A., Dick decided to intern at Cedars to be near Kathy, which didn't please Laura. Fortunately for Dick, Bunny discovered that Laura had filched that letter to Dick from Kathy, and was quick to tell her brother. Bunny was bitter toward Laura for having broken up her recent romance and was drinking heavily because she was now married to a boring man of whom Laura, of course, approved.

kill again. Joe sternly warned Kathy to shape up. Meta, however, feared she would never fit into Joe's family, and they eventually separated. Meta went to New York to visit Trudy and Clyde and began seeing Bruce Banning. When Bruce proposed, Meta realized she belonged with Joe and returned home. To Joe's delight, Joey embraced Meta wholeheartedly as his new mother, but Kathy refused to budge.

Trying to escape her troublesome family situation, Kathy kept writing to Dick, pleading with him to get married. Dick was about to start his medical internship and had no plans for marriage. When one of Kathy's letters to Dick went unanswered, she decided to forget about him and move on with her life. Kathy graduated from high school, and much to her father's dismay, instead of going to Stanford as planned, she took a job in a store and began sharing an apartment with a gold-digging, would-be starlet named Alice Graham.

Another of Kathy's new friends was Bob Lang, a sensitive young man who had been orphaned as a child. Bob was so desperate for a stable home life that he began pressuring Kathy to marry him. Alone and confused, Kathy finally said yes, and they were married by a justice of the peace. The newlyweds told no one of their union, partly because Kathy soon realized she had made a mistake. Within days of the ceremony, Kathy and Bob were talking in the car when Kathy admitted to Bob that

LOVE AND MARRIAGE

Kathy married rich, sheltered Dick Grant and made him believe he had fathered Robin, when in truth the father was the late Bob Lang, to whom Kathy was briefly married.

Bert used to look upon Meta as a scarlet woman who was her competition for Bill's affections, but eventually they became the closest of sisters-in-law.

Determined to keep her brother from following the same path, Bunny urged Dick to stand up to Laura, and to the relief of both Bunny and Richard, he did. Dick lit into his mother for her machinations and told her that he intended to marry Kathy.

As the Roberts and Grant families were coming apart at the seams, the Bauers were struggling to cope with more everyday issues. Charlotte and Ray Brandon had moved to New York and rented their L.A. home to Bert and Bill, who soon celebrated the birth of a baby boy named Michael. Later, Bert read in the newspaper of a development that Bill had withheld from her: Bill had been instrumental in landing Gloria LaRue Harper a television contract! Both Bert and Sid smoldered as they watched Gloria become emotionally dependent on Bill, performing at her best whenever he watched her adoringly from the wings. Bert was relieved when Gloria developed vocal problems, abandoned her new show and moved to New York. Sid replaced Gloria with Alice Graham, whom he had once represented—not to mention taken to bed. But the gig didn't suffice for the greedy Alice, who began filming commercials in violation of her exclusive contract. When Bill threatened to fire Alice, she coolly told him everything about Kathy and Bob's accident and threatened to reveal it to the world if Bill axed her. Cornered, Bill kept Alice on but told Bert and Papa Bauer that Alice had blackmailed him. The Bauers' hearts ached for Kathy, and they decided to keep her

secret. Kathy finally realized that Meta was trying hard to be her friend and confided in Meta about the details surrounding Bob's death. Meta was touched that Kathy had entrusted her with this painful secret but was disappointed when Kathy married Dick without telling him of her previous marriage to Bob. To nobody's surprise, Laura sat out the wedding.

As Kathy's luck would have it, the events she had set into motion began to close in on her. Don Crane, Joe's muckraking colleague at the *City Times*, found a woman's cigarette lighter in Bob's car and suspected he wasn't alone in his fatal accident. Crane traced the lighter to Sid, who had given it to Alice, who in turn had loaned it to Kathy. Investigating the matter further, Crane discovered that Kathy and Bob had secretly married! Crane related this to his and Joe's boss, John (Mac) McIntyre. But when Mac refused to run the story out of loyalty to Joe, Crane angrily defected to a rival tabloid. Mac told Joe, and Joe heard the remainder of the story from Meta. To further complicate matters, Kathy found herself pregnant with Bob's child and led everyone to believe it was Dick's!

Amid all of this turmoil, there were a couple of bright spots. Helen Allen, an employee at the *Times*, discovered that she was Bob Lang's long-lost mother. Saddened by the realization that she would never know her son, Helen formed a close bond with Kathy that lasted for many years, even after Helen moved away to New

York. And Kathy was happy to see brother Joey marry his longtime girlfriend, Lois, and enlist in the Air Corps.

Kathy was arraigned and the police began hammering her with questions about the crash that killed Bob Lang. Meta knew her family could no longer live in denial, and she told Dick the truth about Bob. Kathy left the door open for Dick to divorce her, but Dick loved her enough to stand by her. At this point, everyone except Dick and his parents knew that Kathy's unborn child was Bob Lang's. But Laura suspected the truth and despised Kathy for having dragged the precious Grant name through the mud. When Kathy's bail was set at $25,000, Laura adamantly refused Dick's plea to put up the money. It was Meta who paid the bail, using money she had received after Ted White's death. Kathy's chances for acquittal looked dim at first, as District Attorney Richard Hanley hinged his case on the possibility that she had tampered with Bob's car. However, Joe located a mechanic who admitted he might have left a nut loose when he worked on Bob's brakes earlier. Kathy was cleared of the charges and gave birth to a girl, Robin. She chose that name because the baby was born in the spring, the season of new beginnings.

Unfortunately, a new beginning was forced on Bill when his capricious boss fired him. He formed a new public relations company with a partner, only to lose his shirt and go back to pounding the pavement. Unbeknownst to Bill, Bert received a letter from their landlords, Charlotte and Ray Brandon, announcing their intention to sell the house. Behind Bill's back, Bert convinced a reluctant Meta to loan her the money to buy it! Meta only went along with Bert's scheme because she shared Bert's concern that Bill was already under enough pressure without having to worry about keeping a roof over their heads. But when Bill suggested that they move to another area where his business prospects looked better, Bert was forced to tell her husband that his sister was now technically their landlady! Stung by this revelation and hopeless about finding work, Bill went back to the bottle. For months, he experienced the highs and lows of an alcoholic as he shared delusions of grandeur with the bartender at Blue Moon Lounge, only to feel shame and self-loathing the next day. Papa tried to bring Bill around gently, but Bert gave Bill a firm ultimatum: the bottle or his family. She went so far as to consider divorce until Bill battled his addiction to alcohol at Cedars, where Dick counseled and supported him. Bill's confidence was bolstered when Gloria offered him a job in New York. Bert was not happy about Gloria's reappearance in Bill's

life, not to mention the fact that Bill would be working 3,000 miles away. However, Bert was secure in the belief that he had finally straightened out and agreed to stick by him. He was still Bert's husband and the father of her child, and she loved him. For all Bert's idiosyncrasies—her nagging, her social climbing, her opinionated stubbornness—she remained devoted to her family.

After giving birth to Robin, Kathy came down with viral pneumonia and began to experience hallucinations. To help his wife, Dick called in his cousin, nurse Peggy Regan, who had returned to Cedars. Laura previously had no use for her own middle-class side of the family, but she was now getting chummy with her niece in hopes of learning the identity of Robin's real father. One who shared Laura's suspicions was Janet Johnson, a voluptuous nurse who was attracted to Dick's boyish innocence—and to his money. When Kathy recovered from her pneumonia, she began to pull away from Dick out of guilt for deceiving him, causing Dick to fall prey to Janet's predatory charms. Before long they were having an affair. Tired of her sham of a marriage, Kathy finally told Dick the truth about Robin. Dick tersely replied that he didn't care; he was in love with Janet, and he wanted their marriage annulled.

Although Bill was an alcoholic and prone to womanizing, he was always a good, gentle father who was devoted to his sons. Because family came first, Bert stuck by him.

In actuality, Janet was a mere distraction for Dick, whose true love was the medical profession. Dick was now working for Dr. Baird, chief of plastic surgery at Cedars, and sharing residents' quarters with a young medic named Jim Kelly. The brusque, pipe-smoking son of an eminent Chicago surgeon, Jim had wriggled out from under his father's thumb and moved to Los Angeles to make his own way. Jim was attracted to Peggy, but Peggy was falling for a complex, mysterious man whom Dick and Dr. Baird were preparing for plastic surgery. His name was Dan Peters, and his bitter, nasty demeanor was the talk of Cedars Hospital. When Dan came to realize that Peggy felt affection rather than pity for him, he gradually opened up to her about his tortured past. Dan had been born in Chicago with a disfigured face. All his

In the early days, Bert was a demanding wife and mother. Wise, gentle Papa Bauer was her sounding board and was often the mediator between Bert, Bill and the children.

life, he had felt like the odd person out. Kids called him Scarface, and even his own father rejected him in favor of his good-looking, popular brother. The only person who loved and nurtured Dan was his mother. Because the family was poor, Dan's mother had encouraged him to become successful so he could afford an operation to correct his facial malformation. Young Dan couldn't

wait that long, however, and he dug his nails into his face in hopes of changing his appearance for the better. Sadly, he only made it worse. When Dan was fourteen years old, his mother died of cancer. With no one left to care about him, Dan left his family and struck out on his own. Years later, Dan read of Dr. Baird's excellent reputation as a plastic surgeon and decided to come to Los Angeles. Baird immediately sensed Dan's torment and isolation and told him that he could transform him from a scared little boy into a handsome and secure man. Dan underwent surgery and healed well, but Jim Kelly suspected there was more to Dan's story than he was letting on. He was right.

At this time, Joe and District Attorney Richard Hanley were immersed in the case of Judith Weber, a "lonely spinster" who was found shot to death in a cabin. Joe's newspaper stories of the "Cabin Murder" had the people of Los Angeles both fascinated and baffled, because the murder victim had no known enemies. Upon further investigation, Joe discovered that on the day of her murder, Judith had withdrawn her life savings. As Joe and the police went through Judith's effects, they found a jar of Coverall, a heavy cream for concealing birthmarks and scars. One day in a routine conversation, Joe filled Peggy in on this all-consuming case. Peggy gasped to herself—she had seen a container of Coverall in Dan's room! Telling no one, Peggy took the Coverall and agonized over it for weeks. Meanwhile, Jim couldn't help noticing that Dan was obsessed with the Cabin Murder, clipping articles and listening to all the news reports about the case. Privately, Dan was racking his brain, trying to remember whether or not he had killed Judith Weber!

Finally, Peggy confronted Dan and asked if he knew the murdered woman. Dan blurted out that yes, he had a "marriage pact" with Judith Weber. She would give him the money to finance his plastic surgery, and he would marry her in return. But did he kill her? He couldn't remember. Peggy wanted to believe him, but Dan was in such a tailspin trying to re-create his last moments with Judith that he began yelling and smashing mirrors. Frightened by his temper, Peggy accused Dan of killing Judith and threatened to turn him in. Dan disappeared from the hospital and a few weeks later showed up in Chicago at the office of Paul Avery, a top criminal defense lawyer. Seeking his legal counsel, Dan told Avery that he now remembered having killed Judith Weber. After she had handed him the money for his surgery, Dan backed out on their agreement to marry. Judith pulled a gun, and as they struggled over it, a shot rang out and Judith was dead. Dan had something else to tell Paul Avery, though—they were brothers! Dan's actual last name was Avery, and Paul was the popular brother who'd been groomed for success. Overcome with guilt for rejecting his brother years ago, Paul decided to represent Dan, and the brothers returned to Los Angeles to face the authorities. Before Dan went to prison, Dr. Baird told him that Judith's murder was for naught, as the doctor never intended to charge Dan for the surgery! Peggy was heartbroken by this turn of events and left Cedars once again.

Another source of disappointment for Peggy was Dick and Kathy's annulment, not to mention Janet's shameless quest to marry Dick. Janet was so nervy that she bought an engagement ring for Dick to give to her. He grew tired of her effrontery and broke off the relationship. Bert, Richard and Jim tried to reunite Dick and Kathy, but Dick was using his work as an escape from his ambivalence toward Kathy. Jim began to look in Kathy's direction and realized that the wife his pal had discarded was indeed a desirable woman. Meta was happy to see Kathy and Jim dating, although she was not pleased when Kathy constantly saddled her with Robin's care. The problem was that Jim was falling in love with Kathy, but neither Kathy nor Dick would admit that they still loved each other.

Back at the Bauer house, young Mike began acting out because he missed his dad. Papa Bauer, ever sympathetic, gave Mike the love and gentle discipline he needed, but Bert approached motherhood sternly and would tolerate no nonsense from the boy. When Bert told Papa she wanted to consult a child psychologist, Papa laughed and said, "You're looking at one!" Bill returned from New York and took a job in Los Angeles, only to have Mike reject him. The boy was angry about his father's long absence and called him Bill instead of Dad, because as far as he was concerned, "I have no daddy." Bert and Bill endured months of discipline problems with Mike until Bill realized that Bert's hard-nosed approach wasn't working. In a flash of inspiration, Bill took Mike on an adventure trip to San Francisco to find his "missing daddy." There, in their messy hotel room, father and son bonded, and Bill swore to Mike that his daddy would never leave him again. From then on, they were the best of buddies.

Bill was pleased when his firm landed Richard Grant's company, Acme Construction, as an account. Richard Sr. came to rely on Bill as a confidant when Dick

went through an especially trying period. Dick was frustrated to be reporting to Dr. Baird's new assistant, the pompous and dictatorial Dr. Bart Thompson. Janet was quick to notice the growing enmity between them, and she began dating Bart to get revenge for Dick's rejection of her. Janet gloated as Bart played Machiavellian head games with Dick, keeping him working around the clock and then upstaging him with other interns. When Dick complained, Bart snidely told him that he had a persecution complex and was not cut out to be a doctor. At the same time, Jim confessed to Dick that he was in love with Kathy, and Dick felt he had no right to stand in his friend's way.

Finally, Dick became so physically exhausted and so emotionally demoralized that he "froze" during a skin graft operation and abruptly left Cedars. Holding Bart personally responsible, Richard bitterly confronted the man who had terrorized his son. "You have criticized, harangued—yes, undermined my son until his self-confidence was torn into little shreds," Richard shouted. "You can say you don't understand me because you don't have a son. Well, I'll tell you this, Dr. Thompson—you don't deserve a son."

Bart was chilled by the irony of Richard's statement because he did, indeed, have a son back in San Francisco who knew him only as his mentor. Almost 30 years earlier, Bart had walked out on his wife, Liz, and infant son, John, to devote his life to his prestigious medical career. Liz went on to marry a man named Brooks who adopted John, and the boy grew up never knowing the identity of his biological father. John became a doctor and chose psychiatry as his specialty. When he interned at the hospital where Bart practiced medicine, Bart insinuated himself into John's life and tried to steer him toward plastic surgery. It was Bart's secret hope that one day father and son could work side by side. When Bart transferred to Cedars, he was disappointed that Dr. Baird lacked the budget to create a position for John. It was Bart's intention to force Dick out so he could bring John in. Now with Dick gone, that day had arrived. With his characteristic powers of persuasion, Bart steamrolled John into moving to Los Angeles as his new resident in plastic surgery. John still did not suspect that Bart was his father, but both Jim and Janet detected it when Bart became jealous of Jim and John's budding friendship. Janet began dating John in hopes of getting at the truth. Before long, John began to suspect that he had walked into a strange situation.

While John Brooks struggled to forge a personal

Following Joe's death, Meta had feelings for Bill's friend and business associate Mark Holden. But Mark looked upon Meta only as a friend and was soon to fall for Kathy, her stepdaughter, after Kathy was divorced from Dick.

portrait of him. She called the picture "Dark Echo" to reflect Dick's obvious but inexplicable despair. Soon after, the man who had stolen Dick's wallet sent Dick's medical license to Mrs. Laury's boardinghouse, and the truth about Richard Edmonds was revealed. His secret out, Dick decided to return to Los Angeles, where he walked right into the middle of a tragedy. John Brooks was killed in a car accident and never learned that he was Bart's son. Devastated, Bart admitted the truth to his colleagues at Cedars and apologized to Dick for his diabolical behavior. Bart returned to San Francisco. Janet moved to New York, where, true to form, she married a rich man.

Now back on the Cedars staff, Dick continued to correspond with Marie and flew her to Los Angeles to see an eye specialist. Fascinated that Dick had a new woman in his life, Laura wasted no time in becoming friendly with Marie in hopes that Dick would get over Kathy once and for all. But after Marie and Kathy met, both women realized that Dick was more interested in medicine than he was in either of them. However, Kathy decided to stop leading Jim on and told him they could never be more than friends. Of course, this wasn't enough for Laura, who lied to Kathy that Dick and Marie were engaged. Saddened by the news, Kathy decided to travel around the country with Robin for a while. Dick soon found out about his mother's latest trick and ripped into her. It was resolved somewhat when his sister, Bunny, visited and helped them work out a momentary truce. Marie regained the vision in her one eye and considered going back to New York until Bert, who had become her friend, advised her to stay in Los Angeles. Always the perceptive one, Bert knew that Marie was falling in love with Dick.

As Marie settled into her new life in Los Angeles, she began sketching a blond woman she saw frequently in the park. When Marie introduced herself to her subject, she was struck by the woman's blasé, detached manner. She told Marie only that her name was Lila Taylor and that she hailed from Flint, Michigan. Marie eventually became Lila's roommate and introduced her to Dick and Jim. Dick found Lila amoral and sarcastic, whereas Jim saw in her his own blunt, no-frills qualities, and he liked what he saw. Jim and Lila played it cool at first, but Jim finally summoned the nerve to propose. Lila refused to be tied down, and Jim soon discovered the reason why—she had tuberculosis. Jim stood by her and paid for her treatments, and in time the two were married. The newlyweds moved to Chicago, where Jim

and professional identity, Dick Grant found his own. Under the name Richard Edmonds, Dick moved to New York and lived in a boardinghouse run by the sympathetic Mrs. Laury. One night, he was mugged on a pier and had his wallet stolen. Dick was withdrawn and uncommunicative until he befriended Marie Wallace, a cheerful young woman from Iowa who was also staying at Mrs. Laury's. Despite the fact that she was blind in one eye, Marie was a practicing artist. Gradually, Marie drew Dick out of his shell and painted a

took over his ailing father's medical practice, and they had two children.

Bert and Bill Bauer also celebrated the birth of a second child, William Edward, called Billy, born on New Year's Eve, 1954. As Bert devoted herself to the new baby, she was slow in noticing that Mike was feeling left out. Soon after, Bert's father died in Arizona, and her mother, Elsie Miller, came out to Los Angeles for an extended stay. Papa Bauer graciously went to live at Meta's to make room for Elsie, but Bill and young Mike soon regretted the move. Elsie was a nag and a hypochondriac, spoiling Billy rotten while treating Mike like dirt. Bill, Papa and Meta were furious with Elsie for turning Mike's world upside down, but Elsie countered by accusing them of pampering the boy. Marie became a port in the middle of this storm when she made a charcoal sketch of Mike, and the boy consequently latched onto the family's warm, attractive new friend. Mike also struck up a friendship with a boy named Jock Baker who was several years older than he was, even though Elsie disapproved. Later, Mike overheard an argument between Bert and Bill, in which Bill threatened to leave on account of Elsie. Frightened by the thought of losing his dad again, Mike ran away. The Bauers questioned Jock, who revealed that Mike had talked about running away if Elsie didn't let up on him. With the help of Marie's sketch of Mike, the authorities tracked the boy down in the Hollywood Hills. Bert and Bill confronted Elsie about the damage she'd done to Mike, and Elsie tearfully apologized to the boy. She then began to live her own life, marrying a pleasant man named Albert Franklin in a simple ceremony at the Bauer home. Elsie and Albert then went back to Arizona, much to the family's relief.

On a sad note, Meta was devastated when Joe died of cancer on Christmas Eve, 1955. After the customary mourning period, Bert tried to match Meta up with Mark Holden, a handsome and dynamic structural engineer who had a business relationship with Bill and Richard. Mark was in his early 40s and had never married but was devoted to his younger siblings, Fred and Alice. Mark took a liking to Meta and convinced her to move Joe's favorite chair down to the basement so she could get on with her life. Over the course of a few months, Meta and Mark grew closer and considered marriage, but Meta put him off because she wanted to give Kathy time to adjust to their plans. Mark had not yet met Kathy, who was still traveling, having placed Robin in a school in Switzerland. He became angry with Meta over her inordinate concern for her stepdaughter and insisted on being first in Meta's life. Meta, though, still felt guilty for marrying Joe without Kathy's knowledge, and she didn't want to make the same mistake twice.

Meanwhile, Kathy was spending a lot of time in New York and dating a man named Dan Clark. Dan proposed, but Kathy was still uncertain about her feelings for Dick, so she returned to Los Angeles, where Meta introduced her to Mark. Not only did Mark and Kathy get along, but they were instantly attracted to one another! Fate kept throwing them together at every turn, and Meta never suspected that her fiancé and stepdaughter were harboring intense mutual feelings. Finally, Mark and Kathy had to face the fact that they were both considering marriage to people they didn't love. Kathy also figured out, at long last, where and how Dick fit into her life. They would always be dear friends, having shared a long and rich history in the face of countless problems. Kathy admitted to Dick that she was in love with Mark and that she hated Meta for wanting to marry so soon after Joe's death. To Kathy's great relief, Dick told her to follow her heart and be happy.

Immediately after Kathy and Dick spoke, Dick's car skidded on a rain-slick road and he was badly injured. He was horrified to discover that he'd lost the use of his right hand and faced a doubtful future as a surgeon. Dick's doctor, a newcomer to Cedars named Paul Fletcher, reminded Dick a great deal of Jim Kelly. Like Jim, Paul was from Chicago and had a rough edge to his personality. But Paul was also mysterious, for he was inexplicably determined to conceal the fact that he was Dan Clark's cousin. Dan, who had come out from New York to be with Kathy, realized that Kathy and Mark were in love and bitterly told this to Meta before he left Los Angeles. Meta was heartbroken; she had lost both her husband and her fiancé. Kathy and Mark became engaged, but Mark soon realized that he'd stepped into a sticky situation when Robin returned from school in Switzerland. A spoiled, belligerent preteen, Robin immediately locked horns with Mark. The lives of Meta, Kathy, Mark, Robin and Paul were about to take some fascinating and unexpected turns.

1957-1961

The next five years chronicled a major transition for Meta Roberts, the painful maturation of Mike Bauer and Robin Lang and the revelation of the enigmatic, crusty Dr. Paul Fletcher's true character and background. Central to all of these situations was a violent, though accidental, death.

Bill vehemently objected to Bert's friendship with Kathy, whom he blamed for having made Meta's life a living hell. As the Bauers watched Kathy's daughter, Robin, grow up, it was evident that the apple had not fallen far from the tree. Robin manipulated Kathy insufferably with guilt and threats to run away, all in the interest of keeping Mark and Kathy apart. In truth, Kathy wanted to spare Robin the pain she had known as a teenager when her father married Meta without her approval. Mark was not one to be pushed around, however, and he saw Robin for the precocious and manipulative child she was. Mark convinced Kathy to marry him, but the new Holden household was a battleground from day one. Robin continued to dictate to Kathy, while Meta constantly coddled Robin and undermined Mark's authority. Mark's teenage sister, Alice, came to stay with the Holdens, and Robin took an instant dislike to her despite Alice's efforts to be friendly. When young Mike Bauer became interested in Alice, Robin started flirting with him just out of spite. Kathy learned she was pregnant but held off telling Mark and Robin for fear of escalating the conflict between them. Unfortunately, Robin eavesdropped on a phone conversation between Kathy and her obstetrician and blurted the news to Mark, who was furious with Kathy for keeping it from him!

Robin felt she could count on only two people: Meta and Paul Fletcher. To most people, Paul had all the bedside manners of a process server; Bert Bauer snidely referred to him as a "sour apple." Yet when Paul treated Robin for a high fever, they formed a curious father-daughter bond that was born of a shared loneliness and alienation. Paul's hidden humanity surfaced when he treated Albert Franklin, Bert's terminally ill stepfather, who eventually died in Arizona. But to Dick Grant, with whom Paul shared a practice, Paul remained a curiosity. Paul often boasted that he didn't like people, and he was evasive whenever Dick and Marie asked about his background.

Dick, meanwhile, was finding it difficult to admit to Marie that he loved her. Medicine so defined his identity and his sense of manhood that he felt inadequate because he could no longer perform surgery with his right hand. Dick's reserve finally crumbled and he married Marie, but his first love remained the medical

Mark married Kathy and adopted Robin, a complicated, unhappy child intent on driving a wedge between her mother and new stepfather. It was not a happy home.

profession. Dick's confidence as a doctor was restored when he performed stomach surgery on little Billy Bauer solely with his left hand. Soon he was on staff simultaneously at two local hospitals—Cedars and General—and was working day and night. With Dick absent so often, Marie began to form a close, platonic friendship with Paul, who began to pour out his heart to her. He told Marie that his father had died before he was born, and he'd spent his entire life looking for a father figure. Soon Dick and Paul were at odds over Dick's ongoing neglect of Marie.

At this time, a situation arose that threw Paul into conflict not only with Dick, but with Mark as well. While putting up shelves in her kitchen, Kathy fell, lost her baby and became paralyzed. To complicate matters, Kathy's nurse was her old nemesis Janet Johnson, back in town after a bitter divorce. Dick recommended that Kathy undergo surgery on her legs, but Paul knew Kathy had only one chance in a thousand of walking again and accused Dick of offering her false hope. Kathy and Robin were more comfortable with Paul's direct approach than Mark was. Mark was not happy that Robin had latched on to Paul as a father figure, and he blamed Paul for widening the gap between him and Robin. Fortunately, Kathy's paralysis jolted Robin into accepting

TROUBLED TRIANGLES

Dick Grant married free-spirited artist Marie Wallace over his mother's objections, but his first love remained the medical profession. Soon Dick and his professional rival, Dr. Paul Fletcher, were at odds over Dick's neglect of his new wife.

Bill Bauer's career as a PR man was a checkered one. Whenever he did have success, Bert spent his earnings in her desire to live the good life and impress their affluent neighbors.

Mark as her father, and he happily adopted her. Now that Kathy was paralyzed, Bill began to put aside his resentment of her. He had his own issues to contend with, mainly concerning money. Not only had Bill bought a partnership in his public relations firm, but he had reluctantly let Bert talk him into buying a bigger house. To Bill's dismay, Bert spent what little money they had on clothes and furnishings to impress their affluent neighbors.

Then came an occasion truly worth celebrating in the Bauer household: Papa Bauer's 65th birthday. His daughter and son-in-law, Trudy and Clyde Palmer, surprised him by coming to visit. Afterward, Meta spent some time with Trudy and Clyde at their apartment in New York, where she was reunited with former admirer Dr. Bruce Banning, now a widower. Bruce visited Meta frequently after she returned to Los Angeles and soon proposed marriage, but Meta was noncommittal—she still had not gotten over Mark.

Soon, tragedy struck. While Kathy was outside in her wheelchair, two children on bicycles accidentally

On his 65th birthday, Papa Bauer was toasted by his two favorite women—Meta and Bert.

admitted the truth: He was her illegitimate son by Fred, who was married and had two other children. Paul had lashed out at Marian, telling her that he wished she'd given him up for adoption, because he now considered himself a nobody. Consumed with hatred for his mother, Paul left for New York and began to call himself Paul Fletcher. He never did meet his father, who had been out of Marian's life for many years.

With Marian back in the picture, Paul planned on returning to New York once he had cured a particular patient of her strange illness. Her name was Anne Benedict, and she was wealthy and spoiled but incredibly charming. Anne had been raised in San Francisco, where her parents, Henry and Helene, were country club cronies of Richard and Laura Grant's. Paul was just about to leave for New York when Anne took a bad

knocked her off the sidewalk into heavy traffic. She was killed instantly. Her horrible death brought Meta and Robin even closer together, to the point where Meta took Robin into her home. Certain that Meta would pursue Mark once he got over his grief, Bruce backed off in his courtship of her. He wasn't far off the mark, for Robin, insecure and desperate to have a stable family life, tried to bring Meta and Mark together at every turn.

As the Bauers dealt with Kathy's death, Paul faced an issue that struck at the core of his very being. Paul was stunned to receive a letter from Marian Winters, a nurse in Chicago who wanted to reestablish a relationship with him. He bitterly wrote back, forbidding her to contact him again. Marian was undaunted. She moved to town and took a job as Dick's special nurse without revealing her connection to Paul. For a while Paul managed to avoid her, but after he hung up on her one too many times, Marian confronted him at the hospital. It was then that the real story behind Paul Fletcher emerged. Paul's legal name was Paul Winters, and Marian was his mother. She had worked hard to support him and raised him with much love. For years Marian had told Paul that his father had died before he was born, but Paul suspected otherwise once he found his mother's love letters to Fred Fletcher. When Paul confronted his mother, she

After Kathy's untimely death, Robin looked upon Meta as a mother figure. Desperate for a stable family life, young Robin threw Meta and Mark together every chance she got.

turn. He diagnosed her with endocarditis and saved her life. Reluctantly, Paul allowed Marian to be Anne's special nurse because of her experience, but he was not pleased to see nurse and patient become friendly—after all, Marian and Paul had not told anyone at Cedars that they were mother and son. Soon after, Anne's parents arrived in town along with Anne's fiancé, Tom Sloane. Paul instantly became antagonistic toward Tom, who was to the manner born. Indeed, Paul and Anne were finding themselves very attracted to each other. To the horror of Henry Benedict, a nouveau riche snob, Anne broke her engagement to Tom and agreed to marry Paul.

News of Paul and Anne's engagement reached San Francisco and caught the eye of a man in Santa Clara. That man was Fred Fletcher. Fred was a widower with a daughter, Jane, and he thought Paul bore an uncanny resemblance to the son he had lost in the Korean War. Suspecting that they were related, Fred wrote Paul a letter, which Paul promptly tore up. Anne innocently mentioned this to Marian as well as to her parents. On the sly, Henry went to Chicago to investigate Paul's past, then visited Fred in Santa Clara but was cagey about his purpose. Ashamed to tell Anne he was illegitimate, and feeling his past was closing in on him, Paul asked her to elope.

Suspicious of Henry, Fred came to town, looked up Marian and told her about Henry's visit. She admitted to Fred that Paul was his son. Marian explained that by the time she found out she was pregnant, Fred had already decided to go back to his wife and children, and she felt she had no right to break up his family. In time, Paul established a relationship with Fred and apologized to Marian for being ashamed of both her and himself. Henry also apologized to Paul and went back to San Francisco with Helene, while Marian married Paul's friend, a pharmacist named John Lipsey. At last Paul was able to accept who he was, and he rejoiced when Anne bore him a son, John.

Mark Holden's life also took on a new focus. Although he was being pursued by both Meta and Janet, Mark was quite taken with his soft-spoken new housekeeper, Ruth Jannings. Before long, Ruth agreed to see Mark socially, much to the consternation of Meta and Robin, both of whom still harbored delusions of Mark marrying Meta. Bert tried to make Meta and Robin accept Mark and Ruth's romance, but to no avail. Ruth wanted to cool the relationship for Robin's sake, but

LOVE AND MARRIAGE

Blunt, jaded and hailing from a struggling background, Paul Fletcher fell in love and married rich, spoiled Anne Benedict.

Mark refused to let Robin call the shots. Ever the suffering diva, Robin climbed onto a balcony in the rain and purposely caught pneumonia. Paul placed the blame squarely on Meta for having fed Robin's fantasies about a reconciliation between Meta and Mark. For once, both Bert and Mark agreed with Paul, and the three angrily told Meta to get on with her life. Meta finally came to terms with the fact that Mark would never love her, and she accepted Bruce's long-standing marriage proposal. Mark and Ruth eloped to San Francisco, telling everyone except Alice that it was a business trip.

Bert was delighted when Mike asked Robin to the senior prom. She believed that with a normal teenage existence, Robin would blossom into a fine young lady. But it was not to be. When an excited Robin called Mark's hotel, the operator told her that Mark was out, "but Mrs. Holden is in." Her security shattered once again, Robin ran away. To make Mark feel guilty, she sent him a fake ransom note to lead him to believe she had been kidnapped. Everyone realized it was a hoax, however, when Robin showed up at her grandmother Helen Allen's apartment in New York.

Now that their friends Paul and Anne were new parents, Dick and Marie considered having a child of

rugged fellow artist named Joe Turino. At Joe's suggestion, Marie took a job at the local art school, and they both began working for the highly respected Bowden Art Galleries. Dick and Laura looked down on Joe, a plainspoken man who worked nights as a newspaper pressman, but Marie liked Joe's simplicity and forthrightness and appreciated the way he nurtured her creative spirit. Through her artistic endeavors, Marie met Nora Gibbs, a down-and-out model who was pregnant. Unbeknownst to Dick, Marie and Nora planned for Marie to adopt the child, who was born a girl and named Marie after her prospective mother. Soon after, Nora was killed in a car accident. To ensure a claim on

The Bauers were happy when Meta was courted by and agreed to marry the solid, dependable Dr. Bruce Banning.

their own. Unfortunately, Marie learned she was unable to conceive. She pleaded with Dick to adopt a child, but Dick refused and sent Marie to a bevy of fertility specialists instead. In actuality, Dick feared that becoming a parent would cut into his precious career. To add insult to injury, Laura came for an extended visit and supported Dick's position. Dick later relented and he and Marie consulted an adoption agency, but the caseworker rightly sensed that Dick was halfhearted in his professed desire to have a child. And so Marie busied herself by developing her artistic talent and became friendly with a

the child, Marie lied and said she was Nora's sister. But to Marie's bitter disappointment and Dick's relief, Nora's estranged parents surfaced and took the girl in. It was then that Dick and Marie reached an impasse and separated.

Robin also found a permanent home at long last with Meta and Bruce, who were now happily married. She continued to oppose Mark and Ruth's marriage until Ruth's son, Karl Jannings, arrived in Los Angeles to attend college. Unlike Robin, he was delighted with the marriage and convinced Robin to accept it—or so she led him to believe. Mike Bauer befriended Karl and watched him become emotionally involved with Robin. But Robin had no true feelings for Karl and was only leading him on with the intention of hurting him—all to get back at Ruth for marrying Mark! Mike caught on to Robin's game and told his parents. Bert began to resent Meta for having kept this bad seed in the family. What Mike couldn't admit to himself, however, was that he was becoming intensely attracted to Robin despite his better judgment, and the feeling was mutual. Mike's childhood had been the opposite of Robin's. While he had the secure home base of a loving family, the only family stability Robin had ever experienced was during those periods when she lived with Meta, who was also Mike's aunt. Robin felt trapped, for Karl was a controlling young man who kept his emotions close to the surface. She let Karl press her into an engagement she didn't really want, and soon she began to suffer from fevers and headaches. When Robin consulted Paul for treatment, he instinctively knew that her symptoms were a sign that she didn't love Karl. Dick was helping Robin, too, and advised Karl to postpone the wedding, but Karl angrily refused. Torn and guilty, Mike confided to Bill that he loved Robin but could not bring himself to hurt Karl. Bill was understanding, for he regretted having held a grudge against Robin's mother, Kathy. Both Bill and Mike knew, however, that Bert would not be of the same mind-set.

Robin finally took control of the situation, albeit impulsively. She admitted to Karl that she had never loved him and broke their engagement. Without missing a beat, Robin talked Mike into eloping! When the newlyweds returned and revealed the news to Karl on Meta's patio, Karl lunged at Mike, fell on an iron table and sustained severe head injuries. Karl died on the operating table and Mike was charged with manslaughter. Happily, he was cleared when the death was ruled an accident. Anxious for a new life together without Robin's constant machinations, Mark and Ruth left town.

Back at Cedars, Dick swore Paul to secrecy that he had separated from Marie. Dick was angling to replace the retiring Dr. Ainsley as chief of staff and knew that a failing marriage would make him vulnerable to public attack. Paul urged Dick to come clean; instead, Dick asked Marie to return. Knowing Dick wanted her back only to keep up appearances, Marie refused. When Ainsley found out the truth, he offered Paul the position instead. Paul made no secret of his disinterest in the job but accepted it under pressure from his status-conscious

wife, Anne. Devastated by this blow to his career, Dick told Marie he never wanted to see her again.

Watching all this from the sidelines was Joe Turino. Joe was falling in love with Marie, but he didn't want her on the rebound. Joe persuaded Marie to call Dick, but Laura intercepted the message and informed Marie that Dick was through with her. Ironically, Dick was having second thoughts and was livid when he discovered Laura's latest act of interference. He and Marie got back together, yet reached another impasse when Dick remained adamantly opposed to adopting a child. They planned to divorce, and Marie accepted Joe's marriage proposal. Soon after, Marie and Joe were surprised by the arrival of their boss, the internationally known artist and entrepreneur Alex Bowden. A dapper, 40-year-old womanizer, Alex chanced to meet Robin on a bridge in a park. Robin was depressed because Mike was wrestling with his guilt over the death of Karl. In actuality, they had been too young to marry, and married life

Nora was an unwed mother whose child Marie hoped to adopt, but Dick, unable to accept that they couldn't conceive, was against it. Nora befriended artist Joe Turino (pictured here), Marie's colleague, with whom Marie had a brief flirtation.

In time, Marie came to understand Dick's dedication to medicine, and Dick mellowed. They canceled their divorce, adopted a son and left town to start a new life.

was not what Robin had expected it to be. Alex rudely chided her for being a self-indulgent, spoiled brat—and a curious attraction was born. While Mike was out of town, Robin posed for Alex and he milked her loneliness ostensibly to draw out "that lonely, lost expression."

As Marie and Joe planned their wedding, they considered adopting a likable boy named Philip Collins. When Philip began suffering from fainting spells, Marie brought him to Dick, who discovered the boy had a narrow aorta. Usually indifferent to children, Dick bonded with Philip and performed brilliant surgery on the boy. Marie was deeply moved, for it was through Philip that she finally understood and appreciated Dick's dedication to medicine. To Joe's disappointment, Dick and Marie canceled their divorce, adopted Philip and left town with their new son.

Meanwhile, Bert was fit to be tied over Mike and Robin's marriage! She deeply regretted having promoted a romance between her son and Meta's ward, for Robin had since become a cunning, manipulative brat who orchestrated people's lives according to her whims. Hell-bent on pushing Robin out of the Bauer family fold, Bert

was secretly glad to learn of Robin and Alex's mutual attraction, and she encouraged Alex to woo Robin away from Mike. By the time Bert fully realized what an operator Alex was, she had second thoughts, but it was too late. Robin had fallen under Alex's spell. In Alex Bowden, Robin saw someone whom she thought would always protect her, and he showered her with affection and attention such as she had never known before. Convinced that they were no longer in love, Mike agreed to an annulment, and Robin entered, once again, into an ill-considered marriage that was doomed from the start. As for Mike, he bitterly rejected Bert for her interference and left to take a construction job in Venezuela.

Robin and Alex's Hawaiian honeymoon was a disaster. Alex was a virtual Svengali, planning Robin's every move and becoming jealous if she cast even a glance at another man. Within days, Alex worked himself into a gastric ulcer, and the harried honeymooners returned home, where Alex continued to feel insecure and threatened by Robin's ties to the Bannings and the Bauers. Unable to understand his wife's irrational expectations or evaluate her irresponsible behavior, and tired of his father-figure role, Alex demanded that Robin behave like a wife instead of a child bride. Bert had an attack of conscience and apologized to Robin for her interference, and to Meta's delight the sisters-in-law formed a new bond.

A complex and tragic woman was now to enter the lives of the Bowdens and the Fletchers. One of Alex's ex-wives, the alcoholic Doris Crandall, arrived from San Francisco in hopes of winning Alex back. Alex asked his cynical lawyer pal, George Hayes, to pay her off to get rid of her, but Doris wouldn't accept the money. While renewing a prescription for her medication, Doris consulted Paul and the two formed an instant rapport. Paul hired Doris to be his receptionist, much to the consternation of Anne, who considered Doris a deadbeat drunk. Anne was horrified further when Paul resigned his chief of staff post at Cedars to open a clinic in an impoverished, often violent neighborhood. Even worse, Paul insisted they move into a house next door to the clinic!

At least one patient followed Paul to his new practice: Bert Bauer. Bert had Paul treat her for a virus, and he was shocked to learn that she had not had so much as a general checkup in fourteen years! Paul ordered a complete examination, including a Pap smear. The results indicated the possibility of uterine cancer. Bill called Mike with the news and convinced him to come home. The Bauers were now reunited, albeit in the face of possible tragedy.

1962-1966

The years 1962 to 1966 saw dramatic changes in the lives of the Bauers and the Fletchers, not the least of which was a shift in locale from the West Coast to the Midwest. In doing so, the unity of each of these families would become perilously split by marital and generational problems.

Bert Bauer learned that she was in the early stages of uterine cancer. Happily, her surgery was successful not only in ridding her body of the disease, but also in bringing Mike Bauer back into the family fold. Although he tentatively forgave his mother for her interference in his personal life, Bert and Mike continued to squabble until he felt forced to move out of the house. Thanks to his new job as a law clerk for George Hayes, Mike was able to rent a decent apartment. An added bonus was George's new secretary, who happened to be a captivating young brunette named Julie Conrad. Having escaped bickering parents who dominated and overprotected her, Julie was like a lioness out of her cage, and the handsome, up-and-coming Mike Bauer was her prey. But Mike hadn't given up on Robin, and he was quick to notice Alex's jealous reaction to his return. Mike was confident that the Bowdens' marriage would collapse under its own flimsy weight. Robin didn't help the situation when she played hot and cold with Mike and agreed to a few secret, albeit sexless, meetings with him. In his dual role of Robin's guardian and Alex's doctor, Bruce Banning began to sympathize with Alex and helped him to conquer his jealousy. Banning sternly told Robin to grow up and take responsibility for her life.

Recognizing that his loveless marriage to Robin was on the rocks, Alex began to look once again in the direction of his ex, Doris Crandall, who, much to the pleasant surprise of everyone around her, was showing signs of becoming a strong and independent woman. Bert admired Doris' character and became a close friend. Even Anne Fletcher discovered that they had a great deal in common. Like Anne, Doris came from a finishing school background and had the same understated "old money" tastes. Unfortunately, a friendship between the two was not to be, much to the dismay of Anne's husband, Paul.

The pressure on Paul was becoming unbearable.

Because of his poor patients' inability to pay their medical bills, his clinic was failing. To maximize his chances of getting at least a few solvent patients, Paul worked virtually around the clock. During his few off-hours, Anne bombarded him with complaints that she was unable to afford new clothes, and she hounded him to give

ISSUES

In 1962, Bert had a Pap smear and learned she was in the early stages of uterine cancer. The surgery was a success, and Bert's brush with the disease served to educate several generations of daytime audiences about the value of this simple test.

Charming bachelor Alex Bowden wed the much
younger Robin after her marriage to Mike was
annulled at Bert's insistence. But Mike was still
in love with Robin and confident that her May-
December marriage to Alex would collapse.

up the clinic in favor of a lucrative job back at Cedars.
Anne had a potent ally in her father, Henry Benedict,
who was spending more time in town due to various
business commitments. Henry was horrified by the gang
violence that was erupting in the clinic's neighborhood
and convinced his darling girl to get a gun for her own
protection. Paul was constantly battling his wife and
father-in-law, especially when Henry announced his
plans to buy them a house in a prestigious neighborhood,
complete with a huge playground for his deserving
grandson, Johnny. Fortunately, Anne's mother, Helene,
was more supportive of Paul and his ideals, and she
admonished Anne to stop acting like a child.

As if this wasn't enough, Paul had to contend with
the arrival of his half-sister, Jane Fletcher. A catty, neurotic and bitter young woman, Jane was suffering from
the aftereffects of a disastrous romance she had had during her nurses' training in Boston. She soon became Julie
Conrad's friend and roommate and observed firsthand
Julie's shameless pursuit of Mike. Bert took to Jane immediately and tried to match her up with Mike, but to

her chagrin, she soon discovered that the sexy Julie was
angling to become the next Mrs. Michael Bauer, and
Mike, who was losing patience with Robin's indecisiveness, was beginning to take notice. When Alex finally offered Robin her freedom, Robin's only response was to
become neurotically jealous of Alex's renewed bond
with his ex-wife. Alex's close friend, George Hayes,
warned him to steer clear of Doris because he himself
had feelings for her and had even proposed.

The stage was now set for a jarring chain of events
that had a ripple effect on the Bauers, the Fletchers and
everyone else in their circle. In her determination to save
Paul's clinic, Doris convinced Alex to invest heavily in
the facility. Anne was livid at this development and
served Paul with an ultimatum: the clinic or their marriage. She prevailed upon Robin to change Alex's mind
about the loan, insidiously implying that the business
deal was evidence of a renewed bond between Alex and
Doris. Anne and Robin lashed into Doris so brutally that
Doris went on a prolonged alcoholic bender. When she
finally resurfaced back at the clinic, she got a hold of
Anne's gun and threatened suicide. In an effort to retrieve the gun, Paul grappled with Doris. The gun went
off and the bullet hit Anne. She died on the operating
table. Full of self-recrimination, Paul impulsively confessed to killing his wife. His chances of acquittal looked
dismal because Doris had blocked out the tragic event,
and Henry was snidely feeding the prosecution's case
against his son-in-law. Luckily, George Hayes mounted a
brilliant criminal defense with Mike's eager assistance.
Feeling guilty over their indirect roles in Anne's death,
Alex and Robin agreed to a divorce and dedicated themselves to clearing Paul's name. Robin went to work at the
clinic while Alex scoured the neighborhood bars until he
found a bartender who remembered Doris' alcoholic
bender on the night of the tragedy. Doris' memory finally returned, and she testified that Anne's shooting was
accidental. Soon after, Doris left town and Paul was free
to go on with his life.

Mike Bauer also felt free—for the moment, that is.
Mike pressured Julie into having casual sex, even though
he knew she wanted to hold out for marriage. Mike's
world now revolved around the law, working for George
by day and studying by night, and Julie was merely a
pleasant distraction. So when Julie insisted that they become engaged, Mike cavalierly dropped her. Not long afterward, Julie informed Mike that she was pregnant with
his child! In hopes of keeping this development a secret,
Mike coldly told Julie that he would support her finan-

cially until the baby was born, but he fully expected her to give the child up for adoption. Julie might have gone along with his plan had it not been for Jane Fletcher. Cynical about men in general, Jane wanted everyone to know that Mike was callous and insensitive in his treatment of her friend. Jane told Paul about Julie's pregnancy, then blabbed to Bert that she was going to be a grandmother! Shocked, Bert told Mike in no uncertain terms that her grandchild was not to be given up for adoption! She was somewhat relieved that Bill was away on an extended business trip in Switzerland, because under the circumstances, Bill might have been more sympathetic toward Mike. Recognizing that George was now a father figure to her son, Bert secured George's alliance in pressuring Mike to do the "honorable thing" and marry Julie. They were wed by a justice of the peace, and Mike did not admit to his blushing bride that he was marrying her under duress.

Left without a roommate, Jane moved in with Paul to take care of her little nephew, Johnny. She briefly dated Peter Nelson, an affable young doctor who worked at Paul's clinic, but he soon jilted her because he was more interested in Robin. Paul was also beginning to look at Robin for the first time as a woman rather than as the confused, alienated teenager with whom he had shared a father-daughter kind of kinship. Jane was quick to pick up on the growing attraction between Paul and Robin, and she didn't like it one bit! Wounded once again by a broken romance, Jane sought refuge with Paul and Johnny to the point where she was beginning to look at her brother and nephew more as a husband and son. With uncanny precision, this would-be spinster infected little Johnny with her twisted mind. By the time Paul and Robin announced plans to marry, Johnny was convinced that he was losing his father to an evil woman who had set out to take his mother's place—all thanks to Auntie Dearest, Jane.

One bright spot in Paul's life was the expansion of the Fletcher Clinic, thanks to Alex's loan. Mike served as construction supervisor for the project and thus came into more contact with Robin. By this time, Mike and Robin were nothing more than close friends, but because her marriage to Mike was shaky at best, Julie feared otherwise. They were now living with Bert, who behaved like a member of the gestapo around the newlyweds, and Papa Bauer, who tried his best to mediate Bert and Mike's constant battles. Bill was still away on business, and Mike's brother, William Edward, was away at medical school. Unaware that they already knew, Julie announced her pregnancy to Bert and Papa. Later, she was shattered to overhear Mike tell Robin that he only married her because of the baby! Julie drove away from the house unnoticed and was seriously injured in an automobile accident. When she awoke, she learned that she had given birth prematurely to a baby girl. Embittered by her sham of a marriage, Julie told Mike to take the baby and go! Since Mike's family had known about her pregnancy all along, Julie felt like the Bauer family joke. But once Paul convinced her to hold her new little girl, Julie came around and decided to give her marriage another try. In turn, she named her baby daughter Hope. However, there was little hope of saving Mike and Julie's marriage. Julie resumed her job as secretary to George, while Mike worked slavishly to complete his law education, which George had generously financed. Mike drove himself so hard that he became seriously ill with a viral infection. Instead of being sympathetic, Julie worried that Mike's illness would postpone the degree that would ensure her the privileged life of a lawyer's spouse. Bert helped out by taking care of Hope, but she became

Artist Joe Turino showed his work at the Bowden Gallery. It was there that Turino met and befriended Alex's tragic ex-wife Doris Crandall.

Losing patience with Robin's indecisiveness, Mike turned to Julie Conrad, George Hayes' pretty but neurotic secretary. When Julie became pregnant with Hope, Mike was pressured into a loveless marriage.

so obsessed with the child that when Bill finally returned from his business trip, she barely paid any attention to him. Hope had become Bert's entire world.

While Hope was too young to bear the scars of her family's problems, Johnny Fletcher was becoming quite the little tyrant. Helene Benedict tried to convince her grandson to accept Paul and Robin's engagement, but Henry and Jane kept indulging the boy. Buckling under the child's pressure, Robin called off her engagement to Paul and went to New York. George eventually tracked her down and innocently left her address with Jane while Paul went to fetch his lady love. Salivating at this golden opportunity to wreak more havoc, Jane called Robin and tipped her off that Paul was on his way, adding that she thought she did the right thing by leaving him. Robin eluded Paul, but he caught up with her and they married secretly in New York. Meanwhile, George received a letter from Robin's New York roommate informing him of Jane's phone call. Never one to mince words, George let Jane have it with both barrels and told her to get a life!

At this time, George's buddy Alex Bowden was at loose ends romantically and was surprised to find himself attracted to Julie, by now bored in her marriage. He was even more surprised by his restraint in their offbeat

friendship. The two became confidants and he showered her with expensive gifts, but Alex had grown too fond of Mike to steal another woman from him. One day, Alex asked Julie what she wanted out of life, and without hesitation she replied, "A man who understands me as you do." Alex didn't take the bait. Julie left Mike and Hope and moved into an apartment, only to discover that she was pregnant once again by Mike!

Julie and Alex talked marriage for a while until Alex came to see how twisted she'd become. She tried to pass her unborn child off as Alex's, when in truth they'd never been sexually involved. Once she considered getting an abortion and a quickie divorce, Alex knew he'd had enough and threatened to tell Mike about the baby unless she told him herself. Trapped, Julie became so distraught that she had a miscarriage and tried to jump off the ledge outside her hospital room. When Alex revealed to Mike the truth about the baby, Mike blamed himself for Julie's problems. Yet as far as Bill was concerned, the blame belonged with Bert for having goaded Mike into this loveless marriage. As for Mike, he was disgusted by

Anne's mother, Helene Benedict, disapproved of her husband's attempts to spoil their grandson, Johnny, and tried to get him to accept Paul and Robin's engagement. Johnny lived with them until Helene finally insisted that the boy return home.

his mother's neglect of his father and her "take-charge" attitude with Hope. The only good news in Mike's life at this time was his graduation from law school.

Paul and Robin returned home and told no one about their marriage except for Meta, Bruce and George, who decided not to tell Paul about Jane's damaging phone call to Robin in New York. The newlyweds led separate lives for a while until Robin accompanied Paul to a medical convention. When Jane called Paul's hotel to tell him that Johnny was having problems at school, the desk clerk told her that Paul was with "Mrs. Fletcher." Devastated, Jane told Johnny that his daddy had lied to them and Johnny ran away. When he turned up later at the Children's Zoo, the boy not only rejected Paul and Robin, but added his aunt Jane to the list. Johnny stayed briefly with his grandparents in San Francisco and returned home to Paul at Helene's firm insistence. Determined to salvage both his marriage and his relationship with his son, Paul angrily ordered Jane out of his home and his life!

This was too much for Jane to bear. She wandered around the city, blabbing incoherently until the police finally picked her up. George stepped in and tried to help her, advising her to make the most of her nurturing tendencies and return to nursing. One night, during a heated argument, Jane bolted out onto a dark street. George followed, only to be struck by a car. He underwent a craniotomy and awoke with retrograde amnesia, calling out for his former fiancée, Mary. Racked with guilt, Jane volunteered to be George's special nurse, and she soon realized that she was falling in love. She feared their growing bond would be shattered if George remembered their old antagonism. Gradually, George's memory returned with the help of a specialist, who suggested he play the piano, a pastime he had enjoyed in his youth. Putting his stormy past encounters with Jane aside, George asked her to marry him. When Jane gave birth to a little girl, Amy, their life seemed complete. Seeing how Jane had transformed herself, Paul and Robin found it in their hearts to forgive her as well.

A rash of changes then began to take place. Johnny was so insolent to Robin that Paul reluctantly allowed him to go back to his grandparents for an extended stay. Not long after, Paul learned that Helene had been killed in a car accident. As for Alex Bowden, he left to open new galleries across the country, buoyed by the hope of at long last finding a healthy relationship with a woman. Meta and Bruce Banning moved to New York, where Bruce accepted a prestigious position at Columbia Pres-

After Julie Bauer's sudden death, Bert became totally preoccupied with her granddaughter, Hope. Feeling neglected, Bill turned to his understanding secretary, Maggie Scott, and the two had an affair. The guilt drove Bill back to the bottle.

byterian Hospital. Julie was sent to a mental institution, where she died of injuries that were possibly self-inflicted. With Bill's encouragement, Mike and Hope escaped Bert's dominance and relocated in Bay City. The rest of the Bauers and the Fletchers moved to the Midwestern city of Springfield, where Paul became chief of staff at the Springfield branch of Cedars Hospital.

Bill Bauer also accepted a lucrative transfer to the Springfield office of his public relations firm, where one of his perks was a lovely and dedicated assistant, Maggie Scott. Maggie was a divorcee in her 30s who had single-handedly raised her daughter, Peggy, now fifteen years old. Although Maggie had a loyal suitor in Jason Webber,

was serving in the Korean War. Soon Maggie became pregnant, and she gave birth to Peggy while Ben was overseas. After Ben returned, Maggie realized that the marriage had been a mistake. Ben turned out to be a gambler who passed rubber checks and avoided any opportunity to make an honest living. He ran out on the family and Maggie divorced him for desertion. Shortly after Maggie relayed this story to Bill, Ben Scott returned! His criminal days behind him, Ben bought a restaurant and told Maggie he wanted to reconcile. Maggie was hesitant and tried to keep him from seeing Peggy, so Ben secretly introduced himself to his estranged daughter as a friend of her father, who was on a secret mission in Europe. The impressionable young girl was won over by this charming man, and eventually Maggie discovered that Ben had established contact with Peggy. With Maggie present, Ben revealed to Peggy that he was really her father and that he had done shady things in the past. Peggy was so elated, she could not wait for her parents to get back together! The only hitch was, Maggie and Bill were having an affair, and they were very much in love.

Bert and Bill's marriage was more tenuous than it had been in years. Taking no responsibility for her autocratic ways, Bert constantly sniped at Bill for taking Mike's side against her. She was hopeful about improving the family situation when their younger son, Billy, joined them in Springfield after graduating from medical school, but it soon became evident that the Bauers' cheerful, uncomplicated son had changed into a driven young man. Billy announced that he was now going by the name of Ed, derived from his middle name, Edward. He spent virtually every waking hour at Cedars Hospital, where he aimed to become a brilliant and successful surgeon. Bert was saddened to see that "Billy" was gone forever and that "Ed" was a virtual stranger to her.

The stage was now set for a most trying period in the Bauers' lives. Papa Bauer overheard Bill and Maggie discussing their relationship and warned Maggie not to destroy the family. Bert witnessed Bill and Maggie holding hands, then slipped away unnoticed. This marked the beginning of Bert Bauer's transformation into a mature, caring woman of substance. Taking responsibility for having driven Bill away, Bert made herself more attractive and started paying attention to her husband. The situation might have righted itself more easily had Ben Scott not discovered Bill and Maggie's affair. Later, while they were out driving, Ben confronted Maggie and the car crashed. An injured Ben was rushed to Cedars,

Bert was hopeful about her family situation when their younger son, Ed, returned to Springfield after graduating from medical school. But Ed, sickened by his father's drinking, was anything but sympathetic.

a successful airline executive, she repeatedly turned down his marriage proposals in order to devote her time to Peggy. Eventually, Jason gave up on her, and Maggie began confiding to Bill the details of her difficult life. When she was a senior in high school, Maggie went against her parents' wishes and married Ben Scott, who

where Ed examined him. In his delirium, Ben rambled on about Bill and Maggie's affair in front of Ed. Sickened by this revelation, Ed bitterly confronted his father and demanded that he confess the affair to Bert. What neither Bill nor Ed realized, of course, was that Bert already knew. Bert walked in on the argument and to Ed's surprise, lambasted him for his disrespect and lack of compassion toward his father! In her inimitable way, she told Ed to "start behaving like a son," because right now he wasn't "fit to shine his father's shoes." Touched by Bert's display of love and loyalty, Bill showed her more tenderness than he had in a long time.

The marriage of Paul and Robin Fletcher appeared hopeful when they learned they were expecting a child. Around this time, Johnny, now a tall, handsome teenager, returned from his grandfather's in San Francisco. Like Ed Bauer, he was an anomaly to his family, an insufferably snobbish, preppy golf maven in the mold of his grandfather, Henry Benedict. Paul wisely brought his son back down to earth when he made Johnny attend the public high school in their neighborhood, rather than the private schools he was accustomed to back in San Francisco. Robin and Johnny remained distant but polite to one another. One day, Robin decided to clean up the boy's sloppy bedroom. While she was cleaning, Robin fell off a chair and suffered a miscarriage. Jolted by this tragedy, Johnny made a sincere effort to become closer to his stepmother, but unfortunately, Robin could not respond in kind because she blamed Johnny for the loss of her child. Paul was shocked and hurt by his wife's attitude, as he now saw Johnny in a different light and felt closer than ever to him. Soon Paul and Robin were so frequently at odds that Robin wondered aloud to Papa if Paul would ever love her as much as he did Anne.

Feeling alienated by Robin, Johnny found a new friend in his classmate Peggy Scott, and the two fell in love. Peggy was happy when Maggie remarried Ben, although she was unaware that Ben was blackmailing Maggie with an unmailed love letter he had found addressed to Bill. The marriage was in name only and was further weakened by Ben's strict, overprotective parenting of Peggy. Meanwhile, Bill was so depressed by the loss of Maggie and by Ed's stinging rejection that he let a business associate talk him into having a few drinks to bolster his spirits. After many years of sobriety, Bill was now off the wagon and feeling tremendously guilty because of it. Fighting to regain control, Bill pleaded for Ed's love and forgiveness, but Ed could only respond with lacerating verbal attacks that shattered Bill and infuriated Bert. With chilling detachment, Ed urged Bert to

Peggy Scott, shown here with Robin and Paul Fletcher, was dating Paul's son, Johnny. The teenagers felt alienated from their respective families and found comfort in their friendship, which soon blossomed into love.

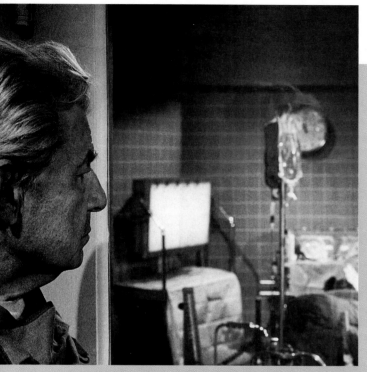

ON CALL AT CEDARS

It didn't take Ed Bauer long to latch on to a father figure far more universally respected than his own. He was Dr. Stephen Jackson, Cedars' eminent chief of surgery, and the two forged a close "father–son" relationship.

looked for new employment...and more important, he stopped drinking.

As impressed as Ed was with Bill's turnaround, he was latching on to a father figure more career-driven, more universally respected and far more authoritarian than Bill Bauer was. He was Dr. Stephen Jackson, Cedars' eminent chief of surgery. Jackson was so married to medicine that he looked on his daughter, Leslie, a nurse's aide, as little more than an inconvenience. All Jackson ever said about his personal life was that his wife had died in childbirth, and his colleagues had the distinct impression that Dr. Jackson was less than devastated by the loss. Out of pure opportunism rather than infatuation, Ed let himself be pursued by the spunky Leslie Jackson. Steve approved of his daughter's budding relationship with the up-and-coming young doctor; now he could marry Leslie off and give his full time and attention to his cherished scalpel. But Ed became far more than a means to an end for Steve. He was the son he never had, the worshipful male successor he'd longed for. Likewise, Steve was a curious source of healing for Ed, who looked on his own father, Bill, as a spineless, job-hopping loser. Time after time, Ed broke dates with Leslie so he could follow Steve around Cedars at all hours of the day and night. To Ed, Steve was his coach, and the operating room was their playing field. Ed Bauer had cast himself in the mold of his successful, though hollow, mentor. The only thing he would do differently from Steve, Ed told Leslie, was that he would never have children, because they were an impediment to his success. Bearing the scars of her father's neglect, Leslie could not help but be offended. She realized that she had fallen in love with a man who was very much like her father.

Enter Joe Werner. Although he was several years older, Joe had been Ed's closest friend in medical school. He had had a less privileged background than Ed and had struggled longer to get where he was. Now a resident at Cedars, Joe was envious that the eminent Dr. Jackson was bestowing so many professional favors on Ed, and that the way was already paved for Ed to become the chief surgeon's son-in-law. Not one to be passed over, Joe vowed to get a piece of Ed's action any way he could.

leave Bill in hopes that he would hit rock bottom and get off the bottle. Bert remained committed to her husband and blamed Ed for driving Bill to drink when he needed his son's love most. During one of Bill's most acute alcoholic stupors, he mistook Peggy for Maggie and revealed their past affair to the confused teenager. Peggy confronted Maggie and then made plans to elope with Johnny, who was fed up with his own sad family situation. Their plan was foiled, however, when Peggy was injured in a car accident. Maggie blamed Bill for her daughter's brush with death, and Bill couldn't argue with her. Sensing that he was about to be fired, Bill quit his job and

1967–1971

The period from 1967 to 1971 marked some surprising departures and shocking deaths in Springfield, not to mention a wrenching conflict between two brothers.

Paul Fletcher was pleasantly surprised when the dedicated research physician Sara McIntyre came to Cedars. They had worked together in Chicago when Paul was a resident and Sara was an intern. Paul had proposed marriage at one point, but Sara opted to remain friends. Personable though she was, Sara used her career as a shield against forming close relationships with men. Independently wealthy, she nonetheless aimed to carve out her own niche in the medical profession. Unlike the other privileged debutantes she grew up with, Sara wanted to prove herself. Though Paul was no longer attracted to Sara, Robin became fanatically jealous of this charming doctor, who seemed to embody everything Paul wanted in a woman. Certain that her marriage was doomed and unable to endure any more heartbreak, Robin threw herself in front of a car! She was killed instantly.

As if this wasn't enough to bear, Paul also had to contend with his son Johnny's teenage romance with Peggy Scott. Once he turned 25, Johnny stood to inherit $3 million from his wealthy grandfather, Henry Benedict. Desperate to marry Peggy, he asked his father and grandfather to advance him the money. Paul thought Johnny was much too young to marry and was relieved when Henry said no. Undaunted, Johnny and Peggy obtained a marriage license on Peggy's eighteenth birthday. Ben Scott found it, went to Johnny and knocked him out cold, and Ben died of a massive coronary as a result. Not long after, Ed reluctantly agreed to operate on Maggie when she was suffering from a serious intestinal ailment. Peggy had finally made her peace with her mother, only to have Maggie die under Ed's scalpel. Bill apologized to the young girl for his indirect role in hurting her, and Peggy became like a daughter to Bert and Bill, as well as Leslie's closest friend and confidante.

Bill had not had any luck in the job-hunting department. To make ends meet, Bert convinced Paul to hire her as a ward secretary at Cedars, which left Bill feeling emasculated. Fortunately, Bill was soon hired by another PR firm. His self-esteem was restored, and Bert came back to home and hearth. Ed shared Bill's relief that Bert was no longer working at Cedars, because she was constantly pushing Ed and Leslie to get married. Convinced that marriage would not serve his illustrious surgical career, Ed broke up with Leslie, leaving the field wide open for Joe Werner, who quickly moved in. Before long, Leslie accepted Joe's proposal of marriage. But when Steve Jackson suffered a coronary, Ed and Leslie, thrown

Sara McIntyre was Paul Fletcher's former flame and colleague from their days as interns in Chicago. Robin was so jealous of their friendship that she threw herself in front of a car and was killed instantly.

together by their mutual concern, realized how much they cared for one another. They were married in a quiet ceremony at Longview Nursing Home, where Steve was convalescing. During Steve's absence, Joe used his chief resident position at the hospital to saddle Ed with menial duties.

The enmity between Ed and Joe reached a climax when the voluptuous Tracy Delmar blew into town. Tracy introduced herself to Sara as her long-lost niece and ingratiated herself with the lonely lady doctor. She was immediately attracted to the coolly ambitious Joe and charmed him into going out on a date one night, when he was supposed to be on duty. While they wined and dined, one of Joe's patients died. Joe seized the opportunity to pin the blame on Ed, who had forgotten to sign out earlier that afternoon when Joe relieved him. But Joe would later prove that he did have a conscience after all. He was awed when Ed saved the life of Marty Dillman, the leader of a neighborhood gang known as the Lords. Marty had been stabbed during a rumble and would

Using the name Tracy Delmar, Charlotte Waring introduced herself to Sara as her long-lost niece. A neurotic schemer, Charlotte planned to take the unsuspecting Sara for everything she was worth.

have died had it not been for Ed's brilliant surgery. As a result, Joe wasted no time in dumping the shallow Tracy and apologizing to Ed, acknowledging him as the fine surgeon he was. The doctors decided to let bygones be bygones and soon became inseparable friends.

It was at this time that Mike Bauer returned to Springfield from Bay City with his daughter, Hope. Both father and daughter took an immediate liking to Leslie, who became the mother figure young Hope had been yearning for. Now a successful criminal defense lawyer, Mike had greatly matured, and he saw a reflection of his younger self in the shabby way Ed treated Leslie. Ed was enraged when Leslie left her nurse's aide job at Cedars, accusing her of secretly planning to get pregnant against his wishes. Mike spoke up about Ed's attitude toward his wife, as well as Ed's surly indifference to their father, who had been experiencing frequent nausea and chest pains. One day, Bill and Ed got into an argument that grew so heated, Bill collapsed of a heart attack! Feeling responsible, Ed recommended that Bill undergo a heart transplant, a risky procedure in those days. Over Bert's objections, Bill agreed, and the brilliant Dr. Gavin

In 1968, Mike Bauer returned to Springfield with his daughter, Hope. Both father and daughter took an instant liking to Leslie, who was the mother figure Hope had always yearned for.

At Leslie's urging, Ed returned to Springfield to help Bert and Papa Bauer through a difficult time following Bill's disappearance in a plane crash.

Hamilton was called in to perform what would be a successful operation.

Ed was full of self-loathing. Even though he had done all he could, he was feeling guilty over Maggie Scott's death, and now he'd almost killed his own father. So it was that this iron-willed, cocksure young surgeon fell victim to the same disease that plagued his father—alcoholism. He became jealous of the growing friendship between Leslie and Mike and picked drunken fights with both of them. Soon his work and concentration slid to the point where even Steve could no longer defend him, and Ed was dismissed from Cedars. He proceeded to go on a binge, sideswiped a car and was jailed for leaving the scene of the accident. Bill bailed him out and desperately tried to help his son, but to no avail. Certain he'd lost everything, Ed left town.

Numbed by the death of both her parents, Peggy was convinced her romance with Johnny Fletcher had caused too much heartache for those around her. She turned her energies toward a nursing career at Cedars, and it was there that she met Marty Dillman. Not your stereotypical gang leader, Marty was an unprincipled, thrill-seeking rich boy who'd been spoiled rotten by his widowed mother, Claudia. Marty took to the innocent Peggy immediately and charmed her with his superficial intelligence and artificial wit. This left Johnny vulnerable to the machinations of Tracy Delmar, who was impressed that he was launching a medical career in the footsteps of his successful father. When Tracy learned that Johnny stood to inherit a fortune, she was no longer merely impressed—she was determined to have him. Paul soon regretted having discouraged Johnny from marrying Peggy, for he rightly sensed that both of these young people were headed for disaster. Indeed, the catalyst for the ensuing tragedy was Johnny and Tracy's announcement of their engagement.

One of Bill Bauer's business associates saw Tracy's picture in the newspaper and told Bill that she resembled a girl named Charlotte Waring, whom he'd known in Oregon. Then Flip Malone, a sleazy garage attendant who was a crony of Marty's, also identified Tracy as Charlotte. Tracy wasn't Sara's long-lost niece; she was a gold-digging impostor who was after Sara's money! When Flip told Marty about the attractive con artist, Marty blackmailed Tracy for big bucks and split the take with Flip. Keeping her identity a secret, Tracy married Johnny. Meanwhile, Marty was not pleased to learn that Peggy was pregnant with his child and he married her reluctantly. Both marriages were mercifully short-lived.

Concerned over her sons' tangled love lives and mourning the loss of Bill, Bert was grateful when her sister-in-law Meta and her husband returned to Springfield.

Peggy overheard a conversation between Marty and Tracy and wrongly suspected they were having an affair. Distraught and weak from her pregnancy, Peggy blacked out. When she came to, Marty had vanished! He was later found near a lake, with a fractured skull and a knife wound to his neck. The police booked Peggy for the murder, and she went on trial with Mike Bauer as her able defense attorney. Mike arranged for Peggy to leave jail temporarily and go to Cedars for the birth of her son. She named him William Bauer Dillman.

With Marty dead and Peggy's life in a shambles, Tracy finally revealed her true identity as Charlotte Waring and confessed that she'd been after Sara's money. Sara bitterly wrote the girl off, and Johnny annulled their charade of a marriage. Charlotte was determined to redeem herself. Sharing Mike's suspicion that Flip Malone was Marty's real killer, she began dating the grease monkey in order to obtain the necessary proof. One night Flip drunkenly revealed to Charlotte that Marty had planned to double-cross him in their blackmail scheme and skip town. He showed her the airplane ticket Marty had intended to use. Guessing correctly that Flip had snuffed out Marty, Charlotte waited until Flip was asleep, then sneaked out with the ticket and turned it over to Mike. Later, when Mike was grilling Flip on

the witness stand, the shrewd lawyer produced the plane ticket and introduced it as evidence. Cornered, Flip confessed to the crime and was jailed. Mike thanked Charlotte for her help in exonerating Peggy, but the former impostor was in no mood to celebrate. The events of the past several months had hit her hard, and Tracy became suicidal. She ran from the courtroom and began driving so wildly that she crashed her car and sustained near-fatal injuries to her lungs. Tracy was operated on at Cedars and recovered, and at long last, Peggy and John were married.

Mike and Leslie's predicament was not only tearing them apart inside, but was dividing the entire Bauer family as well. When Leslie announced her intention to divorce Ed, Bert and Steve implored her to wait for his return. Still closely bonded with his father, Mike confided to Bill that he was in love with Leslie. They tried to keep this a secret from Bert, but she soon caught Mike and Leslie in an embrace and accused them of having an affair. Bill believed Mike when he said that he'd never been sexually involved with Leslie, and warned Bert to tone down her disapproval for Hope's sake. Once again, it was Bert vs. Bill and Mike. Such was the state of Bert and Bill's marriage when Bill left for Alaska on one of his frequent business trips. Bill told

Joe Werner was very much in love with Sara McIntyre. When she turned down his proposal of marriage, he went to England on a lecture tour.

Sara eventually married Lee Gantry, a Bluebeard type who plotted to kill her for her money. His housekeeper, Mildred Foss, knew all about how Gantry had killed his first wife, Alice Rawlings.

Bert he'd be changing planes in Seattle and would call her when he reached Alaska. Sadly, the second leg of Bill's journey met with tragedy. En route to Alaska, his plane went down at sea.

Just as the Bauers were mourning Bill's apparent death, Ed summoned the courage to call Leslie, and at her urging he came back to Springfield. He had been working at Hastings Electrical Supply Warehouse in Tarrywood, where he had become romantically involved with a secretary named Janet Mason. A breath of fresh air in Ed's life, Janet was the sweet, somewhat sheltered daughter of Colonel Grove Mason and his wife, Ellen. When Ed arrived in Springfield in the wake of his father's death, he apologized for the hurt he'd caused and convinced Leslie to give their marriage another try. Janet followed him to Springfield and landed a job as Paul Fletcher's secretary, and she and Ed continued their affair. Ed knew Leslie was really in love with Mike, and he intended to divorce her eventually, but not before he was out of the woods at Cedars. The board had him on probation until they were satisfied that his personal life was

back on track. Once again, Leslie was a means to an end for Ed Bauer's career.

As Bert dealt with her sons' tangled love lives, she was grateful for the arrival of her in-laws, Meta and Bruce Banning. Bruce took a position at Cedars, where he and Meta soon befriended Sara McIntyre. Sara was treating Lee Gantry, a malaria patient whose deceased wife, Alice Rawlings, had grown up with Meta. Alice's wealthy family had a rambling farm near Springfield where Meta had visited as a child. After a sojourn in England, Lee was now living at Rawlings Farm.

Since her "niece" had turned out to be a money-grubbing phony, Sara was more fearful of relationships than ever. Joe Werner found that he had feelings for her and proposed, inviting her to join him on a yearlong sabbatical in England. But Sara was unwilling to commit and offered the excuse that she was hesitant to abandon her practice in Springfield. Joe went to England alone. Paul Fletcher was also interested in Sara, but he was still recovering from his tragic marriages to Robin and Anne, and he decided not to pursue her.

This paved the way for Lee Gantry. A charming and erudite man, Lee made Sara laugh and brought out her long-dormant spontaneity. But there was nothing impulsive about the way he lifted Sara's wallet—or the way he killed his first wife, Alice. Lee's former housekeeper, Mildred Foss, knew how Alice Rawlings Gantry had met her untimely end, and she blackmailed Lee into rehiring her. It wasn't long before Sara's friends were shocked to hear that she'd married the enigmatic Lee. In England, a suspicious Joe investigated his rival and discovered that Lee had fired Mildred Foss when he lived there. Back in Springfield, a sequence of events straight out of the classic film *Gaslight* ensued. In an effort to drive Sara crazy, Lee and Mildred made strange noises in the attic and doctored Sara's appointment book. One night, when Sara was alone during a thunderstorm, she heard one of those noises in the attic. Frightened, she took a gun and went upstairs, where she spotted a shadowy figure and took a shot at it. The figure fell, and when Sara moved in closer, she saw the lifeless body of Mildred Foss! Fortunately for Sara, the D.A.'s office ruled the death an accident and dismissed all charges. But Lee Gantry was still determined to ice his wealthy wife, and he plotted to

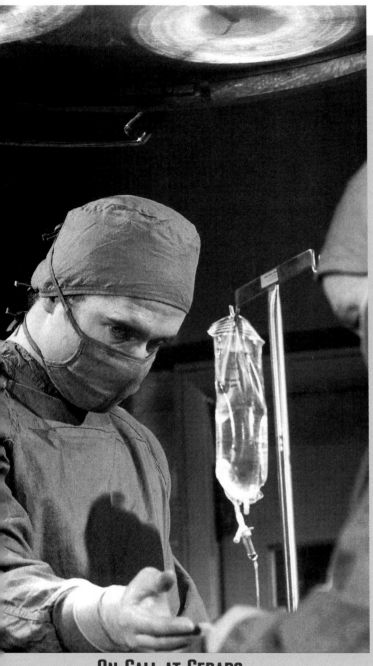

ON CALL AT CEDARS: ISSUES-ALCOHOLISM

Afflicted with the disease that had plagued his father, Ed was dismissed from Cedars. In order to be reinstated, Ed had to perform a successful surgical procedure. Happily, he proved himself up to the task.

make Sara's death look like a suicide. Joe returned to Springfield, and working with Mike, he poked holes in many of Lee's stories. Joe told a disbelieving Sara that "Lee Gantry married you for your money." While searching for evidence against her Bluebeard husband, Sara remembered Meta telling her of the games she'd played with Alice at the farm when they were children. Meta recalled seeing a loose brick in the chimney, and Sara went up into the attic to check it out. Behind the brick, she found Alice Rawlings' diary! At that moment, Lee arrived and tried to murder Sara. Luckily, Joe showed up in the nick of time and saved the life of the woman he'd grown to love. Joe and Lee got into a violent fight that ended when Lee fell out of the attic window to his death. Joe and Sara married shortly after.

The happily married Sara found it in her heart to befriend Charlotte, who had by now convinced everyone that she'd turned over a new leaf. One person who was particularly won over by the "new" Charlotte was Mike, whom she had aided in the Flip Malone caper. Mike was Charlotte's ideal man, handsome, vulnerable and successful, and he was lonely, since he had no guarantee that Leslie would ever wrestle herself away from Ed. In a moment of weakness, Mike married Charlotte. The couple moved in with Bert, who was pained to see how much Charlotte resented Mike's close relationship with his daughter, Hope. Bert and Charlotte quarreled frequently, and Charlotte ran crying to Meta for moral support. Bert was annoyed that Meta was being duped by Charlotte's obviously staged histrionics.

Back at Cedars, Ed performed a successful surgical procedure, which won him back his permanent position. Just as he was ready to divorce Leslie, Janet grew tired of being strung along by Ed. She dropped him and resigned from Cedars to avoid further contact. Then, to Ed's horror, Leslie informed him he was going to be a father! They named their little boy Frederick after Papa Bauer. Janet's protective father, Grove Mason, confronted Ed about his affair with Janet. Their heated meeting caused Mason to have a coronary, which killed him. After overhearing the altercation, Steve Jackson insisted that Ed tell Leslie the truth about Janet, which he did. Leslie was so livid, she not only divorced Ed, but she forbade the Bauers from seeing Freddie.

The staff at Cedars bade a fond goodbye to Paul Fletcher, who had accepted a position in Washington, D.C. At Paul's farewell party, Leslie found herself being wooed by Stanley Norris, Cedars' wealthiest benefactor. Vulnerable after her triangle with the Bauer brothers,

Leslie was charmed by the worldly Stanley. After a whirl-wind courtship, Leslie and Stanley became husband and wife. The news came as a shock to Leslie's friends and family, particularly Steve Jackson, who knew of Norris' dubious reputation with women. Seventeen years earlier, Stanley had walked out on his sympathetic wife, Barbara, and their children, Ken, Andy and Holly. A self-made man, Stanley was absorbed with his business empire, which consisted of several successful companies, including Liberty Airlines. He was a notorious woman-izer who had recently married and divorced a much younger woman, the mentally unstable Kit Vested. Kit's older brother, David, was Stanley's ambitious right-hand man. David played the worshipful employee to the hilt, but in reality he despised Stanley for his treatment of Kit. Stanley himself was unaware that his glamorous ex-lover, Karen Martin, had jilted him because she was re-ally in love with David. Watching this scenario from the sidelines was Linell Conway, Stanley's dutiful but lonely secretary, who was furious that Stanley had married a country bumpkin like Leslie Jackson Bauer. Linell lived with her elderly mother, Marion, who worried about her daughter's neurotic delusions of becoming the next Mrs. Stanley Norris.

After Stanley deserted the family, Barbara promptly divorced him. A talented cook, she wrote a cookbook that soon led to an exciting career as a syndicated food columnist. Barbara was a strong woman with a solid sense of values, and she relied heavily on Ken, her eldest child, who became the "man of the house" after Stanley left. Ken had little contact with his self-absorbed father. With all of his time spent forging a legal career and shouldering the burdens of the family, Ken had no expe-rience in romantic relationships. Yet when he hired the beautiful Janet Mason as his secretary, Ken fell instantly in love for the first time in his life. Janet made it clear that she couldn't reciprocate his affections, but Ken as-sured her he would wait forever for her love. Mean-while, Ed was being pursued by an attractive nurse named Dinah Buckley, but he had to tell her gently that he could not return her love.

Ken and Barbara were concerned when Holly re-fused to go to college and instead sought a glamorous job working for her father. Holly was a mere infant when Stanley walked out on the family, and because he made no effort to be a part of her life, she had never met him. But once Holly introduced herself to her father, he showered her with pricey gifts and matched her up with young Roger Thorpe. Roger's father was the president of

one of Stanley's New York companies. In her naivete, Holly believed that Roger truly cared for her, when in fact Stanley had merely prevailed upon the young man to "show her a good time." Roger was completing busi-ness school, and dating Holly was merely one of the pre-requisites for working at Stanley's firm.

Another divorced father, Ed Bauer, paid barely any attention to his son, Freddie. However, once the boy was living under Stanley Norris' roof, Ed became far more loving and attentive than ever. Although Freddie was un-der the excellent care of baby nurse Leona Herbert, Ed fumed at the idea of a cold fish like Norris raising his son. Ironically, as Steve Jackson continued to voice his disap-proval of Stanley, Leslie was touched. For the first time in her life, she felt that her father truly cared about her.

Young Hope Bauer missed being a part of Leslie's life and was increasingly miserable living with her

After Stanley deserted his first family, his then wife, Barbara, divorced him. A talented cook, Barbara wrote a book, became a syndicated food columnist and worked hard to raise her three children.

On a trip to New York, Holly found her way into Roger Thorpe's bed and lost her virginity. It was the beginning of a long and torturous relationship.

"wicked stepmother," Charlotte. Mike, still starry-eyed over his vivacious new wife, was oblivious to his daughter's sadness. To make matters worse for Hope, Mike and Charlotte were expecting a child! Feeling more alienated than ever, Hope ran away to a deserted cabin, where a desperate Mike eventually found her. No longer in denial, Mike was disgusted by Charlotte's icy treatment of his daughter, and he told his wife they were finished. A distraught Charlotte chased after him and had a serious fall. Their baby boy was stillborn. Hope was grief-stricken, and the tragedy caused Mike and Charlotte to reconcile. It also served as a catalyst in mending fences between Bert and Leslie and in reuniting Mike and Ed.

Fascinated by the convoluted Norris scenario, Charlotte befriended Kit Vested, who'd been admitted to Cedars after a drug overdose. Kit was becoming increasingly worried about her brother, David, who was consumed by ambition and his brewing hatred of Stanley Norris. David knew that Stanley was stripping some of his companies of ready cash in order to bolster Liberty Airlines, which was going through a rough period. David was plotting to gain the controlling shares of Liberty, and at an opportune moment, force Stanley out and marry Karen Martin. But Stanley was a shrewd man, and he knew someone was out to destroy him. After discovering phone calls from David to Karen, Stanley realized David was the enemy. Stanley then shamed Karen into betraying David by signing over a block of her shares.

Meanwhile, Roger Thorpe was tired of pretending that he was in love with Holly. At first he found her boring and immature, but he soon felt guilty for making her a pawn in one of Stanley's games. Holly, blissfully unaware, was basking in the glow of the lavish eighteenth birthday party her father threw for her. Roger boldly told Stanley off for treating his daughter so shabbily, but Stanley refused to let him off the hook. It wasn't long before Holly caught on and confronted her father. Stanley was having trouble from another quarter: Marion Conway was deeply concerned that her daughter Linell's hatred of Leslie was bordering on hysteria. In a pathetic move, Linell told Stanley she was in love with him and they were meant to be together. Stanley's reaction to his loyal secretary was not one of compassion but of disgust, and he fired her.

Stanley Norris was quickly becoming the enemy of the Bauer family. After he prevented Ed from seeing Freddie, Ed told Mike he was planning to sue Leslie for custody. Then Freddie fell deathly ill, and Leslie discovered that Stanley hadn't bothered to tell her that her own father was performing an emergency tracheotomy on Freddie! Leslie went to confront her husband, only to find him dead on their penthouse floor, three bullets in him. Acting D.A. Ira Newton promptly arrested Leslie, and Mike leaped to her defense. Charlotte was jealous that Mike and Leslie were once again thrown together, because she needed him now more than ever—Charlotte had just learned that Flip Malone was out on parole.

There was no end to the suspects in the Stanley Norris murder—so many people had reason to hate him. Ed, Roger, Holly, Barbara, Ken, Kit and David Vested, Karen Martin—the list was a veritable Who's Who. Amid all the anguish and intrigue, on a jaunt to New York City, Holly managed to find her way into Roger Thorpe's bed and lost her virginity to this up-and-coming young hotshot. It was the beginning of a long and torturous relationship.

1972–1976

As the Stanley Norris murder trial drew to a close, it was clear that the intrigue had only just begun for the people Stanley left behind. The Bauers and the Norrises were soon to become further enmeshed with the crafty and complex Roger Thorpe.

The trial came to a shocking conclusion when Marion Conway, Linell's elderly, protective mother, confessed to killing Stanley. Marion collapsed and died of a heart attack, and Linell had an emotional breakdown. Eventually, Linell recovered and left Springfield for a new job and a new life.

Fed up with David Vested's vengeful but failed quest to overtake Stanley's business empire, Karen Martin jilted him. Karen and David blew out of town separately, leaving David's fragile sister, Kit, to salvage her sad life. In her loneliness, Kit found a dubious confidante in the catty and conniving Charlotte Bauer. Charlotte was not happy to see Leslie exonerated of Stanley's murder. When Mike discovered that it was Charlotte who had fed D.A. Newton the dirt on Mike and Leslie's past relationship—which in fact had never been consummated—Mike told Charlotte they were finished for good.

Out on parole, Flip Malone returned to Springfield and took Charlotte hostage. Mike characteristically saved the day, taking a bullet in the chest that was meant

for Charlotte. Flip sped off and was killed in a car wreck. Joe Werner performed the surgery on Mike that saved his life, and Leslie vowed never to leave him again!

Whereas most wives might have been grateful for a husband who took a bullet for them, Charlotte let loose a tornado of revenge on Mike for leaving her. She left his law books out in a rainstorm, dragged Leslie's name through the mud and hired ambulance-chasing lawyer George Kellerman to represent her in a down-and-dirty divorce. She would have left Mike penniless had Hope not spotted her in a liaison with Dick Carey, an egotistical young doctor at Cedars. Eventually the divorce was granted, but Steve Jackson was so incensed by the scandal that he suffered a heart attack and later tried to keep star-crossed lovers Mike and Leslie apart. Thanks to Bert and Ed, who interceded on Mike's behalf, Steve finally gave Mike and Leslie his blessing and they were married at last!

Soon after, the self-centered Dr. Dick Carey indirectly figured into a scenario involving Leslie's closest friends, Peggy and John Fletcher. John irrationally accused Joe Werner of favoring Dick over him at Cedars, and he began pushing himself mercilessly. It wasn't long before John worked himself into a state of physical and mental collapse. When Claudia Dillman, the grandmother of Peggy's son Billy, got wind of John's illness, she threatened to sue Peggy for custody of Billy. Happily, Claudia had an attack of conscience and backed off. John, however, never fully recovered. He left Peggy in hopes of finding himself and was never seen or heard from again. Abandoned and alone, Peggy was forced to obtain a divorce on grounds of desertion.

It was during this period that the marriage of Joe Werner and Sara McIntyre began to show signs of strain. Joe's busy chief of staff position left him little time for Sara, who was saddened to discover that she could not conceive a child. Enter Kit Vested, now working at Cedars and desperately lonely for affection. One look at the cool, sandy-haired Dr. Werner, and Kit was mesmerized. She admitted to her pernicious pal Charlotte that she was secretly in love with Joe. Big mistake, as Charlotte had her eye on him, too! Joe had been Charlotte's first fling when she arrived in Springfield, and by now he had matured into as solid a citizen as her ex, Mike Bauer.

The marriage of Joe Werner and Sara McIntyre went through shaky times when Sara discovered she was unable to conceive a child and Joe began to work long hours at Cedars.

Janet Mason was in love with Ed Bauer but married Ken Norris instead. After she did, she became the object of Roger's unwanted affections.

Sara was fed up with Charlotte because of her treatment of Mike, so Charlotte didn't feel that she owed Sara any loyalty. With cunning duplicity, Charlotte told Kit in a seemingly selfless manner that she would help her break up Joe and Sara's marriage. Charlotte became a volunteer at Cedars and won Joe over with her refreshing new attitude. She was able to catch him at a weak moment and seduced him, and they resumed their affair. Joe became so guilt-ridden that he confided his indiscretion to Ed. Mike also saw the lovers together. Kit saw them from a distance, but she couldn't make out Charlotte's face in the dark. In a typically clumsy move, Kit told Charlotte she knew Joe was fooling around and showed her a note she'd composed from magazine cutouts that she intended to send to Sara. The note read, "Your marriage is a lie! Another woman is stealing your husband from you!" This was just the opening Charlotte needed. She talked Kit out of sending it and then secretly sent it herself! When Sara confronted Joe with the note, he confessed to having a loveless affair but did not reveal Charlotte's name. It wasn't long before Kit learned that Charlotte had tricked her. Kit became deranged and slipped Charlotte a poisoned drink. Charlotte was rushed to Cedars, and Joe was so distraught that he blundered in his treatment of her. Charlotte Waring Bauer was dead.

While Kit was sinking further into her morass, Stanley Norris' other ex-wife, Barbara, was beginning a promising new chapter in her life. Barbara was surprised and charmed to find herself pursued by Adam Thorpe, Roger's widower father. A lifelong workaholic, Adam felt guilty about being a distant and preoccupied parent after the death of his wife, Marjorie. He hoped to hand Roger the reins of his company someday and was happy to see him involved in a relationship with Holly. Adam strongly believed that marriage would help Roger grow up. Barbara didn't trust Roger, however, and feared that where his son was concerned, Adam was wearing blinders. Barbara was right. As soon as her son Ken married Janet Mason, Roger began to make passes at Janet. Ken was becoming increasingly insecure because Janet wasn't returning his affections. His jealousy was directed not at Roger, though, but at Ed! Ed still loved Janet, but he had settled for a good friendship with her in light of her marriage to Ken. Roger capitalized on the situation by taunting Janet about how she wouldn't dare tell her jealous husband if they ever became involved. He even tried to force himself on her, but she fought him off and stormed out of his apartment. When Holly arrived, she saw Janet's gloves on the sofa! Believing Janet to be her rival for

Wilson Frost was a sanctimonious doctor who took a liking to Sara while her husband, Joe Werner, was being pursued simultaneously by Charlotte Bauer and her psychotic friend, Kit Vested.

Roger's affections, Holly ran out in a daze and was hit by a car. After Holly recovered, she sold Ken on her suspicion that Janet and Roger were involved. In short order, Ken beat up Roger, Holly dumped him and Adam fired him from his firm. Roger left Springfield in disgrace.

When she came to Springfield, she tried to pass herself off as Madame Madeline Balenger, but she was in fact Victoria Jackson, Leslie's long-lost mother and the wife Steve Jackson had claimed was dead.

Fortunately, Barbara believed Janet when she insisted that she'd thwarted Roger's advances. Barbara was also hurt when neither Ken nor Holly supported her decision to marry Adam, simply because he was Roger's father. However, realizing that their mother deserved happiness with a decent man, they came around. Barbara and Adam were married, and Adam sold his business so that he could enjoy life with his new bride. Meanwhile, the marriage of Janet and Ken was growing more troubled each day, as Ken's jealous rantings became insufferable. Although Ken was a brilliant lawyer who was now part of Mike Bauer's law firm, he was an emotional wreck in the area of relationships. If she had not become pregnant with his child, Janet would have left him. The couple had a little girl and they named her Emily.

Ed Bauer was extremely lonely and frustrated during Janet's tormented marriage to Ken. To his family's surprise, he formed a bond with Holly, which turned into a relationship on the rebound for both of them—Ed from Janet, Holly from Roger. One night when Ed and Holly were out together, Holly ordered wine, not knowing that Ed was an alcoholic. The next thing Ed remembered, he was in bed with Holly in Las Vegas and she announced that they were married! When Ed insisted on an annulment, Holly lied and said that they'd already

consummated their marriage. The newlyweds returned to Springfield and promptly met with stern disapproval from Bert, but when Ed threatened to break ties with her if she didn't acknowledge his new wife, Bert softened. Meta, usually a soft judge of character, warned Bert that Holly was a conniver.

It didn't take long for Holly to regret having married Ed. In the wake of John Fletcher's disappearance and Charlotte's untimely death, Joe Werner required Ed to work extended hours at Cedars. Joe was in deep trouble due to his bungling of Charlotte's case, and although Ed tried desperately to salvage his friend's career, Bruce Banning, Meta's husband, pushed for Joe's demotion. Hard-nosed osteopath Dr. Wilson Frost went so far as to insist that Joe be dismissed from the staff. Unbeknownst to Joe, Wilson had feelings for Sara. Under pressure from the medical review board, Joe resigned from Cedars and Ed became a reluctant chief of staff. Ed felt doubly guilty when Adam Thorpe came to Cedars as an independent contractor to analyze the hospital's efficiency and recommended that Ed remain in Joe's former position. Adam eventually became president of Cedars' board of trustees. Over the years, Adam and Barbara Thorpe were to become Ed's staunchest supporters and closest friends.

Ed was concerned for his beloved mentor, Steve

Barbara looked upon Ed as another son and hoped his shaky marriage to her daughter, Holly, would survive.

Holly might have been pregnant with his child, but it was Peggy Dillman Fletcher whom Roger wanted as his wife, and the two were married.

Jackson, who had become preoccupied and irritable. The truth was, Steve was being hounded by a woman from Switzerland who was passing herself off as Madame Madeline Balenger, but who was in fact Victoria Jackson, the wife Steve had claimed was dead! Madeline insinuated herself into the lives of her daughter and son-in-law, Leslie and Mike Bauer. Leslie eventually figured out that the mystery woman was her mother when she studied an old photo of Victoria. Steve tried to bribe Victoria to leave town but changed his mind when Leslie warned that she would have nothing more to do with him if he interfered in her life again. When Hope went off to college, Mike and Leslie welcomed Victoria into their home, and the three became a family unit—for a while. Something about Victoria did not sit right with Mike, and he decided to investigate. He soon discovered that she was taking money from Steve supposedly to operate a shop she had in London, but it was really meant for Victoria's dilettante lover, who was languishing in a sanitarium! Mike convinced Leslie that her mother was a fake. Leslie confronted Victoria, only for her mother to blurt out that Steve Jackson was not her biological father! Because he was an obsessive workaholic, Victoria had felt lonely and neglected during their marriage, and she conceived Leslie with another man. She then breezed off to Europe, saddling Steve with raising a child whom he knew wasn't his. At long last, Leslie realized why

Steve had been so cold toward her while she was growing up. When she confronted him, Steve tearfully told her that he loved her as much as if they were connected by blood. Father and daughter became closer than ever, and Victoria left Springfield for good.

The Bauers were happy for Steve and Leslie, but they were concerned for Sara and Joe. Despite Ed's attempts to turn him around, Joe took to drink and holed up in a cabin with the unstable Kit as his only link to the outside world. Kit didn't waste any time in telling Joe that Wilson Frost was pursuing Sara, but she left out the part about Sara not reciprocating Wilson's feelings. Eventually, Kit completely lost her mind. She poisoned Sara and shot Joe, only to be fatally wounded while struggling with Joe over the gun. Both Sara and Joe survived, and galvanized by these events, they worked hard to save their marriage.

The marriage of Janet and Ken Norris, however, was not worth saving. Ken was so infernally possessive of Janet that he even resented her attentions to their little daughter, Emily! When Janet consulted Ed about Emily's urinary tract infection, Ken and Holly accused their spouses of plotting to run off together into the sunset. Barbara was horrified by her children's unfounded suspicions of Ed and Janet—both of whom were the son and daughter she wished she had—and she warned Ken

Roger became manager of the Metro, a restaurant/hangout popular with Springfield's "younger" set.

and Holly to curb their jealous behavior. Ken did consult a psychiatrist, the eminent Dr. Bertrand Mandel, just long enough to convince Janet to stay with him. For hours on end, he would talk into a tape recorder and pour out his morbid fantasies about Janet and Ed. Janet soon discovered Ken was no longer in therapy. They had an altercation while out driving and got into a horrible accident. Ken was temporarily blinded, and when Janet refused to come back to him, he convalesced at Barbara and Adam's. Ken's eyesight returned, but he kept the development a secret. He had plans and they included killing Ed. A man obsessed, Ken shadowed Ed and Janet, then confronted them both. He pulled out a gun and shot Ed, leaving the bullet critically lodged in his spine. Ken was carted away to a sanitarium in a state of catatonia. Janet and Emily left Springfield to begin anew, and Ken eventually recovered and settled in California.

Ed and Holly's marriage didn't fare much better than Ken and Janet's. Ed was angry that the shooting had left him physically unable to perform surgery. He pressured Steve to perform a revolutionary new operation on him, but in the middle of the procedure Steve halted the surgery because he knew it was too risky. Ed was also disappointed to see that Holly had no rapport with Frederick, his and Leslie's son. At Ed's urging, Holly and little Freddie went on a picnic. The outing ended when Freddie's clothes caught fire. Afterward, Leslie insisted that Holly never care for her son again unless Ed was present. Then Mike took Freddie, who was both his nephew and stepson, on a canoe trip. During the trip, Freddie was washed downstream. The frightened boy was rescued by a mountain man and suffered from a brief bout with amnesia. This near tragedy caused a temporary rift between Mike and Ed, but the brothers eventually reconciled.

Between Ed's chief of staff position and his family entanglements, Holly was becoming increasingly bored in their marriage. She was excited by the return of former flame Roger Thorpe, who had been involved with a string of loose women and ill-fated business schemes in Texas. Holly seduced Roger and soon discovered she was pregnant. But Roger wanted no part of it; he was falling in love with Peggy Fletcher and becoming attached to her son Billy, and was intent on proving to both Peggy and Adam that he was now a mature, successful man. Unfortunately, Roger got himself into such a financial hole that he became indebted to loan sharks, who threatened Peggy and Billy's lives. With money from various odd jobs and help from Adam and Mike, Roger paid off the

YOUNG LOVE

Hope Bauer and artist Ben McFarren were an item for a while, but Mike disapproved because Ben was an ex-con.

goons. Soon he became the manager of the Metro, a restaurant that attracted the "younger" set.

Ed was delighted when Holly gave birth to a daughter, Christina, unaware, of course, that the child was Roger's. Soon after, Holly's other brother, Andy Norris, arrived in Springfield. A writer with an almost diabolical grasp on what made people tick, Andy picked up on vibes between Holly and Roger. When Andy asked her what the story was, Holly admitted that Christina was Roger's child. Recognizing that truth was often more entertaining than fiction, Andy wrote a thinly disguised book about Holly's predicament, calling it *Valerie's Story*. He later tore up the manuscript and decided to leave Springfield rather than cause Holly any trouble. However, Barbara pieced the manuscript together and figured out the entire sordid scenario!

As Roger picked up the pieces of his life at the Metro, he became friendly with the young people who frequented and worked there. They were Pam Chandler, a perky single mother who also befriended Leslie and

Mike; Dr. Tim Ryan, a cocky young neurosurgeon whom Pam loved, but who didn't fully reciprocate her feelings; Ann Jeffers, a hostess who had been abused by her husband and was now searching for her little boy, Jimmy; and Chad Richards, a folk-singing guitar player who had known Leslie back in high school. Chad had a tumor, which caused him to act out, and he made advances toward Leslie, angering Mike. One day Chad lunged at Leslie and Mike had to fight him off, prompting Chad to leave Springfield and obtain medical treatment elsewhere. But it was Ann Jeffers who would indirectly mean tragedy for Mike and Leslie. When Mike tracked down Ann's husband, a volatile drunk named Spence Jeffers, the two men had a violent showdown at Mike's house. Spence stormed out and accidentally ran over Leslie with his car, killing her. After Spence turned himself in, Ann became Mike's secretary and began to develop feelings for him, but it would be a long time before Mike got over the one true love of his life.

Ann hoped that an orphaned little boy named T.J. would turn out to be her long-lost son, but sadly, this was not the case. The boy was eventually adopted by Sara McIntyre and Joe Werner, who had finally accepted the fact that they could not have children. Joe was now

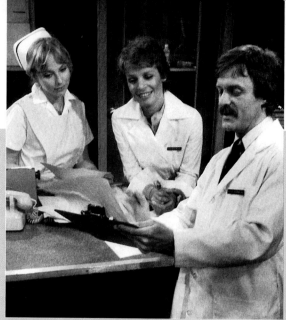

ON CALL AT CEDARS

When Malcolm Granger suffered a stroke, Peggy Thorpe, shown here with Sara McIntyre and Dr. Peter Chapman, was his attending nurse.

back at Cedars and working so hard that he suffered a heart attack. His life was saved by a brilliant yet abrasive cardiac surgeon named Justin Marler. Justin had dated Sara back in his native Chicago but ended up marrying the daughter of the famous surgeon who was advancing Justin's career. A pragmatic man, Justin was the product of an indolent father and a dominating mother. He was recently divorced and heading up Cedars' new cardiac unit. Justin regretted having lost his chance to be with Sara—that is, until Joe died of a massive coronary.

In the midst of all this tragedy, Mike Bauer had to deal with his fast maturing daughter, Hope. A protective father, Mike had extricated his daughter from a dead-end relationship with a married professor, Alex McDaniels, back in Bay City. Now settled in Springfield, Hope became a waitress at the Metro and fell in love with Ben McFarren, a hotheaded young artist who had little respect for Mike. Some years earlier, Mike had represented Ben in a case involving a robbery Ben didn't commit. Mike lost the case, and Ben was sentenced to prison. Now Ben was out and sporting a massive chip on his shoulder. However, thanks to Hope, he soon mellowed, and in the process drew a nude portrait of her for which she had posed fully clothed. Eventually, Hope and Ben made love and became engaged, but his misfit brother, Jerry, turned out to be the fly in the ointment. Jerry borrowed Ben's car and used it to rob a deli. Ben withdrew money from his and Hope's new joint account to pay the deli owner

Seductive Rita Stapleton and her sweet sister, Eve, arrived in Springfield with their mother, Viola, and shook things up romantically.

back. Hope discovered the withdrawal, and Ben, hesitant to implicate his brother, took the heat for the crime. A tearful Hope broke off the engagement and gave him back his ring.

As Mike dealt with the loss of his beloved Leslie and the difficulties of dealing with the grown-up Hope, his brother, Ed, came to realize that his marriage to Holly was a sham. Christina contracted pneumonia, necessitating a blood transfusion that could come only from her natural father—Roger Thorpe! Holly was forced to come clean about Christina's true parentage, and the two decided to divorce. This development anguished Barbara to the point where she developed migraines and ordered Roger out of her home. When Roger married Peggy, Barbara sat out the ceremony, claiming she was sick. Barbara's attitude soon drove a wedge between her and Adam, who believed he owed his only son some loyalty despite all he'd done in the past. It was becoming clear that both Barbara and Adam were placing their children before their marriage.

A new family, the Stapletons, arrived in Springfield. Rita Stapleton was an alluring brunette nurse from the coal-mining town of Bluefield, West Virginia. She soon had a fling with Dr. Tim Ryan, which cost him his relationship with Pam Chandler, but ultimately she set her sights on Ed Bauer. Rita was thrilled when Ed saved the life of her ailing widowed mother, Viola, and became like a big brother to her demure younger sister, Eve. When Holly had a change of heart and tried to stop her divorce from Ed, Rita intercepted the call, determined to land the well-connected medic for herself. Eve became

infatuated with Tim Ryan, only to find out that he had slept with her sister. Tim left Springfield, and Eve refused any further financial help from Rita. Eve quit school and went to work for a flamboyant newcomer to Springfield, Jackie Scott Marler, Justin's ex-wife!

The source of Rita's seemingly limitless funds was to provide the basis for an intriguing tale. Roger recognized Rita as the former private nurse of Cyrus Granger, a millionaire from Abilene, Texas, for whom Roger had also worked. Cyrus was now dead, and his son, Malcolm, came to Springfield to accuse Rita of his murder. Indeed, Rita had come into a handsome inheritance from the grateful Texan, and Roger was resentful that he had not been cut in on the gravy train. One night, after a con-

Bert, shown here with Mike, had learned her lesson and was trying hard not to interfere in the lives of her children.

frontation with Rita, Malcolm suffered a stroke and was rushed to Cedars. Peggy was the attending nurse, and Malcolm, unable to speak, scrawled Rita's name on Peggy's pad of paper. Shortly thereafter, when Rita was on duty, she accidentally misplaced Malcolm's chart. As a result, the medication nurse was misled, and Malcolm died of an overdose. The hospital did not blame Rita, but Raymond Shafer, the Granger family lawyer, was far from satisfied with the outcome. Rita was arrested for Malcolm Granger's murder, and Mike defended her. Ed rushed to Rita's side and proposed. It was not one of his wisest decisions. Bert was happy for Ed, though. By now, she had learned not to interfere in her children's lives. Her beloved Papa Bauer was gone, having died in his sleep, and Meta and Bruce Banning had left Springfield once again. Bert was growing closer to her dear old friend Steve Jackson, who had mellowed considerably ever since Leslie's tragic death. What Bert did not yet realize was that her serene life was about to be turned inside out.

When Rita was arrested for Malcolm Granger's murder, Ed rushed to her side. It was an impulsive move he would come to regret.

1977

The year 1977 was one of unprecedented upheaval in Springfield: The convoluted secret behind a young boy's parentage would touch many lives, the Thorpe family disintegrated and the Bauer family tree was shaken to its very roots.

The catalyst for much of the action was Rita Stapleton's trial for the murder of Malcolm Granger. Peggy, who was Granger's attending nurse, was forced to reveal on the witness stand that Malcolm was afraid to see Rita on the night he died and had written her name on Peggy's notepad. In truth, Peggy shared Barbara Thorpe's conviction that Ed had made a mistake when he became engaged to Rita. There was another cloud over the proceedings: Georgene Granger, Malcolm's spiteful widow, accused Rita of killing not only Malcolm, but his father, Cyrus, as well! Panicked at the thought of Ed discovering her racy past, Rita concealed the fact that on the night Cyrus Granger died in Abilene, Texas, she was having a tryst with none other than Roger Thorpe! The trial dragged on as Rita obscured facts, much to the annoyance of her lawyer and future brother-in-law, Mike Bauer. Eventually, Rita confided to Mike that Roger was her secret alibi in Cyrus' death.

Finance magazine

Exclusive Interview with Alan Spaulding

WHEELING AND DEALING

Spaulding Enterprises came to Springfield in 1977 and made itself known. This huge conglomerate was headed by a powerful young millionaire named Alan Spaulding.

Jury Finds Rita Stapleton Innocent in Granger Death:
New Evidence Entered in Eleventh Hour

Rita Stapleton: Saved by Thorpe's Testimony

A surprising revelation by Roger Thorpe cleared his ex-lover, Rita Stapleton, of Cyrus Granger's murder.

Unable to live with the fact that Rita could be sent to prison, Roger uncharacteristically risked everything by admitting that he was with Rita on the night Cyrus died. He added that Rita genuinely cared for Cyrus as an employer and a father figure.

Although Rita was cleared of the charges, Ed began to doubt whether he had a future with her. He looked once again in the direction of Holly, who had matured into a strong young woman of substance. Barbara was encouraged by Ed and Holly's new bond but was appalled that Adam stood by Roger and agreed to rehire Rita at Cedars. Acknowledging that they would probably never agree about his deceitful son, Barbara and

Phillip's four parents: birth parents Jackie and Justin Marler; adoptive parents Elizabeth and Alan Spaulding.

Adam sadly divorced. Equally disillusioned, Peggy divorced Roger and moved to Boise, Idaho, with Billy.

Trying to come to terms with his failed marriage, Adam once again busied himself with his work. He became general manager of Spaulding Enterprises, one of Mike Bauer's latest clients. Mike warned Adam that he would need to jump through the proverbial hoops to please his new boss, a charismatic and demanding young millionaire named Alan Spaulding. In his personal life, Alan relentlessly dominated his beautiful wife, Elizabeth, a photographer who was becoming increasingly impatient with her husband's attempts to crush her free spirit. When Mike refused to represent Alan in an industrial park project that would harm the environment, Elizabeth applauded Mike's stand against her powerful husband. Indeed, Mike and Elizabeth found they had much in common and were becoming quite entranced with one another. Watching this budding triangle with great interest was Jackie Marler. A feisty, assertive woman with a cutting edge, Jackie was also drawn to Mike. But Jackie had a secret, one that would affect many lives in Springfield.

Years earlier in Chicago, Jackie had fallen deeply in love with the rugged Dr. Justin Marler and married him.

Unfortunately, Jackie was initially blind to the fact that Justin married her only to score points with her father, Dr. Emmet Scott, who was his mentor in cardiac surgery. On their honeymoon, Jackie was devastated when she caught Justin in bed with a young reporter named Brandy Shellooe. Jackie bitterly filed for divorce, only to learn she was pregnant by her errant husband! Determined to have a life without Justin, Jackie never told him about the child. She gave birth to a son in Amsterdam, where she made the painful decision to give the child up for adoption. At the same time, Jackie's obstetrician, Dr. Paul LaCrosse, had been treating Elizabeth Spaulding during her difficult pregnancy. As was then the custom, Elizabeth was placed under general anesthesia, then gave birth to a stillborn baby boy. Before Elizabeth was revived, Alan told Dr. LaCrosse that his wife was too fragile to handle the death of this child. Without revealing Jackie's name, LaCrosse told Alan about a woman who wanted to put up her baby for adoption. Alan paid LaCrosse to pass Jackie's baby off as the boy to whom Elizabeth had given birth. To assure Jackie that he had found a good home for her son, Dr. LaCrosse told her that he'd been adopted by the Spauldings. The boy was named Phillip.

Cut to Springfield 1977, where Jackie opened a thrift shop and soon became mother confessor to Eve Stapleton, who was disillusioned with her older sister, Rita. Although she was dating Mike Bauer casually, Jackie was hurt when neither he nor Justin returned her affections. By now, Justin had reason to hope for a relationship with Sara McIntyre and considered his ex-wife Jackie merely an annoyance. Ironically, Dr. Emmet Scott came to join the staff at Cedars and competed with Justin for Sara! Justin decided to level with Sara and told her about the sleazy Brandy Shellooe caper. Just then Brandy breezed into Springfield on assignment. Jackie finally told Emmet the sad story behind Phillip's birth. Revealing the secret to no one else, Jackie decided to befriend Elizabeth for the sole purpose of getting to know the son she had given up.

While Mike tried to sort out his feelings for both Jackie and Elizabeth, his neurotic secretary, Ann Jeffers, continued to pine away for him. One day, Ann happened upon a tape of a conversation between Justin and Jackie which, unbeknownst to Mike, had accidentally been saved. On the tape Jackie implied to Justin that she was pursuing Mike on the rebound. When Ann finally summoned the nerve to confront Jackie about the tape, Jackie viciously told her to forget any notions of a romance with Mike. After all, it was Ann's abusive husband, Spence, who had killed Mike's beloved wife, Leslie. Realizing that she wasn't in Jackie's league, Ann destroyed the tape.

Almost everyone in Springfield was happy about the budding romance between Eve Stapleton and Ben McFarren. Due to a misunderstanding, however, the young pair soon suffered a tragic setback. Before she left for an extended stay in France, Mike's daughter, Hope, bade an emotional farewell to her ex-fiancé, Ben. Eve saw them together and mistakenly believed that Hope and Ben were still involved. She ran from the scene and fell, hitting her head. Sometime later, when a reassured Eve became engaged to Ben, she began to experience blurred vision as a result of her fall. Soon Eve was completely blind and was diagnosed with a rare disease known as Blake-Carney syndrome.

By now, Eve had reconciled with Rita, who was extremely concerned for her sister. Rita was being pursued by a bright young doctor named Peter Chapman, but she held him off in hopes that Ed would come back to her. Peter turned to Holly, who was preoccupied with the growing enmity between Ed and Roger. The ego-driven Roger, dismayed to learn that he was infertile, became obsessed with spending time with his daughter, Christina. Ed was so livid at this development that he and Roger got into a fierce fistfight. Rita doubted that Ed would ever pry himself loose from Holly and marry her. She also had to contend with the return of the vengeful Georgene Granger, who ransacked her apartment and sent her threatening notes.

Unbeknownst to Rita, she was about to stumble into a situation more complex and far-reaching than anything she had ever encountered. She befriended Hillary Kincaid, a young nursing student from Vancouver, Canada. When Hillary needed an emergency appendectomy, her adoring stepfather, Bill Morey, came to Springfield to be at her side. Morey was cordial to Rita but was curiously hesitant to meet any of Hillary's other friends. He had good reason. Bill Morey was really Bill Bauer!

Many years earlier, Bill had spent several months working on a public relations project in Switzerland. There he met a soft-spoken, attractive young woman named Simone and instantly fell in love. It was during this alpine assignation that Bill and Simone conceived Hillary. Once his work was completed, Bill returned to Bert, but he and Simone never forgot one another. Simone moved to Vancouver, and on the rebound married an abusive lout named Victor Kincaid. Together they raised Hillary and led her to believe that Victor was her natural father. Some years later, Bill located Simone while on a business trip in Canada and they resumed their affair, conceiving another child named Paul. Again,

Romance was in the air for Eve Stapleton and talented artist Ben McFarren.

A proud Bert and Ed congratulated Mike on being named Man of the Year by the Springfield Chamber of Commerce.

Simone led Paul to believe that Victor was his father. In short, Bill was leading a double life, and he resigned himself to the idea that Simone would never be truly his—until that fateful plane trip to Alaska. Bill had changed planes in Seattle, and when the plane stopped in Vancouver to refuel on the second leg of the flight, Bill went to call Simone. The plane left without him and crashed!

Learning that he was presumed dead, Bill felt so guilty about not contacting his family that he went on a bender and nearly perished of frostbite in a deserted cabin. He was rescued by Simone, who, after his phone call, had managed to track him down. Unfortunately, Simone was still married to the crafty Kincaid, but Bill stayed on in Vancouver to be close to her. In time, Kincaid discovered Bill and Simone's affair and threatened to reveal that Bill was alive. Bill in turn was livid because Victor was being physically abusive to his wife and children. Bill and Victor got into a violent fight that resulted in Victor's death. Although a cloud of suspicion hung over Bill, he went ahead and set up house with Simone, Hillary and Paul. Simone knew Bill's true identity and understood that he could not legally remarry under the circumstances, but she and Bill led the children to believe they had gotten married anyway. Together they owned and operated a mill that brought them a modest but steady income.

Now Bill had returned to Springfield to see Hillary. Mike Bauer's family and friends gathered to celebrate Mike's Man of the Year award from the Springfield Chamber of Commerce. Bill got wind of the event and observed it unnoticed from behind a curtain, longing to acknowledge the son who had always believed in him

and who had loved him unconditionally. After the ceremony, Bill left the scene to return to Vancouver but accidentally dropped an old photo of himself and his family. Rita found it and, recognizing Hillary's "dad" as Bill Bauer, returned it to him confidentially. Bill shared his story with Rita and swore her to secrecy, determined not to hurt, yet again, the family who believed him long dead. It was too late. After Hillary recovered from her surgery, she invited the Bauers to a housewarming party at the apartment she shared with Katie Parker, a fellow nurse at Cedars. At the party, Mike saw a photo of Hillary's "stepfather" and recognized him as Bill. Telling no one of his discovery, Mike flew to Vancouver and

Longing to acknowledge his son, Bill Bauer watched unnoticed as Mike accepted his prestigious and well-earned award.

confronted the father who had so spinelessly and cruelly abandoned him and his family. Bill admitted everything and agreed to reveal himself in the new year. Christmas was approaching, and he did not wish for either of his "families" to be plagued by his situation over the holidays. Reluctantly, Mike ceded to his father's wishes.

That Christmas, Mike sang "O Holy Night" at vespers, as he did every year. He sang about the miracle of the Christ child and the virtue of family, but this time the inspirational lyrics he was delivering to the misty-eyed parishioners carried a bitter irony, for Mike knew his own family was a sham. Needless to say, Mike wasn't looking forward to the new year.

1978

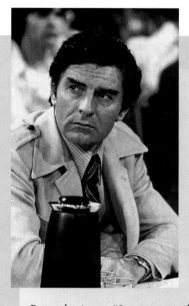

ON TRIAL

Deeply moved by his father's attempts to redeem himself, Mike insisted on defending him for Victor Kincaid's murder. His impassioned plea was a tribute to the loyalty of family and the strength of the Bauer heritage. "I say to you that the evidence we will present will show that William Bauer, despite certain personal weaknesses, and he had some...is an honorable man, a respected man. A man who never was in trouble with the law. A man whose family and friends could not believe he would deliberately kill another human being. I believe the evidence will show that the confession and the self-accusatory statements are made by a man who is tormented by his own guilt...not the guilt resulting from the crime of which he is accused, but guilt built up over days and weeks and months and years. Guilt over other actions, actions that would not be considered to be a crime in this court of law, but which, in his own mind, my client has convicted himself of...I believe that the evidence will show a memory clouded by guilt and a need for penance and forgiveness. This does not make him untruthful or unreliable. It makes him a man like every one of us...a man who regrets some actions in his life...which one of you has not? A man who would like to correct them if he could and, without knowing how, seeks some form of absolution."*

As the new year began, Mike told Bert that Bill was still alive. Bert was civil but guarded when she went to see the husband she had assumed was dead. Both she and Mike dreaded telling Ed, who had never shaken the memory of his father as a weak-willed womanizer. As luck would have it, they were spared this unpleasant task, for Ann Jeffers heard Mike and Steve Jackson discussing Bill, and she innocently commented to Ed how wonderful it must have been to learn that his father was still alive. Ed bitterly confronted Bill, and the old family wounds were opened once again.

Bill could no longer hide when Max Chapman, the hard-nosed publisher of the *Springfield Journal*, plastered the revelation all over the front page. The Bauers' insurer took one look at the *Journal* headline and demanded that Bill repay the indemnity that had been awarded to Bert upon his supposed death. Determined to right the wrongs he had committed, Bill convinced Simone to sell their home and the mill in Vancouver to pay the insurance company. He then confessed to the murder of Victor Kincaid. Deeply moved by his father's attempts to make amends, Mike insisted on defending him for

Blind Woman Saved From Fiery Inferno By Local Artist

Eve Stapleton, recently blinded, rescued by Ben McFarren

The demented widow of Cyrus Granger held a blind Eve hostage after setting fire to the house. Eve was saved by husband-to-be Ben McFarren.

Kincaid's murder. Ed, however, swore off his father and went back to the bottle. Ed was also pained to learn that Rita had known about Bill's presence in Springfield before Mike did.

With Mike's help, Bill pieced together the events of his tragic fight with Kincaid and proved that the death was accidental. Bill was cleared of the charges and prepared to leave Springfield, but before he did, he made one last attempt to reconcile with Ed, only to be rejected. Shaken by the encounter, Bill left Ed's apartment in such a daze that he was hit by a car. This was the jolt Ed needed. Witnessing the accident, Ed raced into the street, held his father in his arms and rushed him to Cedars. When Bill recovered, Bert, Mike, Ed and Hillary bade him a bittersweet farewell. Bert filed for divorce, and Bill moved to Chicago with Simone. Soon after, Hillary learned that Simone had left Bill and returned to her native Switzerland.

By this time, Hillary knew that Bill was her natural father and that he had never been legally married to Simone. These revelations threw the innocent Hillary to a tailspin, and she lost her virginity to that most charming but undeserving of men, Roger Thorpe! More cocky and insufferable than ever, Roger was now working for the powerful Alan Spaulding and was well on his way to becoming the millionaire's fair-haired boy. Roger sorely needed this new corporate gig to help him feel like a man. Feeling protective of Hillary, Rita threatened to tell her that Roger was sterile, but Roger laughed in her face and taunted her about their "hot" past in Texas. The most painful reminder of Rita's Texas sojourn, however, was Georgene Granger. Georgene blamed Rita for being disinherited by Cyrus, a fact that Rita didn't know. Furthermore, it was not Rita but Georgene who had killed old Cyrus Granger, smothering him with a pillow. On a demented rampage, Georgene set fire to Rita's curtains and held a blind Eve hostage. Happily, Ben saved Eve and Springfield's finest carted the unstable Georgene away. Eve and Ben married, and Eve underwent surgery and regained her eyesight.

Ed, now off the bottle, realized he loved Rita after all and they became engaged. In actuality, Ed was not completely over his feelings for Holly, but he didn't want to stand in the way of her healthy new relationship with Dr. Peter Chapman. For a while their romance appeared to be headed for the altar and was further helped along when Holly's mother, Barbara, began keeping company with Peter's father, newspaperman Max Chapman. But like many others in Springfield, Peter was wrestling with

LOVE AND MARRIAGE

Eve and Ben were married, and Eve regained her eyesight soon after.

a demon from his past: He felt guilty for not having saved the life of a drowning girl, Linette Waterman, back in Santo Domingo. Peter had been engaged to Linette's older sister, Maya, whose physician father had been a mentor of Peter's, but he broke it off after Linette's untimely death. To resolve the questions in his own mind, Peter went to Santo Domingo and finally came to accept the fact that he had done everything possible to save the girl. He and Maya reconciled and planned to marry, but Maya felt out of place in Peter's button-down, Midwestern world, and she returned to Santo Domingo, leaving Peter once again confused.

Peter's closest friend at Cedars was Justin Marler, whom he assisted in the cardiac unit. However, Adam demoted Justin when he fatally bungled an operation on a key member of Cedars' board of directors. He was replaced by Emmet Scott, Justin's ex–father-in-law, who was now aware of how poorly Justin had treated Jackie. Justin wasn't faring much better in his personal life, as he was frustrated that Sara was unwilling to go to bed with him. Despite his better judgment, Justin found

ON LOCATION

In a first for a soap, "Guiding Light" went to Nassau to shoot underwater footage of Dr. Peter Chapman, who was haunted by memories of a disturbing incident while scuba diving, which resulted in the drowning of his fiancée's younger sister.

himself enjoying a flirtation with Brandy Shellooe, the alluring young writer who had seduced him on his honeymoon with Jackie. One day, Sara went to Justin's office to make up with him after a heated argument, only to find Brandy waiting there, too. Wrongly suspecting that Justin and Brandy were having an affair, Sara berated herself for having been, yet again, too cautious in love. She took off to Hawaii, where she found herself in a whirlwind courtship with a dashing attorney named Dean Blackford. Resolving to take a risk for once in her life, Sara married this handsome stranger and they returned to Springfield together. Both Mike and Justin took a dim view of the marriage. Justin rightly sensed that Sara had married Dean on the rebound, and Mike knew through his legal connections that Dean, a social climber from an impoverished background, had had some shady dealings. Dean purchased a slick, contemporary condo in which Sara felt ill at ease, and he put his law career on the back burner to work for Alan Spaulding.

Rounding out Alan's inner circle was Diane Ballard, a cunning and ambitious young woman who harbored fantasies of becoming Alan's spouse and right-hand person. Diane started out as Phillip's nanny, but Elizabeth was on to her immediately and insisted that Alan remove her from their household. Alan made her his secretary.

He liked Diane's loyalty, and of course her looks weren't bad, either. Alan also flirted with Brandy, who was compiling material for a book about Spaulding Enterprises. Because Alan had grown up in a world of men's clubs, a world that didn't value women, his behavior was normal to him. However, he felt it was not acceptable for his wife, Elizabeth, to be openly interested in Mike Bauer. The chemistry between Mike and Elizabeth was not lost on Alan, and he fought loudly and bitterly about it with Elizabeth. Alan also resented Elizabeth's devotion to her new job as a photographer for Max Chapman's newspaper. Phillip overheard his parents fighting and, much to Alan's delight, turned against his mother and Mike. Alan took Phillip and Diane on a trip to Africa, purposely leaving Elizabeth behind. While they were gone, Elizabeth decided she wanted a divorce and went to Madrid to think it over. Shortly after she returned, she was mugged while on a photo shoot and spent a long time recovering from her injuries. Alan won temporary custody of Phillip—but the real custody battle between Alan and Elizabeth was about to begin! Mike represented Elizabeth in the suit, being careful not to reveal that they were very much in love.

This complicated mess worried Jackie terribly because it was so hard on Phillip. He began experiencing chest pains and shortness of breath. Jackie knew that these were the first signs of the congenital heart problem that had plagued her father, Emmet. Deeply concerned about the son she could not acknowledge, Jackie became so obsessed with Phillip that Elizabeth questioned her new friend's all-consuming interest in the boy. The situation grew more complicated when, on Jackie's recommendation, Elizabeth chose Justin as Phillip's cardiac physician. Justin was surprised by how easily he bonded with this bright but lonely young boy, not to mention his beautiful mother. In effect, Justin finally grew up. He barely noticed when Brandy left town, because he was falling in love for the first time in his life—with Elizabeth.

A tawdry twist was now about to take place. To gain permanent custody of Phillip, Alan had Dean Blackford bribe the crafty Ramon del Villar to say that he had had a fling with Elizabeth during her trip to Madrid. One glance at del Villar's sworn statement and Mike smelled something fishy. He soon came up with evidence of bribery. Mike privately warned Alan to back down in the custody suit, threatening to reveal his collusion with del Villar. But Alan had a trump card. He told Mike that Phillip had been switched at birth, and that Elizabeth had no idea that she hadn't been able to bring a child to term. If Mike nailed him on del Villar, Alan would destroy Elizabeth with these revelations. Because he loved Elizabeth, Mike backed off, but his hatred of Alan was stronger than ever.

As the custody suit progressed, Elizabeth buckled under the pressure and became addicted to pain medication. When Dean gleefully discussed this aspect of the case with Sara, she was appalled by his insensitivity and began to realize that her new marriage was a mistake. She had no idea how grave a mistake it was, as Dean was soon embroiled in a fatal fiasco. Learning that del Villar wanted to change his story, Dean killed him and made his death look like the result of a robbery. Representing Alan in the suit, Dean produced del Villar's original affidavit, and the court awarded custody of Phillip to Alan. Determined to be a part of Phillip's life, Jackie pursued Alan and the two became engaged and soon tied the knot!

Rallying herself, Elizabeth conquered her drug habit in hopes of winning back Phillip. Much to Justin's disappointment, she planned to marry Mike, who was still holding the secret of her stillborn child. Mike was also certain that Dean had murdered del Villar, and he was

Phillip became embroiled in a custody battle, which caused his "mother," Elizabeth, to turn to pills to ease the pain.

THE WOMEN IN ALAN SPAULDING'S LIFE

Three of the women who played a significant role in Alan Spaulding's life were his wife, Elizabeth; his future wife and the mother of his adopted son, Phillip, Jackie Marler; and his loyal nanny turned secretary, Diane Ballard.

bent on proving it, partly to save his good friend Sara from a sorry fate. Meanwhile, Roger got his hands on the new affidavit from del Villar, which told the truth about Alan and Dean's bribe, and made a photocopy for his files! Roger and Dean were fierce competitors at Spaulding, so Alan concocted a plan for the two of them to vie for a vice presidential position. Alan was determined to purchase a choice piece of property on Thornway Road owned by Lucille Wexler, a wealthy eccentric who had long been an adversary of Alan's family. Whichever man was able to charm Lucille into selling her creepy mansion to Alan would win the post.

Lucille had a daughter named Amanda, a talented classical pianist whom Lucille sheltered and treated like a little girl. Amanda had been married to a handsome architect named Gordon Middleton, but she left him on their wedding night because she couldn't bring herself to consummate the marriage. Amanda was now beginning to blossom into a woman, thanks to artist Ben McFarren. Ben and Eve were renting Lucille's guest cottage, and Eve noticed that Amanda was mesmerized by her dashing husband. Ben did a painting of Amanda that stirred such deep, frightening feelings in her that one stormy night she slashed it to shreds. When Ben witnessed this scene, Amanda admitted to him that she couldn't shake the memory of being twelve years old and overhearing a man beating Lucille in her bedroom. This horrible episode ended with Lucille telling Amanda firmly that she must never trust a man. Lucille continued to nurture this fear throughout her daughter's life, to the extent that Amanda remained essentially a child, talking to dolls and avoiding intimate contact with men. With Ben's help, Amanda threw away her dolls and became her own person. Lucille was livid! A twisted woman, she decided to make Ben and Eve her virtual slaves and burned down the art gallery where Ben was having a showing. Had the showing been successful, Ben would have been able to send Eve to college so she could fulfill her dream of becoming a teacher. Now that their hopes were dashed, Lucille came to the "rescue." She hired Eve to manage her real estate holdings and gave Ben household chores to perform at the mansion.

While Eve resigned herself to her fate, her sister,

Lucille Wexler, a wealthy eccentric and longtime adversary of the Spauldings, lived in an eerie mansion with her sheltered daughter, Amanda.

LOVE AND MARRIAGE

When Rita and Ed were finally wed, Rita resolved to shake her mining-town roots and live the good life.

Rita, was going through a private hell. After Hillary dumped Roger, he arrived drunk at Rita's apartment and ranted on about how he was a better man than Ed. Then he raped Rita! Instead of going to the police, Rita kept the crime a secret for fear of losing Ed once again. Ed and Rita were married and moved into a sprawling Spanish-style villa on Skyline Drive, right next door to Alan.

Soon after, Roger was run over by a car in a parking garage. While he recovered, he was surprised to see Holly come to his side. Now that Ed was married to Rita and Peter was sorting out his feelings, Holly was lonely. As for Roger, he finally saw the opportunity to take a woman away from Ed. Roger played on Holly's sympathies as he reminisced about the good old days. Holly's visits to Roger's hospital room became more frequent and one day, they decided to get married! Another wrong move....

1979

It was a banner year for intertwined intrigue in Springfield as brothers Mike and Ed Bauer fought the machinations of their respective adversaries, Alan Spaulding and Roger Thorpe.

Holly married Roger in a quiet civil ceremony with Sara McIntyre and Adam Thorpe in attendance. Adam was furious with Barbara for sitting out the wedding, as he was still blind to his son's treachery. But Adam saw right through Alan and minced no words with his egomaniacal boss, who responded by firing him. Roger now became Alan's number one man, thanks to a climactic incident involving Dean Blackford.

Sara was becoming increasingly suspicious of Dean and was particularly curious about a key she found in his possession. She turned it over to Mike, who traced it to Dean's locker at the Springfield Athletic Club. Inside the locker, Mike discovered the gun that killed Ramon del Villar! Dean learned that Sara was on to him and confessed his crimes to her just as he was preparing to shove her off a cliff! Mike arrived in the nick of time and fought with Dean, who plunged to his death. Sara was devastated that she'd repeated with Dean her tragic marriage to the murderous Lee Gantry, and she was determined never to make the same mistake again. Subsequently, Mike proved that Dean was the hit-and-run driver who had plowed into Roger.

Both Alan and Roger were relieved to see Dean meet his end. Alan was glad that Dean did not live to incriminate him in del Villar's murder, even though Alan hadn't ordered or even known about the hit in advance. Now that he was minus his adversary, Roger was sitting pretty at Spaulding Enterprises. However, he was frustrated by his lack of a sex life, as Holly, realizing she'd erred in marrying him, assiduously avoided sex. So Roger charmed Hillary into resuming their affair, but Hillary felt guilty about being the other woman and quickly ended it once and for all. Roger was also livid that Holly let Christina maintain a close relationship with Ed, whom she had originally known as her father.

Roger was like a volcano ready to erupt, and he did so in the most grotesque and brutal way imaginable: He raped Holly!

In an unprecedented show of fortitude and maturity, Holly fought back by suing Roger for marital rape. She was represented by Mike Bauer and the eminent Clarence Bailey, while Roger engaged the services of a brash young barrister new to Springfield. He was Ross Marler, Justin's younger brother, who had left the streets of Chicago to become a legal whiz kid in New York. Ross was every bit as materialistic and ambitious as Justin was prior to his metamorphosis. Justin saw a reflection of his former self in his kid brother and was appalled that Ross would stake his career on a sleazeball like Roger Thorpe. Other lives were deeply affected by the rape. Rita was guilt-ridden about not coming forward about her own attack at Roger's hands, and admitted this in confidence to Eve. Adam was initially opposed to Holly's lawsuit against Roger until Sara convinced him from a medical standpoint that Holly's allegations were true. A devastated Adam finally saw how

Even after he found out that Christina was Roger's child, Ed never stopped loving her like a daughter, and Roger was furious that Holly let the relationship continue.

ISSUES

In a landmark case that garnered much attention, Holly sued Roger for marital rape.

be an amusing challenge, telling her, "Even a thorough-bred needs someone to hold the reins." Jackie's hopes soon faded when Alan lost custody of Phillip to Elizabeth. Mike and Elizabeth reconciled briefly, but when Phillip's heart condition flared up at the sight of Mike with his mother, they decided they could never marry. By now, Alan had completely poisoned Phillip's mind against Mike, and this pitted Jackie against Alan. Jackie was infuriated when Alan considered telling Elizabeth that Phillip was not her natural son. Jackie contemplated leaving Alan until she found herself pregnant with his child. The scenario came full circle when Justin proposed to Elizabeth. At first she hesitated, but the prospect of raising Phillip with a loving husband won her over. Elizabeth and Justin were married, and Phillip was content.

At this time, Jackie was also worried about her friends Ben and Eve McFarren. Ben was now a staff artist for Alan and was being overworked, while Eve was being slave-driven by the demanding and deranged Lucille Wexler. And Lucille's daughter, Amanda, was obviously smitten with Ben. Lucille falsely insinuated to Eve that Ben and Amanda were sexually involved. Since Ben insisted on keeping their friendship strictly platonic, Amanda returned to her estranged husband, architect Gordon Middleton, and finally consummated

Justin couldn't understand why his feisty ex, Jackie, would marry a man as tyrannical as Alan Spaulding. Of course, neither Justin nor Alan knew that Jackie was Phillip's biological mother.

twisted Roger was and confronted his son, urging him to get psychiatric help. Roger angrily rejected him. Adam came to rely on Sara as a confidante, and the two became close and dear friends.

Elsewhere in Springfield, the saga of Phillip Spaulding's parentage took on new twists and turns. Flush with excitement over his new marriage to Jackie, Alan callously lied to Elizabeth that she was infertile, and that Mike knew all about it! This revelation brought Elizabeth closer to Justin, who began to investigate her medical background. To Justin's puzzlement, Alan tried to block his investigation. And when Justin went to Amsterdam to meet with Paul LaCrosse, the obstetrician avoided him. Justin's suspicions grew when he couldn't trace Phillip's congenital heart condition to either Alan's or Elizabeth's medical histories. He also couldn't figure out why his feisty ex, Jackie, would marry a man as dominating and insufferable as Alan. Of course, she had only done so to be near Phillip. Alan had no idea that Jackie was Phillip's natural mother, and he found her to

their marriage. The next morning, she awoke and realized she'd made a mistake. Amanda divorced Gordon, while Ben and Eve's marriage deteriorated to the point where Diane seduced a lonely Ben. When Diane came to the Wexler estate to return Ben's wallet, Lucille overheard them discussing their night of passion and told a horrified Amanda! Ben admitted his indiscretion to Eve, who promptly filed for divorce and resigned from Wexler Properties.

Eve found an unexpected new friend in Ross Marler, who saw that she brought out his softer side. Certainly no one else at the Springfield Superior Court building saw that facet of Ross' personality, as he mounted a masterful defense of Roger Thorpe. Ross brought to the fore Holly's thwarted attempt to stop her divorce from Ed, and depicted Roger as an upstanding husband whose relations with his wife were consensual. Certain of victory, Roger was brash enough to boast to Diane that he had the true del Villar affidavits. As it turned out, Diane was too shrewd even for Roger. She broke into his apartment and stole the documents in order to protect Alan.

The case swung in Holly's favor when Rita finally admitted that Roger had raped her. This revelation left Ed hurt and confused, and Roger cornered. While Barbara listened on the other side of the door, Roger told Christina that he was planning to take her far away from Springfield. Barbara told Holly, who ran to Roger's office and found him engaged in a brutal fistfight with Ed. Overcome with hatred and determined to save Ed, Holly shot Roger! When Roger regained consciousness at Cedars, he summoned Alan to his bedside. Now under Roger's thumb because of the del Villar caper, Alan had Roger whisked away to his private clinic in Puerto Rico, where he enlisted Dr. Gonzalo Moreno to operate. Adam followed, only to find Roger's body covered with a sheet. A grim Dr. Moreno informed him that his son was dead.

One of many who did *not* mourn Roger was Hillary Bauer, who had matured into a capable nurse at Cedars. Hillary was rooming with Katie Parker, another young nurse who fell hard for a cool, collected, noncommittal surgeon named Mark Hamilton. Katie's brother, Floyd Parker, was a well-meaning blowhard who sponged off Katie until he landed a job on the custodial staff at Cedars. There he befriended a new patient, Lainie Marler, Justin and Ross' younger sister. Lainie was a sweet, dedicated track star who had been hit by a car and was temporarily paralyzed. When Ed participated in a surgical procedure that restored her mobility, Lainie developed a brief but harmless crush on him.

LOVE AND MARRIAGE

Elizabeth had been in love with Mike, but Phillip's reaction to their relationship was so extreme that she accepted Justin's proposal in the hopes that they could be a loving family.

Another arrival in town was Hope Bauer, fresh from a New York design school. Hope was hired to work on some of Gordon Middleton's architectural projects, including a villa on the island of St. Lucia that Alan had bought for Jackie. The barbs flew between Hope and Alan, who was not pleased that Gordon was working with Mike Bauer's daughter on his project. The two men were archenemies, and Mike was still investigating Roger's "death." One day, Hope and Gordon were puzzled to find an IV unit in the villa and even more baffled when Alan was secretive about it. Before Hope and Gordon could pursue this mystery, Gordon learned that his brother had been seriously injured in a car accident, and he decided to go back to his family home far from Springfield. This development left Hope and Alan to slug it out until the interior of the villa was finally completed. They then boarded a small plane bound for Puerto Rico, where they would catch a connecting flight to Springfield. The plane went down in the ocean, killing the pilot and leaving Hope and Alan adrift on one wing. Eventually, they came to a deserted island, where Alan became feverish from an infected wound. He rambled on deliriously about del Villar as a curious Hope listened in wonderment. Hope nursed Alan back to health and asked him about what he had said, but Alan avoided the subject. He did apologize for his rude treatment of her and found himself talking to

On the run, Roger landed in France, where he did his best to charm pretty plastic surgeon Renee DuBois into changing his face so that he could return to Springfield with a new identity. The good doctor made only small adjustments, however.

this genuine young woman about his life. Alan admitted his dislike for his manipulative father, Brandon Spaulding, who was now in a nursing home. Hope got Alan to see how much like his father he'd become, and he resolved to change once he returned to Springfield. Thanks to Hope, Alan became more human. Then the unthinkable happened—Hope and Alan made passionate love on the beach!

While Hope and Alan were missing, Lucille was angered to discover that Brandon Spaulding had initiated contact with Amanda. Ben found a letter revealing that Brandon and Lucille were former lovers. What neither Ben nor Amanda knew, however, was that Amanda was not Lucille's biological daughter. Brandon had led Lucille to believe that the girl was his illegitimate daughter by another woman, and Lucille had adopted her in hopes of

becoming closer to Brandon, but to no avail. When Brandon fell ill and was hovering close to death, he admitted to Lucille that Amanda was in fact Alan's *daughter* by a woman whose name Brandon whispered to Lucille. Brandon insisted that Lucille tell Amanda the truth, but Lucille adamantly refused, fearing that she would lose her beloved daughter. During this intense confrontation in his room at the nursing home, Brandon became short of breath and Lucille brusquely left the scene without summoning his nurse. Moments later, Lucille heard on her car radio that the legendary millionaire Brandon Spaulding was dead.

Alan's absence brought to a boil the long-simmering animosity between Jackie and Diane. During one of their confrontations, Jackie fell and lost her baby. She then rallied and assumed control of Spaulding Enterprises, with Ross as her ambitious adviser and Diane as her target for eventual dismissal. Diane had one friend, Mike Bauer's secretary, Ann Jeffers. Both Ann and Diane pined for their dashing bosses and occasionally commiserated over drinks. During one of their bull sessions, Diane let it slip that Alan was inexplicably getting phone calls from Puerto Rico on his private line. When Ann relayed this information to Mike, he immediately suspected that Alan had a part in Roger's death. But in truth, Roger was alive! It was Roger who was responsible for the phone calls from Puerto Rico and the mystery IV in the villa on St. Lucia. Roger was now in France, charming plastic surgeon Renee DuBois into altering his face so he could return to Springfield with a new identity. Renee made only minor adjustments, but Roger was too smitten by the beautiful doctor to let her go. Won over by his sincere longing to be with Christina, Renee agreed to marry him and help raise his daughter!

But that task, meanwhile, had fallen to Ed and Rita. Over Rita's objections, Ed insisted on raising Christina while Holly was imprisoned for Roger's supposed murder. In jail, Holly had the support of a sympathetic cellmate named Clara Jones, as well as her former suitor Peter Chapman, who volunteered at the jail one day a week just to be near her. Rita resented having to care for Christina, and she was furious with Ed for refusing Barbara's offer to take the girl temporarily. Ed had never stopped loving Christina as a daughter, but as Bert wisely pointed out, he was wrong to expect Rita to care for Roger's child.

Enter Dr. Greg Fairbanks, Rita's old flame from Bluefield. Greg was a cocky medic who was at Cedars for a short-term project. One look at Greg and Rita started feeling sorry for herself because Ed was boring in bed. She consulted Sara McIntyre, who was now a certified sex therapist, about her dissatisfaction with her sex life. On Sara's advice, Ed and Rita went to St. Lucia on a second honeymoon, but it was a disaster, for Ed wanted to spend more time on sightseeing buses than between the sheets. While they were on the island, Ed received word that Holly had been stabbed in jail by a hardened con named Gail, and he rushed back home to be with her. Rita stayed behind on St. Lucia, where Greg found her and seduced her. Once back in Springfield, Rita admitted to Ed that she was in therapy with Sara and that her dissatisfaction had led her to have a one-night stand with a man whom she refused to name. Later, she found herself pregnant and told Ed truthfully that she didn't know who the father was. This event would have brought Ed back to Holly, had she not just accepted Peter's marriage proposal. Holly was happily cleared of all charges when, under hypnosis, she revealed that her "fatal" confrontation with Roger was interlaced with flashes of her rape by him.

As Ed wrestled with his confusion, he and his family were relieved when Hope and Alan were discovered safe and sound. The castaways did not reveal their growing love for one another, but eyebrows were raised by a newspaper photo of Hope and Alan hand in hand during their rescue. When Jackie discovered that Hope and Alan were carrying on an affair, she divorced Alan, much to the disappointment of Phillip, who adored his "aunt Jackie." Fortunately, Phillip also adored his "stepdad," Justin, and the two spent a great deal of time together. Justin even took Phillip to New York for a medical convention so they could enjoy the sights together. While they were gone, Mike and Elizabeth ran into one another—and ended up in bed. Obviously the spark was still there, but Jackie had also become interested in Mike again. When she found Mike and Elizabeth together, she was both hurt and furious, but she agreed not to tell Justin. This romantic roundelay came full circle when Hope admitted to Mike that she was in love with Alan, his archnemesis, and that they planned to be married. Shocked, Mike vowed to prove to his daughter what a duplicitous, amoral man Alan Spaulding really was.

Alan was trying to deal with the death of his domineering father. The reading of Brandon Spaulding's will unleashed a furor. Instead of leaving everything to his son, Brandon bequeathed the bulk of his estate to Amanda Wexler! When he learned that Brandon and Lucille were once involved, Alan suspected that Amanda was

ON LOCATION

Hope was hired to decorate Alan's villa, and he was not pleased to be working with Mike Bauer's daughter. But when the two were later stranded on a desert island, they grew closer, and before long they fell in love.

Brandon's illegitimate daughter. As for Lucille, she prayed that no one would learn the truth about Amanda's parentage. Lucille made no secret of her hatred of Alan but wouldn't explain to him the reason behind it. When she realized that Ben was becoming increasingly suspicious about Amanda's parentage, Lucille set him up to fall from a window at her estate. Ben took the tumble but lived, and was more suspicious of Lucille than ever.

Enter Ross Marler. Mike respected his legal skills enough to hire him as his new partner, but Ross had far grander ambitions. He yearned for a high-profile life in politics and saw Amanda's money as the perfect springboard. With Lucille as his ally, he struck up a friendship with Amanda in hopes of diverting her attention away from Ben. But Ross was ambivalent, because his true feelings were for Eve, Ben's soon-to-be ex! To Ross' credit, he deeply regretted having defended Roger, whom people were gradually beginning to suspect was still alive. One night, Roger broke into Alan's home and greeted his shocked host calmly by saying, "I'll take a scotch if you've got it." Alan thought Roger was in France and hoped he'd never return. As Alan stood dumbfounded, Roger let him in on his plan to kidnap Christina away from Holly. Alan offered Roger a million dollars to leave Holly and Christina alone, but Roger turned him down. Christina was the only person in his life who loved him, and he was determined that he and his little girl would be together forever!

1980

DASTARDLY DEEDS

At the Cedars Hospital circus bazaar, Rita had the misfortune of recognizing Roger, who was disguised as a clown. After a harrowing chase through the Hall of Mirrors, he abducted her to a deserted cabin. As a result, Rita lost her baby, and Roger was on the run again.

A time of major transition was in store for the Bauers, the Thorpes and the Marlers. Shocking secrets would be revealed, depraved villains would receive their comeuppance and some exciting new people would pepper the Springfield landscape.

The holiday season was over, and Jackie was on a ladder removing ornaments from her Christmas tree when she fell and hit her head. Justin saved her life by rushing her to Cedars, where, in her delirium, she mut-

tered, "Phillip...my baby." After she recovered, Jackie finally admitted the bittersweet truth to Justin: Phillip, the boy they both loved, was their son. This revelation brought Justin and Jackie closer together than ever, but he grew tense and irritable around Elizabeth because of this momentous secret. Elizabeth picked up on Justin's new bond with Jackie and accused him of having an affair with his ex. Later, during a medical checkup, Elizabeth learned that it was impossible for her to have given birth to Phillip! Just then, Dr. Paul LaCrosse came to Springfield and talked to Alan about Elizabeth's growing curiosity regarding Phillip's parentage. Conveniently, the omnipresent Diane overheard the conversation! Elizabeth stumbled upon a tape of Justin telling Mike that Jackie knew Elizabeth was not Phillip's biological mother. Feeling deceived, Elizabeth underwent extensive psychotherapy and subsequently initiated an amicable divorce from Justin. Jackie's divorce from Alan was also finalized. Phillip's parents were finally free, and Jackie and Justin were married again!

Alan now had to deal with Roger, who had returned to Springfield with plans to steal Christina. He disguised himself as an elderly European professor named Schneider and took a room at a boardinghouse on Seventh Street. The wily impostor planted a listening device in Barbara Thorpe's home and was soon devastated to hear Adam tell Barbara that he wished he had a son like Ed. Roger was appalled. Everyone in his life preferred Ed over him: Holly still loved Ed...Rita married him... Christina looked to him as a father figure. Now, his own father was glorifying the man whom Roger paranoically considered a threat to his manhood.

It was ultimately through Rita that Roger got revenge on Ed. Rita had Sara McIntyre arrange for a paternity test to determine whether Ed or Greg had fathered her unborn child. Soon after, Rita and many others in Springfield attended the Cedars Hospital circus bazaar. Rita noticed one of the clowns getting particularly chummy with little Christina. Rita looked carefully into the clown's piercing dark eyes, and Roger knew immediately that he had been recognized. Roger chased Rita through the Hall of Mirrors, caught her and brought her to a cabin on Indian Lake. Anguished by

It was nosy Nola Reardon who discovered "Professor Schneider's" listening device and identified him as Roger Thorpe. As soon as Mike and Ed got wind of what was happening, they traced Roger to Santo Domingo.

Rita's disappearance, Ed got Sara to reveal the results of Rita's test. Ed, not Greg, was the father of Rita's baby. When the police traced Roger to Indian Lake, he ran, abandoning Rita, who he'd tied to a bedpost. Racked with abdominal pain, Rita tried to free herself, and in the process accidentally knocked over a kerosene lamp, setting the cabin on fire. Ed arrived in time to help the police save Rita, but was devastated when she tragically miscarried their baby boy.

Back in France, Renee DuBois was shocked to see news reports revealing that Roger was an international fugitive, and she came to Springfield to help Mike Bauer with his investigation. The two became instantly attracted to one another. Mike was lonely without Elizabeth, and Renee felt foolish for falling for a criminal like Roger. But a long-term romance was not to be, for Roger—via the bug he had put in Barbara's apartment—eavesdropped on Mike and Renee when they visited Barbara. Renee mentioned that Holly and Christina were away from Springfield but did not say where they had gone. Holly and Christina (Chrissy) were actually in Santo Domingo with Peter Chapman. Roger confronted Renee in her hotel room, but she refused to tell him Holly and Chrissy's whereabouts. During the altercation, Renee bolted and fell down a stairwell to her death.

The adventures of rotten Roger reached their ulti-

mate climax. When Roger overheard Ed mention the Santo Domingo hotel where Holly and Chrissy were staying, he wasted no time in finding them. Holly prevented Roger from abducting Chrissy, and he angrily forced Holly into a stolen Jeep and took her for a wild ride through the streets of Santo Domingo and into the jungle. Roger told a terrified Holly that they were going to the Island of Lost Souls, where no one would be able to find them, ever. When Mike and Ed discovered that Roger had bugged Barbara's house, they knew that Holly was in imminent danger. They notified the Santo Domingo police and flew there immediately. Ed and Mike followed Roger's trail, and when they found him, he was holding Holly hostage on top of a cliff. The intrepid Bauer brothers engaged in a struggle with Roger that left the crafty criminal dangling perilously from the edge of the cliff. In an incredible show of humanity, Ed grabbed Roger's hand and tried to save the man who hated him so deeply, but it was too late. The lethal, tormented Roger Thorpe fell to his death.

Holly's life was changed forever. She decided to leave her job as Steve Jackson's secretary at Cedars and

MORE DASTARDLY DEEDS

By the time Ed and Mike caught up with him, Roger was holding Holly hostage perilously close to the edge of a cliff.

open a child care center in Zurich, Switzerland. Before she and Chrissy departed, Holly broke her engagement to Peter, who later reconciled with Maya back in Santo Domingo. She then bade a sad farewell to Ed and told him that she had never stopped loving him.

In the meantime, Greg Fairbanks was pursuing Eve with the express purpose of arousing Rita's jealousy. Rita warned Greg not to hurt her sister, or she would tell Ed what a louse Greg was, and his career would be finished. Greg managed to convince Eve to go to bed with him, and Eve believed this was a sign of something permanent. Sex meant commitment as far as Eve was concerned, and was not to be treated lightly. But Eve soon discovered that Greg was carrying on with Diane Ballard, whose seduction of Ben had led to his divorce from

When handsome med school student Kelly Nelson moved into the boardinghouse, Nola was more than intrigued.

Eve! Not only did Greg lose Eve, but he let it slip to Ed that he had recently been on St. Lucia. Putting two and two together, Ed realized that Greg was the other man in Rita's life and promptly fired him from Cedars. Greg moved back to Bluefield, West Virginia, and Ed and Rita decided to give their marriage another try. Barbara called a truce with Rita for Ed's sake, and hoped that Roger's death would open the door for a reconciliation with Adam. Although Adam remained friendly with his ex-wife, he was starting to look upon Sara McIntyre as more than just a friend.

Eve felt she'd been too hasty in divorcing Ben and tried to make it up to him by introducing him to the influential Carter Bowden, who'd inherited an art gallery empire from his late estranged father, Alex Bowden. Insecure over the renewed bond between Ben and Eve, Amanda secretly paid Carter Bowden a princely sum to subsidize an art contract for Ben. Ross was handling Amanda's business affairs at the time and was quick to tell Lucille that Amanda was evasive about a sizable withdrawal she'd made from her account. Lucille rightly feared that the money was a loan for Ben, whom she distrusted and despised with a vengeance. Amanda continued to pursue Ben until he finally gave in to her romantic overtures. Ben was convinced that Amanda was now a strong woman with earthly desires, not the sheltered girl who retreated into a world of dolls. When Eve visited Ben at the Wexler cottage to ask him to consider a reconciliation, it was too late—Ben and Amanda had just married! Lucille and Ross immediately conspired to break up the couple by trying to get Ben and Eve back together again, but there was a sinister undercurrent to this scheme. Ross was too blinded by ambition to admit, even to himself, that he had feelings for Eve, and he had no idea Lucille was plotting to kill the unsuspecting Ben. Lucille was deathly afraid that Ben would somehow discover the truth about Amanda's parentage.

As he lay dying, Brandon Spaulding had whispered the name of Amanda's natural mother to Lucille. It was Jane Marie Stafford. Lucille investigated the woman's background and discovered that her sister, Janice, had been involved with Alan Spaulding. Janice drowned in a lake after discovering Alan in a tryst with Jane Marie. Lucille traced Jane Marie's widowed father, Logan Stafford, to Toronto and paid him a visit. Logan gave Lucille a chilly reception and tersely informed her that Jane Marie was dead.

Unaware that Lucille was trying to uncover yet another skeleton in his closet, Alan married Hope in a ceremony in Bert's backyard. This did not please Mike, who was hell-bent on proving Alan guilty of collusion with the devious Roger Thorpe. Mike believed his investigation hinged on Roger's surgeon, Dr. Gonzalo Moreno, who was now at large. Moreno was slipping in and out of the United States, hitting Alan up for money to stay on the run. When Hope discovered the extent of Mike's efforts to nail Alan, she bitterly broke all ties with her father. Hope had her grandmother's sympathetic approval. Now older and wiser, Bert was not happy to see her old interfering tendencies in Mike.

When Jennifer found out that Morgan was really on a picnic with Tim instead of studying, Morgan was forbidden to see him for a while. Jennifer was determined that Morgan not make the same mistakes she did.

Mike's life took another turn when his car collided with that of Walter and Jennifer Richards and their spirited teenage daughter, Morgan. Jennifer was injured and Walter was killed instantly. Morgan, who had loved her father dearly, blamed Mike for his death. As fate would have it, Jennifer Richards was on her way to Springfield to become Lucille Wexler's household manager. Morgan eventually mellowed toward Mike when Bert kindly took her under her wing while her mother recovered at Cedars. It wasn't long before Mike began to enjoy the company of the lovely, soft-spoken Jennifer.

At the request of his good friend Sara McIntyre, Mike agreed to help her volatile adopted son, T.J. (Tim) Werner out of a major mess. After Joe Werner's sudden death, Tim went away to Lincoln Prep boarding school and saw his mother only on vacations and weekends. At Lincoln Prep Tim was accused of being an accessory to a young girl's suicide. The accusations were proved false, but Tim left school and returned to Springfield. Now

Morgan and Tim were both students at Springfield High School, and before long they began to date. Tim had befriended Kelly Nelson, Ed's godson, who had transferred to Springfield University as a pre-med student. Kelly's widowed father, Dr. Frank Nelson, had been Ed's closest friend in medical school. Kelly moved into the boardinghouse on Seventh Street, where Roger had masqueraded as Professor Schneider. The establishment was owned by Bea Reardon, a woman whose good nature and positive outlook belied her circumstances. Bea had been deserted by her husband, Hugh Thomas (Tom) Reardon, with whom she had seven children. Her youngest, Nola, was known to spout endless trivia about old movies, as they were her only refuge from the downtrodden existence she longed to escape. Nola immediately set her sights on handsome, straight-arrow Kelly. It didn't hurt that Kelly had a very promising medical career. But Kelly spent most of his time with his new confidante, Hillary Bauer, who found him to be the most honest and compassionate man she'd ever known. Floyd Parker, Katie's brother, teased Hillary about being smitten with Kelly, when in reality Floyd had a crush on Hillary himself. Nola took a job at Cedars, where Floyd worked as an orderly, and Floyd soon found himself falling in love with this quirky young woman. Steve Jackson, however, found Nola to

Magical Laurel Falls was a favorite meeting place for Springfield's teenage set. Here Morgan Richards, Tim Werner, Kelly Nelson, Floyd Parker, Hillary Bauer, Nola Reardon and Katie Parker enjoy a perfect summer day.

In 1980, Vanessa Chamberlain and her doting father, Henry, came to Springfield to join forces with Spaulding. The darkly beautiful Vanessa had once been deeply involved with Ross.

be insufferably nosy. After the old doctor retired and left Springfield, Ed learned that his mentor's diagnosis was correct—Nola was not as sweet as she led people to believe.

As Morgan and Tim grew closer, Jennifer warned her daughter to proceed with caution. Morgan assured her mother that she was not having sex with Tim, but told her in no uncertain terms that it was her life and she would live it as she pleased. When Morgan's grades dropped, Tim asked Kelly to help her with her studies. At first there was friction between them, especially when Morgan called Kelly "Mr. Perfect." Kelly's old girlfriend had called him that, and it brought back painful memories to this sensitive young man. Soon Kelly developed feelings for Morgan, even though she was his good friend's girlfriend. Perhaps it was her combined maturity and vulnerability that attracted him to her. Kelly decided to do the honorable thing, though, and backed out of their tutoring sessions with no explanation, leaving Morgan hurt and confused.

One day Morgan saw Kelly at Laurel Falls, a beautiful spot where the young people of Springfield enjoyed summer picnics and swims. As they talked in this magical setting, Kelly and Morgan could no longer hide their true feelings, and they made love. Although they tried to conceal their blossoming romance from Tim and their friends, Nola observed them together and wasted no time in plotting her strategy. Morgan and Nola had become chummy, and Morgan looked upon the older Nola as a confidante and friend. Nola helped her "friend" get birth control pills in hopes that Morgan would consummate her relationship with Tim. Kelly didn't want Morgan to take the pills because he thought it was irresponsible, and as a medical student he knew the pills had possible side effects. When Jennifer discovered Morgan's pills, she was furious! To add to Morgan's misery, she saw Kelly and Hillary on a date and feared she'd lost him forever. Saddened, Morgan fled to Chicago, where she met the unsavory Duke Lafferty. The innocent Morgan thought Duke had hired her to be a waitress, but the club was for swingers, and waitressing turned out to be the least of her duties. Morgan was saved in the nick of time by Jennifer, Mike, Tim and Kelly, who, distraught over her disappearance, tracked her down and brought her home. The police hauled Duke away.

Floyd proposed marriage to Nola, but the social-climbing Nola refused, telling him she was close to getting what she *really* wanted. She then lied to Morgan that Kelly and Hillary were having an affair. Stung by what she thought was Kelly's rejection, Morgan told Tim that she'd once had a relationship with Kelly. Tim wasted no time in picking a fight with his former friend, and destructively turned to drink for solace. Soon after, Sara and Adam confided to Ed that they were engaged, but made it clear that they were waiting to tell Tim until he was more stable. Ed told Rita and warned her to keep the news under wraps. Fat chance. Rita threw a lavish party, got tipsy and brazenly announced the engagement. The news shocked and saddened Barbara, who'd hoped for a reconciliation with Adam, and she promptly left the party. When Ed angrily confronted Rita, she coldly replied, "Barbara had her chance with Adam and she blew it!"

It was Nola's turn to be insensitive as she broke the news to Tim. Pushed over the edge, Tim was arrested for drunk driving. Ed, himself a recovered alcoholic, helped the troubled teen conquer his addiction. But Nola didn't make it easy, plying Tim with booze so he would pick another fight with Kelly. Then Nola made her ultimate move by lying to Kelly that Morgan and Tim were sexually involved. Depressed and lonely, Kelly fell under Nola's spell for one fateful night in bed.

Jennifer and Morgan continued to be at odds over Morgan's impulsive behavior. The truth was, Jennifer had a valid and potent reason for protecting her daughter from growing up too fast. Jennifer was in fact Jane Marie Stafford! For months, Jennifer went to great lengths to avoid meeting Alan, who was settling into married life with Hope. One day, Hope found letters in the attic of Alan's mansion pertaining to a Janice and Jane Marie Stafford. She gave them only a cursory glance, but when she asked Alan about them, he promptly burned the letters and told her the Stafford sisters were in the past. Soon after, Jennifer discovered that $25,000 had been mysteriously deposited to her account. When Mike offered to investigate, he was surprised by Jennifer's evasiveness. Lucille was also surprised to find that her new employee had musical talent just like Amanda. Jennifer often played "Misty" on the piano, because it reminded her of her night of passion with Alan, when the Johnny Mathis recording played softly in the background.

Ross started to have second thoughts about working for the Wexler family when Ben was almost gassed to death in his cottage. Ross secretly—and rightly—suspected Lucille. At this time, Ross was once again dating Eve, with whom he felt he could be himself, without ambitions or pretensions getting in the way. He was soon to be knocked for a loop when Vanessa Chamberlain, his darkly beautiful ex-fiancée, came to Springfield. Vanessa and her doting father, Henry, were wealthy Chicago businesspeople in the process of joining forces with Spaulding Enterprises. Iron-willed and sensuous, Vanessa was every bit the lady in the boardroom and the animal in the bedroom. Years before, Ross had courted her for her wealth and connections, then fell deeply in love with her. But Vanessa had ditched Ross for a rich, drab preppy who was more comfortable in her world. Now she was divorced, and Ross once again came face-to-face with the woman who represented his darker and baser instincts. For old times' sake, they made love.

Vanessa immediately made an impression on the people of Springfield. Hope was jealous when Vanessa flirted with Alan, even though Vanessa was more taken with Ben. Pragmatic to the core, Ross told Lucille that he'd picked up on Vanessa's attraction to her son-in-law and planned to use it to break up Amanda and Ben—a move that pleased Lucille, who hated Ben, and Ross

himself, who wanted Amanda for her money. Ross soon stumbled upon more ammunition: He discovered that Amanda had secretly paid Carter Bowden to bankroll Ben's contract at the gallery. When Ben politely rebuffed Vanessa, Ross relayed this information to her, and she took the liberty of telling Ben! Feeling emasculated and deceived, Ben flew into a rage and left Amanda, who later found herself pregnant with his child.

Vanessa found her next night of recreational sex with someone who was familiar to many in Springfield—Andy Norris, Barbara's son, a cunning writer who never remained in one place for very long. Vanessa knew Andy was trying to get out of a disastrous marriage to Trish Lewis, Vanessa's debutante friend. Barbara didn't know about the marriage and was happy to see Andy with Katie Parker. Recovering from her recent breakup with Mark Hamilton, Katie was now working as Sara's assistant and was therefore privy to confidential information about patients' sexual dysfunctions and assignations. The trusting, upbeat Katie didn't realize that Andy was an opportunistic cad who was only dating her to gain access to the keys to Sara's files. Andy planned to write not only an exposé on the sexual secrets of

Naive Katie Parker didn't realize that opportunistic Andy Norris was only dating her to gain access to Sara McIntyre's private files.

Springfield, but also a tell-all book about Alan! The latter could have been made into a miniseries!

Despite his marriage to Hope, Alan's eye was beginning to roam toward Rita. Her marriage to Ed hit the rocks when Ed invested in the Copper Lantern, a restaurant that Andy had bought for Barbara. Rita resented any connection Ed had with Holly's family and was extremely bored with her life as a doctor's wife. She and Alan became friendly because they were next-door neighbors. It also didn't hurt that Alan was handsome and wealthy. One minor problem: Alan was married to Rita's husband's niece.

His curiosity aroused by Hope's discovery of his letters regarding Jane Marie Stafford, Alan hired slimy private eye Joe Bradley to find her. At the same time, Ross located Logan Stafford and his son, Chet, who admitted that Jane Marie was alive but missing. Chet told Ross that Jane Marie had a distinctive birthmark on her arm. By now Jane Marie/Jennifer was forming such a close bond with Amanda that Lucille was becoming insanely jealous of their relationship. Lucille also knew that Jennifer had caught on to her scheme to separate Ben and Amanda. A deranged Lucille began terrorizing Amanda with phone calls and hanging up whenever Amanda answered. She also began to remove items from her mansion so that she could frame Jennifer for theft. The stage was now set for Lucille's ignominious downfall. Lucille spotted a picture of Jane Marie in the hotel room of Chet Stafford—who had come to Springfield to look for his

Marler to Become D.A.

When District Attorney Clarence Bailey returned to private practice, he handed the reins over to Ross, launching the ambitious lawyer toward the political career he always wanted.

missing sister—and recognized her as Jennifer! Raving mad, Lucille rushed home and confronted Jennifer. "Jane Marie Stafford!" she shrieked, lunging at Jennifer with a letter opener. As the two struggled, Lucille fell on the blunt instrument. When Amanda heard the commotion and rushed in, Lucille weakly murmured that Jennifer had tried to kill her. Lucille died on the operating table, and Jennifer was booked for murder. Ben learned he was going to be a father and reconciled with Amanda, who had completely turned against Jennifer.

Although Ross was angry to have been left out of Lucille's will, he found another way to capitalize on this tragedy when D.A. Clarence Bailey returned to private practice and named Ross as his successor. It was now Ross' civic duty to prosecute Jennifer's case, and he did so in his usual bloodthirsty manner. When Jennifer took the stand, Ross so relentlessly accused her of thievery and murder that she hysterically confessed to the crime! Everyone in the courtroom gasped in shock, not realizing that Jennifer was only protecting Amanda from the truth. Ross became such an instant celebrity that Henry Chamberlain wowed him with a promise to back the political career Ross had always wanted. Jennifer was found guilty of second-degree murder, leaving Mike mystified as to why she would blurt out a dishonest confession. Determined to clear her name, Mike got his hands on tapes from a local bank that revealed who deposited the $25,000 in Jennifer's account. It was Neil Blake, the Spaulding family attorney!

Other secrets were beginning to close in on Alan Spaulding. On his deathbed in Amsterdam, Paul LaCrosse told Elizabeth that he'd switched Phillip with her deceased child at Alan's instigation, and that Phillip was really the son of Justin and Jackie Marler. Elizabeth graciously wanted Justin and Jackie to have custody of Phillip, and the three prepared to fight Alan's inevitable resistance. Meanwhile, Diane led Alan to believe she'd destroyed the del Villar evidence, when in fact she'd saved it. More slippery than ever, Diane got into cahoots—and into bed—with Joe Bradley. Mike then learned that Dr. Moreno had been hospitalized for a heart attack in St. Lucia, and his medical bills were being paid by a tall, well-dressed American man. As Hope and Alan headed to their private island for a vacation, they were blissfully unaware that they had a stowaway aboard their yacht—Dr. Moreno!

1981

Secrets, murders and two mysterious newcomers made 1981 a year of action-packed adventure in Springfield.

The big news at the beginning of the year involved Jennifer Richards. Still determined to keep Amanda from learning that they were mother and daughter, Jennifer resisted lawyer Neil Blake's advice to tell the truth. She was unaware that Logan and Chet Stafford, her estranged father and brother, were now in Springfield. Then evidence came to light about Lucille's past antics, which indicated that Jennifer might not have stolen the money or items after all. A new trial was scheduled, and Chet saw Jennifer's photo in the newspaper! When the trial began and Jennifer took the stand, she saw both Chet and Alan in the courtroom crowd. In a heart-wrenching monologue, Jennifer confessed that Alan Spaulding had been her teenage lover and that Amanda Wexler McFadden was the result of that affair! She had never wanted her daughter to know, but on that fateful, stormy afternoon, when Lucille found out the truth, she tried to kill Jennifer. Jennifer was subsequently acquitted of Lucille's murder, while a guilt-ridden Alan vowed to be a father to Amanda, who was so shocked by the revelation that she suffered a miscarriage.

As Alan gained one child, he was on his way toward losing another. He was livid to learn that Elizabeth wanted Justin and Jackie to have custody of Phillip, and he planned to fight Elizabeth tooth and nail in court! Hope was sympathetic to Alan until he told her he intended to exploit Elizabeth's shaky mental history. When Elizabeth told Hope part of the convoluted LaCrosse baby-swapping story, Hope began to realize that her father was right—Alan had a cruel side after all. The situation grew uglier when Andy Norris, disguising his voice, blackmailed Alan to the tune of twenty-five grand for the revelation that Elizabeth had once cheated on Justin with Mike. Andy, of course, had stolen the information from Sara McIntyre's patient files. To redeem herself, Elizabeth told Justin about her night with Mike and he forgave her.

Hope soon became so sickened by Alan's behavior that she threatened to testify against him in the custody battle. Placing his marriage before his desire for revenge,

Alan backed down and allowed Justin and Jackie to take Phillip. But Hope had serious enough doubts about her husband to turn him out of their bed. As for Elizabeth, she left for Switzerland to continue her psychiatric treatment, while Justin and Jackie discovered they were expecting a child of their own. The latter piece of news did not sit well with Phillip, who was looking forward to having Justin and Jackie all to himself now that Alan, the father he idolized, had abandoned him. Sadly for Phillip, he was of no further use to Alan as a pawn in his vendettas and schemes. Of course, Phillip had no idea that the people who had adopted him were, in fact, his natural parents.

Other developments in early 1981 included the marriage and departure of Lainie Marler and gallery owner Carter Bowden, the marriage of Sara McIntyre and Adam Thorpe and the separation of Ed and Rita Bauer. To clear her head, Rita took Alan up on his offer to use his Caribbean villa. When she arrived, she was puzzled

ON LOCATION

He was married to Hope and she was married to Ed, but that didn't stop Alan and Rita from having an island fling. When they returned home, they continued their affair.

to see a Hispanic man run in panic upon seeing her. That man was—who else?—Dr. Moreno. Rita was delighted when Alan surprised her at the villa, and within hours the millionaire and the social climber were making passionate love amid the crashing waves. Meanwhile, back in Springfield, a distressed Hope learned that she and Alan were expecting a baby. Alan and Rita continued their affair after they returned to Springfield, and Rita confided to Sara about it during one of their sessions. As luck would have it, Andy found out about the affair in one of his midnight raids on Sara's files. After Alan told Andy that he'd changed his mind about agreeing to the tell-all biography Andy was writing, a vengeful Andy, again using his disguised voice, called Alan and threatened to blackmail him about his affair with Rita. Sara grew so concerned about her missing files that she nearly fired Katie for her supposed carelessness. Once Katie convinced her that she was as perplexed as Sara was about the missing files, Sara called in her old friend Mike Bauer to investigate. Mike had noticed the chemistry between Rita and Alan and suspected they were involved. He confronted Alan and warned him that he'd reveal the affair if Alan was ever again unfaithful to his daughter!

TROUBLED TRIANGLES

Floyd loved Nola, but Nola loved Kelly—and Nola would stop at nothing to get what she wanted.

Deception was rampant on the other side of the tracks in Springfield, where the scheming Nola seduced Kelly in hopes of becoming pregnant. Although both Kelly and Floyd were dupes in Nola's schemes, Bea had the nagging suspicion that Nola was manipulating the trusting Kelly. Nola's games reached the ultimate low when, in hopes of bedding Kelly, she plied him with so much liquor that he passed out. Not about to be a victim of circumstance, Nola first seduced an ecstatic Floyd that same night, then slipped back into Kelly's bed. The next morning, she lied to Kelly that they had made passionate love! To make sure she got pregnant, Nola slept with the unsuspecting Floyd once again.

While this was going on, Morgan was wrestling with the revelation that Amanda was her half-sister, and the two were slowly working to build a close relationship. Morgan was once again dating Tim, who was still battling his addiction to alcohol. Duke Lafferty, the notorious Chicago sleazeball, saw Morgan's picture in the paper and vowed to make her pay for ruining his life. Duke broke out of jail and abducted a terrified Morgan to a deserted farmhouse, where he savagely raped her. With the aid of Tim, Mike Bauer and the fearless Lt. Larry Wyatt, Kelly saved Morgan, and Duke was again brought to justice. In his characteristically kind manner, Kelly helped the girl he knew and loved come to terms

ISSUES: TEENAGE DRINKING

When Morgan turned to Kelly, Tim turned to drink. A car crash that badly injured Morgan led Tim to get the help he needed from Alcoholics Anonymous.

Hope and Alan mended their marriage in time to welcome a son into the world. They named him Alan Michael Spaulding.

Morgan soon became concerned about a new mystery at the Wexler mansion. Items from Amanda's childhood were being stolen, and at the same time, someone was anonymously threatening Eve's life. Subsequently, Vanessa was becoming neurotically insecure about Ross and Eve's growing relationship. When Ross wanted no part of Vanessa, she downed pills and booze in a phony suicide attempt to get him back. Instead, she found a new relationship with the man who saved her life—Ed Bauer! When a terrified Eve received a dead mouse in the mail, it was clear that someone was trying to force her out of town. Ross accused Vanessa, but Ben suspected Amanda, who was filing for divorce. Soon after, Amanda had occasion to see her uncle Chet Stafford's room. There she found all of the items that had been stolen from her house, including a fur hat and muff she'd worn as a little girl! It was now clear that Chet was a deeply disturbed man who had obsessively built a shrine to his niece. Amanda also discovered a letter from Chet confessing to terrorizing Eve because she was a threat to Amanda's love for Ben. He ended the letter by saying that he planned to get rid of Eve once and for all! Knowing something bad was about to happen, Amanda ran to the cottage in search of Chet or Eve. Just as she arrived,

with her rape and resume a normal life. Quick to pick up on Kelly and Morgan's renewed bond, Nola got Tim drunk and fed him more lies about Morgan and Kelly, knowing it would drive him mad! Later, a drunk Tim picked Morgan up to take her to a dance, and as he drove wildly at top speed, he got her to admit that she was still in love with Kelly. The car crashed, leaving Morgan briefly comatose and Tim realizing that he desperately needed help. Tim started going to Alcoholics Anonymous and went on to have a healthy relationship with Trudy Wilson, a down-to-earth volunteer at Cedars. Kelly and Morgan reconciled. But Nola wasn't through with Kelly—not yet! To her delight, Nola learned that she was pregnant, and she rushed to tell Kelly he was going to be a father. Always one to do the right thing, Kelly agreed to marry Nola, until Bea realized it was impossible for Kelly to have fathered Nola's child on the night he passed out in a drunken stupor. Disgusted by her daughter's deceitfulness, Bea told Kelly the truth and he denounced Nola as a contemptible liar. It was a triumph of love over adversity when Kelly and Morgan were married at Laurel Falls, the beautiful setting where they had first found love.

DASTARDLY DEEDS

Diane Ballard was on a rampage of revenge against Alan, while Joe Bradley tried to blackmail the wealthy financier for millions. Diane and Joe had once been involved in business and pleasure, and soon they would both be dead.

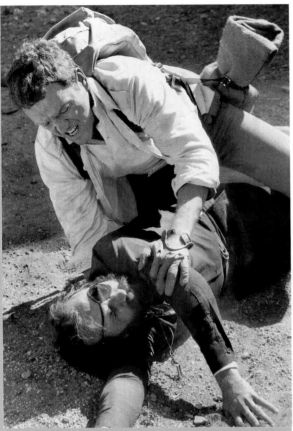

ON LOCATION

On the run in Tenerife, Alan was pursued by a one-eyed stranger. When they met up in the crater of a volcano, the two fought fiercely, and then the one-eyed man vanished.

Chet appeared and pulled out a gun. Amanda was struggling to stop him from shooting Eve when Ben showed up with the police, and Eve was saved from imminent death. Chet fled and was shot and wounded by the cops. As he lay in Cedars, Chet told Amanda that all he wanted was to make her happy. Chet died, and another tragic chapter was closed in the lives of the Stafford family.

Opening a new chapter at this time was Nola, who was finally acquiring a conscience and a sense of maturity. Nola almost went through with an abortion until Floyd learned of her pregnancy and realized he was the father. Floyd proposed and Nola said yes mostly out of a sense of defeat, but when they stood before the justice of the peace, Nola suddenly backed out. She'd made too many mistakes already to enter into marriage with a man she didn't love. Nola moved out of the boarding-

house and took a job as housekeeper/assistant to the mysterious Quinton R. McCord, an archaeologist whose imposing mansion was next door to the Wexlers' on Thornway Road. Nola was at once scared and intrigued when she found a human skeleton in McCord's library, and she became curious about her boss' secret phone calls and inexplicable headaches. The only one who seemed privy to McCord's strange activities was Violet Renfield, the dour head housekeeper.

As Quinton McCord's web of secrets grew more baffling, Rita and Alan's clandestine affair gradually came to light. Matters got more complicated when Hope was injured in a car accident after Andy, once again disguising his voice, told her over the phone that Alan had had an affair at his Caribbean villa. It was at the hospital that Alan learned Hope was pregnant!

Vanessa overheard Mike Bauer mention Alan's affair and hired PI Joe Bradley to determine the mystery woman's identity. Vanessa was hungry for more power at Spaulding and was looking for something she could hold over Alan's head. Within a few days, Joe reported to Vanessa that he had evidence that Alan had bought Rita a diamond-and-ruby necklace. Salivating, Vanessa told her father, Henry, that she had proof of Rita and Alan's affair. The wily Henry used this information to blackmail Alan into buying a company whose owner had secretly promised the Chamberlains $2 million for the sale!

Andy Norris also stood to gain from Alan and Rita's fling. He considered extorting money from Hope, but then she generously volunteered to give him a loan to keep the Copper Lantern's creditors at bay. Then Andy hit on Rita with his phony telephone voice, and she dutifully dropped off a handsome sum to keep her blackmailer from telling Ed about her affair. Ed put the pieces together anyway and furiously confronted Rita, who left for San Francisco soon after.

A reversal of fortune was in store for Andy when his estranged wife, Trish Lewis, arrived in Springfield. Trish accused Andy of stealing half a million dollars from her father, the powerful Oklahoma oil magnate Harlan (H.B.) Lewis. H.B. and his wife, Martha, had disowned Trish for marrying the opportunistic Andy, so Andy stole the money to make up for the loss. When Trish threatened to take Andy to court, he cruelly roughed her up and plied her with liquor until she passed out. Andy soon got the shock of his life when he picked up the latest money drop from Alan: His blackmail victim was waiting in ambush with a flashlight! With sneering contempt, Alan called Andy a contemptible and pathetic little nobody. Andy was further devastated when Alan brought up his late, unlamented father, Stanley Norris. As self-destructive people are apt to do, Andy finally caused his own undoing when he accidentally let it slip to Hope that the woman Alan was having an affair with was none other than her aunt Rita. After Hope tearfully relayed this to her father, Mike put the pieces together and realized that Andy was the guilty party who'd stolen Sara's files and spread the story. Mike forced Andy to reveal that he knew about Mike's night with Elizabeth, information that could have been found only in Sara's files. Andy was arrested for blackmail and theft, and as a heartbroken Barbara looked on, the Copper Lantern was awarded to Trish Lewis in the divorce settlement. Barbara was doubly regretful—not only did she discover what a deceitful, tormented young man her son was, but she also realized how sanctimonious she'd been with Adam over his loyalty to Roger. Putting the past behind her, Barbara joined Holly in Switzerland before settling in California to be near her oldest son, Ken, and his new family.

Once Hope recovered from the revelation of Alan and Rita's affair, Alan convinced her of his love and swore that he'd be faithful from now on. Hope touched Alan in a way no one ever had before and brought out his tender, sensitive side, while he showed Hope a kind of passion she'd never known. Hope relented, and soon after, they celebrated the birth of a son, Alan Michael Spaulding. Ironically, at the same time Justin and Jackie had a daughter, Samantha Marler.

Ross also turned over a new leaf when he met a refreshing and vivacious young woman, Carrie Todd, the new head of graphics at Spaulding Enterprises. Humanized by their whirlwind courtship, Ross confessed to Amanda that he'd manipulated her for her money. This revelation proved too much for Amanda to handle, as she was still in shock about her late uncle, Chet Stafford. She eerily reverted to her childlike state, cavorting around her mansion in little-girl dresses and ankle socks and playing with dolls. Pained by guilt over Amanda, Ross could not bring himself to admit to Carrie how devious he'd been before he met her.

With Andy Norris out of the way, it was now Diane Ballard who posed the greatest threat to the Marlers, the Spauldings and the Chamberlains. As Alan's right-hand

ON LOCATION

Even though Mike Bauer had been Alan Spaulding's archenemy for many years, Alan's conscience wouldn't let him leave the father of his beloved Hope alone in the desert to die. Alan brought Mike safely home.

woman, Diane ordered Ross to see to it that Phillip was cut out of Alan's will, or she would tell Carrie that Ross had manipulated Amanda. Then Diane confronted Henry with the knowledge of an affair he'd had with one Stephanie Ryan which produced an illegitimate son named Sean! Diane used this information to blackmail Henry into cementing a business deal with his old pal, H.B. Lewis, that was favorable to Spaulding Enterprises. The unscrupulous Diane soon learned that Joe Bradley was working for the Chamberlains. To extricate himself from his business and sexual arrangements with Diane, Joe confessed to Mike that Diane had paid him to steal Rita's San Francisco address. Alan finally fired Diane. Stung by Alan's disloyalty and rejection, Diane icily threatened to reveal his collusion with Roger Thorpe, Dr. Gonzalo Moreno and Ramon del Villar. Justin and Jackie also rushed to confront Diane after she made noises about revealing Phillip's true parentage. Concerned when Diane didn't show up for a scheduled meeting, Vanessa went to her apartment. There she found Diane's lifeless body, her battered head laying against the fireplace.

The suspects were numerous: Justin, Jackie, Ross, Alan, Henry, Vanessa and Joe, to name but a few. More

An aura of mystery swirled around the enigmatic Quinton McCord, new to Springfield. When the inquisitive Nola went to work for him, she was instantly intrigued.

slimy than ever, Joe demanded $10 million from Alan in exchange for tapes of him and Dr. Moreno. But Joe never lived to be a millionaire, for he, too, ended up dead in his apartment of a gunshot wound to the chest. In his typewriter was an unfinished letter to Alan, referring to the Moreno tapes, which were now conveniently missing. Alan was now the prime suspect in the murders of both Diane Ballard and Joe Bradley. Feeling the world closing in on him, Alan convinced Hope that they should take Alan Michael and flee to the exotic island paradise of Tenerife. The three left Springfield quickly, and Mike and Lt. Larry Wyatt followed in hot pursuit. On the island, Hope told Alan that a man she'd never seen before was following them. Offering no clues about their mysterious pursuer, Alan urged Hope to take Alan Michael back home without him.

In Springfield, some bizarre facts about Diane's past began to come to light. When the authorities went through her personal effects, they found an unnotarized will drawn up by an attorney in St. Paul, Minnesota. The will left all of her Spaulding stock to a stranger named Curtis McNeil of San Diego, not to Alan, as was expected, given her obsession with him. Diane also left

$5,000 to a Mrs. Edward MacKenzie, who was mute due to a stroke and living in a nursing home in Milwaukee. It was revealed that Diane had worked not only in St. Paul, but also in Omaha—at the same company as Carrie Todd! At the time, Carrie's last name was Anderson. Curious as to why Carrie had never revealed this, Ross looked into her past and discovered that for ten years, Carrie had been paying Mrs. MacKenzie's nursing-home bills. Ross worked with Mike to get to the bottom of this mystery. They found a picture of a young man in Carrie's house and brought it to Mrs. MacKenzie, whose eyes indicated that she recognized him. Could the man be Curtis McNeil? Mike also learned that Carrie had angrily torn up a check that Diane had offered to the nursing home for Mrs. MacKenzie's care.

Back in Tenerife, Alan went on the run to evade both Mike and his mysterious pursuer, but the mystery man caught up with him and engaged him in a fierce struggle. After the man disappeared, it was Mike Bauer's turn to meet up with Alan. Mike and Alan got into a violent fight that left Mike badly injured. Alan quickly left on his private plane, his pilot Wayne Jennings at the controls. Once aboard, Alan had a change of heart; he couldn't leave the father of his beloved Hope to die, no matter what threat Mike posed to him. Alan had Wayne return to the scene and lifted the injured Mike onto the plane. Just then, the stranger appeared in the distance, aiming a gun. A shot rang out and Wayne was critically injured, leaving Alan to pilot the plane and bring them back safely to Springfield.

Meanwhile, on Thornway Road, Amanda emerged from her childlike state when Ben stormed into the mansion and made love to her! They were still uncertain about their future together, but Amanda soon found a new purpose in life as a driving force at Spaulding Enterprises, much to Vanessa's chagrin. Jennifer also began working at Spaulding, where she was being trained to take over the late Diane Ballard's position.

Mike and Alan returned to Springfield with Alan's confession to conspiring with Roger and Dr. Moreno. Amanda was so disillusioned by the father she was just growing to love that she turned completely against him. In an ironic twist, Mike defended Alan, and his pleas for leniency won Alan a reduced jail sentence of eighteen months to two years. The pieces were now falling into place for an upcoming stockholders' meeting, which promised to be a showdown. On top of all this, Alan's mysterious enemy was now in Springfield and sending Alan death threats! Alan was cleared of suspicion in the murders of Diane and Joe, thanks to a shocking confession. In Carrie's apartment, Ross found Diane's briefcase, which contained letters about Henry's illegitimate son, Sean Ryan. Carrie admitted to having confronted Diane because Diane was threatening Ross. Diane and Carrie had engaged in a shoving match that ended when Diane fell and hit her head on the fire iron. Panicked, Carrie lifted all the evidence from Diane's apartment. Carrie also confessed to having accidentally shot Joe Bradley in a struggle over a gun. A trial date was set for January, but Ross was certain that Carrie would be cleared because the deaths were accidental. However, there were other complications. Carrie almost died from a drug overdose and began having inexplicable memory lapses. Then she disappeared.

As the year drew to a close, Mike and Ed discovered among Joe Bradley's notes that Vanessa had paid him to steal Rita's address. Ed angrily broke off with Vanessa and went to San Francisco in search of Rita, but to no avail. Josh Lewis, Trish's younger brother, came to town. An entrepreneur and the black sheep of the oil-rich Lewises, Josh decided to back Floyd Parker in his new rock-singing career. Floyd was trying to put Nola in the past and had begun a new relationship with a sweet young nurse named Lesley Ann Monroe. As for Nola, she was taken with Josh's wealth and charm, but he seemed more interested in Morgan, much to the horror of a jealous Kelly!

Nola's older brother, the macho but sympathetic Tony Reardon, arrived in town and went to work for Trish at her restaurant, the old Copper Lantern, now known as the Hideout. Tony dated Katie Parker, even though he was secretly more interested in her good pal Hillary Bauer. The feeling was mutual, but Hillary also kept the attraction to herself because she was dating Derek Colby, Mike Bauer's earnest new associate, who had grown up in the Reardons' neighborhood. Tony went on to become the manager of a local disco, Wired for Sound.

The most intriguing mystery in Springfield at this point was the story behind the enigmatic Quinton McCord, whose mansion on Thornway Road was replete with skeletons and secret passageways. Quinton seemed disturbed by the mention of various women from his past, especially Blanche Bouvier, a friend of Trish Lewis', who wrote him that she would soon be visiting Springfield. When Quinton learned of this, he left with Nola on a business trip to San Francisco to avoid her. Nola enjoyed the taste of the rich life in San Francisco and Quinton laid on the charm. Ever curious, Nola heard Quinton on the phone telling someone to "stop the great man." Nola wondered if Quint was referring to Alan, who was still being terrorized by a shadowy figure. When they returned from San Francisco, Quinton got word that yet another woman from his past was coming to Springfield. It was then that he had one of his "strange headaches" and disappeared. As his staff ventured out in a snowstorm to find him, Nola, alone in the mansion, collapsed with abdominal pains—her labor had begun.

1982

Loyalties, both familial and corporate, were tested in 1982, as some people turned out not to be what they seemed.

Ross finally located Carrie in Milwaukee and brought her back to Springfield, where she was immediately put in jail to await trial for the murders of Diane Ballard and Joe Bradley. Carrie was unable to account for a portion of the time she was gone. Jackie learned that Carrie had gone to Milwaukee via Chicago—where she had tried to hit up Jackie's father, Emmet, for $5,000! A photo then surfaced of Carrie, alluringly attired, tripping the light fantastic with a blond hunk in a Chicago nightclub!

LOVE AND MARRIAGE

After months of fighting desperately to save Carrie from a prison sentence, Ross wed his beloved fiancée in a moving ceremony surrounded by family and friends. Ross was convinced that their troubles were behind them, but Carrie's past would soon come back to haunt them.

During Carrie's trial, some of the truth came out about this enigmatic and tormented woman. After the court was cleared of spectators, Carrie took the stand and revealed that when she worked at Laird & Sogard in Milwaukee some years ago, she'd fallen in love with a junior accountant named Todd MacKenzie. They eloped and were happy until Carrie overheard pieces of a conversation between Todd and Diane Ballard, who also worked for Laird & Sogard, which led her to believe they were having an affair. In truth, Diane had pressured Todd to cook the company books, and strong-armed his mother into mortgaging her home to make up for the shortfall. Just as Carrie learned she was pregnant, Todd was driven to suicide over Diane's duplicitous scheme, and as a result, his mother had a stroke. Emotionally devastated, Carrie spent time in a mental institution, where she gave birth to a baby boy. Because of her unstable condition, she felt unfit to raise the child and willingly gave him up for adoption to a couple named Howard and Betty Long. In the courtroom, Carrie explained that Diane's blackmail of Ross was a replay of the Todd MacKenzie situation, and it triggered Carrie's renewed and deep-seated hatred of Diane. Ross pleaded with the jury to consider the emotional issues involved and to remember that Carrie's motive was to protect the people she loved. To his relief, Carrie was found not guilty.

Carrie and Ross were married and spent their honeymoon in Seattle, where—from a distance—Ross arranged for Carrie to see her little boy, Todd Jr., dining happily with the Longs in a restaurant. Overcome by a new sense of peace and contentment, Carrie quietly wept, but the feeling was not to last. Her belongings were vandalized, and Carrie felt a strange presence shadowing her, undermining her attempts to get on with her life. The presence turned out to be Carrie herself! Carrie had multiple-personality disorder. "Carrie #1" was the essential Carrie, open, vivacious and positive. "Carrie #2" was the vamp, the painted woman seeking pleasure at all costs. And "Carrie #3" was shy and insecure, the embodiment of low self-esteem.

The Carrie saga ultimately peaked when "Carrie #2" seduced a teenage neighbor, Ron Kennedy, as well as Josh Lewis, who was always up for a good time. She

Not long after her marriage to Ross, it became clear that Carrie had alter egos whom she was unable to control.

then attempted to lure Justin to bed, but when her horrified brother-in-law refused, Carrie told Jackie and Ross that she and Justin were having an affair! With the Marler family at loose ends, Jackie went to visit Emmet in Chicago for a while. When Sara placed Carrie under hypnosis to get to the root of her memory lapses, the three faces of Carrie came to the fore. Carrie called Jackie to apologize and filled her in on the truth behind "Carrie #2's" near destruction of her family. Jackie promptly boarded a plane for Springfield. Sadly, the plane crashed, leaving no survivors. Anguished, Carrie left Springfield to undergo extensive treatment in England, then wrote to Ross and insisted they divorce so he could get on with his life. Both Justin and Ross, bereft of the women they loved, now had to start new chapters in their lives.

Back on Thornway Road, Kelly saved Nola's life when she went into labor and gave birth to a baby girl, Kelly Louise, named for Kelly and for Floyd's deceased mother. Nola and Kelly made amends, but Kelly gently told Nola that because of all that had passed between them, their friendship was over. As a result, Nola changed her daughter's first name to Anastasia, after one of her favorite movies, calling her Stacey for short. Nola had a runaway imagination fueled by all the old movies she'd watched and memorized. She was becoming more fascinated with Quinton McCord, who was training her in his archaeological work. Ever nosy, Nola and her wacky sidekick, hairdresser Gracie Middleton, were increasingly baffled by the spooky goings-on at the McCord mansion. A secret passageway and an ancient gold cradle were just two of the strange things Nola stumbled upon, leading her to believe that Quint was part of an evil cult

à la Rosemary's Baby and was plotting to perform a mysterious rite on Stacey. Her curiosity at an all-time high, and still confused about her feelings for Kelly and Quint, Nola began to have fantasies about the two men drawn from such classic films as Casablanca, Shipmates Forever, Now, Voyager, Rebecca and It Happened One Night.

The real story behind Quinton R. McCord began to unfold in London, where Nola accompanied him on an archaeological mission. Upon arrival, Quint was reunited with his former fiancée Helena Manzini, a scheming, hot-blooded Italian. Helena had helped Quint in his work, only to desert him on the eve of their marriage for his unscrupulous competitor, Silas Crocker. When Helena saw Nola, whom she dubbed "that little American tramp," wearing a fur coat that Quint had originally intended for Helena, the two women erupted into a catfight on the spot! But the real intrigue involved Quint and Silas' competing quests to find the temple of gold from which the ancient gold cradle came. Quint had been searching for this early civilization for many years. The adventure brought Nola, Quint, Helena and Silas to an uninhabited island near St. Croix, where Silas abducted Nola and held her hostage on the edge of a volcano. After fighting off Silas, Quint went to rescue Nola just as the volcano started to erupt! Through a crack in the rock, Quint spied the golden temple of the lost civilization he'd been searching for. Unable to save both Nola and the temple, a devastated Quint watched his years of work disappear in the volcanic fire. Nola assumed Quint blamed her for the loss and returned to Springfield ahead of him. Helena accompanied Quint,

ON CALL AT CEDARS

Carrie tried to seduce her brother-in-law, Justin, causing turmoil in the Marler family. When Sara McIntyre put her under hypnosis, the three faces of Carrie were finally revealed.

presumably to realign herself with her former love, but she actually intended to double-cross both Quint and Silas! Silas stole into Springfield and kidnapped Nola yet again, this time taking her to a rotting boat teeming with rats who ate whatever food he saw fit to provide. Nola was rescued by a distraught Quint. As she lay in Cedars, dehydrated from her ordeal, Nola pretended to be asleep while an emotional Quint professed his love for her.

Meanwhile, Nola's former love, Kelly, and his wife, Morgan, were hitting rocky times. Because of her budding modeling career, Morgan started taking birth control pills, even though she knew Kelly wanted to start a family. Kelly resented his wife's new and glamorous career, and when Morgan went to St. Croix to film her first television commercial, Kelly managed to get time off and followed her there. Josh was on the island as well, and Kelly was furious to learn that Josh and Morgan had gone sailing together. Even though nothing had happened, Kelly suspected the worst. When he caught up with them, he knocked Josh out cold in a jealous rage. As a result, Kelly and Morgan separated.

Under the circumstances, Josh decided not to pressure Morgan into a relationship. Besides, he was much too busy managing Floyd's thriving career as a rock singer. This venture brought Josh into contact with the new woman in Floyd's life, nurse Lesley Ann Monroe. Josh remembered Lesley Ann as a hooker named Candy

ON LOCATION: ST. CROIX

In hopes of having a second honeymoon, Kelly joined Morgan on St. Croix, where she was filming her first TV commercial. But after hearing that she'd gone sailing with Josh, Kelly flew into a jealous rage that led to the couple's separation.

ON LOCATION: ST. CROIX

Washed up on the shores of St. Croix after a volcanic eruption, Quint and Nola finally shared their first kiss.

whom Andy Norris had hired back in Tulsa to steal Josh's money after the two had slept together. An embittered and vengeful Josh warned Lesley Ann to keep Floyd happy and productive or he would reveal her past. Josh reasoned that as long as he could be a successful show business manager, he would be free from the pressures of the family oil company, which he had long eschewed. With Josh's help, Floyd's singing career took off, and Josh started bringing big-name acts such as Crystal Gayle, Judy Collins, the B-52s, Quarterflash and Maurice Gibb into Wired for Sound. It was Maurice Gibb who convinced the Sour Grapes to record one of Floyd's songs. Floyd's career made him and Josh so wealthy that Floyd was able to rent the Spaulding mansion while Alan was doing prison time for his conspiratorial activities.

As Alan was paying his debt to society, the mysterious plot against him became more complex by the minute, as did developments at Spaulding Enterprises during his absence. Spaulding took on two new employees. Brenda Lowry was an attractive and soft-spoken research analyst who, unknown to the others, was really FBI agent Ivy Pierce. She had been investigating Alan's case ever since the unknown assassin followed him to Springfield from Tenerife. The other new employee was Mark Evans, a handsome foreign affairs expert who became involved with Vanessa until he grew tired of her manipulative games. When Alan was briefly released from prison to advise the governor on state financial matters, Alan's mysterious tormentor managed to abduct him to a cabin despite the heavy security Mike had arranged. Once there, the assassin revealed his identity to his would-be victim: He was Lucien Goff, a disgruntled ex-employee whom Alan had fired for illegally profiting from the company's foreign trade. To Alan's horror, his pilot Wayne Jennings entered the cabin and admitted that he and Goff were in cahoots. Mike managed to trace Alan to the cabin, and when he arrived with Ivy, they struggled with Goff on a moving tramway. Goff fell off the tramway to his death. A penitent Wayne was sent to prison, where he was later fatally poisoned.

It was obvious that at least one other person was involved in the scheme. Ivy believed it was Samuel Pasquin, a former cohort of Goff's who had disappeared after his wife, the former Mona Enright, had fallen off a cliff to her "death." When Quint purchased the Spaulding stocks that Diane Ballard had left behind, Ivy strongly suspected that Quint was, in reality, Samuel Pasquin. Nola also became suspicious when she spotted Quint and his housekeeper, Violet Renfield, in a secret third-floor room with a bandaged young woman who had lost the use of her vocal chords. Not realizing that Nola was snooping, Quint sneaked the woman into Cedars to be

Tony, Floyd, Lesley Ann and Josh hang out with Maurice Gibb of the Bee Gees at Springfield's popular night spot, Wired for Sound.

treated by Ed and Justin, giving her name as Rebecca Cartwright. What the authorities did not yet know was that Rebecca was the missing Mona. When Quint brought Mona back home, Nola overheard the "mute" patient tell herself that she planned on having Quint back in her life for keeps! As for the "Samuel Pasquin" alias, it belonged not to Quint, but to Mark Evans.

A lethal opportunist, Mark moved in on the lonely Jennifer Richards and married her, only to seduce her daughter Amanda! Now that Amanda was president of Spaulding in Alan's absence, she had considerable cash, stocks and corporate clout, all of which Mark dearly coveted. Jennifer was a mere cover for Mark's intentions toward Amanda, who felt guilty and cheap for betraying her mother, and it wasn't long before Mark became verbally abusive to his baffled new wife. Mark Evans' ultimate plan was to kill both Alan and Amanda and make Spaulding his own.

Amanda was torn between her love for her mother and her intense attraction to Mark. Her personal life in a shambles, she began making costly mistakes at the company. Amanda's biggest snafu was a Madrid oil-drilling operation in association with Lewis Oil that failed when a storm destroyed the rigs and killed several workers. Henry was livid and convinced Quint to organize a stockholders' revolt against Amanda. Vanessa was not happy to see these two men bond. Vanessa had found an old letter indicating that Henry had an illegitimate son, Sean Ryan. When she investigated further, Vanessa found a picture of Sean and was shocked to see that he was none other than Quinton McCord! Vanessa confronted Quint and blackmailed him into giving her

Josh was intensely attracted to the beautiful Morgan, and after the breakup of her marriage, they had a brief fling.

TROUBLED TRIANGLES

Mark Evans was not a man to be trusted. He married Jennifer Richards, then seduced her daughter Amanda.

his stocks, but he later reclaimed them after threatening to reveal Vanessa and Henry's previous double-dealings against Alan with Jocelyn Electronics.

As pretentious and scheming as she was, Vanessa showed her hidden earthy side in a brief relationship with the working-class Tony Reardon. At the same time, Henry found himself lonely and began squiring Tony's lovable mom, Bea, around town. As for Tony, his heart truly belonged to Hillary Bauer, and in time they became open about their feelings. Katie was happy for them despite her own feelings for Tony. Derek, Hillary's former love, was not. When Tony proposed, however, Hillary could not commit to him because she still had not resolved her feelings about Kelly.

Lesley Ann told Floyd about her past, and Floyd angrily turned on Josh and decked him. Josh promptly ended their business arrangement. Soon after, a truck transporting a house crashed into the Reardon boardinghouse. Tony cleverly turned the house into a bar, naming it Tony's Place. No longer the singing sensation of Springfield, Floyd was hired as Tony's bartender.

Alan was eventually cleared of all charges and re-

leased from prison. He assured Hope they would now have a simpler life. When Amanda almost sunk the company along with Lewis Oil, though, Alan could not sit back and watch his empire be destroyed. Behind Amanda's back, Alan made a deal with Josh's older brother, Billy Lewis, to sell him Lewis Oil and help him wrestle control away from Amanda. Josh was not happy to see Billy—who was their father's favorite—in Springfield. When Josh discovered Alan and Billy's plot to push Amanda aside, he was furious. To spite the other Spauldings and Lewises, Josh, Amanda and Ross formed their own oil exploration firm, Los Tres Amigos, known as LTA. Ross had dated Trish Lewis, however, and they found that they enjoyed one another's company, which created an uncomfortable situation.

Alan and Morgan eventually discovered Amanda and Mark's affair, but held off telling Jennifer because she was pregnant. When Amanda's divorce from Ben became final, Ben reconciled with Eve and they left Springfield together.

There was still the matter of Phillip Spaulding's parentage to resolve. Justin told Alan that he and Jackie were Phillip's natural parents and convinced Alan to let the boy stay with Justin now that Jackie was dead. Value clashes soon broke out, however, when Phillip was expelled from Lincoln Prep for cheating. While Alan covered for the boy, Justin insisted that Phillip own up and take responsibility for his actions. Phillip transferred to Springfield High School, where he befriended Ed's son Frederick, who was now calling himself Rick. When Alan gifted Phillip with a flashy sports car, Phillip and Rick promptly went joyriding with Rick behind the wheel. The police pulled them over for speeding. Rick was not carrying his driver's license, so Phillip quickly got into the driver's seat and took the rap for his new buddy. The bond between Rick and Phillip was now set for life.

After Ed finally received Rita's divorce papers from Toronto, he formed a promising new relationship with Nola and Tony's eldest sister, Maureen, who was back in Springfield following a disastrous marriage. Nola resented Maureen because she was always the "perfect" daughter, but Tony adored her. Ed made Maureen his secretary at Cedars and they worked beautifully together. He knew she still carried a torch for an old boyfriend, Dr. Matt Davenport, whose father was the Reardon family physician, but Ed was determined. "You make me want to live up to the very best there is in myself," he told Maureen. "You've given me back to myself, whole and healthy."

1983

The Bauers and the Reardons, now free from the past, entered a new phase in their lives, while Phillip Spaulding was forced to come to terms with a past he had never known.

Quint realized that Mona was only pretending to be mute in order to manipulate him. Out driving one snowy day, the two were arguing when their car skidded off the road. Both were injured and rushed to Cedars, where Nola and Violet Renfield kept a vigil as Quint lay unconscious. Fearing that Quint was dying, Violet admitted to Nola that Quint was really Sean Ryan, Henry's illegitimate son. Violet and her husband, the late archaeology professor Archibald Renfield, had been friends of Sean's mother, Stephanie Ryan. When Stephanie died, she left Sean in the Renfields' care and Sean became Archibald's protégé. Then Archibald was fatally injured in a cave explosion, and Sean was implicated. To evade the authorities and investigate Archibald's death on his own, Sean had assumed the name of Quinton McCord.

Despite Violet's fears, Quint recovered from his injuries and later proved that Silas Crocker was the one responsible for the explosion that killed Archibald years ago. Quint and Silas ended up in Tanquir, where—in a stroke of poetic justice—a cave collapsed on Silas, killing him. It was in Tanquir that Quint discovered a buried city, which he named after his beloved mentor, Archibald Renfield.

But intrigue continued to surround Quinton McCord. Mona told Nola that she'd been engaged to Quint and pregnant with his child. When Quint left on a long archaeological dig, Mona had an affair with Samuel Pasquin and married him. After Quint returned, Mona told him of her marriage and they had an argument atop a cliff. Quint was so agitated that he lost his balance, fell off the cliff and was knocked unconscious. What Mona didn't tell Nola was that while Quint was out cold, Samuel Pasquin arrived at the scene and pushed Mona

off the cliff, hoping to collect on her life insurance policy. Pasquin thought she was dead, but Mona had fallen only a few feet. Mona lost the baby, and to play on Quint's guilt, she pretended to be severely injured so he would take care of her.

Meanwhile, Mark Evans, alias Samuel Pasquin, finally showed a trace of humanity when he realized he was truly in love with Amanda. He confessed to her that he hated the Spaulding family because years earlier, Brandon Spaulding had swindled Mark's father when they were partners in the shipping industry. The betrayal drove his father to suicide—or so he thought. Mark believed he was entitled to half of Spaulding Enterprises by virtue of his father's prior relationship with Brandon. Amanda was sympathetic and helped Mark investigate the matter, only to discover that the senior Mr. Evans hadn't killed himself after all. He'd been murdered by Bryan Lister, one of Brandon's white-collar henchmen, who was now Mark's accomplice! Mark's world then began to crumble. He confronted Bryan and killed him. In the meantime, Morgan told Jennifer of Mark's affair with Amanda. Then Mark discovered that Mona was still alive, and in an eerie turn of events, Mona tried to push both him and Amanda off a cliff to right the wrongs supposedly done to her in the past. Mark tried to restrain Mona, and in the ensuing scuffle they both plunged off the cliff to their deaths. An embittered Jennifer left Springfield and gave birth to a son, Matthew,

He had pursued Amanda in the past, but that was only for her money. Now forging a solid career as Springfield's district attorney, the new and improved Ross briefly renewed his relationship with Amanda (pictured here), but he soon became more interested in Trish.

while Morgan moved to New York and became a successful model. Amanda had a brief relationship with a new and improved Ross, who was forging a solid career as Springfield's district attorney, but by this time he was more interested in Trish. As a result, Amanda sold her share of LTA to Trish's brother Billy and moved to California to start a new life. Helena Manzini moved to Arizona, and Violet Renfield left for Scotland. Finally cleared of suspicion in Archibald Renfield's death, Quint freely and proudly acknowledged Henry as his father and legally took the surname of Chamberlain. Nola and Quint married in a wacky ceremony. The bride arrived in a fire engine, and they took off on their honeymoon in a hot-air balloon! Vanessa was left to accept begrudgingly the zaniest Reardon of them all as her sister-in-law.

A dark secret was about to unfold that involved several families in Springfield. Tony Reardon found a roll of film in an old camera left behind by his father, Tom, who had deserted the family years ago. When Tony developed the roll, he was curious about one picture, which showed Tom on a fishing trip alongside Bill Bauer, Brandon Spaulding, Henry Chamberlain and another man who turned out to be H.B. Lewis! The men were posing with a pretty young woman. Soon after, Tony was shocked to meet someone who strongly resembled the woman in the picture. She was Annabelle Sims, an attractive but somewhat aloof college professor. Tony and Annabelle fell in

Tony found himself falling in love with Annabelle Sims, a woman who strongly resembled the girl in the mysterious picture.

love, but Tony couldn't get the photograph out of his mind. He was also puzzled by Annabelle's discomfort around her dour father, Eli, a naval officer. When the ever inquisitive Nola saw the mystery picture, she was so fascinated that she decided to play detective and convinced Quint to go to Chicago with her to question Bill Bauer. Nola phoned Bill, and Bill became so nervous at the mention of the long-ago fishing trip that he went back to the bottle after years of sobriety! But before he could meet with Nola and Quint, a mysterious figure appeared and pushed Bill out a hotel window. The tormented, self-destructive Bill Bauer was dead.

One of the other men in the picture, Henry Chamberlain, then had a near brush with death. On the eve of Quint and Nola's housewarming party, a messenger delivered a photograph to Henry. It was a picture of Annabelle and her mother. Henry took one look at the picture, saw Annabelle coming through the door and suddenly had a severe heart attack. While convalescing at Cedars, Henry scribbled on a notepad the name of his old friend, H.B. Lewis. Soon the boisterous patriarch from Tulsa made his grand entrance in Springfield to give Henry the will to live. A frightening chain of events followed. Annabelle's psychiatrist, Dr. Gwen Harding, was fatally strangled. Billy Lewis' car exploded, but luckily no one was in it. Finally, H.B. was shot and slightly wounded. Terror began running rampant in Springfield! Fearing for his loved ones, Henry finally admitted the truth behind the photograph. Unbeknownst to the Bauers and the Reardons, he and the other men had known one another through business connections. Some 20 years ago they

When Tony Reardon developed this 20-year-old photograph, he unwittingly brought to light a tragic incident buried deep in the past of the Bauers, Spauldings, Reardons, Chamberlains and Lewises—prominent Springfield families, all.

had taken a fishing trip together on Lake Elizabeth, where they drunkenly but harmlessly caroused with a good-time girl named Annie. One night all the men, except for Tom Reardon, took Annie out on a boat. They dared her to strip down and jump into the lake, which she did. Later her dead body was found on the shore. The jittery and embarrassed men took an oath of secrecy and swore never to discuss the incident.

As Mike and Ross investigated the events surrounding the photo, it came to light that Annie was Annabelle's mother, and that the murderous culprit was Eli Sims. When Eli learned about Annie's romp with the jolly fishermen, he assaulted her with an oar and left her to drown. Annabelle suddenly remembered witnessing this grisly scene after years of having blocked it out. Now completely insane, Eli revealed to Annabelle that he'd killed Tom Reardon, then tried to drown her just as he

DASTARDLY DEEDS

When Eli Sims discovered his wife had been with the fishermen, he attacked her with an oar and left her in the lake to drown. Little Annabelle saw the whole thing.

Henry Chamberlain took one look at this picture of Annabelle and her mother and suffered a severe heart attack.

had done with Annie. Eli was tracked down and killed by the authorities. Bea was hurt that Henry had not revealed his connection to Tom earlier, but she was secure in the knowledge that Tom had not willfully deserted their family, as they had long believed. Coming to terms with both their fathers' deaths, Ed and Maureen resolved to get on with their lives, and they were married.

A rash of new developments would now take place at Cedars Hospital. Sara McIntyre accepted an exciting new position in Oregon and left Springfield with Adam. Best buddies Phillip and Rick became orderlies, and Rick decided that he wanted to become a doctor like his father, Ed. Rick needed to take basic German for his medical studies and sought the tutelage of a curmudgeonly patient named Martin Bruhner. Bert, who was now a patient advocate and was also of German descent, took a liking to Martin and gave him a positive new outlook that brightened his final days.

The hospital also welcomed several newcomers. Dr. Claire Ramsey, a brusque and ambitious resident, roomed with Kelly Nelson and had a brief affair with him. Lillian Raines was a compassionate nurse with an abusive second husband, Bradley, and a sweet teenage daughter named Beth. Social-climbing hospital administrator Warren Andrews had a reputation as a womanizer. Also new to Cedars was John Stephens, an intense young research doctor who was secretly working on a project for Alan Spaulding's pharmaceutical division. John Stephens was quick to attract the eye of Cedars' women. Katie developed a wild crush on him. Soon after,

LOVE AND MARRIAGE

The Bauer and Reardon families were united when Ed and Maureen were married. They would have their ups and downs, but it was by all accounts a strong and stable union.

he met Hillary Bauer on a camping retreat. Not realizing Katie and Hillary were friends, John had a fling with Hillary that blossomed into love. True to form, the good-natured Katie let her pal have John. Maureen, however, had a different interest in John Stephens: She recognized him as her brother, Jim Reardon! John begged Maureen to keep their relationship a secret for reasons he refused to reveal. Alone in his room, Jim thought back to that day in San Rios, when the real Dr.

ON CALL AT CEDARS

Her children now grown, Bert put her considerable skills to use and became a patient advocate at Cedars.

John Stephens, who was dying, gave Jim an ancient Incan necklace with a heavy talisman. This artifact had great significance in Jim's research work for Alan.

At this point Alan, savoring his new power, was resorting to his old tricks. Alan found himself attracted to Trish Lewis and hired her to redecorate his mansion, even though his wife, Hope, was an accomplished decorator herself! Hope was so distraught by Alan's insensitivity that she began drinking heavily. Fortunately, with Ed's help, Hope went to Alcoholics Anonymous and divorced Alan soon after. Hope then left with her son, Alan Michael, to begin life anew in New York. Meanwhile, Trish was repulsed by Alan's affections and was

He was married to Hope, but that didn't stop Alan Spaulding from hiring lovely Trish Lewis to redecorate his home. Alan had more than decorating in mind, but Trish preferred Ross over him.

determined to salvage her relationship with Ross, but Alan was just as determined to destroy it, along with Ross' political career. Alan set Ross up with a hooker and had cocaine planted in his car. Springfield was shocked when the picture of Ross and the hooker hit the front page of the newspaper. Alan's romantic interest shifted when Trish's pal Vanessa acquired more shares of his company. To ensure that he would remain in power, Alan put aside his reluctant tolerance of Vanessa and made her executive vice president of Spaulding over Trish, then began to pursue her in earnest. Vanessa, however, was embarking on a stormy, hilarious courtship with Billy Lewis, and before long the debutante and the redneck announced their unlikely engagement, to the great delight of Henry and H.B., who relished the prospect of becoming in-laws.

Determined to ruin Ross' political career, Alan set him up with a hooker and planted drugs in his car. The scandal, complete with pictures, made front-page news.

But Alan was not about to lie down and accept this potential threat to his corporate fiefdom, and he proceeded to investigate Billy's past. Alan hit paydirt when he located Billy's second wife, the randy, raunchy Reva Shayne. Alan wasted no time in paying Reva to come to

Springfield, armed with the news that her divorce decree from Billy was invalid! Billy also had a teenage daughter, Melinda Sue (Mindy) Lewis, from his first marriage. Mindy was spoiled rotten by all the Lewis men, but she adored Vanessa and wanted her beloved "daddy" to marry her. Immediately after she arrived in Springfield, Mindy began dating the handsome, wealthy Phillip Spaulding. Phillip didn't give Mindy the attention she felt she deserved, so she devised a ploy to keep him at her side. She made it look like her horse, Boss, had trampled her! Mindy was briefly hospitalized at Cedars, where her roommate was the innocent young Beth Raines. Beth had supposedly taken a bad fall, but in fact her twisted stepfather, Bradley, had beaten her during one of his frequent rages. The frightened girl kept this a secret from her mother, Lillian, who was herself abused by Bradley. Hospital orderlies Phillip and Rick both found themselves quite taken with Beth, but Phillip nobly backed off and continued to endure Mindy's childish shenanigans. These four young people spent a great deal of time together and soon came to be affectionately known as "the Four Musketeers." At the senior prom, Phillip and Beth were named king and queen, even though they were dating other people. It was a prophetic moment indeed.

The most dramatic moment of Phillip's life was soon to come. Alan hired slimy Bradley Raines to work

WHEELING AND DEALING

Alan's romantic interests shifted when Vanessa Chamberlain acquired more shares of Spaulding Enterprises. Vanessa and Trish vied for the position of executive vice president. Vanessa won.

Vanessa had eyes for redneck Billy Lewis. À la Rhett Butler and Scarlett O'Hara, they met at the Antebellum Ball.

in his security department, then fired him when one of his underlings got into a bar fight with Phillip. Bradley later chanced to overhear Rick and Mindy discuss a nagging suspicion they had about Phillip. Mindy couldn't understand why Phillip was living with Justin if Alan was his father. Curious, she had snooped around Justin's house and found a note in Phillip's bedroom expressing Justin's feelings for Phillip. Could Phillip be Justin's biological son? Seeing dollar signs, Bradley sent anonymous blackmail notes to Alan and hit him up for $100,000. Meanwhile, Phillip and Beth were finding it difficult to deny their mutual feelings. During Mindy's lavish surprise eighteenth-birthday party at the Springfield Country Club, Phillip and Beth sneaked out to the stables and confessed their love to each other. Bradley followed them and started a fistfight with Phillip, then made the unkindest cut of all. "You're not a Spaulding!" Bradley sneered at the bewildered young man. "You're no better than the rest of us!"

Devastated to hear the long-hidden truth about his origin, Phillip told Bradley he would not name him as the source, provided that Bradley let him continue to see Beth. Phillip then stormed into the ballroom and confronted Alan and Justin, who guiltily confirmed what he'd just learned. Hurt to discover that Rick also knew the truth, Phillip bitterly told him that he and Beth were in love. Soon after, Justin moved to Arizona with his asthmatic young daughter, Samantha, and Phillip moved in with Ross, his uncle and confidant. Ross was pained

to hear Phillip voice his biggest regret—that he had never had the chance to call Jackie Mom.

Bradley became more abusive than ever. He believed Mindy's lie that Beth and Phillip were sexually involved and brutally raped his stepdaughter. Frightened and ashamed, Beth told no one of this ugly incident and rejected a broken-hearted Phillip. Phillip turned to Mindy, who, after months of taunting and teasing him, proceeded to seduce the lonely and confused Phillip without using birth control. Alan shared Mindy's relief about the growing schism between Phillip and Beth; after all, Beth was from a "lower class" and might impede Phillip's potential success at Spaulding.

Beth moved into Bea's boardinghouse to get away from Bradley, but Bradley got a court order to force his stepdaughter to return home. Luckily for Beth, Phillip was at the scene when she came home. He grabbed her and they jumped out a window and ran, destination New York. It was Christmastime, and they were without friends, family or funds. In the true spirit of the season, a sidewalk Santa Claus gave them refuge. Rick and Mindy soon followed in hot pursuit, and the Four Musketeers were about to embark on the adventure of their lives!

The romantic adventures of Beth, Phillip, Mindy and Rick earned them the title of "the Four Musketeers." For the senior prom, Phillip took Mindy and Rick escorted Beth, but Phillip was drawn to the shy, sweet Beth as well. As class valedictorian, Beth later spoke these words at the graduation ceremonies: "Fellow graduates, teachers, parents, friends. Today we, the class of '83, celebrate the beginning of our education, for we have just begun to learn. We celebrate the beginning of adulthood, for we have just begun to grow. We celebrate the beginning of our future, for we have just begun to live." Prophetic words indeed.

1984

The year 1984 ushered in a time when still more dark family secrets would be revealed, along with some shocking deaths, surprising departures and spicy romances.

In New York, Rick and Mindy bonded as they finally caught up with Phillip and Beth. The four took odd jobs in order to survive, and for a while they enjoyed the sights and sounds of the Big Apple. With the help and support of Nick, the sidewalk Santa, Beth told Phillip about Bradley's rape of her. Phillip promised to protect her always, and they pledged never to let anything come between them again. The party was over, though, when Bradley tracked them down. To evade him, Phillip and Beth dressed up as clowns and engaged in a mime act in the park, but Bradley eventually saw through their ruse.

LOVE ON THE RUN

Pushed to the breaking point by Bradley, her lascivious stepfather, Beth and Phillip escaped to exciting New York, where, with the help of a sidewalk Santa named Nick, they disguised themselves as clowns to avoid Bradley.

Phillip and Bradley got into a violent struggle in Central Park that ended when Bradley fell off a cliff. Fighting the temptation to leave the despicable Bradley for dead, Phillip and Beth rescued him, then warned him to back off. Later, back in Springfield, Alan rehired Bradley with the intention of transferring him and his family out of town so Beth would be out of Phillip's life. Of course, Alan was still unaware that Bradley was the one responsible for telling Phillip that he was not a Spaulding by blood.

However, Alan's brittle elder sister, Alexandra, was every bit a Spaulding. Alan was delighted to welcome Alex to Springfield after her divorce from self-proclaimed count Baron Von Halkein in Europe. Alex played the adoring sister to the hilt, but in reality she hated Alan. She had never forgiven him for helping their father, Brandon, sabotage her romance with a struggling musician named Eric Luvonaczek, and for pressuring her to give up the baby boy she and Eric had conceived. Alex confided this to Ross, who became her closest confidant, and entreated him to find her son, whom she'd named Brandon after her father.

Before Ross was able to do so, Alex got her revenge on Alan. She discovered—and revealed—his conspiracy with Bradley to separate Phillip and Beth. Alan was shocked and saddened to learn that his sister despised him, and he felt guilty when Beth told him that Bradley had raped her. Alex had become extremely protective of Phillip and Beth, and the resolute Ms. Spaulding had Ross arrest Bradley immediately. Bradley denied the charge until his trial, when Ross extracted his confession. "No one could love Beth like I did," Bradley said in a pathetic attempt to justify his crime. "That's why I had to mark her. I had to make sure no one else would ever want her." Bradley was remanded to a psychiatric hospital, and Lillian divorced him. Now, she and Beth were free of his toxic influence for good.

Further revelations were to strengthen Ross and Alex's alliance against Alan. Floyd won the lottery and stashed his winnings at Company, Tony's bar. This well-publicized event caught the attention of an enterprising teenage tough named Lujack, leader of a street gang called the Galahads. Lujack stole the money but later

TROUBLED TRIANGLES

Torn between two lovers: Beth loved Phillip, who was honor-bound to Mindy, while Lujack was drawn to Beth's sweetness and warmth.

had a change of heart and gave it back to Floyd. While he was in jail, Lujack overheard a crooked cop tell someone that Alan Spaulding had hired him to plant cocaine in Ross' car. Lujack hated wealthy, privileged people like the Spauldings, so to spite them he came forward and

LOVE AND MARRIAGE

When Alan Spaulding proposed to Vanessa at the height of the masquerade ball, wild and woolly Billy Lewis threw her over his shoulder, shouting, "No one leaves until this woman is my wife!" The two were married on the spot.

cleared Ross' name. It soon became evident that Lujack had a soft, tender side, and he was deeply moved when Tony took him under his wing and hired him to work at Company. Lujack met Beth, who began tutoring him in hopes that he would swear off the Galahads. But Darcy, Lujack's jealous girlfriend and fellow gang member, had other ideas. Phillip was a bit jealous as well, but he and Beth still planned to marry, and they believed the worst was behind them. Enter Mindy, who was pregnant with Phillip's child! At first Rick convinced her to say that he was the father, and they announced their engagement. When Billy railed at Ed that Rick had impregnated his little girl, though, Ed set him straight by saying he had evidence that the child was really Phillip's. Feeling foolish, Billy barged in on Rick and Mindy's quickie wedding ceremony and broke it up in his usual straightforward way: "Why didn't you tell me Phillip Spaulding is the father of your baby?"

Phillip was trapped. He loved Beth but felt he had to marry Mindy so that, unlike himself, his child could be raised by its natural parents. "I love you more than I'll ever love anyone else," Phillip told Beth gently, "but I've asked Mindy to be my wife." Phillip married Mindy, but his heart still belonged to Beth. Meanwhile, Mindy was pining for Rick. A crushed Beth began to date Lujack in earnest. One night they went to a dance together, only for Darcy and the other gang members to crash it. With Darcy's coarse battle cry of "Look out, preppies, the Galahads are back!" a fight broke out that compromised Lujack's parole.

Mindy had another reason to be miserable. Reva was demanding $5 million from a Swiss bank account in exchange for a divorce from Billy, and it looked like Billy and Vanessa would never be together! Billy ultimately found the divorce decree that Reva had willfully withheld, but by that time Vanessa was beginning to fall for Alan's shallow charms. The situation climaxed at Alan's masquerade ball, where Alan made a big show of proposing to Vanessa in front of all the guests. Suddenly Billy leaped forward, grabbed Vanessa and threw her over his shoulder, yelling, "No one leaves until this woman is my wife!" A minister was summoned, and Vanessa and Billy enjoyed an impromptu wedding ceremony as a defeated Alan seethed.

Now that Alan was officially persona non grata with Billy, he insisted that his family put up a united front against their enemy. Knowing that Reva and Josh had once been lovers, Billy convinced Reva to charm Josh into merging LTA with Lewis Oil so they could

TROUBLED TRIANGLES Reva NOV3 2006.

She'd been married to Billy Lewis, but deep down Reva had always loved her childhood sweetheart, Josh. An argument forced her into the arms of Lewis patriarch H.B., and they were married, but Josh and Reva's story wasn't over...not yet.

fight Spaulding Enterprises. Josh and Reva rekindled their romance and enjoyed a rendezvous at the place where they first made love—Cross Creek, the Lewis family's retreat in Tulsa. These two had always loved each other. They planned to marry until Reva's maid, Anita, revealed that Alan had bribed Reva to come to town. H.B. was relieved when Josh bitterly called off the wedding. But when Reva was mugged by two of the Galahads, H.B. began to soften toward his confused ex–daughter-in-law, and the two impulsively married! Josh was so disgusted, he went for a wild drive and got into an accident that left him paralyzed from the waist down. He had surgery and was disheartened by the long road of physical therapy that lay ahead. At that point a special person gave Josh the courage and the will to live: The indomitable Bert Bauer pulled her wheelchair right up alongside his and told him, "It takes time. You're at the beginning—so am I. Look at how far we've come already. Don't look at the distance that's left to go." An inconsolable Josh replied, "Don't expect miracles—is that what you're saying?" Bert had an answer ready: "No, I'm not telling you that, because life itself is a miracle, and don't you ever forget it!" Bert had been in near-perfect health since her bout with uterine cancer, until a blood clot necessitated the removal of one of her legs. As the valiant Bert was wheeled into the OR, she informed

her doctors, "Save as much of me as you possibly can. I've got a long life to lead and more grandchildren to raise." With spunk and determination, Bert learned to walk with a prosthesis and did her physical therapy side by side with Josh.

Bert missed Mike, who had left Springfield on an investigative mission, and young Kelly Nelson, who was now working in Boston. Her main concern was Ed's marriage to Maureen, which was facing the first of many trials. Ed felt emasculated when Maureen became Cedars' administrator and, therefore, his boss. Fortunately, a firm lecture from Bert knocked some sense into Ed, and he subsequently pledged his love and support to Maureen in her new position. However, he was still uncomfortable with his wife's inexplicable interest in Dr. John Stephens. One day, Tony collapsed from a strange illness. Dr. Stephens saved his life and revealed that he was the long-missing Dr. Jim Reardon—Maureen and Tony's brother!

Quint was paid a visit by a young boy, Jonathan

ISSUES

Mirroring the true-life story of actress Charita Bauer, a blood clot due to circulatory problems caused Bert Bauer to lose a leg. Said Charita, "You know what? I've been damn lucky. I have nothing to be bitter about. My foot's gone, but I'm still here." Proclaimed Bert as she was being wheeled into surgery, "Save as much of me as you possibly can. I've got a long life to lead and more grandchildren to raise."

ON CALL AT CEDARS

Claire Ramsey was attracted to John Stephens, aka Jim Reardon, but the feelings weren't mutual. However, they would soon be working together to uncover the origins of a strange virus known as "the Dreaming Death."

Brooks, who had corresponded with him on-line. Quint had thought Jonathan was an adult colleague and was surprised to find out that he was only twelve years old. Jonathan wanted to be everything that Quint was, including his adopted "son." This exceptionally intelligent young man told Quint and Nola that his adoptive parents had died in a plane crash. With Nola on the case, the boy's natural parents were soon found.

Jim decided to consult Quint, his archaeologist brother-in-law, about the Incan necklace, which the real Dr. Stephens had given to Jim on his deathbed. The necklace held the key to a vaccine for a deadly disease known as "the Dreaming Death." The unscrupulous Warren Andrews overheard the men talking and stole the necklace, hoping it would make him a fortune. Completely amoral, Warren took Lesley Ann as his trophy wife and set out to become as rich and powerful as Alan. Meanwhile, Alan pressured Jim to keep working on the vaccine for reasons he refused to explain. Bent on sabotaging Jim's work, Warren set free the infected mice from

Jim's lab. Warren's plot tragically backfired when one of the mice bit Lesley Ann and infected her with the Dreaming Death. A penitent Warren returned the necklace to Jim in hopes that Jim could save Lesley Ann. Jim had planned to go to San Rios to investigate the Dreaming Death, but instead he locked himself in his lab and worked around the clock to find the vaccine.

Unaware that Jim was still at Cedars, Hillary went to San Rios in search of him. There she met a glib young reporter named Fletcher Reade, who, by coincidence, worked for the *Springfield Journal*. Fletcher was intrigued by the Dreaming Death story and called it in before returning to Springfield with Hillary. Hillary contracted the Dreaming Death, but Jim saved her life and the two continued their romance. Standing on the sidelines were Fletcher, who had developed feelings for Hillary, and Claire Ramsey, who was secretly attracted to Jim.

Unfortunately, Jim was unable to save Lesley Ann. Racked with guilt and thoughts of revenge, Warren hired a private detective who discovered that Alan was planning to patent the vaccine to use in biological warfare! Warren allied himself with Alex, who secretly taped Alan's admission of his part in the conspiracy, and turned Alan in to the FBI. Devoid of family, company and worldwide repute, Alan managed to escape the authorities and disappeared into the jungles of San Rios.

Alex was overjoyed to find her long-lost son, but after a lifetime of antagonism toward the wealthy and privileged, Lujack was anything but pleased to be a Spaulding.

Alex took over Spaulding Enterprises and offered Ross the position of president. Ironically, this was the honor that the "old" Ross had once craved. Now a reputable public servant, Ross accepted Alex's offer for one reason: to protect the interests of his nephew, Phillip. Trish cooled her relationship with Ross once she sensed his growing attraction to Alex, and the two enjoyed a passionate affair. The bond between Ross and Alex was further strengthened when Ross finally located Alex's long-lost son. He was living in Springfield—and his name was Lujack!

When Alex tearfully told Lujack that they were mother and son, he was horrified. He'd spent his entire life striking out against wealthy autocrats like the Spauldings, only to discover that the same blue blood ran in his veins! Nonetheless, Alex was happy that he intended to leave the Galahads for a clean life with Beth. Meanwhile, Mindy lost her baby and divorced Phillip, while Rick, pessimistic about his chances with Mindy, lost his virginity to the lonely and slightly older Claire Ramsey. When the Galahads terrorized Mindy and Phillip, Rick brazenly trashed the gang's garage in retaliation. Darcy was running the Galahads now, and Lujack went undercover to infiltrate the gang. He refused to tell Beth why he was back with the gang, leaving her to turn once again to Phillip. When Darcy caught on to Lujack's plan, she went on a rampage, shooting Lujack and holding Beth and Alex hostage at Cedars. Lujack talked her into giving up the fight, and she was arrested. A few of the other Galahads—Lucky, I.Q. and Gina—were proud of Lujack's heroics and went straight.

Phillip, however, was less than impressed. He deeply resented the fact that Lujack had blood ties to the Spauldings when Phillip himself did not. Slowly, the false values and condescending affectations of the missing Alan began to visit themselves upon his adoptive son. He pursued Beth with all his might, damning Lujack as scum. Beth wouldn't budge. When Phillip discovered that Lujack and Floyd were turning the Galahads' garage into a nightclub, he hatched a scheme. Phillip hired a crooked tradesman named Andy Ferris to sabotage the construction of the club. But Andy went too far and blew up the building, injuring and blinding Beth! A guilty Phillip could not bring himself to admit his wrongdoing, so he enrolled Beth in a school for the blind, where she befriended Andy's sight-impaired sister, Nancy. Suspicious of Andy, Lujack went undercover as a blind man named Lenny to find out the true story.

Another catalyst was about to impact the triangle of Phillip, Beth and Lujack. It was Alex's newly arrived former stepdaughter, Baroness India Von Halkein, a poised and scheming young lady of leisure. Secretly broke, India began to charm Phillip in hopes of marrying him and sharing the Spaulding fortune. At the same time, Ross was outraged not only to catch Alex in a fling with Warren, but also to learn that Alex plotted to force Vanessa and Henry out of the company by threatening to reveal their bogus buyout deal several years earlier. Sickened by the warped Spaulding values that were now corrupting Phillip, Ross dumped Alex and quit his position at Spaulding. Alex promptly brought in Warren. After Alex and Warren became engaged, though, Warren had an affair with India when they both discovered Phillip's collusion with Andy. India used a tape of Phillip and Andy to blackmail Phillip into marriage, but Phillip refused to consummate the union. On their honeymoon night, Phillip coldly told India, "You married a company, not a man." Alex discovered India and Warren's affair and told Warren to take a hike, but reconsidered when she realized he was in the best position to find out what India's hold on Phillip really was. Alex still loved her nephew and felt caught in the middle of his conflict with Lujack.

Alex was about to have one of the most jarring episodes of her life. It began—as events in Springfield were apt to do—as a predicament involving people Alex barely knew. Tony and Annabelle were married and

Greedy and corrupt realtor Susan Piper knew Annabelle and Tony's cottage was worth millions, and she would do anything to get it.

moved into a cottage that Annabelle insisted was haunted. Tony thought his new wife was nuts, but his brother, Jim, believed her. Jim and Annabelle formed a close friendship that left Tony feeling excluded and angry. Soon Jim, Hillary, Fletcher and Claire were caught up in an investigation of the cottage. They were particularly struck by a picture of a woman, whom an elderly librarian named Miss Emma identified as Victoria. The librarian added that the dress Victoria was wearing in the portrait was the same one she had worn some 40 years ago at a Founders' Day picnic.

At the same time, Annabelle was having visions of a young black woman named Sharina. Then Miss Emma was brutally assaulted by henchmen working for Susan Piper, an officious realtor who was trying to seize the cottage from Tony and Annabelle. On her deathbed Miss Emma eerily posed a riddle: "What's thicker than water and runs uphill, straight to the heart of a rich man's will?" Shortly thereafter, Hillary was staring out the front window of the cottage, thinking, when she figured out the answer to the riddle—only to have a music box blow up in her face. She was killed instantly.

Once Jim was able to work through his grief, he added up the clues. The front window Hillary had been

Family secrets were exposed when a shocked Alex discovered her presumed-dead father, Brandon, was alive and well and living with his true love in Barbados.

ON LOCATION

Reporter Fletcher Reade and Dr. Claire Ramsey got caught up in the mystery surrounding Annabelle and Tony's cottage, and it wasn't long before the two became lovers.

looking out of faced the Spaulding mansion, and the "rich man" was Brandon Spaulding! Jim's investigation revealed that Alan was born on Founders' Day, and Victoria was Alan and Alex's half-sister. The situation grew more dangerous as Annabelle explored a secret passageway, where she found a skeleton clinging to a doll! Then Quint discovered that Brandon Spaulding's shipping business had been based in Barbados, where Susan Piper had connections. A chaotic chain of events ensued, climaxing in Barbados, where Susan kidnapped Jim and Annabelle and threatened to throw Annabelle into quicksand. Claire and Fletcher, now lovers, were also present, along with Alex. It was then revealed that Susan wanted the cottage so she could sell it to the Spaulding family for millions. Susan met her end in the quicksand, and Alex met with a ghost—her father, Brandon Spaulding, was actually alive and well and living in Barbados!

Brandon revealed the long-hidden story of his life. He had been in love with a black woman named Sharina, but for the sake of propriety he married a debutante named Penelope, Alex and Alan's mother. Brandon never stopped loving Sharina, though, and he put her and her brother, Conrad, up in the cottage, which faced his mansion. In time Brandon and Sharina conceived their own child, Victoria, who was now living with him and Sharina in Barbados. Just after Brandon signed papers recognizing Victoria as his heir, a pregnant Penelope discovered his double life and brandished a gun, threatening the lovers. Conrad stepped into the line of fire and was killed. His was the skeleton holding the doll. Inside the doll were the papers guaranteeing young Victoria a share in Spaulding Enterprises. Penelope died while giving birth to Alan on Founders' Day. Much later, when Lucille Wexler left Brandon for dead, he seized the opportunity to fake his own demise. He slipped out of Springfield and joined Sharina and Victoria in Barbados. Brandon apologized to Alex for the pain he'd caused her in the past and walked off into the sunset with Sharina. Later, Brandon and Sharina's bodies were found together. Victoria opted to stay in Barbados and gladly signed over her share of the company to Alex. A chapter in the Spaulding family was now closed, with Alan ironically absent from the proceedings.

Back at the Lewis household, Billy vowed to remove Reva from his family, taunting her for having "sampled" all the Lewis men. Vanessa feared that Billy's vendetta against Reva was a cover for any lingering feelings he might have for her, and she decided to leave him. She packed her bags but then found that she was carrying Billy's child. Josh learned to walk again and began to mellow toward H.B. and Reva, while Reva couldn't help being enamored of her newly virile true love, who was now her stepson. One night, Reva climbed into Josh's bed when H.B. was not around—but Billy pulled her out!

Feeling like a loser, Reva went back to Tulsa, where she sang tortured country-western ballads at her old hangout, Wily Coyote's. There she was reunited with her somewhat dizzy but sweet younger sister, Roxie Shayne, who was now living with an abusive redneck named Johnny "Dub" Taylor. Josh found Reva in Tulsa and wanted to run away with her. Just then they heard from Trish that a heartsick H.B. was in failing health. The lovers returned to Springfield with Roxie in tow and gave H.B. the will to live. After Reva discovered she was pregnant with H.B.'s child, Josh sadly told her to take good care of his "daddy" and left to work on an oil rig in the Gulf of Mexico.

Vanessa gave birth to a son, Harlan Billy Lewis III,

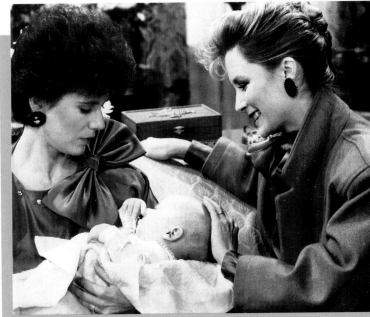

ISSUES

After Vanessa gave birth to Harlan Billy Lewis III, known affectionately as "Little Bill," she became fixated on the child and turned to tranquilizers to ease her growing anxiety.

and became unhealthily fixated on the child. Unwilling to trust anyone else with his care, Vanessa grew increasingly dependent on tranquilizers. Roxie became smitten with Rick, the first "nice guy" in her life. In response, a jealous Mindy brought Dub to Springfield. Fortunately, Dub revealed that Mindy was behind his arrival. Roxie tried to better herself and became Billy's assistant at Lewis Oil, only to be blackmailed into sex by one of his business associates, handsome newcomer Kyle Sampson, who remembered her from her days as a hooker in Tulsa. Kyle Sampson had an agenda, and it centered on the Lewis family.

1985

Crime was the number one issue in Springfield during 1985. Murder, conspiracy and devious mind-control tactics pervaded this once sedate Midwest city. As a result, good people went bad, bad people redeemed themselves and the Spaulding and Lewis families became bitter enemies.

At the Horizon School for the Blind, Beth regained her sight and was thrilled to discover that her new friend Lenny was really Lujack. Andy did not share Beth's joy, however, when he spotted Lujack during a visit with his blind sister, Nancy. Andy went gunning for Lujack and was arrested, but Alex bailed him out in exchange for his silence about his involvement in Phillip's scheme. Noticing that Phillip and Beth were renewing their old friendship, India told Beth about Phillip's sabotage plot, which had resulted in her blindness. Beth angrily rejected Phillip but didn't tell him she knew the truth in order to prevent further bad blood between him and Lujack. Lu-

She had wanted the Spaulding fortune and blackmailed the Spaulding heir into marriage, but in time Baroness India Von Halkein and Phillip Spaulding came to an understanding—inside and outside the bedroom.

jack was suspicious, though, and convinced Andy to crash Alex's Valentine's Day soiree with the intent to reveal Phillip's duplicity. But once he was at the party, Andy began having second thoughts. A fuming Lujack warned, "If you back out on me now, Ferris, I'll kill you!" Suddenly the ballroom was plunged into darkness. A shot rang out. A few moments later, the lights came on—and Lujack, gun in hand, was standing over Andy's dead body.

Lujack stood trial and was convicted of Andy's murder despite Ross' brilliant defense. In prison, he found an unlikely ally in a fellow inmate—Bradley Raines! Lillian had written a letter to Bradley asking him to look after Lujack. Bradley was grateful for the opportunity to right some of the wrongs he had committed. Meanwhile, Beth convinced Phillip to come clean about his collusion with Andy, and they became friends once again. Ironically, the authorities didn't even believe Phillip's story. By now, Phillip shared Alex and Warren's suspicion that India was Andy's murderer. The real culprit, however, was holding India hostage in a cabin, where he forced her to sign a false confession. He was none other than Floyd Parker! Once a jovial, uncomplicated guy, Floyd's romantic and financial roller-coaster ride left him lost and confused as to who or what he was. The pitiful young man revealed to India that he had killed Andy out of his secret love for Beth. Beth and Lujack tracked down Floyd and India, and a tearful Floyd was taken to jail. Strengthened by this turn of events, Phillip and India realized they had a great deal in common and finally consummated their marriage.

As Phillip tried to put the pieces of his life back together, his friend Rick rejected Mindy for having brought Johnny "Dub" Taylor to Springfield. Mindy turned to Kyle Sampson, whose winning charm concealed his dark side. Kyle's sole reason for dating Mindy was that she was a link to Billy, whose Alaskan oil leases he planned to steal for Sampson Industries. His other connection to Billy was Roxie, Mindy's rival for Rick's affections. Back in Tulsa, Mindy and Roxie had been high school rivals, and now history was repeating itself. Roxie was now proving herself as Billy's assistant at Lewis Oil. Threatening to tell Rick that she was once a

Kyle's mother, former madam Sally Gleason, shared a colorful past and more with H.B. Lewis.

prostitute, Kyle blackmailed Roxie into feeding him information on Lewis Oil. Billy caught on but remained loyal to Roxie after she flew to Alaska to save him from a bad deal of Kyle's making. Roxie was headed for the airport to fly back home when her snowmobile overturned during a blizzard. Suffering from a concussion and amnesia, she wandered aimlessly in the snow and disappeared into the Alaskan wilderness.

Back in Springfield, Kyle succeeded in wrestling Lewis Oil away from Billy. Consumed with revenge over Kyle's deceit, Mindy got drunk and shot Kyle. This brought Kyle's estranged mother, Sally Gleason, to Springfield. Unlike the slick, urbane Kyle, Sally was a raunchy, redheaded Southern gal who had a colorful past with H.B. Sally told H.B. that Kyle suspected him of being the father who had deserted him, and that Kyle resented Billy's position as a favored Lewis son. Billy and Kyle were indeed brothers, but not in the way Kyle believed. Sally was also Billy's mother! H.B.'s deceased wife, Miss Martha, had agreed to raise Billy after Sally blew out of H.B.'s life. Neither H.B. nor Sally had the heart to reveal the truth, given the hatred between Billy and Kyle. Billy, meanwhile, was trying to deal with Vanessa's growing addiction to prescription drugs and her obsession with Little Billy. One night, a dazed and drugged Vanessa ran Reva over with a car. As a result, Reva tragically lost the baby she and H.B. were expecting. Reva forgave Vanessa, however, and was happy to see her conquer her addiction. It was now Billy's turn to become addicted—to gambling.

Up in Alaska, an amnesiac Roxie ended up in a brothel run by the lovable Diamond Lil. The madam nicknamed Roxie "Rosie Cheeks" and immediately gave her gainful employment servicing the lonely men who worked on the Alaska Pipeline. One such customer was a soft-spoken young man named Kurt Corday, who got the surprise of his life during his session with Rosie. Having tracked down Roxie to Alaska, Rick suddenly stormed in and denounced his girlfriend as a whore! Rosie was dumbfounded, as she had no idea who Rick was. Kurt soon fell for Rosie, who took the last name of Smith, and surprised her with an Eskimo marriage festival and a honeymoon in an igloo!

A despondent Rick returned to Springfield and informed Reva he had found Roxie. Reva then appealed to a new friend for help—Kyle! To H.B.'s consternation, Reva was forming a bond with the Lewis family enemy. It was to Reva that Kyle showed his hidden humanity, and Reva could not help but be attracted to such a charismatic man so close to her in age. Kyle generously flew Reva to Alaska on his jet to retrieve Roxie, but while they were flying the confused girl back to Springfield, Kurt, who had stowed aboard, appeared with a

Her past revealed, Roxie felt unworthy of Rick's affections, but Rick refused to give up on her.

Claire Ramsey followed Fletcher Reade to Beirut to confront a difficult piece of his past. When a worried Maureen and Ed followed, their lives were changed forever.

spear gun! After a struggle with Kurt, Kyle jumped out of the plane with Reva and the two parachuted to safety. They ended up crashing through the roof of a barn owned by a farm couple named Yoder. Embarrassed, Kyle and Reva convinced the Yoders to let them work on the farm to make up for the damage. Kyle and Reva slept side by side in the Yoders' barn, and Reva tried hard to fight her growing attraction to Kyle. In truth, they were soul mates. Billy eventually caught up with them and engaged Kyle in a fierce fistfight before they all returned to Springfield. Desperate to salvage his family's honor, Billy warned H.B. that Kyle was not only after Lewis Oil, he was out to steal Reva as well! When H.B. confronted Reva, she admitted that she loved Kyle, but H.B. vowed to fight for her.

Roxie and Kurt settled in Springfield and began working for Tony Reardon at Company. Mindy also got a job at Company. Rick helped Roxie regain her memory, but in doing so he unearthed in her the sad memory that she had been raped at age twelve. Roxie felt unworthy of Rick's affections, not to mention the love of such a close family as the Bauers. Rick refused to give up on Roxie and became increasingly suspicious of Kurt. Investigating the newcomer, Rick discovered that Kurt was an illegal alien from Canada who had worked for Lewis Oil. The situation came full circle when Mindy and Kurt fell in love and became engaged! Rick warned

Mindy that Kurt may only be after her money so he could stay in the United States. He had been allowed to live in the country simply because he was married to Rosie Smith. To guarantee Kurt's American citizenship, Roxie crashed Mindy and Kurt's wedding ceremony and had the minister marry her off to Kurt! The immigration officials eventually realized they'd been had. Fortunately, they gave Kurt a reprieve and his marriage to Roxie was annulled.

As Rick coped with his chaotic love life, he painfully bore witness to the near destruction of his father, Ed. It began when Claire Ramsey followed Fletcher Reade to Beirut, where he confronted a piece of his past. Several years earlier, he had fathered a daughter, Rebecca, with a Beirut woman named Leah. One day, Fletcher took Rebecca to the local market, where she was killed in a terrorist attack. Now, with terrorism once again rampant in the region, Ed and Maureen feared for their friends' safety and flew to Beirut to join Claire and

TROUBLED TRIANGLES

Thinking his beloved Mo was dead, a grief-stricken Ed slept with Claire. A daughter, Michelle, was conceived, which was a blow to the infertile Maureen and her marriage to Ed.

Just as Kyle and Reva's romance was blooming, Kyle's former lover, Maeve Stoddard, came to town and shook things up.

Fletcher. Maureen and Fletcher were soon caught in terrorist crossfire and presumed dead. A grieving Ed and Claire were left to share a room, where a dazed Ed mistook Claire for Maureen and made love to her. Shortly thereafter, Maureen and Fletcher turned up alive and the four returned to Springfield. Claire and Fletcher made wedding plans, but their joy came to a halt when Claire learned she was pregnant! Having had a vasectomy following Rebecca's death, Fletcher realized Ed was the father. Fletcher and Claire continued with their plans to marry, but a guilty Claire stood Fletcher up at the altar. Fletcher was furious that Ed could not bring himself to tell Maureen the truth. However, Maureen stumbled upon Fletcher's medical records at Cedars and put two and two together. Feeling deceived by both her husband and her friends, Maureen lit into Fletcher and left Ed. Ed became so racked with self-hatred that he went on a drinking binge. As hospital administrator at Cedars, Maureen had no choice but to place her husband on probation.

Ed's condition did not escape a gossipy nurse named Charlotte Wheaton. Suspecting Ed had fathered Claire's child, Charlotte leaked Ed's alcoholism to newswoman Alicia Rhomer, and he was suspended from Cedars. Reveling in her victory, Charlotte and her boyfriend, Harry,

enjoyed a night of champagne and sex in a vacant hospital room. After Harry left, Charlotte fell asleep. Before leaving on suspension, Ed had issued a medication order to Lillian for a patient whom neither knew had been moved from the room in which Charlotte was now snoozing. In the darkened room, Lillian injected the sleeping woman. Later, in the cold light of day, she realized she had injected Charlotte—who now lay dead!

Lillian felt responsible for Charlotte's death, but Lt. Jeff Saunders, who took a fancy to Lillian, had other sus-

When long-absent Hawk Shayne returned, he tried to make peace with daughters Reva and Roxie.

pects in mind. He discovered Charlotte had died after being struck by a blunt object, and Ed and Claire were at the top of his list of suspects. Fletcher was determined to clear them of blame, however, and he investigated Charlotte in her home city of Philadelphia. There he learned that Charlotte and Alicia Rhomer were sisters! Charlotte had blackmailed Alicia with the knowledge that she had launched her television news career by falsely accusing a local doctor of being a lush. Although Charlotte had studied to become a doctor, she couldn't make the grade, so she settled for becoming a nurse. Consequently, she had resented the success of doctors like Ed. Armed with this knowledge, Fletcher lured Alicia to her TV studio late one night as police officers hid in the wings. With great flourish, Fletcher presented the neurotic telejournalist with a private show of his own titled, "This Is Your Life, Alicia Rhomer." Reduced to a sobbing wreck, Alicia confessed to killing Charlotte, and the police arrested her. Ed got off the bottle and rejoiced when Claire gave birth to a baby girl, Michelle.

Several people close to Ed and Maureen were now to depart from Springfield. Katie Parker was so shocked by her brother Floyd's murder confession that she turned down a marriage proposal from Rick's good-natured roommate, Dr. Louie Darnell, and left town. Tony Reardon left Company in Kurt's capable hands to travel around the country with Annabelle, while Tony's brother, Jim, went to join a think tank in Aspen. Nola and Quint Chamberlain set off on more archaeological adventures. Trish Lewis, whose business acumen was never appreciated by her macho family, took an executive position with Spaulding Enterprises in Europe. Bert Bauer went on an extended trip to visit her sister-in-law, Meta, in Washington, D.C. These developments brought several newcomers to Springfield, two of whom arrived at the behest of Sally Gleason.

Disgusted by Reva and Kyle's romance, Sally convinced Kyle's wealthy and refined former lover, Maeve Stoddard, to come to Springfield. The unsinkable Miss Sally then brought Reva's estranged father, a wily wildcatter named Hawk Shayne, to town. Hawk had deserted his family long ago, but he was determined to win back their affection. In hopes that Kyle and Billy would end their feud, H.B. and Sally lied to Kyle that his suspicions were correct: H.B. was his father. As Kyle struggled with his ambivalence toward H.B., Reva sadly told him they must end their romance for H.B.'s sake. Kyle went

Lillian's sister, Calla Matthews, an old flame of Ross', came to Springfield, and Ross was glad to see her.

back to Maeve on the rebound, while Reva began keeping platonic company with a younger man—Phillip! Kyle and Reva eventually found their way back to one another and made love. Maeve suffered in silence, for she was now pregnant with Kyle's baby.

Also among the new arrivals were Lillian's sister, Calla Matthews, and her beautiful teenage daughter, Jessie. Calla was a brash social climber who had dated Ross back in Chicago after Vanessa jilted him. Ross was pleasantly surprised to be reunited with his old flame, even though she still harbored the false values he had once held dear.

India, Trish, Mindy and Kurt attended opening night at Warren Andrews' new club, the Blue Orchid, where Lujack was soon to become the singing sensation of Springfield.

Two other newcomers were David Preston, Kyle's ambitious right-hand man, and his equally aggressive live-in lover, record producer Suzette Saxon. Suzette frequented the Blue Orchid, Warren Andrews' new nightclub, and was quick to notice its unlikely new singing sensation—Lujack! Alex feared that Lujack's growing fascination with show business would threaten his marriage plans with Beth. To bring Lujack back down to earth, Alex introduced him to her former lover, Locke Walls, a musician who had become a substance abuser. Lujack ended up idolizing the man and grieved when Locke later died of a terminal ailment.

Satisfied to see Lujack committed to his singing career, Suzette offered him a record contract. She brought in a suave rock promoter named Jackson Freemont to work with Lujack. Jackson soon became friendly with Beth, who had always been a talented artist, and Jackson himself had an artistic bent. He encouraged her to be more free and sensual in her brush strokes. Suzette was

Record producer Suzette Saxon was quick to recognize Lujack's talent and brought in rock promoter Jackson Freemont to advance his promising career.

pleased by this, for she made no secret of it that a girlfriend did not fit into the plans she had for her new star, Lujack. Suzette was so preoccupied with Lujack's career that she was unaware David was fending off a threat that had been made on her life. Bea Reardon's latest boarder, Daryl, was in fact a vicious criminal named Largo who aimed to take over Sampson Industries. Largo forced David to help him in his scheme by threatening to kill both him and Suzette. Noticing the enmity between Billy and Kyle, Largo and David engaged Billy in a poker game and hypnotized him with Largo's unusual ring. Their mission was to control Billy's mind and manipulate him into killing Kyle. Billy indeed had subliminal thoughts of murdering his half-brother, but strangely, the programming was ruined whenever Billy saw the ringed symbol of Largo's organization, known as Infinity. Coincidentally, Beth and Jackson had designed the same logo for Lujack's music video.

This eerie scenario came to a head during Mindy and Kurt's lavish wedding. At the reception, Lujack proudly screened his video, complete with the ringed symbol. A programmed Billy pulled a gun and aimed it at Kyle, but when H.B. called out Billy's name in the ensuing melee, David was shot instead! During Billy's trial, Suzette came forward to confess that she had fired the

shot which killed David. Beth was then held hostage aboard Largo's ship but was saved by Lujack, Kyle and Kurt. The boat exploded, taking Largo's life and injuring Lujack severely. Lujack was rushed to Cedars, where he died tragically in the arms of his beloved Beth. Consumed with grief, Alex swore never to forgive Kyle or the Lewises.

The love between Reva and Kyle also reached a crossroads. H.B. graciously gave Reva the divorce she wanted, but Kyle learned of Maeve's pregnancy and married her instead. Reva then saw Sally with Billy's baby picture and found the birth certificate that indicated Sally was Billy's mother. Confronted, Sally told a shocked Kyle that his father was not H.B. but a prominent cleric named Cardinal Malone. Kyle and Billy finally resolved to be brothers in every sense, merging their enterprises into Sampson-Lewis Industries.

Reva had lost in love once again and could take no more. After suffering in silence outside the church as Maeve and Kyle were married, she walked in a daze onto a suspension bridge, disrobed and threw herself into the icy waters below.

On Location

For his first music video, Lujack performed Bruce Springsteen's "Out in the Street." The video embroiled Lujack and Beth in a sinister plot involving the symbol known as Infinity. Kidnapping, murder and a missing $10 million were all part of the deadly scheme.

1986

ON CALL AT CEDARS

Determined to make it on her own after her aborted suicide attempt, Reva accepted help from no one and went to work as a nurse's aide at Cedars.

stubborn Reva was determined to make it on her own without Kyle or the Lewises bailing her out. She rented a bungalow in the Reardons' run-down neighborhood and named it Reva Bend as an expression of her newfound independence. However, in hopes of staying connected to her, Kyle secretly bought the bungalow, telling no one, including Reva. Meanwhile, Kyle's wife, Maeve, bought the *Springfield Journal* and formed a close friendship with her star reporter, Fletcher. She was particularly impressed by Fletcher's new series of articles titled "Woman on the Ledge," in which he interviewed a woman named Laura who had tried unsuccessfully to end her life. Maeve had no idea that Laura was really her rival, Reva!

Kyle was struggling to come up with a gimmick to make his new Sampson-Lewis holding company a household name, and he grew jealous of his wife's newfound professional status. He came up with a beauty-and-brains campaign called "The Sampson Girl" and hired promo-

Family secrets continued to unravel in 1986 amid several dramatic departures and one shocking return.

Reva was saved from her suicide attempt by a mysterious stranger. While recovering at Cedars, she talked Maureen into hiring her as a nurse's aide. The

tional wizard Jackson Freemont to run it. Kyle held a contest to find a woman to be the Sampson Girl. Jackson was still pursuing Beth at the time and convinced her to enter the competition. Mindy, Roxie and Jessie Matthews also signed up. Hawk wanted Roxie to win, and when he discovered Kyle secretly owned Reva

Bend, he tried to blackmail Kyle into throwing the contest Roxie's way. But Kyle just laughed in his face. A jubilant Mindy was announced as the winner. Roxie was disappointed and had an impulsive one-night stand with Jackson, only to feel like a bigger loser the next morning. Then she found a victory poster that

Kyle, fabricated evidence that the Sampson Girl contest was a fraud. Suddenly, Mindy's name was mud. Ready to roll up her sleeves, Mindy went to the construction site of the new house, where she found Kurt and Roxie asleep in each other's arms! Mindy didn't know Roxie had been helping Kurt with the house, and they had

In an effort to get national exposure for his new company, Kyle created the Sampson Girl contest. The winner was Mindy Lewis Corday, and it would change her life. First runner-up was Jessie Matthews.

Jackson had prematurely made for Beth!

But Mindy had more to lose—namely, her marriage. As the Sampson Girl, she traveled, schmoozed and interviewed with the likes of Dick Cavett, while hubby Kurt was busy building their dream house and keeping Company running smoothly. He looked forward to the day when Mindy would become a full-time wife and they could start a family. Kurt was blissfully unaware that Jackson had talked Mindy into signing a no-pregnancy clause! Mindy's party suddenly ended when Alex and Hawk, out of a mutual enmity toward

varnished themselves into a corner and had to remain there until the varnish dried. Jealous and angry, Mindy beat a hasty exit, knocking over a kerosene lamp in the process. A fire broke out, and Hawk risked his life to save Roxie and Kurt. The house was destroyed, but the incident prompted Hawk and Roxie to reconcile as father and daughter. Eventually, Mindy realized she couldn't play housewife to a traditional, working-class husband and admitted to starting the fire. A disillusioned Kurt left to work on an oil rig in Venezuela, where he was later killed in an explosion. Mindy's granddad, H.B., mellowed toward Hawk and helped him buy Company from Bea Reardon.

As for the other Sampson Girl contenders, Beth wrote Jackson off upon realizing what a slick operator he was. She was touched when Phillip wrote a novel titled *Zanzibar*, which chronicled their love story against a Roaring '20s backdrop. Having come full circle, Phillip and Beth once again became engaged. This aroused the envy of Beth's aunt Calla, a wanna-be who was bent on making sure that her daughter, Jessie, had the same advantages her niece, Beth, was enjoying. Calla soon wormed her way into Alex's life and became her live-in assistant, bringing Jessie to live at the Spaulding mansion with her. This put a crimp in Ross' renewed interest in Calla, as Alex intensely disliked Ross. Ever the pragmatist, Calla didn't want to compromise her esteemed new position by dating a Spaulding adversary. In time, Calla gave in to her feelings for

Both Phillip and Jackson Freemont graced the pages of Phillip's novel, *Zanzibar*, set in the Roaring '20s. At the time, Phillip and Beth were finding their way back to each other, and he wrote the book as a celebration of their love.

Ross, and the two became concerned over an offbeat newcomer to the Spaulding family circle.

A charming young magician named Simon had begun performing at Warren Andrews' Blue Orchid club.

An old lover of India's, he told Alex that he was the illegitimate son of Brandon Spaulding! When Phillip walked in on Simon and India in an embrace, he told his wife that he wanted a divorce. By the time India was available to Simon, though, he had already fallen in love with someone else—the sweeter, more innocent Jessie Matthews. Calla disapproved of the romance, for she was certain that Simon was an impostor. Alex, however, was torn between her own suspicions and her sisterly feelings toward Simon. One day Alex spotted Simon at Lujack's grave

When India's ex-lover Simon Hall came to town, he claimed to be the son of Brandon Spaulding. India was not pleased when he chose sweet young Jessie Matthews over her.

Calla panicked when she heard that her ex-husband, Gordon Matthews, was remarrying. She confided to Lillian that a few years after Jessie was born, Gordon had infected her with venereal disease, which left her sterile. Calla never told Jessie the truth about why the marriage broke up. Calla's growing anxiety turned into psychosomatic symptoms and eventually landed her at Cedars. There Jessie happened upon her mother's chart and discovered the ugly truth about her family. A confused Jessie ran away, and Simon frantically searched for her. India thought this was the perfect opening for her to reconcile with Simon, until Alex came forward with a heretofore secret document. It was a written promise by Simon never to marry India, or he would lose his position at Spaulding! "I never forced him to sign this," Alex smugly informed India. "It was all his idea."

Eventually Simon located Jessie and brought her back to Springfield. This development pleased Alex, who encouraged their romance, and she gifted Simon with one third of Spaulding Enterprises. But Ross had been investigating him and learned he was really Simon Hall from Baltimore, Maryland. Cornered, Simon performed the ultimate disappearing act. One night he announced to the Blue Orchid audience, "Simon Spaulding is a fantasy. I'm a bastard. My father isn't and never was Brandon Spaulding!" With this bombshell, Springfield's answer to Mandrake the Magician vanished in a puff of smoke. Sometime thereafter, Simon resurfaced and admitted his connection to Alex: He was the son of Eric Luvonaczek by another woman and was

and was moved beyond measure. "Now you're a true Spaulding," Alex told him. "But if you are lying, please don't ever tell me." In a gesture of good faith, Alex made Simon executive vice president of Spaulding Enterprises and threw a lavish party in his honor. Desperate to get Simon back and land the Spaulding fortune one way or another, India tried to enlist his help in bilking Alex, but he was strangely noncommittal.

An unusual secret began to haunt Calla and Jessie.

therefore Lujack's half brother. Alex felt Simon had betrayed her trust, but he set out to make amends with her anyway.

Meanwhile, Fletcher discovered that India was embezzling Spaulding Foundation monies in tandem with her father, Baron Von Halkein of Andora. As punishment, India was sentenced to 30 days of community service at the Stony Lake Reformatory, where she befriended a gutsy little orphan named Dorie. This unlikely relationship brought out a refreshing new side to India, but she had not completely reformed. She was hiding the identity of a third party who was in cahoots

Sentenced to do community service for embezzling funds from Spaulding, India worked at the Stony Lake Reformatory, where she befriended a spirited orphan named Dorie. The two instantly formed a bond.

It was her father, Baron Von Halkein, for whom India was embezzling Spaulding money. And who was the third man in this scheme? None other than Alan Spaulding, long believed dead, who was about to make a surprise return to Springfield!

with her and her father, a man whom many in Springfield assumed was dead. He would soon reveal himself at a masquerade ball, in front of everyone who was anyone in Springfield. It was Alan Spaulding!

Now the proud owner of mineral rights in the war-torn country of San Rios, Alan intended to rebuild his power base in Springfield. He outbid Billy and Kyle for the *Mirror*, a sensationalistic competitor of the *Springfield Journal*, and plotted to take over Sampson-Lewis. He schemed with India to boot Alex out of Spaulding Enterprises, and he muscled his way onto Cedars' board of directors and tried to oust both Ed and Maureen, claiming that both were inefficient. Ed and his beloved Mo did not appreciate Alan's manipulations, for they already had their hands full with Claire Ramsey.

After giving birth to Michelle, Claire lapped up Ed and Maureen's generous hospitality during an extended stay in their home. It was a disastrous arrangement. Maureen was left to care for Michelle while Claire carried on a series of trysts with her medical students. Then Rick entered Cedars' accelerated medical program and learned his teacher would be Claire, his ex-lover and now the mother of his half sister. Claire was still attracted to Rick and was not happy to see his romance with Roxie heating up again. At the same time, Ed and Maureen were appalled by Claire's callous neglect of Michelle and engaged her in a battle for the girl's custody. More vindictive than ever, Claire put Rick under so much pressure that he became addicted to amphetamines. She then threatened to report him to the medical board unless he dissuaded Ed and Maureen from proceeding with their case against her. Ironically, Claire was alternating her teaching duties with a cushy new gig as Maeve's personal physician and thus had no time for little Michelle.

When Kyle sympathized with Claire in Michelle's custody situation, the neurotic doctor fantasized that he would leave Maeve for her. But Kyle's help was to no avail, for two events strengthened Ed's resolve to win his daughter away from Claire. Rick overheard Claire threaten Michelle with physical violence, and he relayed this to Ed, along with Claire's blackmail scheme. Rick struggled to conquer his drug addiction and was able to complete his intensive rehab program. The Bauers then received word from Meta that their beloved Bert had died. Determined to pass Bert's loving legacy on to his daughter, Ed vowed that Michelle would grow up in their home. Claire eventually handed over custody of Michelle to Ed and Maureen but retaliated by giving Rick an undeserved F on his final exam. An added blow came when Roxie told Rick she was pregnant with Jackson's child!

Claire was now to become further enmeshed in the triangle of Reva, Kyle and Maeve. Reva was reunited with the mystery man who had pulled her out of the icy water during her suicide attempt. His name was Cain Harris, and he was now tattered and feverish. She let him stay at Reva Bend and pawned her engagement ring to pay his medical bills at Cedars. Reva thought Cain was a decent fellow, but neither Kyle nor Fletcher was convinced. Fletcher investigated and learned that Cain was a former Hollywood stunt director who was implicated in the murder of his starlet wife. After Cain had discovered his wife carrying on with a fellow actor, he orchestrated a stunt that ultimately killed her.

As Kyle agonized over this stranger living in Reva's house, Claire found out Kyle owned Reva Bend and tried to blackmail him into an affair. When he refused, Claire told Maeve that Kyle owned the place—and that meant he must be having an affair with Reva. Claire then overheard Fletcher warn Reva that Cain was a murderer. Aware that several people in Springfield now had his number, Cain went completely insane and threw Claire off a bridge. Kyle grappled with Cain, who fell to his death. Claire was rescued by Kyle. After lying in a coma for weeks, Claire regained consciousness and admitted Rick had aced his final exam. She soon collapsed with a brain seizure. Her condition caught the eye of a charismatic and controversial

In the tragic aftermath of the Andoran art heist, Beth disappeared, and the lovers were separated once again.

Von Halkein Artifact Stolen Spaulding Heir Injured

neurologist, Dr. Mark Jarrett. Ed objected when Mark made Claire a test case for an experimental procedure. However, Ed came around after Mark cured Claire and became a media celebrity as a result. But Kyle had a hunch about Mark that proved to be correct: Mark was a pawn in Alan's attempt to take over Cedars. To beat Alan at his own game, Kyle himself set his sights on the institution. Alan was chagrined to discover Mark's new bond with Ed and yanked his funding. Alex stepped in as Mark's new benefactor, while India opened a gallery and held an art showing to benefit Mark's research. Both women were attracted to the doctor, but he grew weary of being caught in their constant crossfire. He romanced Claire, his miracle patient, and they left Springfield together as husband and wife!

The Spauldings became embroiled in a madcap though ultimately tragic adventure. Beth began working at the local museum for a Professor Blackburn, who got his hands on the cornerstone of the Von Halkein estate in Andora. India knew the cornerstone contained gold, and she tried to steal it from the professor. Blackburn knew he was sitting on a treasure and defended it literally to the death. He knocked India unconscious, shot Phillip and held Beth hostage aboard a boat on Stony Lake. Sometime later, Blackburn's dead body turned up. Beth's shoe and some fabric from her dress were found, but she was nowhere in sight. Phillip was devastated and vowed to find her. But Alan, who had always looked down on Beth, fabricated evidence to make it appear that she had indeed died.

At this time, Reva was working as Alan's photographer at the *Mirror* so she could keep tabs on him for Kyle. One of her first assignments was to shoot underwater photos of Stony Lake, which had become flooded. There she found Professor Blackburn's boat, which contained evidence inconsistent with Alan's claims that Beth was dead. Reva confronted Alan with her findings but agreed not to reveal them when he backed off on an article he was planning to write—a slam piece on Kyle's parentage. But Reva was soon to make an even more dramatic discovery in the flooded waters: the Von Halkein gold! To Alan's horror, Kyle nobly gave the treasure to its rightful owner, the ambassador of Andora. Alan and India then hoodwinked the dignitary into giving it back to India, and the two subsequently became lovers as well as cohorts.

India was not entirely comfortable with the relationship, though. Her art gallery was, in fact, a front for stolen masterpieces that Alan was peddling! During Alan's absence from Springfield, he had been involved with a pair of art smugglers named Paul and Christine Valere. Now that the Valeres were separated, Christine turned to a former lover for help in the operation. He was Johnny Bauer, Ed's distant cousin, a handsome pilot who was now based at Springfield Airport. Christine hoped Johnny would act as a courier for the hot goods, but Johnny had integrity and was hesitant. Then India's old flame, Warren Andrews, caught on to the scheme. India and Warren set out to turn the tables on Alan and another of his cohorts, a handsome Frenchman named Jean-Claude Laval. By coincidence, Jean-Claude was engaged to one of Maureen's younger sisters, vivacious singer Chelsea Reardon. It was at this time that yet another secret was revealed, this one involving Ross and Vanessa.

Vanessa had never told Ross that she had given birth to a daughter by him when she was seventeen years old. She had put the girl up for adoption with the help of a Chamberlain family friend named Grace who lived in Maine. Feeling unfulfilled in her marriage to the boisterous Billy, Vanessa began a search for the child and found out she was linked to Calla and Gordon Matthews! Vanessa concluded that Jessie was her daughter, but Calla and Gordon proved otherwise, explaining that Gordon was the child's adoptive uncle.

Chelsea and Jean-Claude came to Springfield and crashed their car into Phillip's as he was driving two teenagers, Dinah and Kelly Ann, home from a party. Jean-Claude would later die at Cedars under Rick's care, leaving Chelsea to sue Rick—her sister's stepson—for malpractice. Fortunately, Phillip convinced Chelsea to reconsider and drop the suit. When Dinah donated blood to an injured Kelly Ann, Ed discovered that Dinah had the same rare blood type as Ross! Vanessa realized that it was Dinah who was her child by Ross, and she told both him and Billy. Although Ross was delighted to have a daughter, Billy was jealous that Vanessa had yet one more link to Ross.

By now Ross and Vanessa had matured, and their relationship was one of deep, abiding friendship based on a shared past. Billy couldn't handle it and began to wonder if divorce was in the cards for him and Vanessa. Dinah, meanwhile, was kidnapped by a couple named Joe and Shelley Carney, who wanted the handsome ransom that the wealthy Henry Chamberlain could afford to pay. With Phillip's help, Ross saved Dinah and welcomed her into his home. Dinah adored Ross, but because it was her mother who had

was also unhappy to see Jessie and Simon grow even closer in San Rios, where they tried to save Alex from guerrilla leader Tito Montoya. Tito wanted the Spauldings dead because Alan had seized the rights to his mineral deposits. Alex, Simon and Jessie were able to escape, and Alex finally forgave Simon for his past con games. Simon, however, realized Jessie was too young and immature for a committed relationship. Jessie went off to college, and a lonely and defeated Calla decided to leave town.

During these high adventures, Maeve could not help noticing that Kyle was always by Reva's side. Unwilling to live with a man who didn't love her, Maeve told Kyle that their child had been stillborn and that she wanted a divorce. Reva and Kyle soon became engaged. They had no idea Maeve had secretly given birth to a son, Ben, whom her friend Louie Darnell agreed to pass off as his orphaned cousin. When Maeve talked of "adopting" him, an unsuspecting Kyle also made moves to adopt the boy for himself and Reva. Finally, Maeve crashed Kyle and Reva's wedding ceremony and revealed that Ben was her natural son by Kyle.

Vanessa and Ross were teenage lovers and had a child, whom Ross never knew about. When Vanessa launched an intensive search, she found daughter Dinah right in Springfield! Ross was delighted, but Vanessa's marriage to Billy was damaged beyond repair.

In the meantime, Josh Lewis had returned to Springfield, and Reva realized that her love for him was stronger than it ever was for Kyle. A bitter Kyle left Springfield, and Josh and Reva were soon fending off mobsters Gebhart and Cat, who were threatening Josh. The Lewises had reason to believe these thugs were acting as agents for—who else?—Alan Spaulding. Indeed, Alan was already engineering a hostile takeover of Kyle's shares in Sampson-Lewis.

abandoned her, she had a difficult time bonding with Vanessa. She also found it hard to fit in with the "normal" teens at Springfield High until she began dating a popular young man named Cameron Stewart.

As Ross struggled with his new role as bachelor father, Calla realized she had no place in his life, and he in turn was fed up with her shallowness. Calla

But the big news in the Lewis family was that another baby was on the way. The proud parents? Reva and Josh!

1987

Alan Spaulding continued to be an ever-present catalyst to the action in Springfield throughout 1987, as he forced two long-standing relationships toward a crossroads—those of Ross and Vanessa, and Josh and Reva.

India was pleased to see the growing bond between her young ward, Dorie, and her fellow waif, Dinah. Now that Dinah was contentedly living with Ross after years of being shuttled from pillar to post, India convinced Ross to split Dorie's care with her. But upon learning her father was in failing health, India returned to Andora with Dorie in tow. With Ross relegated to the role of bachelor father, Vanessa began to feel like an outsider. Dinah continued to have no use for her, and Ross showed no interest in marriage despite Vanessa's divorce from Billy, who was now in Venezuela. The rift between Vanessa and Dinah grew when Vanessa expressed her disapproval of Dinah's drunken teenage parties. Vanessa started throwing herself into her new job at the Spaulding Foundation, where she found herself enjoying Alan's flirtatious advances. Ross was disheartened to see Vanessa use Alan to try to make him jealous. This was the old, manipulative Vanessa, and he wanted no part of her. Ross issued her an ultimatum: Alan and the Spaulding Foundation, or him. Because Billy had left Vanessa with nothing but child support for little Billy, Vanessa took the pragmatic route and chose Spaulding.

Alan confided to Vanessa that Henry's finances were in bad shape. Furious that Alan had alarmed her, Henry confronted him, and the showdown caused Henry to suffer his second heart attack. To Vanessa's great relief, her beloved father survived. Henry then had Ross change his will to include Dinah, as well as to name Vanessa as his successor on the Spaulding board. Dinah finally accepted Vanessa and formed a close bond with Henry, whom she considered her grandfather and adviser. Dinah needed advice more than ever, now that her boyfriend, sensitive Cameron Stewart, had been busted for drug possession. What Cameron hadn't revealed was

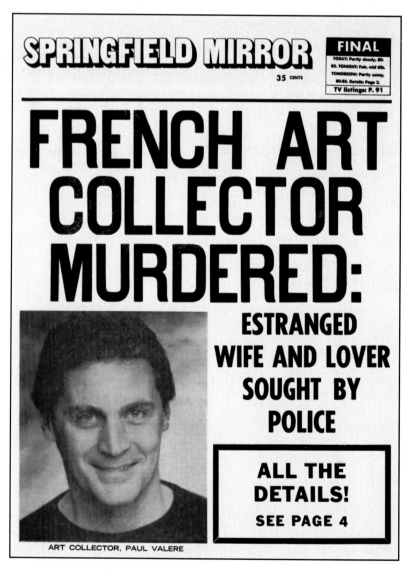

SPRINGFIELD MIRROR

35 CENTS

FINAL

TODAY: Partly cloudy, 80-85. TONIGHT: Fair, mid 60s. TOMORROW: Partly sunny, 80-85. Details: Page 2.

TV listings: P. 91

FRENCH ART COLLECTOR MURDERED:

ESTRANGED WIFE AND LOVER SOUGHT BY POLICE

ALL THE DETAILS! SEE PAGE 4

ART COLLECTOR, PAUL VALERE

After art smuggler Paul Valere was found dead, it was discovered that he had ordered a hit on Phillip prior to his death.

that the drugs belonged to his father, George, a coke-addicted loser. Neither Dinah nor Cameron suspected that George was the one behind a major robbery that had occurred at the Chamberlain house.

Compared to Paul Valere, though, George Stewart was a petty crook. The insidious international art smuggler arrived to keep his estranged wife, Christine, in line, along with his American partner, Alan Spaulding. Meanwhile, an unsuspecting Phillip became a columnist at Alan's newspaper, the *Mirror*, and began a series of investigative pieces on the stolen-art syndicate. As a warning, Paul had Phillip's apartment ransacked, prompting Phillip's gal friday Chelsea Reardon to destroy Phillip's exposé in order to protect him. Phillip rewrote the piece in a blander version, only to have the original turn up and make the front page! Alan told Paul not to hurt Phillip, so instead, Paul tried to ice Chelsea by rigging a microphone to electrocute her. Luckily Jackson saved her in the nick of time and began developing feelings for Chelsea when Phillip didn't seem to be returning her affections.

Also involved in the Paul Valere chaos was Johnny Bauer, who was trying to live down his past dubious connections with Paul and the late Jean-Claude Laval. The sneaky Alan had a dossier on Johnny, however, and blackmailed him into being his courier. Johnny made it clear to Alan that he didn't know what was in the crates he was transporting from Europe to Springfield, nor did he want to. Although Johnny was unable to fight his lingering attraction to Christine, whom he had known intimately in Europe, he ultimately chose his love for Roxie over her. When Paul threatened Johnny and Christine, Johnny swore he would kill Paul if Paul ever lay a hand on Christine again. Not long afterward, Paul was shot! The slew of suspects included Johnny, Christine and Alan. But an unlikely party confessed to the crime: Warren Andrews. Paul had discovered that Andrews was double-crossing him.

As the Valere imbroglio came to an end, the ripple effect was widely felt. Before Warren was moved to an out-of-state prison, he warned Alan that Paul had ordered a hit on Phillip prior to his death. Alan confessed to his part in the scam, leaving Phillip to feel betrayed once again by the man he'd always known as his father. Phillip moved into the lighthouse and staked Johnny in an exciting new venture: a hot-air balloon flight center. The grand opening was celebrated at Ed and Mo's annual barbecue, where two bold and daring teenagers arrived with a bang. Alan-Michael Spaulding, Ed's nephew and Alan's biological son with Hope, parachuted into the party and immediately charmed all the young ladies present. Aspiring gymnast Lacey Bauer, Johnny's sister, also made a splashy entrance and took Cameron on a wild balloon ride.

A few weeks later, Warren's warning materialized. Paul's paid assassin kidnapped Alan and demanded he lure Phillip into a deadly trap. When Alan refused to give Phillip up, Phillip found himself infected with botulism from a poisoned steak. Ed and Rick worked feverishly to save him and finally succeeded, while Alan-Michael begrudged his uncle and cousin's concern for his adoptive brother. Alan-Michael yearned to have a relationship with Alan after years of distance, but it seemed Phillip was all Alan cared about. Alan-Michael secured Phillip's reluctant assistance, however, in helping the police rescue Alan from the assassin's clutches. The goon was vanquished, and Alan expressed his deep gratitude to his sons. But Phillip would have none of it and bitterly swore off Alan. Having risked his life to protect Phillip from the assassin, Alan was so hurt by his son's rejection that he disowned him.

Alan was also displeased to learn that Alex was involved in a hilarious and unlikely new romance—with H.B. Lewis! Alex was once again on good terms with Simon Hall, who became the trucking coordinator at Sampson-Lewis. But Simon realized he missed Jessie, so he left to join her in North Carolina, where she was attending college. He was replaced at Sampson-Lewis by Rusty Shayne, Reva and Roxie's brother, who was soon embroiled in a hot romance with Mindy. Unbeknownst to most, Rusty was really a cop secretly hired by H.B. to infiltrate Cat Brixton's gang. When Cat held Hawk hostage, Rusty saved his father and killed Cat. Cat represented an organization called Diamondhead, which planned to take over Sampson-Lewis—and which had no connection to Alan.

Rusty saw his heroics as strictly part of his job. Though Reva and Roxie knew Hawk had reformed, Rusty was stubbornly unconvinced. Lillian Raines thought Hawk was pretty terrific, though, and they became engaged. Yet Lillian would soon wonder about their future together when Hawk's ex-wife, Sarah Shayne, joined her three children in Springfield. A no-nonsense woman with an innate sense of fairness, Sarah recognized the change in Hawk and convinced Rusty to acknowledge his father's love. At the same time, Mindy couldn't accept Rusty as a professional crime fighter and was unsure about the prospect of becoming a cop's wife.

Rusty and Mindy embarked on a hot romance, but Mindy soon became concerned about the repercussions of being a policeman's wife.

A new chapter was to begin for the Lewis family. After a business disagreement with H.B., Josh resigned and spent some time back in Venezuela. There he was reunited with Dr. Will Jeffries, a psychiatrist he had befriended earlier while he was living in the South American country. Josh returned to Springfield with Will just in time for Reva to give birth to a daughter, Marah, named after Josh and Reva's mothers, Martha and Sarah. Will took a position at Cedars, and Josh started managing a construction company owned by the ailing Koz Kowolski. Happy with his new niche, Josh looked forward to leading the simple life with Reva and Marah, his buddy Will

at his side. He had no inkling of the nightmare to come.

Sally Gleason suspected that Marah's father was really her son, Kyle, who had remarried out of town. Picking up on the tension surrounding Marah's birth, Will—for reasons he did not yet reveal—altered the birth records to indicate that Josh was not Marah's father. Josh eventually saw the records and told Reva they were finished. He also hastened to add that he had been married in Venezuela to a psychiatrist named Sonni Carrera. Sonni had since died in a hiking accident, having plunged to her death off a suspension bridge. Reva was angry that Josh had withheld this from her, but the attraction between them was so strong that in time they decided to make a go of their romance once again. It was then that Sonni turned up alive, and Alan got into the act.

After Rusty saved his father's life, nurse Lillian Raines and Hawk became engaged.

Alan was still pursuing Vanessa in hopes that they could build a corporate dynasty together. But Reva had a raw energy and an unpretentious quality that Alan found irresistible. He hired Reva and prevailed upon her to break up Alex and H.B. In return, he offered to have paternity tests performed on Marah to get to the bottom of the mystery. Alan was shocked to discover that Marah was, indeed, Josh's child! He considered telling Reva the truth but couldn't bring himself to do it, for he wanted Reva to himself. Alan lied and told Reva that Marah was Kyle's, adding that he wanted a relationship with her. Reva

Josh brought his psychiatrist pal Will Jeffries from Venezuela to Springfield. He would soon live to regret it.

LOVE AND MARRIAGE

Josh had married Sonni Carrera in Venezuela, but she had been presumed dead after a hiking accident. Once she resurfaced in Springfield, Josh remarried her, even though his heart belonged to Reva.

Reva pretended to understand, but she was so livid she planned to take Alan for all he was worth.

Reva had no idea that others in Springfield had determined the truth behind Marah's parentage. Sally felt guilty for having inadvertently perpetuated the lie, and she rushed to Josh and Sonni's wedding in Hawaii to reveal the truth. However, Alan made Alex intercept her under threat of telling H.B. that Alex knew the truth and had kept it from him. Alex talked Sally into holding off until after the ceremony. As the guests danced and celebrated, Sally was about to drop the bombshell when she dropped dead of a massive coronary! A shocked H.B. realized that life was short, and he proposed to a receptive Alex.

Back in Springfield, Alan hired George Stewart to bring his car fleet up to emissions standards. Alan didn't realize he had done the equivalent of hiring a rat to bring a restaurant up to the health code. In exchange for a discount on cocaine, George arranged to help dope dealer Nicky Sutton smuggle drugs by conceal-

was shocked. "Why would you want someone who doesn't want you?" she asked Alan. Alan could only reply, "Why would you?" Knowing Josh still had feelings for Sonni, Reva set him free to remarry her and took up with Alan. But Alan's first love was still business, and he ultimately proposed to Vanessa.

ing them in the car door panels. George conducted his business at a garage owned by a hard-edged young mechanic named Frank Cooper. While Frank himself wasn't totally on the level, he had no idea George was using his garage as a way station for drugs. Another figure in the drug scenario was Nicky Sutton's attractive, fragile girlfriend, Rose McLaren, an addict who was struggling to go straight. Frightened of Nicky, Rose secretly gave Rusty evidence that would incriminate the slimy dealer. Rusty realized he had more than protective feelings for Rose when Nicky found her out and savagely attacked her. Nicky then framed Rusty for drug possession, resulting in Rusty's arrest and dismissal from the force. As a confused Mindy looked on in jealous anger, Rusty kidnapped Rose in order to shield her from Nicky. Mindy soon found herself enjoying the company of Will Jeffries.

The teenagers of Springfield also had their hands full in the romantic quadrangle department. As Lacey bulldozed her way into Cameron's life, Alan-Michael and Dinah began dating, much to the dismay of their feuding fathers, Alan and Ross. One day Alan-Michael took Dinah joyriding on a motorcycle he "borrowed" from Frank's garage—only to collide with Frank's car! Frank was rushing his pregnant younger sister—aptly named Harley Davidson Cooper—to the hospital. Dinah bravely delivered Harley's baby girl right at the scene. The girls became such close friends that Dinah was present when Harley handed her daughter over to her new adoptive parents. As she watched, Dinah was stung on a

TEENAGE TRIANGLES

When Dinah Marler came to town, she and Cameron Stewart formed a bond, but after dashing Alan-Michael Spaulding parachuted into town, he more than caught her eye. Their fathers, Alan and Ross, were fierce rivals and were furious to see them together.

gut level, for she had been given up as well. She was also pained to realize that her parents, Ross and Vanessa, would probably never marry.

Phillip was wrestling with his own demons in regards to his strange background. He reestablished ties with Alan and took a demeaning job in the Spaulding publicity department. Although Alan was pleased to see Phillip humbling himself, he had no idea his son was secretly plotting his ruin. With Spaulding-like precision, Phillip sold Alex on the idea of merging Spaulding

Strong-willed Dr. Meredith Reade and easygoing Rick Bauer were an unlikely pair. Something about this slightly older woman intrigued him, and they became involved. It was a complex relationship from the start.

Enterprises with Sampson-Lewis and forcing Alan out. Alex now owned Cachet, the gallery India had opened with Alan's help, but she was tempted by Phillip's proposal to get back into the corporate power game. Phillip grew so obsessed with destroying Alan that he neglected his promising relationship with Chelsea. Seeing an opening for himself, Jackson became Chelsea's show

business manager as well as her boss at the Blue Orchid, which he had taken over in Warren's absence. Chelsea was far from flattered, however, when Phillip and Jackson fought over her. She knew the two men were continuing their old rivalry for Beth, and that she was a mere substitute! Phillip did some hard thinking and wrote Chelsea a love letter in which he swore he had put Beth behind him. But Jackson, who was controlling Chelsea's every move, quickly intercepted it. Jackson was also harboring the secret that he was a British earl, a distinction the rock promoter considered uncool. He could no longer ignore his noblesse, however, when his ailing mother, Lady Agnes Freemont, came to visit him in Springfield.

Another new arrival was Dr. Meredith Reade, Fletcher's sister, a brilliant cardiac surgeon new to the Cedars staff. Meredith moved in with Fletcher and Maeve, who were now living together and providing a stable home for her little son, Ben. Maeve found Meredith to be brusque and self-involved, but Rick Bauer liked what he saw in this attractive, somewhat older doctor. Rick and Meredith began a relationship that was soon complicated by their differing approaches to a sensitive case. Johnny Bauer was diagnosed with malignant throat cancer, and Rick was appalled by Meredith's clinical approach to his ailing cousin. Meredith insisted on surgery, whereas Rick supported Johnny's decision to undergo holistic treatment suggested by Roxie. Meredith picked up on the lingering chemistry between Rick and Roxie and spitefully thrust Rick before Cedars' review board because of his opposition to the surgery. Johnny also sensed the chemistry but tried to get Rick and Roxie together at every turn. As Johnny explained to Ed, "I want them to have each other when I'm gone."

Fletcher knew the real reason behind his sister's behavior. When their mother was dying of cancer, Meredith pulled the plug from her mother's life support system. Fletcher and Maeve worried that if Meredith didn't come clean about this painful episode, her past could destroy Rick's professional future. Against Fletcher's wishes, Maeve went to Ed and told him Meredith's secret.

Of course, more secrets were yet to be revealed. As the year drew to a close, Sonni adjusted to life in Springfield as Josh's wife but was plagued by a recurring nightmare in which a group of South Americans surrounded her, chanting "Bad girl! Bad girl!" Each time she was saved by Will, clad in a monk's robe, who absolved her of her sins?

1988

It was merger mania in Springfield as Alex and Phillip plotted to join forces with the Lewises to bring Alan to ruin. H.B. and Josh were hesitant until Alex revealed that Alan had tampered with Marah's paternity test. What neither the Spauldings nor the Lewises knew was that two other people stood to gain from the proposed merger: Sonni and Will.

Sonni was not the shy shrinking violet she appeared to be. Not only was she involved in an ongoing affair with Will, but she was actually Sonni's evil twin sister, Solita! "Sonni" and Will had hatched an elaborate plot in which she was to remarry Josh and encourage the merger with Spaulding Enterprises. The crafty lovers would then kill Josh and make off with a fortune. Sonni and Will enjoyed several rendezvous in Springfield, one of which Reva witnessed and photographed from a neighboring apartment. Although she didn't have the heart to show Josh the pictures, she nonetheless told him she suspected Will and Sonni were carrying on. When Josh confronted the lovers, Sonni innocently replied that she and Will were just planning Josh's surprise birthday party! Josh bought the story.

Sonni, however, was beginning to care for Josh in earnest and started to waver about the idea of murdering him. Determined to see it through, Will unilaterally stepped up the plan and set Josh up to plummet to his

While Sonni and Will plotted Josh's murder, Reva caught them on film and alerted Josh, but Sonni cleverly managed to avoid detection.

death in icy waters in a malfunctioning Jeep. Josh's Jeep plunged off a bridge, but as luck would have it, Reva and Alan were skating nearby. Reva jumped into the freezing water and saved her love, then fought for her own life at Cedars, where she suffered cardiac arrest. One night Sonni sneaked into Reva's room and found her choking on a tube. Sonni considered killing her, but instead she inexplicably saved her life!

Reva's ordeal jolted Alan into realizing how much he loved her, and he brought in a minister to marry them while Reva lay half-conscious in her hospital bed. He was stunned the next day, though, when Reva came to and thought she'd married Josh. The marriage was annulled, and Alan and Reva planned to have a proper wedding.

Then came a new wrinkle—Sonni was pregnant! Will pressured her to have an abortion and she refused. The conspirators then panicked at the arrival of Will's parents, Anita and Esteban Jeffries, and Sonni's estranged father, Welles Carrera. Will told his parents that Sonni (whom they knew as Solita) had married Josh because he was terminally ill, and that she would marry Will after Josh's inevitable death! A hard-nosed man who had no sympathy for his errant daughter, Welles Carrera figured out the scheme but was fatally struck by a car shortly after. Sonni feared for Josh's life and begged him not to go through with the Spaulding merger, knowing it would seal his fate at Will's hands.

LOVE AND MARRIAGE

In the summer of 1988, Fletcher and Maeve were married at the annual Bauer barbecue. Maeve died tragically in a helicopter crash soon after.

In the meantime, Phillip was sealing Alan's fate in a most contemptuous manner. Unbeknownst to Alex or the Lewises, he set Alan up to lose a fortune in an illegal emerald mine venture. Nonetheless, they still planned to surprise Alan with news of the merger at an upcoming gala. Moments before Alan was to make a speech at the event, Phillip took Alan aside. "The IRS has frozen all your assets," Phillip quietly and delightedly told his father. "The board has had it. You're out."

Mistakenly thinking that Reva was in on the maneuver, a devastated and vilified Alan fled to Mexico. H.B. felt so guilty over his part in Alan's downfall that he called off the merger and sadly informed Alex he couldn't go through with their marriage plans. Alex blamed Phillip, and after discovering the emerald mine scam, she lit into her callous nephew. Sometime later, Phillip and Chelsea called it quits when she accused him of demanding perfection of everyone but himself. Rick and Alan-Michael were also furious with Phillip, who

Will over the head in self-defense. Thinking he was dead, she set his lifeless body adrift in his boat. With Will missing, Reva blurted out to Josh that Sonni and Will had had an affair. Then she tracked Alan to Mexico, where she found him working at a seedy bar. Pained to see the mighty Alan Spaulding so down and out, Reva convinced him she had nothing to do with the merger plot and brought him back to Springfield to fight for what was his.

Reva and her family were saddened when Roxie suffered a breakdown and was institutionalized. Johnny's cancer was too much for her to bear, and she had buckled under the pressure. Ironically, the cancer went

Maeve's mother, Julia, fought for custody of little Ben and offered Fletcher the *Journal* in exchange. Fletcher refused, secured a loan from Alexandra to buy the paper and kept the boy. It was Maeve's wish.

condescendingly reminded Alan-Michael that he, too, would be part of Spaulding Enterprises someday. "Part of?" Alan-Michael said incredulously. "I'm Alan's real son. Spaulding is mine to begin with."

Lewis Oil was back in its original form, and Josh became its president. Reva confronted Sonni, saying she intended to tell Josh about the affair, but changed her mind when Sonni lost the baby during their heated argument. Sonni then pleaded with Will to call off his plot against Josh. They got into a struggle, and Sonni hit

into remission after her breakdown. Johnny's parents, Jack and Lainie Bauer, came in from Wisconsin and encouraged him to date Chelsea, which he did. Now that Jackson had returned to England with his mother, Chelsea felt more free than ever to find real love in her

LOVE AND MARRIAGE

When Rick married Meredith, he had no idea she was pregnant with his best friend Phillip's child.

a news story and went down with the chopper! An instant widower, Fletcher now had to fight Julia Stoddard, Maeve's prickly, well-to-do mother, for custody of little Ben. Julia had hidden Maeve's letter indicating her wish to have Ben remain with Fletcher. She offered to sign over Maeve's ownership of the *Journal* to Fletcher in exchange for Ben, but Fletcher refused and secured a loan from Alex to purchase the newspaper.

The ambitious Meredith was about to put Rick and Phillip's friendship to the ultimate test. Meredith criticized Rick for his desire to be a family physician rather than an eminent surgeon like she was. Now that Phillip had returned to his former position with the Spaulding Foundation, Meredith applied for and won a research grant from the organization. After an argument with Rick, Meredith got drunk with Phillip and they had hot sex in the lighthouse. The next morning Phillip loathed himself for having sunk to a new low—bedding his best friend's woman! When an apologetic Rick told Meredith he regretted their disagreements and proposed, she accepted. Meredith didn't know it then, but she was pregnant with Phillip's child!

Into Phillip's irresolute life came a new and mysterious character. A bright, attractive young woman named Blake Lindsey joined Spaulding Enterprises as

life. Johnny's doctors, Rick and Meredith, also had a stronger relationship now that her mother's cancer and the mercy killing at Meredith's hands were out in the open. That summer Fletcher and Maeve were happily married at the annual Bauer barbecue. Sadly, only moments later, Maeve hopped into a helicopter to cover

public relations director and set her sights on Phillip. Blake overheard Phillip and Meredith discuss their fateful encounter in the lighthouse. Projecting his guilt onto Meredith, Phillip threatened to yank her research grant if she married Rick. He did this not to win Meredith for himself, but to save Rick from entering a sham of a marriage. Feeling cornered, Meredith told everything to Fletcher and Blake.

As it turned out, Blake herself had an angle on the situation. She had been briefly involved with Alan during his sojourn in Mexico and had been sent by him to spy on Phillip. In essence, Blake was Alan's vehicle for winning back Spaulding Enterprises. Alan sensed correctly that Blake was falling for Phillip, and he began to distrust her. Alex discovered Alan and Blake's affair and told Reva in hopes of keeping her from marrying into the family.

Reva wasn't the only undesired would-be Mrs. Spaulding. After Dinah and Cameron had George Stew-

art arrested on drug charges, they departed Springfield, leaving Alan-Michael to date wild, working-class Harley Cooper. Alex and Phillip were horrified, to put it mildly. They knew that if Alan-Michael were to marry by the age of 25, he stood to inherit a sizable trust fund—and they didn't want it in Harley's grubby little hands. Thus, when Alan-Michael and Harley became engaged, Phillip made it appear that Harley had slept with him. Alan-Michael was hurt and furious, but eventually the truth came out. A remorseful Phillip became Harley's Pygmalion, teaching her how to be refined and fit into Alan-Michael's upper-crust world.

Alex found an unlikely new friend in Sonni. Desperate for a confidante, Sonni broke down and admitted to Alex that she'd killed Will. Just as Sonni feared that prison was imminent, however, Will turned up alive and with amnesia! At the same time, Ed—not suspecting Sonni was Solita—heard of Sonni's background as a psychiatrist and hired her at Cedars. Sonni now had to

They made a diverse foursome: Cameron, who had to deal with an abusive, drug-addicted father; Harley, who had something to prove; spoiled Alan-Michael; and virginal Dinah Marler. After Cameron left town, Harley and Alan-Michael became an item.

act like a real doctor, so she took on Will as her first patient. Her aim was to toy with Will's mind and make him remember events as she colored them. It was during this time that Will and Mindy became involved again. Mindy had helped Rusty and Rose get Nicky Sutton arrested, only to see Rusty and Rose become a pair. On the rebound, Mindy married the confused Will as her disapproving family watched helplessly.

Time was running out for Sonni and Will. Reva finally showed Josh the pictures of his wife and pal in a tight embrace, and together they went to Venezuela to investigate Sonni. There they soon met up with Sonni and Will and figured out the criminal lovers' master plan. Thinking fast, Sonni tricked Will into telling the Venezuela police that Josh, not Sonni, had tried to kill him.

Meanwhile, Josh and Reva made passionate love on the beach as Alan's photographer snapped pictures of them unnoticed. Josh was arrested for trying to kill Will, but as Will's memory slowly returned, Reva ex-tracted an anguished confession from him and got it all on tape. Then Alan showed up to throw his usual monkey wrench into the proceedings by becoming Sonni's lover and co-conspirator. Josh confronted them with his shocking discovery that Sonni was not Solita after all, but Sonni herself! Frantic, Sonni fired a gun and Alan caught the bullet, which left him paralyzed. Will then injected Alan with a needle, while Sonni knocked out Reva and prepared to inject her as well!

As Alan hovered on the brink of death in Venezuela, another ghost loomed over the people of Springfield. Blake was so guilt-ridden for having used Phillip that she took an overdose of sleeping pills. Ed saved her life and was touched to learn his patient's true identity. Blake was really Christina Thorpe, the girl he had once considered his daughter! Christina's mother, the recently divorced Holly Lindsey, arrived in Springfield to be at her side. Correspondence then surfaced that confirmed Alan's suspicion that Christina's "late" un-lamented father, Roger Thorpe, was alive!

Josh followed Sonni and Will to Venezuela, where he uncovered their master plan. The conniving Sonni tricked Will into telling the police that Josh, not she, had tried to kill him, and Josh was arrested.

1989

For the families of Springfield, 1989 was a banner year. The Bauers survived another test of their unity, the Lewises welcomed a relative they never knew they had, the Coopers became assimilated into Springfield society and the Spauldings were reunited with two people who, in effect, had come back from the dead.

Ed, Fletcher, Alex and Rusty raced to Venezuela to save Reva and Alan from the murderous Sonni and Will. Ed performed surgery on Alan, but he remained paralyzed and convalesced in Venezuela. Rusty hauled Sonni back to Springfield, where she stood trial for Will's attempted murder. When Sonni's inconsistent testimony left everyone baffled, Reva and Rusty investigated her in Venezuela and found her twin sister Solita's remains in a grave. Sonni had evidently killed Solita and taken on her personality as an alter ego! Back in Springfield, Sonni finally unraveled and lost her "Solita" persona. She spent some time in an institution but made such a fine recovery that Ed rehired her at Cedars. Ed fired Will, however, when he admitted to tampering with Marah's birth records.

During Sonni's trial, Alex and Fletcher left Venezuela together in the Spaulding jet. The plane crashed, killing the pilot. Stranded on an island, Alex and Fletcher became friends, and passion soon began growing between them. They had no idea that a mysterious man was watching their every move. When Alex and Fletcher were separated during a storm, the man sprang into action and convinced each of the two castaways that the other was dead. The stranger then held Alex hostage but made himself out to be her "host" rather than her captor. Alex was being subtly romanced by this stranger, who called himself Adam Malik. She found it puzzling, however, that he always sat in a dark corner and refused to approach her.

Spaulding/Reade Survival Doubtful

After Alex and Fletcher's plane crashed on a desert island, they became intensely attracted to each other. Unbeknownst to them, they were being watched by a mysterious stranger.

Fletcher made it back to Springfield and was able to secure custody of his stepson, Ben. His longtime pal, Maureen, was relieved to see him alive and began to fantasize about a future with him. She was uncomfortable with Ed's renewed bond with Holly, who had become more vibrant and assertive since she was last in Springfield. But Fletcher told her they could never be more than friends. This made no difference to Ed, who so distrusted Fletcher that he declared their friendship over and he and Maureen separated. Ed now relied on Ross as his closest confidant.

On the other side of the tracks, a justice of the peace performed a double ceremony for the Shayne family: the wedding of Rusty and Rose, and the remarriage of Hawk and Sarah. But Rusty was still haunted by thoughts of Mindy, who had disappeared when Will's treachery came to the fore. Desperate to get Mindy back, Will kidnapped Marah, framing Sonni for the deed, and left her in the care of his mentally unbalanced mother,

Anita Ybarra. Will planned to play hero and "save" the child so that a grateful Josh would tell him Mindy's whereabouts! Rose suspected he was the culprit and confronted him. A struggle ensued, and Rose hit her head on a rock and died. Sonni found Marah and convinced Reva she was not the kidnapper. An anguished Rusty was certain that Will had iced Rose, but the D.A.'s office dismissed the evidence as circumstantial and let Will off. Determined to nab him, Rusty turned in his badge and became a private eye. When Billy and Mindy returned to Springfield, Rusty was able to convince Mindy to help him get the goods on Will. Panicked by Rusty's investigation, Will had Anita confess to Marah's kidnapping,

and she was duly committed. But Will himself seemed to be in need of a padded room, as he began hearing Rose's voice. In time Will realized Mindy was gaslighting him, and he drugged her and held her at gunpoint. Rusty arrived at the scene with Josh and Sonni and shot Will, who grabbed Mindy's hand as he fell off a balcony. Will plunged to his death, but Josh and Sonni were able to pull Mindy to safety. Although Billy hoped Mindy would settle down with Rusty, she elected to remain behind with her family when Rusty went to Tulsa to become chief of detectives.

With Alex presumed dead, Phillip seized control of Spaulding Enterprises. This distressed Alan-Michael,

Like a cat with nine lives, Roger had survived his plunge off a cliff in Santo Domingo and had resurfaced as "Adam Malik" on the island on which Alex and Fletcher were stranded.

who flew to Venezuela and convinced the recovering Alan to come home and reclaim his empire. Alan was touched by his son's concern and hopeful about his chances at Spaulding. The Spauldings had no clue that Alex was at that moment pouring out her heart to her friendly captor, Adam Malik. One night Malik finally showed himself to Alex, albeit wearing a mask. He explained that he had been disfigured in an accident, which he considered retribution for the horrible things he had done to his family. Moved by Malik's soul baring, Alex told him about her own family and mentioned Phillip's romance with Blake, whose father was a rotten loser named Roger Thorpe. Malik was deeply affected by what he heard. After he bade Alex goodnight, he took off his mask in the dark. Adam Malik was Roger Thorpe!

Like a cat with nine lives, Roger had miraculously survived his fall off the cliff in Santo Domingo. He had since taken his father's first name and become an agent for the CIA. When Roger tracked the Spaulding jet to its island location, he had set out to torment Alex to get back at Alan. He found he was becoming attached to the iron-willed but lonely Alexandra despite himself. He would have kept Alex on the island forever had Phillip, Blake and Fletcher not tracked her down. When they arrived, a masked Roger, still calling himself Adam Malik, introduced himself as Alex's benevolent host. Roger ached to reveal himself to Blake, his "little Chrissy," who was now all grown up. He accompanied the group back to Springfield, where a grateful but confused Alex sequestered him in her wine cellar.

Alex returned just in time for Alan-Michael and Harley's wedding. It was a classic case of oil and water as the refined Spauldings met the tacky mother of the bride, Nadine Cooper. A brash, blond nurse with a social-climbing bent, Nadine had raised Frank and Harley alone, but only for a while, after her husband, Buzz Cooper, deserted her. Now she was back in Springfield evading a thug named Louie, to whom she owed a

Her daughter's marriage into the Spaulding family brought Nadine Cooper back to Springfield. Looking to marry into money herself, Nadine set her sights on Alan Spaulding, and when that didn't work out, she turned to Ross.

bundle of cash. Louie arrived moments before the ceremony began. To avoid an embarrassing scene, Phillip paid him off. Also in attendance was teenager Samantha Marler, Phillip's biological sister and Ross' niece. Samantha was staying with Ross for an extended period of time.

The wedding of Alan-Michael and Harley begat another Spaulding family schism. Phillip and Alex set out to postpone the release of Alan-Michael's inheritance, considering him too immature to handle it. Alan caught on and told Alan-Michael, who replied that he had overheard conversations to the effect that Phillip had fathered Meredith's baby. Shortly after Rick married Meredith, a spiteful Alan sent Rick a letter revealing that Phillip had fathered the child he and his wife were expecting. Meredith lost the child as a result and left Rick out of guilt. Devastated, Rick punched Phillip out and told him he hated him. "I know," Phillip calmly told his friend, "but I still love you, and there's a fine

Blake and Phillip's dueling fathers brought their children's nuptials to a halt before they could say "I do." To the horror of everyone present, Adam Malik was revealed to be none other than Roger Thorpe!

line between the two." As in the past, Rick and Phillip's friendship proved rock-solid and could not be torn asunder.

Blake admitted to Phillip that she had slept with Alan, but Phillip forgave her and they became engaged. The love triangles then grew more tangled. Blake moved in with Holly and got her hired at WSPR. Holly slept with Ed, and it was unsatisfying for both of them. Ed was still in love with Mo, and Holly was attracted to Ed's cousin, Johnny. She even gave him his own talk show at the station. But Johnny moved in with Chelsea, and the two became alarmed when a "fan" of Johnny's began threatening Chelsea. As for Ed, he and Mo consulted Sonni for marriage counseling. Thanks to her expert coaching, the Bauers reconciled and reaffirmed their marriage in a beautiful ceremony.

Nadine also had an eye toward marriage—to Alan! When she helped the millionaire in his physical therapy, a revitalized Alan took the proverbial turn for the nurse. But Nadine's true feelings were for Ross, Alan's longtime adversary. Picking up on Nadine's inherent greed, Phillip paid her to spy on Alan. She was hurt to overhear Alan say he switched Marah's test results out of love for Reva. Feeling rejected, Nadine became lovers with Ross and moved in with him. The arrangement proved short-lived, however, when Nadine began to doubt that Vanessa was out of Ross' system.

Alan, meanwhile, was able to walk again sooner than he let on. One day, while alone in his basement, he stretched his legs, only to be confronted by Adam Malik! Alan recognized Roger's voice immediately, but his masked enemy refused to confirm his suspicion. To draw Roger out, Alan engineered a series of accidents supposedly targeted at Blake. Roger eventually caught on and got his revenge: He dumped Alan out of his wheelchair and proved that he could walk!

The ultimate climax occurred at Phillip and Blake's wedding. As the couple began reciting their vows, Alan confronted Malik in the loft and shot him. Attending to the victim, Ed pulled off his mask. To the shock and horror of all present, including Blake's grandparents Barbara and Adam, Roger's true identity was revealed! "Kill him," a smoldering Holly icily told Ed. But Ed was first and foremost a doctor, and despite his painful history with Roger, he operated on his old rival. Phillip and Blake's nuptials were never completed. Roger's father, Adam, swore off his son and left Springfield for good. Alan was arrested for shooting Roger. Before going to prison, he told Phillip that Beth might still be alive!

To Holly's horror, Roger began doting on Blake. He admired Phillip for his machinations toward Alan and made a big show of offering to find Beth for him. For Blake's sake, though, Roger secretly hoped Beth was dead. When he saw a coroner's report indicating Beth might be alive, Roger showed it to Blake, who promptly burned it. A jubilant Blake then eloped with Phillip, but the groom was growing more obsessed with finding the missing Beth.

Around this time, Phillip was startled to see a series of paintings matching Beth's style turn up in Springfield. The paintings were being funneled through an agent of Alan's named Bruce Daly, who had impregnated a confused teenager named Dana Jones. Dana aroused Rick's interest when she checked into Cedars for an abortion, only to have a drug-induced miscarriage. Frank Cooper also became intrigued with this mystery girl. Dana looked strikingly like Beth. The sleazy Bruce sent Phillip anonymous ransom notes demanding a million dollars for Beth's release. Phillip convinced Alan-Michael to give up his inheritance to pay the ransom, but when Bruce went to collect the money, it was gone! Roger had caught wind of the plan and lifted the cash. Bruce confessed to the scam but did not implicate Alan. Phillip began to give up hope of finding Beth until Bradley Raines was released from jail and told Lillian that he had witnessed Alan trafficking Beth's paintings in prison.

Not suspecting Roger was playing both sides against the middle, Alex and Phillip made Roger a vice president at his old stomping ground, Spaulding Enterprises. Roger also expressed an interest in purchasing WSPR, but Ross and Holly became partners and beat him to it. Roger and Alex continued to flirt, even though Alex was still confused about her feelings for Fletcher. After a brief involvement with Sonni, Roger realized Holly was still, and would always be, under his skin. He sparred with her, sweet-talked her, even jumped off a bridge to get her attention. Holly eventually showed signs of succumbing to Roger's charm and told a hopeful Blake that she was mellowing toward him.

When Alex went on an extended cruise, she appointed Vanessa as her surrogate at Spaulding. Vanessa was less than pleased to have Roger as an employee, because she and Henry had known Roger from when he was a cocky kid worming his way up the corporate ladder. Nonetheless, Vanessa approved Roger's latest project, Blakewood Towers, a middle-income housing project to be built in an abandoned factory. Vanessa assigned the engineering duties to Gary Swanson, an ambitious Spaulding golden boy who had a past with Blake. Now a force to be reckoned with, Vanessa ordered Gary to keep an eye on Roger and Blake, unaware that Gary was concealing dubious connections of his own.

Gary was surprised to see Neil Everest, a former Spaulding architect whom he had fired for incompetence. Neil was back in Springfield with a new friend, a young woman who had lost her memory and was stricken with aphasia, the trauma-induced inability to speak. Neil's companion was Beth! As Beth looked around Springfield, places and people began to appear familiar to her. Trying to piece together her memories, she went to the country club stables, where she encountered Bradley. Overcome with emotion upon seeing his former stepdaughter alive, Bradley apologized for the horrible things he'd done to her and Phillip. Suddenly

It was a miracle for Phillip and for everyone who loved her when Beth turned up alive. She had lost her memory and was suffering from aphasia, and her traveling companion was the questionable architect Neil Everest.

When Hampton Speakes retired from the NFL, he came to Springfield to join his football buddy, Billy Lewis. Together they opened a country-western bar and called it Heartbreaker's after—who else?— Reva Shayne Lewis, now Billy's brother's wife.

Beth had a memory flash of Bradley beating her, and she clubbed him with a shovel and ran out. Bradley was admitted to Cedars and informed Phillip and Lillian that Beth had attacked him. Lillian didn't believe him, but Phillip was convinced.

By now, Blake was livid about Phillip's obsession with his lost love, so she hit the sheets with Gary again. She was also appalled when Phillip rehired Neil. Suspicious of Neil, Blake went to his trailer and saw Beth! She was relieved to find that Beth didn't know her true identity. However, Vanessa discovered Blake had burned the coroner's report, and she told Phillip. Now

every bit her father's daughter, a vengeful Blake committed Phillip to Willow Hills Sanitarium for his "delusions" about Beth. Gary and Neil were pleased with this development—Gary, because Blake now had Phillip's power of attorney, and Neil, because the field was clear for him to marry Beth.

Then came the miracle. While Rick was visiting Phillip at Willow Hills, the two spotted Beth on the grounds! Beth had come to the institution for treatment. When Phillip approached her, she showed him a picture of Neil, which Phillip, of course, recognized. Shortly after, just as Beth was about to marry Neil,

Rick and Phillip crashed the ceremony and whisked her away! Beth eventually regained her memory and the ability to speak, and she and Bradley made amends.

It was at this time that Sonni caught on to Roger's modus operandi and decided she was through with people of his ilk. She divorced Josh and accepted a new psychiatric position in San Francisco. Finally free, Josh married the love of his life, Reva, at Cross Creek, with the Lewises and Billy's longtime friend, Hampton Speakes, in attendance. Hamp had come to Springfield and was pursuing Gilly Grant, Nadine's stage manager, who came from an upper-crust African-American family. Together Billy and Hamp opened a country-western bar called Heartbreaker's, a name inspired by Billy's ex-wife, his lifetime friend, his "Reva girl." Hamp and Reva shared a secret they had long kept from Billy: Reva had given birth to Billy's baby boy when the two were teenagers and had put the child up for adoption. All Reva could recall about the infant was that he had a tiny birthmark above one of his knees. Reva's mother, Sarah, had been by her side during this painful period of her life. Sarah and Hawk were now running Company as well as the adjoining boardinghouse they had purchased from the Reardon family. One of the Shaynes' boarders was a young drifter named Dylan, who had fathered a daughter of his own with Harley Cooper Spaulding. Dylan immediately clashed with Harley's rich husband, Alan-Michael, and slugged the arrogant young heir. Alan-Michael promptly had his attacker arrested, but Dylan was released to the custody of Billy, who took him under his wing. When Hawk and Sarah cleared out Dylan's room, Sarah found a tattered old blanket that their boarder had left behind. She had seen that blanket before—on Reva and Billy's baby boy!

As Hamp and the Shaynes wrestled with this discovery, Dylan made his mark in Springfield. Ross fumed when Dylan dated Sam and taught her how to do shots and guzzle beer. Dylan promised not to have sex with the underaged Sam and found it difficult to handle his and Harley's lingering mutual attraction. The ex-lovers became obsessed with their little girl, Daisy, who had been adopted by a couple named Lemay and renamed Susan. Without revealing he was Susan's father, Dylan got himself hired by the Lemays to do yardwork. He was relieved to see how happy Susan was with the Lemays and thought she should be allowed to stay with them. But Harley and Alan-Michael thought otherwise. They offered the Lemays a

fortune for the little girl. The horrified adoptive parents refused. A pouting Alan-Michael then squealed to the Lemays that their yardboy was Susan's biological father. Harley was furious with Alan-Michael and set out to take him to the cleaners in a messy divorce. Still unaware that he was Susan's grandfather, Billy ordered Dylan to write a letter of apology to the Lemays. When Dylan sat down to try to compose the note, Sarah realized that Dylan couldn't write.

As Sarah grappled with her secret about Dylan, Reva and Josh were now expecting their own baby boy. But Reva was plagued by memories of her first child and grew distant with Josh. Ironically, she became closer to Billy, who hired her to sing at Heartbreaker's. Soon Reva's recurring heart condition flared up under the pressure, and she told Billy the truth about the child she had by him. Billy then admitted to Reva that he had fallen for her all over again but refused to pursue her out of respect for Josh.

Coincidentally, Dylan told Samantha he had been raised by adoptive parents in Tulsa. His mother was now dead, and his father, Cody, was a hateful person. Determined to learn his origins, Dylan stole cash from Company's register and headed to Tulsa with Samantha. Cody, meanwhile, knew what Dylan wanted and blackmailed Reva for hush money. Reva had not yet made the connection that Dylan was the son she had given up. Josh sensed Reva's torment and became fearful for both her and their baby's health, so Reva finally confessed to Josh that she had given birth to a little boy when she was a teenager. However, she left Billy's name out of the scenario, implying that the child was the result of a rape. Reva and Josh went to Tulsa, where Josh confronted Cody and threatened him. A sniveling Cody told Josh that Dylan was Reva's son. Later Reva accidentally hit Dylan with her car and saw the birthmark above his knee. Back in Springfield, Reva told Dylan that she was his mother, and he reacted cautiously to the news.

Hoping to shore up his failing marriage to Harley, Alan-Michael kidnapped Susan from the Lemays. Harley bravely returned her, and Alan-Michael was sentenced to community service. Harley and Dylan finally gave in to their sexual urges, but she was hurt to learn that Dylan was really in love with Samantha. Vanessa upbraided Billy for being more attentive to Dylan than to little Billy and began to notice a resemblance between Billy and Dylan. Vanessa and Josh finally guessed that Billy was Dylan's father, and Josh

ISSUES: ADOPTION

When they were teenagers, Dylan Shayne Lewis and Harley Cooper Spaulding had a baby. Harley gave the child up for adoption and then became obsessed with getting her back. Eventually Dylan and Harley realized that little Daisy, now called Susan, was better off with her adoptive parents.

bitterly confronted Reva. Marah and little Billy overheard the argument and ran away. Dylan located them and brought them safely home. Little Billy blurted out to Dylan that they were brothers. A newly mature Dylan proudly took the name of Dylan Shayne Lewis. Josh forgave both Reva and Billy, and Vanessa and Billy got back together.

A new complication arose in Vanessa and Billy's roller-coaster relationship when they found themselves on opposite sides of a Saudi Arabian business alliance that both Spaulding Enterprises and Lewis Oil were competing for. Billy became obsessed with getting the better of Roger, who was representing Spaulding in the negotiations. In Billy, Roger was about to find a powerful new adversary, one who was determined to put him in his place.

1990

The year 1990 ushered in a moment of truth for Phillip and Beth, surprising new romances for Josh and Alan-Michael and an escalation in the antagonism between Roger and Billy.

Although Beth tried to explain otherwise, Phillip was convinced that Neil had been involved in Beth's kidnapping and fired him from Spaulding. Determined to prove his innocence, Neil helped Beth relive her kidnapping at the hands of Professor Blackburn. Beth recalled killing Blackburn when he tried to attack her, and she realized her aphasia stemmed from her lack of guilt over his death.

Neil's past also came to light when he told the Spaulding board that the company had previously fired him after a building he'd designed collapsed and killed his wife and stepchildren. Neil was able to prove that the collapse was due not to his design, but to the faulty materials Spaulding had purchased. Grateful to Neil for helping Beth, Phillip voted for him to be reinstated. Anxious to have a future with Beth, Phillip ended his

TROUBLED TRIANGLES

Phillip was married to Blake when Beth miraculously returned to Springfield, but Blake had no intention of letting the Spaulding heir off easy.

calamitous marriage to Blake. Alan-Michael comforted Blake, which led to a kiss, but Gary intervened before it went any further. Because of his growing attraction to Blake and her lingering feelings for Dylan, Alan-Michael and Harley decided to divorce. Harley thought she could take Alan-Michael for a fortune but learned she didn't have a case unless Alan-Michael was unfaithful. Alan-Michael ended up in Blake's bed, and when Harley found out, she went to Blake's and set up a videocamera. Alan-Michael caught her just as she was leaving, and she promptly seduced him to shut him up. Afterward, neither would admit he or she still loved the other, although Alan-Michael did confess to Ed that he loved Harley.

Alan-Michael wasn't the only man sleeping with Blake. She bedded Gary after he accused her of fooling around with Alan-Michael. She convinced Gary to spy on Phillip and Beth for her, hoping to get evidence of Phillip's unfaithfulness. A devious Gary agreed, then tried to score points with Phillip by telling him Blake was having an affair. Despite her extracurricular activities with both Gary and Alan-Michael, Blake vehemently refused when Beth asked her to give Phillip an amicable divorce. Phillip asked Beth to marry him anyway. Not wanting to rush into anything, Beth said no, but their feelings ran deep and they made love. Beth kept working on Blake to let Phillip go. One day she collapsed and was shocked to learn she was pregnant! Beth assumed the baby was Neil's and told Phillip, who suggested they pass the child off as his. Unaware that the baby really was Phillip's, Beth decided to be honest with Neil, but Blake told Neil before Beth could. A furious Neil refused to allow Phillip to raise his child. Beth was ecstatic when a sonogram revealed her child had been conceived in February, not December, which meant the child was Phillip's.

Neil learned Gary was the one responsible for the collapse of the building that killed his family, but because he was so devastated that he was not the father of Beth's baby, he was vulnerable to Gary's suggestion that they join forces to bring down the Spauldings. Blake refused his proposal, determined to get Alan-Michael to marry her. However, Alan-Michael wanted nothing to do with her after discovering that Blake had had Phillip committed even though she'd known Phillip was right about Beth being alive. Trying to get back on Alan-Michael's good side, Blake agreed to give Phillip a divorce, no strings attached. Roger warned her about crossing Gary, but Blake thought she could keep him under control by blackmailing him about the building collapse. A clever Gary tricked her into destroying the evidence of his misdeeds.

Thanks to her hidden camera, Harley learned that Blake was Alan-Michael's mistress, but when she tried to blackmail Alan-Michael, the tape vanished. A worried Blake realized Gary had taken it. Harley and Alan-Michael considered a reconciliation when Harley suspected she might be pregnant, but went through with the divorce after the test came back negative. Blake, on the other hand, got a positive test result. Not knowing Blake had doctored her pregnancy test, Alan-Michael proposed. Upon learning of Blake's engagement, a furious Gary considered letting Blake die in the explosion that he and Neil were arranging for the opening of the Blakewood Towers, but he changed his mind after the videotape showed that she had doctored her pregnancy test. Gary rushed to the Towers, got Blake to safety and declared his love for her. Beth went to the Towers after she learned Phillip was planning to meet Neil there. Neil kissed her to scare her off. When Phillip showed up, Neil knocked him out and left him to die. A double-crossing Gary confronted Neil and pushed him down a flight of stairs, then carried Phillip to safety, leaving Neil to perish in the explosion. The last thing Neil said before he died was "Phillip." This, coupled with the threats Phillip had made against Neil's life, was enough to get Phillip arrested for Neil's murder. Gary took over Phillip's position as vice president of Spaulding. His luck did not hold out, however. Believing he was behind Alan-Michael's kidnapping during their honeymoon in Costa Verde, Blake shot him. Gary decided to hold the shooting over Blake's head rather than turn her in to the police. Holly and Roger shared a tender moment after they flew to Costa Verde to comfort Blake and rescue Alan-Michael. Blake later faked a miscarriage.

Phillip decided to stage his own death to buy some time to prove his innocence. Rick agreed to help, and the two friends stole a corpse from the Cedars morgue. After resigning from Spaulding, Phillip faked a drunken scene and raced off in his car, which moments later crashed and burned. Phillip's plans were thwarted, though, when he stopped to help a woman stranded on the side of the road and discovered it was his ex-wife, India!

At this time an enterprising young cop named A.C. Mallet showed up in Springfield posing as a writer interested in Phillip's life, and encouraged a distraught Mindy to open up to him. Rick got nervous when Mallet started questioning Phillip's autopsy. Rick then

India surprised Rick and Beth when she showed up in Springfield, knowing everything about their scheme to fake Phillip's death.

proposed to Mindy, unaware that she was seeing another man—Roger Thorpe! Mindy turned him down, but Rick still warned Mallet to watch his step around the vulnerable Mindy. Mallet learned from Mindy that Beth was going to Paris to forget the pain of Phillip's death and followed her. He was foiled when Beth became ill and had to get off the plane. India was having fun torturing Phillip by threatening to reveal that he was alive. Phillip tried to drug India but inadvertently ingested the drug instead. Realizing she was on to him, Phillip agreed to give India his Spaulding stock if she agreed to go to Springfield to check on Beth. On her way, India met up with Gary, and they hit it off. When India got to town, she informed Roger that she was Phillip's heir and visited a surprised Beth.

Following an encounter with Mallet, Roger found his phone bugged and warned Rick and Beth that Mallet was a cop. Roger also gave Alex proof that Phillip was alive. Mindy found out that Mallet was a cop just as he discovered from his phone tap that she was sleeping with Roger. Unaware that Mallet was listening,

Gary threatened Blake over the phone, thinking she had tipped off the police about his connection to Neil's murder. As Mallet got closer to the truth about Phillip, Rick got closer to Beth. One night after her Lamaze class they shared a kiss. Mindy decided Rick was the man for her after all and rushed to profess her love. She was devastated when he announced that he had married Beth, unaware that they'd only done it to throw Mallet off track. Mindy turned to Mallet for comfort.

Unable to get ahold of India and desperate for information about Beth, Phillip returned to Springfield and heard the news of Beth and Rick's marriage. He revealed himself to Beth and was understanding when she explained why she'd wed his best friend. Rick agreed to allow Phillip to be present at the baby's delivery. Convinced she had a future with Mallet, Mindy tried unsuccessfully to end her relationship with Roger. Meanwhile, Mallet was busy trying to prove that Phillip was alive and back in Springfield.

While hiding out at India's, Phillip overheard Gary send a threatening telegram to Blake. Ross learned of the telegram and questioned Blake about her relationship with Gary. Alan-Michael, Ross and Samantha then began to piece together Gary's involvement in Neil's murder, as well as Blake's involvement with Gary.

When India insisted on being appointed a Spaulding vice president, Alex had no choice but to comply when she learned that India was helping Phillip. Gary discovered Phillip was still alive and ordered a hit on him, but Phillip managed to escape. Mindy warned Beth that Mallet was on to her. As Mallet questioned Beth, she went into labor. A frantic Mallet tried to drive her to the hospital in a raging snowstorm, but the car slid off the road into a ditch. Mallet carried her to the hospital right before she delivered a daughter, Elizabeth (Lizzie) Spaulding. Phillip realized that Rick had fallen in love with Beth. Mallet caught Phillip visiting Beth and Lizzie and had him arrested.

The brakes failed on Alan-Michael's car, nearly killing him, and a vengeful Blake went after Gary with a gun. Alan-Michael secretly followed her and was accidentally shot instead, while Gary fled undetected. With Alan-Michael in a coma, Blake was arrested for attempted murder and put into a psychiatric ward for observation. Posing as a cop, Gary got her out and took her to an abandoned warehouse. Soon Roger got a call from Gary demanding $4 million for Blake's return. Alan-Michael came out of his coma and said that Blake had shot him accidentally. He fled the hospital and went with Mallet to rescue Blake. A spiteful Gary revealed to Alan-Michael that Blake had faked her pregnancy. India posted Gary's bail, but he was "kidnapped" on his way to freedom by Mallet and Roger, who forced him to confess what really happened the night of the Towers explosion. With the truth finally out, Phillip was released.

Fed up with her games and lies, Alan-Michael told Blake their marriage was over. Rick's career looked to be over, too, as he faced charges for stealing the corpse and was sus-

pended from practicing medicine pending a criminal investigation. Despite all their personal and legal troubles, Phillip and Beth asked Rick to be Lizzie's godfather.

Chelsea and Johnny were almost as troubled as Phillip and Beth, thanks to the obsessed fan who continued to stalk Chelsea. Frank tried to trace the

DASTARDLY DEEDS

Chelsea had no idea that the dangerous fan stalking her was actually her old roommate and best friend, Rae Rooney

threatening calls, but the fan remained one step ahead of him. Johnny and Chelsea came home one night to find their bedroom ransacked and her engagement ring missing. Dana looked guilty when the ring fell out of her clothes and Nadine secretly saw her imitating Chelsea. After a scary encounter with the fan in a gazebo, Chelsea asked her old roommate Rae if she could borrow her gun. Johnny was furious when he found the weapon and took it away from her. Johnny and Chelsea proceeded with their plans for a Valentine's Day wedding, but Chelsea collapsed before they could say "I do." She'd been poisoned. To protect Chelsea, Johnny broke up with her. Frank suspected that Dana might be the culprit but asked her to marry him anyway. Nadine couldn't stand the thought of Frank marrying a woman who might be a criminal, and she went to the police. When she saw that Frank believed the accusations against her, Dana broke up with him. Later, after Chelsea was attacked in her car, Dana was arrested. Thinking their ordeal was over, Johnny and Chelsea got engaged again. Meanwhile, an unknown person posted Dana's bail. Dana went to WSPR, saw Rae setting a trap for Chelsea and realized Rae was the demented fan. Rae shot Dana, who slipped into a coma. When Dana started to recover, Rae paid her a visit. Upon awakening and seeing Rae, Dana went into shock and died.

HEROIC DEEDS

Volunteer firefighter Alan-Michael helped Dylan, Harley and Sam escape when Harley's store went up in flames. Harley's grandfather, Pops, perished in the fire.

Rae's reason for wanting to hurt Chelsea was revealed when she went to see her brother, Bobby, in a mental institution. Rae blamed Chelsea for Bobby's condition because Chelsea had not returned his love for her. Soon after, Bobby killed himself, strengthening Rae's resolve. Johnny, Rick and Frank showed up just as Rae was about to shoot Chelsea, and Rae was arrested. The path was finally clear for Johnny and Chelsea to wed. However, Johnny learned that Roxie Shayne, his former girlfriend, was making progress in her psychiatric treatments and was being transferred to Chicago. Realizing Johnny was still in love with Roxie, Chelsea called off the engagement and Johnny left for Chicago. Chelsea eventually accepted an offer from Jackson Freemont to go to London to pursue her singing career.

Roger Thorpe had plans to take over Spaulding Enterprises and launch a massive development project on Fifth Street. He hired a henchman named Scully to buy up the property. Harley was a holdout, so Scully tied her up and set fire to her store. The blaze spread quickly to nearby homes. Sam got trapped trying to help Harley, and Dylan (who was doing community service as a volunteer fireman with Alan-Michael) rescued both of them. He also tried to rescue Harley's grandfather but was overcome by smoke. Alan-Michael rescued Dylan, but sadly Pops died. Dylan got Lewis Oil to agree to fund a shelter for the victims of Fifth Street in memory of Pops. Fletcher was determined to prove Roger was behind the fire and caught him with Scully. When Scully pulled a gun on Fletcher, Roger shot Scully. Before he died, Scully confessed to setting the fire but refused to implicate Roger. Alex questioned Roger's involvement with Scully but defended him to the police. She then told her nephew that she was in love with the nefarious Thorpe.

Alex wasn't the only one Roger was using to get to Spaulding. After losing his Spaulding stock to Roger in a poker game, Henry planned to commit suicide and left a goodbye note for Vanessa. Fortunately, Vanessa and Billy found him in time and gave him the will to live. Complicating Roger's pursuit of Spaulding were his lingering feelings for Holly. Now lovers, Holly and Ross discovered Roger owned half of WSPR, and Holly suspected he'd bought it so he would have an excuse to be near her. To prove her theory, Holly played up to Roger, but when he tried to kiss her, she exploded. Ross couldn't figure out which was stronger—Holly's hate for Roger, or her love for Ross.

Roger got Alex to agree to go away with him and shocked her with a proposal. They then negotiated an intricate prenuptial agreement. Upon Alex's return, Fletcher proposed and was shocked to learn she was now married to Roger! She then tried to buy Fletcher out of the *Journal* so they wouldn't have to work together. Meanwhile, Roger hired Blake to promote his new image for Fifth Street. He also gave Nadine the money she wanted to turn her diner into a bistro in exchange for stealing the Lewis Shelter blueprints from Billy. Roger set a trap for Vanessa to see if she would betray Spaulding to help Billy, and Vanessa fell right into it, leading Roger to fire her. Phillip sided with the Lewis family at the zoning board meeting where Roger, Blake and the Lewises battled it out.

Billy didn't realize he had the key to bringing down Roger right under his nose. His housekeeper, Ruth, who had been left homeless by the fire, had a deed that proved she owned the land on which Spaulding had built the Towers. After suffering a heart attack, she ended up at Roger's apartment, where she died. Billy was unable to find the deed, which Reva later found. Vanessa learned Reva had the deed and gave it to Billy. Billy tricked Roger into burning the pictures by making him think the envelope contained the deed. Alex was stunned when Billy flashed the deed and announced that he was the owner of the Towers! After she learned of his actions with Ruth, Alex started regretting her marriage to Roger. Per their prenuptial agreement, adultery was the only way to get out of her marriage without having to give Roger control of Spaulding, so Alex asked Holly to seduce Roger for her. But Roger was already committing adultery—with Mindy! Holly convinced Roger to go to a convention in Acapulco. Once there, Holly began to seduce him. Alex learned of Holly's situation and insisted to Ross that the two of them go to Acapulco. Holly panicked when her seduction of Roger brought back memories of his rape of her. Alex and Ross burst in only to find Holly and Roger laughing and having a good time. They had finally come to terms with the rape and were enjoying each other's company. Later, a disgusted Ross broke off with Holly and told Roger how Holly and Alex had tried to set him up. A furious Roger told Mindy he wanted to marry her, but Alex didn't want to lose too much of Spaulding and refused to let him go.

Billy and Vanessa decided to remarry, but the night before the wedding Billy fell off the wagon and woke up next to Nadine. Not knowing the reason for his absence, Vanessa agreed to postpone the wedding. Ed called Billy on his drinking, but Billy insisted it was a one-time slip. It wasn't—nor was Nadine. Little Billy saw his dad with Nadine, and Billy convinced him to lie to his mother. Billy couldn't choose between Vanessa and Nadine and continued his relationship with both, although his real love was the bottle. Vanessa finally broke off with Billy, and H.B. and Josh stripped him of his power at Lewis Oil.

Josh had much more to worry about than Billy's drinking. A car accident almost stopped him from attending the birth of his and Reva's baby at Cross Creek, but he arrived just in time to help deliver his son, Joshua Shayne Lewis. Reva soon started acting strangely, going on shopping sprees and leaving the

ON LOCATION

As Josh watched in horror, Reva drove off a bridge and into the murky waters of the Florida Keys. Her last words were "I'm coming, Bud!"

however, when she got a letter from her father, Dr. Justin Marler, now working in India. Justin wanted her to attend Harvard in the fall. Sam decided to get married anyway, and a manic Reva helped the couple plan their elopement. Harley learned of their plans and told Ross, and Ross, Billy and Josh caught Dylan and Sam en route and dragged them back to Springfield. Samantha went to India to get her father's permission to marry Dylan, and Reva impulsively went with her. Justin refused to give his blessing when he learned of Dylan's police record and returned to Springfield to keep an eye on his daughter. His colleague, Dr. Daniel St. John, joined him, telling no one that he was treating Justin for a potentially fatal case of malaria.

At a party to welcome Justin, it became obvious that something was very wrong with Reva. She made a fool of herself with her flirtatious behavior and embarrassed Josh with her jealousy of him and Vanessa. Ed diagnosed Reva as having a severe

baby unattended. When Reva hired Harley to help her take care of the kids, Harley was glad for the distraction now that she had divorced Alan-Michael and Dylan had chosen Sam over her. Ross disapproved of Sam moving in with Dylan, so the young lovers decided to get married. Samantha had second thoughts, case of postpartum depression and gave her medication, but a paranoid Reva didn't want to take it. Her condition became worse, and she started getting promiscuous. One night she even picked up Roger! Roger took provocative photos of her and tried to use them to blackmail her, but Billy stopped him. Josh decided a

On Location

Before she went off the bridge, Reva pushed Dylan out of the car. Fearing for her life, Sam jumped out of the car, too. The injury left her paralyzed.

vacation might be just what Reva needed, so the family headed to the Florida Keys with Harley, Dylan and Samantha. Reva had a seizure and collapsed on the beach. After recovering, she went on a shopping spree and bought everything in red. Later, hearing strange voices in her head, Reva drove off with Sam and Dylan. She stopped and forced Dylan out, then tore off with Sam. Sam jumped from the speeding car only moments before Reva drove through a barricade and off an unfinished bridge into the water below as Josh watched in horror. He dove into the water, but neither he nor the Coast Guard was able to find her.

It was left to Harley to talk to Marah about Reva, death and heaven when a devastated Josh retreated into himself. Unable to face the reality of losing Reva, Josh fired Harley for talking about Reva's death. However, he soon asked her to return. Sam was left paralyzed by her jump from Reva's car. After her doctors told her the operation to reverse her paralysis could cost her her life, she decided to forgo surgery and face life in a wheelchair. Dylan assured Justin he would stick by Sam, and at a surprise party for Sam's eighteenth birthday he gave her an engagement ring. Depressed about being wheelchair bound, Sam told Dylan she couldn't marry him. Dylan left town in frustration, while Daniel St. John comforted Sam. Daniel and Sam grew closer when he found a cure for Justin's malaria. Daniel bought Samantha a sophisticated stand-up wheelchair with his own money, and later the two shared a romantic dance. Ed noticed that Daniel's interest in Samantha had gone beyond a professional one and chastised him for it. Sam was hurt when she later saw Daniel out with another woman.

When Josh accidentally called her Reva, Harley was understanding but continued to try to get Josh to accept Reva's death. Meanwhile, Marah grew more and more attached to Harley. Harley decided to take matters into her own hands by throwing Reva's clothes out the window and setting them on fire. Josh was furious, and their confrontation led to a heated kiss, followed by wild lovemaking. Harley thought Josh had only made love to her because he thought she was Reva, so she moved out. But Josh told Harley it was her he wanted and convinced her to come back. A frustrated Harley finally decided to leave Josh for good and talked Mindy into giving her a job selling Mindy's fashion line. Harley flew to New York to meet with famous designer Matt Weiss. Josh tracked her down, and they made love again. When Mindy saw one of her designs in Matt Weiss' new line, she accused Harley of selling her out and fired her. Harley followed Matt to a Chanukah celebration at his grandparents' house and confronted him about the theft, but she got snowed in and was unable to return home, where Josh was waiting with an engagement ring. Harley was stunned when Josh surprised her in New York and proposed, and she agreed to be his wife.

1991

After Gary blabbed that Blake had faked her pregnancy, Alan-Michael left her in disgust. But later, as they recalled happier times while finalizing their divorce, Blake and Alan-Michael patched things up between them, and Blake decided not to take any money from him.

D.A. Lisa Dravecky brought charges against Phillip, Beth and Rick for faking Phillip's death. She offered to get Rick's suspension reversed in exchange for his testimony against Phillip. Rick agreed, but when he was on the stand, he remembered their longtime friendship and instead pleaded guilty. Phillip, Beth and Rick were sentenced to community service to be served outside of Springfield. Rick left for Chicago, and after their Valentine's Day wedding, Phillip and Beth packed up Lizzie and headed for Arizona to serve out their sentences.

Holly and Blake rented Reva Bend together. She had hoped Ross would eventually move in, too, and was hurt when he said he needed a clean break. Sam and Dylan's relationship was headed for trouble as well, thanks to her growing feelings for Daniel. She asked Daniel to perform the surgery that would help her walk again, but he didn't think she was ready. Dylan changed Daniel's mind, and Daniel told Sam that the operation was technically a success, but he wasn't sure whether she would walk again. Sam continued to be confused over her feelings for Daniel and became upset when Dylan confronted her about it. After Sam took her first steps, Daniel decided to drop her case, which only made the troubled teen more emotional. Dylan broke up with her and Justin moved back to India, so Sam was left all alone. As it turned out, Daniel was more interested in Holly, and the two became lovers. Blake felt their relationship was a conflict of interest, since Holly was producing a story on Daniel's neurorobotics project in conjunction with Spaulding, and told her mother that Daniel was using her for the publicity. Sam overheard Holly blurt out to Ross that she was seeing Daniel. Sam began to dig into Daniel's past, hoping it would bring them closer, but he told her to butt out. Ed began to wonder about some discrepancies on Daniel's résumé. Roger was also suspicious and tracked down Daniel's former sister-in-law, Jean Weatherill.

Holly was left to deal with Roger at WSPR when Ross accepted an offer to become district attorney. When Fletcher offered Holly an exclusive on Roger's dirty dealings, both relished the idea of Roger's own station funding Fletcher's investigation. Daniel jumped in and wanted to get a loan to help Holly buy Ross' shares of the station. Ed ended up floating him the loan, infuriating Maureen, whose brother had also asked Ed for money but was turned down. Roger learned from Jean that Daniel had killed her sister, who had been married to St. John. Soon after, Daniel started getting crank phone calls and told Holly he thought it was Sam. He was shocked to find out it was Jean. Jean then began stalking Daniel and Holly, while Daniel campaigned to be promoted to head of neurology at Cedars and tried to make peace with Sam. He also tried to get Holly to speak to Ed about the promotion and even told an insecure Maureen that he would marry Holly if his future were more secure.

Meanwhile, Ross' assistant, Suzanne, sold Holly on doing a show about solving crimes. Holly was unaware that Roger had Suzanne set this up in hopes of exposing Daniel. Roger couldn't get Holly to listen to his warnings about Daniel. Daniel figured out that Jean was working with Thorpe. Ed reprimanded Daniel when his preoccupation with Jean led to his slacking off at work, but Daniel was promoted anyway. Blake made Daniel think Holly still wanted Roger, which Daniel began to believe after seeing Holly come out of Roger's apartment. Blake got scared when she witnessed Daniel's temper and tried to talk to Holly about it, to no avail. Just before Jean was about to accuse Daniel of her sister's death, Daniel set off the fire alarm at WSPR, preventing Holly from learning about his past. Daniel threatened Roger, and Roger vowed to protect Holly no matter what, even if it meant killing Daniel. Holly was unnerved when she and Roger got locked in the basement together at WSPR, but she soon realized he was not the monster he used to be. However, she began to wonder about Daniel, who went into a jealous rage when he found them together.

DASTARDLY DEEDS

Daniel St. John seemed like a fine, upstanding doctor when he accepted his promotion to head of neurology at Cedars. Later his sister-in-law, Jean Weatherill, was found floating in the country club pool. If you look closely at this picture, you can see the murder weapon.

Jean told Roger that she planned to take Daniel down during a party to celebrate his promotion, and Roger warned her not to reveal his part in it. Daniel got a gullible Sam to intercept Jean before she incriminated him. A disappointed Jean decided to punish Daniel by killing Holly. When Roger found out, he threatened Jean. A short time later, Blake saw Jean floating face down in the country club pool. After Jean's death, Sam caught Daniel in a lie about his sister-in-law. She shared the information with Harley, and the two started their own investigation. Holly and Gilly were suspicious when the tape of Jean's appearance on WSPR disappeared. Although the police thought Jean's murder was an accident, Mallet kept the investigation open.

Roger agreed to Alex's request to try to start their relationship over, but he couldn't get Mindy out of his mind, and he convinced Mindy that they would someday marry. At the same time, Holly remained a big part of Roger's life due to his partnership with her and Ross in WSPR. Roger tried to get the upper hand with Holly by threatening to tell Blake about the Acapulco incident. Fed up with the Roger/Holly animosity, Ross tried to get out of the station but refused to sell his shares to Roger. An angry Roger launched a series of personal attacks against Ross.

A man named Peter Jessup presented Ross with ammunition against Roger: Jessup's grandson, Hart, was Roger's son! Unaware of this, Roger and his henchman, Davis, were using a dummy corporation to trick Jessup out of his farm. Jessup suffered a heart attack after losing his beloved land, and Hart sold his prized horse to Alex to finance the trip to Ireland that his grandfather had always wanted to take. When he returned, he was devastated to find that his grandfather had passed away.

Roger and Mindy's affair was discovered when they got into a car accident, and Mallet, who had been hired by Alex to track down Roger, rescued them. Roger threatened to expose Mallet's mysterious past if he said anything to Alex. But Alex found out about the affair on her own, and a devastated Mindy miscarried the child she just learned she was carrying—it was a boy, and it was Roger's. Just then, Roger was informed by Hart Jessup that *he* was Roger's son! Alex told Mindy, and Mindy ended the relationship. Victory was bittersweet for Alex, because she also had to deal with the revelation that someone was embezzling from Spaulding.

Another surprise was about to threaten Alex's stability. While on business in New York, Mindy was shocked to see a man who was a dead ringer for Alex's late son, Lujack. Mindy discovered that the man was an investigative reporter named Nick McHenry. Intrigued when Mindy told him of his resemblance to someone she'd once known, Nick followed her to Springfield. Stunned upon seeing a picture of Lujack, Nick decided to stay in town. As he and Mindy grew closer, Nick saw an article on Lujack that Fletcher had written and went to him for answers. Fletcher knew Nick's parents, who were also journalists. At the airport, Alex fainted when she spotted Nick.

Alex was having a hard time deciding on a new president for Spaulding. She finally appointed Vanessa interim president and confronted Alan-Michael about Blake, saying he'd better lose her or forget about ever becoming president of Spaulding. Vanessa had left a letter for Alex from Nick, but Alan-Michael had found the letter and burned it. Alex wondered if Nick was really her son, especially after hearing that at the moment of Lujack's death, Nick had been suddenly overwhelmed by grief. Alex asked Nick if he was sure that Mary McHenry was his natural mother. An irritated Nick fired back, asking if she was sure Lujack was really her natural son. Mindy warned Nick that Alex wouldn't be satisfied until she owned him heart and soul. Sure enough, Alex offered Nick the *Springfield Journal*. He declined. He was planning to return to New York, but Alex secretly sabotaged his job there. Mindy resisted telling Alex that she planned to move to New York with Nick. Alex told her that if she didn't stay away from Nick, all her dirty little secrets would come out. Mindy told Alex she was leaving town, but when Alex heard where she was headed, she vowed to follow Mindy's every move. Mindy didn't tell Billy she was leaving. She went to the airport but just missed Nick's plane. When Nick got to New York and learned he no longer had a job thanks to Alex, he headed back to Springfield, where he found Mindy desperately trying to book a flight to be with him. The two went to the lighthouse and made love.

When Alex discovered Nick and Mindy had become lovers, she sought out Billy at the Blue Moon and told him and Nick and everyone else present about Mindy's affair with Roger. That was it for Fletcher—he washed his hands of Alex after her public display. Billy found Roger, beat him to a pulp and then told Mindy he was writing her off as his daughter.

Blake was shocked and insecure when she learned Hart was her brother. Attempting to earn Roger's respect, she unwittingly ended up causing his downfall

TROUBLED TRIANGLES

Mindy was stunned when she met Lujack look-alike Nick McHenry, and the two fell in love. Alex was sure he was her son and couldn't tolerate his affair with the woman who had helped break up her marriage to Roger.

when she inadvertently tipped off the Spauldings that Roger was embezzling from the company. Alex rebuffed his advances, and Roger realized she knew the truth. Hart heard about Roger's past from Ed, Holly and Ross, but Roger managed to whitewash all his crimes to Hart and vowed revenge against the threesome for almost costing him his son.

Roger asked Alex for a divorce and moved out, but Hart stayed on in the Spaulding stables, having been hired by Alex. Alex finally got her revenge on Roger by publicly roasting him in front of a large crowd at the country club. She got to keep almost everything in the divorce settlement, but she let Roger keep the farm and take credit for its return to Hart. Alex gave back everything else that Roger had stolen from her friends and family. Holly was enraged, though, when Alex allowed Roger to keep his shares in WSPR. Without Roger's support, Blake lost her job at Spaulding and set out to help Hart learn who had stolen his grandfather's farm, knowing it was Roger. She also helped Alan-Michael try to get the presidency of Spaulding, hoping he would give her her job back.

Vanessa insisted that Billy stay away from little Billy until he got his drinking under control. Nadine saw them together and moved out of Billy's house. Billy won Nadine back by vowing not to drink for 90 days. He was furious when he learned Josh and H.B. had brought Vanessa in as acting CEO at Lewis Oil, and he ran off with Nadine to Las Vegas. Henry convinced Vanessa to fight to get Billy back, but it was too late—Billy had married Nadine following a drunken winning streak in Vegas. Frank and Harley were stunned by the news, and Frank punched Billy out. Vanessa overheard Billy tell Frank that he had wanted to marry Nadine. But later Billy admitted to Ed that

he still loved Vanessa, while she told Henry she still loved Billy.

Vanessa learned it was Roger who had caused Mindy all her pain but kept the information from Billy at Mindy's request. She also discovered that Billy, who had been reinstated at Lewis Oil at her urging, had been cutting deals behind her back. After a confrontation with Vanessa and H.B., Billy ran off and Vanessa found him at Cross Creek. After pouring out her heart

When Billy left Vanessa and married Nadine on a drunken spree, Vanessa turned to Fletcher, and they had a brief affair.

Mallet, who had left New York after seeing his girlfriend Francesca die in an explosion, was stunned to find her alive and well in Springfield.

to him, they made love and were caught by Nadine. Nadine was devastated, but she and Billy later reconciled. An angry Vanessa left Lewis Oil and returned to Spaulding. Billy and Nadine bought Josh's house and remarried in a ceremony there. Vanessa began spending more time with Fletcher. Billy was upset when he was asked to present the Man of the Year award—which he'd strived to win—to Vanessa.

Josh and Harley planned to marry until Billy told Josh that he'd spotted Reva on a travel show about Italy. Sarah saw the same show and agreed it was Reva, but Josh refused to believe it. Billy had the shot of the woman on the video made into a photo and showed it

to Harley at her bridal shower. She was even more hurt when she later saw Josh watching the supposed video of Reva over and over again. Josh left town to search for Reva.

As Josh was leaving Springfield, Mallet was getting settled in by joining Frank in a private detective agency. Their first order of business was to retrieve Mindy's stolen design from Matt Weiss in New York. Being in New York had a strange effect on Mallet, and he began to have nightmares about his past. Mallet went to see the priest from his old church, who encouraged him to put his former life behind him. Back in Springfield, Mallet's cop friend, Levy, was arrested, and Mallet was certain that Levy had been framed. Levy had been investigating attorney Jeffrey Battles before his arrest. Fletcher told Frank of the role Battles had played in Roger's attempt to take the waterfront property from Billy, and he, Fletcher and Mallet decided to work together to nail Roger. Mallet also opened up to Frank about his past. They managed to clear Levy's name—and get Hamp a liquor license for the Blue Moon—by setting up a crooked poker game with Battles, who incriminated himself on tape.

Not knowing Mallet was in Springfield, his supposedly dead love, Francesca, arrived there to care for her sick aunt. Roger borrowed money from Francesca's father in exchange for tracking down Francesca's former love, one Anthony Camaletti. The truth was, A.C. Mallet was Anthony Camaletti, and Roger knew it. As a cop in New York, Mallet/Anthony had been trying to bring down a mobster named Marco when he fell in love with Marco's daughter, Francesca. He and Francesca decided to run away after Marco threatened to have Tony killed. Marco made Mallet believe Francesca had died in an explosion. When Mallet saw Francesca alive and well in Springfield, he wanted to renew their relationship, but she was convinced they couldn't have a future together. Roger exposed Mallet to Marco after Mallet and Levy arrested Davis, Roger's partner in the Jessup farm scam. Marco had Mallet beaten to a pulp, but he recovered. Francesca was ordered to marry a man named Giancarlo. Mallet tried to stop the wedding but was too late. As the newlyweds pulled away, a girl got out of a limo. She was Mallet's younger sister, Julie, who revealed that Marco had used her to force Francesca to marry Giancarlo. Mallet brought Julie back to Springfield, where she soon caught Hart's eye.

Mallet warned Roger that he'd pay for ruining Mallet's life. Ross asked Mallet to help him get the goods on some dirty politicians, and Mallet agreed when he learned it could bring down Roger. Meanwhile, Harley was going after dirty cops. She succeeded, impressing both Ross and Judge Collier. Harley decided to follow Judge Collier's suggestion that she become a cop. Mallet joined the Springfield police force, too, as a detective and immediately clashed with hot-headed Hart over Roger. Mallet forbade Julie to see Roger Thorpe's son and threatened to send her

back to New York. Julie and Hart decided to continue to meet in private.

Hutchins, one of the bad cops Harley had brought down, started following her and warned Battles to stop Harley from testifying at his trial. Hutchins also met with Mallet and told him that if he wanted to be part of the "in" group, he should take care of Harley. Harley was shocked to see Mallet with the crooked cop. Later Mallet unknowingly hit on a dolled-up Harley, and both of them were surprised by the mutual attraction. Thanks to Harley, Mallet was able to arrest Hutchins and his partners in crime.

Hart and Julie decided to run away together; however, they got only as far as the farm. As they were about to make love, Mallet and Harley showed up. Mallet was furious, but he allowed her to continue seeing Hart. Harley opened up to Mallet about the baby she'd had with Dylan, and their relationship grew more passionate.

Frank's love life looked like it was about to pick up, too, when his uncle Stavros wrote to say he was arriving soon with a wife for him. Frank turned down his uncle's offer, but Stavros tricked him into paying the passage for a beautiful Greek goddess named Eleni. Frank insisted Eleni work at the diner to pay him back. Catching on fast to American dating rituals, Eleni attempted to make Frank jealous of her and Dylan. After lack of business forced Frank to close his detective agency, Eleni encouraged him to focus on the diner, and the two grew closer. When Eleni planned an intimate dinner with Frank, he ended up having it with Blake. Alan-Michael took advantage of the incident and whisked Eleni away on the Spaulding yacht. Frank realized his mistake and wanted to make it up to Eleni. Without her knowledge, he raised money to hire an immigration lawyer. He also confessed his feelings for her to Mallet. Thinking Frank was dating Blake, Eleni continued to see Alan-Michael, but she backed off when he bought her an extravagant statue.

Upset over Alex's delay in naming the permanent head of Spaulding until after the new year, Alan-Michael allowed himself to be seduced by Blake. He lied to Eleni that he and Blake were just friends, but Blake told her differently. Even as he continued sleeping with Blake, Alan-Michael's feelings for Eleni were growing deeper. Eleni was given a three-month extension on her visa thanks to the lawyer Frank hired, but she thought Alan-Michael was her benefactor. Frank planned to show his love for Eleni by buying a house and fixing it up for them to live in once they were married.

Kat and Bridget became fast friends. Kat helped Bridget handle her psycho boyfriend, Elvis, and Bridget lent a hand in Kat's scheme to break up Gilly and Hamp.

Maureen learned of a new procedure that could finally enable her to have the child she so wanted, only to find that Ed didn't want another child. Ed finally changed his mind. Obstetrician Margaret Sedwick performed the operation and said Maureen and Ed had a one in three chance to conceive within the year. Their attempts to conceive were unsuccessful, however, and in her emotional state, Mo's jealousy over Holly resurfaced. When their continued attempts at conception failed, Maureen took a job as Vanessa's assistant to get her mind off the pain. She was also distracted by the arrival of her spitfire niece Bridget Reardon, who came to live with the Bauers for the summer. Bridget's boyfriend, Elvis, forced Bridget to give him the keys to the Bauer house, then spied on Ed to get the security code for the alarm system. While the Bauers were out celebrating Bridget's birthday, Dylan caught Elvis breaking into their home. Bridget developed a crush on Dylan. She wrote herself a threatening note from Elvis, hoping Dylan would help her. Unfortunately, Elvis began threatening Bridget and everyone around her for real. Hart rescued Bridget when Elvis tried to rape her. Mallet mistakenly thought Hart was the one who had

attacked Bridget and warned him to stay away from Bridget and Julie. Finally, Elvis kidnapped Bridget. After Hart rescued her again, Bridget told Ed and Maureen everything, and they agreed to let Bridget stay with them. Ed tricked Elvis into admitting his crimes, and he was arrested.

Bridget's scheming wasn't over, though. Kat came to live with Hamp and took an immediate dislike to Gilly. Bridget agreed to help Kat get rid of Gilly. The girls were shocked when they discovered Gilly had once worked for an escort service. Kat tried to blackmail Gilly with this information, and on the eve of their engagement party, Gilly told Hamp about Kat's blackmail attempt. An upset Kat took off and got into a car accident. Hamp blamed Gilly, and the two called off the engagement.

For the residents of Springfield, their lives were about to take some new twists and turns...

1992

TROUBLED TRIANGLES

Ed saw Lillian through a cancer scare after she discovered a lump in her breast. Their friendship turned into an affair, which led to the breakup of Ed's marriage and Maureen's eventual death.

The year started on an alarming note for Lillian Raines when she found a lump in her breast that turned out to be malignant. Lillian told her good friend Ed but no one else. Maureen noticed their closeness and thought they were having an affair. After the surgery to treat her cancer was successful, Lillian realized she was indeed attracted to Ed. During a citywide blackout, when they got trapped together in the parking garage of the Towers, Ed admitted that the feeling was mutual, and they shared a tender kiss. Lillian found another lump in her breast but was hesitant to confide in Ed this time. Ed found out anyway and was supportive. The biopsy revealed the lump was benign. Upon receiving the good news, Lillian impulsively kissed Ed, and things turned passionate. Ed refused to continue their affair because he did not want to divorce Maureen. An upset Lillian decided to leave town and penned a farewell letter to Ed, which fell behind the counter in Ed's kitchen. Ed talked Lillian into staying in Springfield, and they agreed to be just friends. Months later Maureen found Lillian's letter.

Alex hired Frank to track down her ex, Eric Luvonaczek, in Paris. Thrilled when Eric admitted that she had actually given birth to twins, Alex was convinced that Nick was her son. Nick refused to listen, even when Alex told him that the doctor named on his birth certificate had been treating his mother for depression, not a pregnancy. Nick declined to take a test to disprove he was Alex's son. Eric revealed that he had lied and that Alex really hadn't had twins, but he left a DNA sample at Cedars in case Nick ever wanted to have the test done.

Alex's world continued to fall apart when Nick proposed to Mindy, and Alex turned to Roger for help in breaking them up. He agreed to do so in exchange for her help in getting back his empire. Roger told Alex that the key to separating Nick and Mindy lay in Cambrai. Although no one believed Nick was her son, Alex made him her heir. Mindy found a picture of Nick's mother dated just a month before his birth, in which she was obviously not pregnant. Mindy quickly erased the date. When Nick decided to take the DNA test and get Alex

Nick was shocked to learn his presumed-dead love, Eve, was alive and married to his best friend, Paul. After Paul explained it was only a marriage of convenience, Nick and Eve were reunited.

off his back, Mindy broke into the computer at Cedars and changed the results. Roger discovered what she'd done and told Alex that the tests were wrong, but he didn't rat on Mindy.

Roger's next move was to go to Cambrai to look for Eve Guthrie, a woman from Nick's past whom Nick

Eve was married to Paul. Nick helped Eve rescue Paul, and Paul told Nick that Eve had only married him to try to save him from jail. Eve decided to return to Springfield and started working at Cedars.

Miffed that Roger hadn't stopped Nick and Mindy's wedding plans, Alex threatened to tell Hart that Roger

ISSUES: SEXUAL HARASSMENT

It was a brave move when Vanessa took business client Jack Kiley to court for attempted rape. An outraged Billy, still harboring feelings for her, punched Kiley out.

thought was dead. Roger found the beautiful young doctor hiding in a convent and offered to help her escape to Springfield. Eve ended up going to Springfield on her own. Nick was stunned when he saw Eve at the Blue Moon and ran straight into her arms. Roger made sure Mindy witnessed the ex-lovers' reunion. Eve told Nick she was trying to get his best friend, Paul, out of a political prison in Cambrai. Nick was shocked to learn that

Attempted Rape Trial Date Set

JACK KILEY

had swindled the Jessup farm away from his grandfather. Roger quieted her by telling her about Mindy changing the DNA results. He also arranged for Nick to be arrested on his way back from Cambrai so he wouldn't get home in time for the wedding. Alex then convinced Mindy that Nick had left her because he'd learned she'd tampered with his DNA test. Mindy left town. Nick arrived at the church to find Alex, who told him Mindy had changed the results of the test. Nick refused to believe it, but after he got a letter from Mindy in which she returned her engagement ring and admitted to changing the test, Nick finally acknowledged to Alex that she was his mother. She was elated until he said he couldn't forgive her for all she'd done.

In an attempt to keep Nick out of Spaulding, Alan-Michael told him that Roger and Alex were behind Mindy's departure. Nick decided to pursue a job in New York. Once again, Alex made sure he didn't get it. As Nick was trying to find his identity and put Mindy behind him, Eve was waiting patiently. She wanted a future with Nick but didn't want to hurt Paul. Paul gave Eve a divorce and his blessing to marry Nick. Meanwhile, Nick learned Mindy was in New York, but she left before he could talk to her. Nick put Eve off but rediscovered his feelings for her after seeing her with another man. Just as he and Eve were making love, Mindy called home.

Gilly and Hamp reconciled and decided to marry in April. Just before the wedding, Gilly got flowers from a mysterious man, who was also following her. Football players Gale Sayers, Harry Carson and Bart Oates were surprise guests at Hamp and Gilly's nuptials, as was singer Roberta Flack, who performed for Gilly as a wedding gift from Hamp. The mysterious man also attended the wedding and later showed up in their honeymoon suite. Gilly recognized him as her brother, David. Unaware of their relationship, Hamp was furious when he found David and Gilly horsing around on the bed. Even after he learned David's identity, Hamp had doubts, especially when Gilly and David refused to discuss David's past. Hamp learned David had a criminal record when David was arrested for stealing Ed's credit card. Gilly got him out by agreeing to take him in. Hamp was upset when he saw the sparks fly between Kat and David. Hamp attacked him after Kat accused David of betting that he could be the first to sleep with her, and David moved out. After Bridget set her straight, Kat realized how much she missed David. Kat moved out, and her battle with David over a room at the boardinghouse led to a kiss.

An illicit kiss with a client gave Vanessa quite a reputation and threatened her new position as president of Spaulding. Fletcher came to her rescue when one lecherous client, Jack Kiley, tried to rape her. Holly talked Vanessa into pressing charges. Billy did not take kindly to Jack's treatment of his ex and punched him out. A jealous Nadine leaked the story of Vanessa's attempted rape to a tabloid reporter, who began to harass Vanessa. Billy vowed to destroy the person who had tipped off the press, and Frank discovered it was Nadine. Alan-Michael also learned what Nadine had done and blackmailed her into giving him information on one of Billy's clients. At Jack's trial, Fletcher was forced to admit his feelings for Vanessa on the stand. When Nadine saw Billy's reaction to this declaration, she gave the tabloid reporter back the hidden camera he had given her to take pictures of the trial. Jack painted himself as the victim, and the trial ended with a hung jury. Hamp later got Jack's confession on video, forcing Jack to plead guilty, but to a lesser charge. Vanessa and Fletcher celebrated by making love. Billy learned Nadine was the one who'd tipped off the reporter, and he walked out on her. Billy noticed Fletcher in Vanessa's bedroom. Little Billy was just as unhappy as Billy about Vanessa's relationship with Fletcher and ran away. Vanessa and Billy grew closer during the search for him, and their excitement over finding the boy at Cross Creek led to a passionate kiss.

Nadine was determined to win Billy back, even after he served her with divorce papers, and decided a baby was just the way to do it. As Nadine was trying to figure out how to get pregnant, Bridget learned her one-night stand with a drunken Hart had left her expecting. Nadine talked Bridget into letting her take the baby so she could pass it off as hers and Billy's.

Tired of waiting for Vanessa to commit, Fletcher told her to meet him at the justice of the peace or they were through. Vanessa got into an accident on the way there, and Fletcher believed he'd been stood up. Even after he learned the truth, he decided to end things with Vanessa anyway, because she wasn't over Billy. When Vanessa informed Nadine that she was going to fight for Billy, Nadine countered with the news that she was pregnant. Billy wanted to move back in with Nadine after learning about the baby, but she refused, afraid he would discover her ruse. David began to suspect that something was wrong with Bridget, but she wouldn't open up to him. Nadine worried that David, not Hart, was the father of Bridget's child. Once her pregnancy became more noticeable, Bridget told Ed and Mo that she was going to Appalachia on a class trip, then secretly moved into Nadine's attic.

Julie had been all set to give up her virginity to Hart until she learned of his night with Bridget. She and Dylan started to get closer when they were trapped in an elevator during the Springfield blackout. Although Mallet gave Julie a talk about safe sex when he found condoms in her room, he was too preoccupied with solving the Jean Weatherill murder to get further involved. Roger thought Daniel was the murderer. Sam

TEENAGE TRIANGLES

Hart loved Julie, but a drunken roll in the hay with Bridget cost him his first love and left Bridget pregnant.

also thought Daniel was the culprit and begged Harley to help her prove it. Daniel pressed a reluctant Holly to set a wedding date. When Roger tried to talk her out of it, a defiant Holly told Daniel she'd marry him on Valentine's Day.

Ross wanted to pin Jean's murder on Roger and urged Mallet to find the murder weapon. Suzanne told Ross and Mallet that Roger had killed Jean and asked Ross to protect her from him. Mallet suspended Harley when she continued to work on the Weatherill case even after he told her not to. Harley didn't give up and found the murder weapon in Daniel's office. Harley had the lab test the soiled felt from the back of the nameplate on Daniel's desk and learned it matched Jean's blood. When she heard Holly and Daniel were planning to elope at the Bauer cabin, Harley followed to try to warn Holly. Daniel locked Harley in a root cellar and took Holly hostage. Mallet rescued Harley, who was suffering from

Murder Suspect Killed in Shootout — Fiancee Rescued Unharmed

In an ironic twist of fate, Roger saved Holly from her crazed fiancé, Daniel St. John, but Holly turned to Ross, not Roger, after the ordeal.

These steamy photos of Ross and Blake fell into Roger's hands. However, it was Holly, not Roger, who ended up using them to hurt Ross. When the pictures made front-page news, Ross knew his days in office were numbered.

hypothermia. As he lay in a sleeping bag with her to keep her warm, a delirious Harley said she was in love with him. Meanwhile, Roger, disguised as a minister, came to the cabin, armed with a pistol. Roger and Daniel struggled, and when Daniel tried to turn the gun on Holly, Roger shot and killed him. Roger thought a grateful Holly would come back to him, but once again she turned to Ross.

Angry because she thought her mother had cost her Alan-Michael, Blake decided to get back at Holly by seducing Ross. On the night of the blackout, Ross was stunned when a naked Blake came on to him. Ross resisted at first, but Blake wore him down. Ross quickly regretted his indiscretion. Blake was upset when he asked Holly to a charity dance instead of her because it would look better for his senatorial campaign, but that didn't keep her out of Ross' bed. When Holly showed up one morning to surprise Ross with breakfast, she was the one who got the surprise! Holly confronted

Blake and Blake ran off, but Ross tracked her down and apologized. Not realizing Ross was sleeping with his daughter, Roger had Gilly investigate the possibility that Ross had a secret lover. Gilly got her hands on photos of Blake and Ross together, and David accidentally left the photos on Roger's desk. Roger exploded when he saw them, but Blake claimed she had only seduced Ross to make him look bad. Blake told Ross that she was in love with him. Ross realized he felt the same way after he broke up a fight between Blake and Holly. He berated Holly for her treatment of Blake, then kissed Blake as Holly and Roger looked on. Roger felt betrayed and considered exposing the photos of her and Ross. Holly stumbled on the photos and took them to a tabloid.

The night before the election, Ross had an elaborate dream in which he was searching desperately for the one vote he needed to win, and none of the women in his life would give it to him. To test Blake, Roger let her know

On election eve, Ross had a surreal dream in which he needed one vote to win, and none of the women in his life would give it to him.

that there was evidence in Leo Flynn's office that could help Ross win the election. Blake took the bait and broke into Flynn's office. After Ross won the election, Roger showed him the tape of Blake's crime and threatened to make it public if Ross didn't become his pawn. Ross destroyed the tape. Holly was upset when Ross gave up his senatorial career for Blake. Blake tried to make amends with Holly, but Holly told her daughter she no longer loved her.

Harley saw Mallet being friendly with another woman, unaware that he was just trying to get Harley's job back for her. Mallet tracked her down and told her he loved her. Harley got more good news when she learned she'd passed the police exam. She and Mallet decided to celebrate with a vacation. At their hotel, they ran into a jewel thief named Jenna Bradshaw. Jenna hid a brooch in Mallet's luggage and followed him and Harley back to Springfield. Harley couldn't tell anyone that she had passed the exam because she was working undercover to catch Jenna. She took a job as Jenna's personal assistant. Thinking Harley was involved with Frank, Jenna told her she was attracted to Mallet. Frank learned about Harley's undercover work and her relationship with Mallet. Jenna started snooping around and found a police manual among Harley's possessions. She also learned from Nadine that Harley and Frank were siblings, not lovers, and that Mallet was a cop. Jenna went to the Spauldings' home to rob them. There she heard Roger and Alex plotting to break up Mindy and Nick. Jenna hid the stolen Spaulding jewels in Harley's bag, then tipped off a reporter. Despite Jenna's actions, Harley was officially sworn in as a cop. Instead of escaping when she had the chance during the blackout, Jenna stayed with Michelle in a stalled elevator. She was arrested, but after she blackmailed Alex by threatening to reveal that Alex had been responsible for Nick missing his wedding, Alex dropped the charges.

Jenna soon started receiving gifts from a mysterious benefactor, whom she learned was Roger. Roger encouraged Jenna to search for her father. He had a photo of a man in a car whom Jenna thought was her father. Henry recognized the man as Brandon Spaulding but didn't tell Jenna. Ross and Jenna learned the car had belonged to Henry. Jenna confronted Henry about whether he was really her father, and he said he was. A stunned Vanessa overheard, and Henry later told her that he'd lied to Jenna to protect Spaulding. Vanessa found it almost impossible to make nice with her new

"sister." Roger didn't believe Henry was Jenna's father, so Jenna broke up with him. Roger then uncovered proof that Jenna wasn't Henry's daughter and spitefully told Jenna.

Frank was nursing a heartbreak of his own after Alan-Michael stole Eleni away from him. In Paris searching for Eric, Frank called Eleni and told her he loved her. Alan-Michael agreed to fly Eleni to Paris to surprise Frank, then arranged for her to find another woman in Frank's bed. A devastated Eleni went back to Springfield but was detained at the airport by Immigration thanks to a tip from Blake. Alan-Michael came to Eleni's rescue by marrying her. Not knowing what Eleni had seen in Paris, Frank returned home and hurried to finish the house he was building for her. Imagine his surprise when he learned his true love was now Alan-Michael's wife! Eleni's family didn't consider her wedding valid since there was no church ceremony, so she married Alan-Michael again at the church in her family's village in Greece. Frank was convinced that he'd lost Eleni forever, but Blake refused to give up on Alan-Michael. She played up Eleni's feelings for Frank and pushed Alan-Michael to go after the Spaulding presidency.

To get Alex on her side, Blake told Alex that Roger had stolen Hart's grandfather's farm. Alex still ordered Blake to stay away from Alan-Michael. At the diner, Blake accidentally dropped Alan-Michael's folder containing information on Billy's clients. Frank attacked Alan-Michael after learning he'd blackmailed Nadine to get this confidential information. Eleni, who thought Blake had stolen the file, forced Alan-Michael to fire her. Frank saved Eleni and Stavros when they were caught in a fire at the diner, and during the blackout he joined Alan-Michael's search for a missing Eleni, whom they found trapped in the diner's freezer. Frank realized he could never compete with Alan-Michael's money and power, but he told Eleni he still loved her. She was grateful when he agreed not to interfere in her marriage, even though she knew she still had feelings for him, too. Meanwhile, Musette, the girl Alan-Michael had planted in Frank's bed in Paris, was threatening to come to Springfield. Her arrival was bad timing, because it came just as Alex agreed to give Alan-Michael control of a critical division of Spaulding. Alan-Michael hired a man named Pierre to get rid of Musette. Pierre planned to kill Musette with a car bomb, but not wanting anyone to be killed, Alan-Michael tipped off the police. The bomb went off anyway and both Musette and Mallet were hurt.

ISSUES

When an explosion left Mallet deaf, Harley got him a hearing-assistance dog named Xyla from Canine Companions for Independence. The dog helped Mallet communicate and made the public aware of this important service.

Mallet awoke from surgery unable to hear or to move his legs. Harley got Mallet a dog that was trained to help disabled people, but Mallet felt like a burden and decided to move out of the apartment she'd gotten for them. Harley talked him out of it, and they made love for the first time since the accident. As the two of them started talking about starting a family, Lillian learned that Mallet might be sterile. Mallet's hearing started to return, and he overheard Lillian and Ed discussing this possibility. Mallet had surgery to try to correct his sterility. Although it went well, Ed could not guarantee that he would be able to father children. Discouraged, Mallet ended his relationship with Harley. She finally learned the true story and assured him of her desire to be with him. The two reunited, and Mallet surprised her with his mother's engagement ring.

Things were not going as well for Alan-Michael and Eleni. Eve was suspicious after finding Alan-Michael at Musette's hospital bed, and Nick's investigation into the car bombing linked Musette to Spaulding. Stavros gave Frank a letter from Musette detailing how Alan-Michael had used her to break up Frank and Eleni. Frank confronted Alan-Michael but didn't show Eleni the letter after seeing that she really loved Alan-Michael. Knowing Eleni would never leave him if she was pregnant, Alan-Michael switched her birth control pills with placebos. Eleni eventually found Musette's letter. Devastated, she made love with

Frank. She was ready to end her marriage to Alan-Michael when she learned her mother had suffered a stroke. She rushed to Greece, and Alan-Michael followed. Zoned out on sleeping pills, Eleni slept with her husband, but the next day said she needed some time alone. She went to a remote island, where Frank tracked her down, and the pair made love again.

A tip from Henry led Nick to believe that Alan-Michael could have been behind the bombing. He revealed this to Harley, who told Mallet. Eleni tried once again to end her marriage but learned she was pregnant. Frank thought the child was Alan-Michael's and told Eleni he would raise the baby as his if she left Springfield with him. Before they could go, Alan-Michael learned of Eleni's condition. Afraid of losing the child, Eleni decided not to go through with the divorce.

Pierre showed up in Springfield again, and Alan-Michael hid him in the Spaulding stables. Nick planted a bug at the Spaulding mansion to get evidence implicating Alan-Michael in the bombing. When Harley came to the stables looking for more evidence, Pierre took her hostage. Nick and Mallet overheard Alan-Michael arrange to meet Pierre at the airport. They followed him, and the three teamed up to save Harley. Because of Alan-Michael's heroism, Harley, Mallet and Nick decided not to tell Eleni of his role in the bombing. Eleni discovered the truth anyway and went running into Frank's open arms.

1993

After finding Lillian's letter to Ed, Maureen had an emotional confrontation with her, then went to the Bauer cabin. When Ed came looking for her, Maureen fled and got into a serious car accident on the icy road. Ed was anguished when his colleagues couldn't save her. A guilty Lillian tried to comfort him, but Vanessa—who had already gotten the whole story from Maureen—warned Lillian to stay away. Holly was supportive when Ed told her about his affair, but when Holly started to take a motherly interest in Michelle, Blake became jealous. A confused Michelle ran away, and Ed found her at Vanessa's.

Despite her closeness to Ed, Roger admitted his feelings for Holly. Needing time to think, Holly took

Michelle to a resort called Cliff House. Roger followed. Davis, Roger's cohort in the Jessup farm swindle, tailed Roger and was bent on revenge because he thought Roger had cheated him. After Holly kicked Roger out, Davis took her and Michelle hostage. Ed arrived just as Roger was trying to help Holly. Ed jumped Davis, who fell off a cliff to his death. Roger grabbed Ed in time and pulled him to safety. Roger and Holly impulsively made love. He asked Holly to marry him, but she refused. Thinking Ed was standing between him and Holly, Roger told Ed that he'd slept with Holly. Ed punched him out and told Holly that they could never have a relationship because of her obsession with Roger. Roger tried one last time to get through to

Blake was reeling from Ross' rejection, and Alan-Michael was nursing his wounds after finding out Eleni's baby wasn't his when they met at the Bauer cabin and made love.

Holly by breaking into her house. When she rejected him again, Roger said his best revenge would be to let her go, convinced she wouldn't be able to live without him. Blake offered Holly support, and they began to mend their relationship.

Mindy came home to patch up her relationship with Nick just as he was surprising Eve with two tickets to the Caribbean. Eve warned Mindy to stay away from Nick. Later, Eve found photos of Nick with Mindy, and Ed watched as Eve ripped them to shreds. Mindy later found the pictures Eve had tried to destroy. Nick confronted Eve, who denied any involvement. Ed caught Eve trying to break into Mindy's medical records and threatened to suspend her. After a fight with Mindy at the Towers, Eve smashed her own windshield with a shovel and claimed Mindy had done it. Nick stood by Eve but began to doubt her when she donned a blond wig and dressed up like Mindy for a date with him. When Nick caught Eve lying about Mindy, he broke up with her, which sent Eve on a rampage. At a bridal fashion show to mark Mindy's return as a designer, Eve drugged Mindy's water bottle, and Mindy got into an accident while driving home with little Billy. Nick found evidence linking Eve to the crash, but it disappeared before the police investigation. Eve tried to attack Mindy at the lighthouse. When Nick and Ed arrived, Eve threatened to jump off the observation deck. Ed talked her down and took her to a psychiatric center for treatment. After Billy and Vanessa's wedding, Nick and Mindy rediscovered their romantic feelings and made love.

Ed helped get Eve released from the psychiatric center and offered her the garage apartment to live in. One night the two kissed just as Michelle and Holly walked in. Ed helped Eve get her job back at Cedars. Nick and Mindy got into a fight when Mindy questioned whether Eve had really recovered. Mindy accepted a date with detective Macauley West. Eve spotted them kissing and told Nick, who thought he'd lost Mindy. When Macauley asked her to go to Chicago with him, Mindy said no and made up with Nick. Holly was convinced that Eve had it in for her after someone broke into her house and stole her gun. Holly asked Ross for a restraining order against Eve. Ed started to have doubts about Eve's mental stability and suggested they slow things down.

Ross told Blake to slow down as well when she showed up at his house with a suitcase. Blake went to the Bauer cabin, where she ran into Alan-Michael, who was reeling from the news that Eleni's baby was Frank's

and not his. They spent the night together. Eleni later saw them but agreed to keep quiet if Alan-Michael would give her a divorce. He reluctantly agreed.

Blake returned home to find Ross had changed his mind about them living together. Although she felt guilty about her night with Alan-Michael, Blake moved in. She was excited when she found an engagement ring in Ross' drawer, until she learned it was the one he had bought for Holly. Blake finally gave Ross an ultimatum. She went to the Bauer cabin to wait for his response and ran into Eleni, who had had a fight with Frank about the money Alan-Michael wanted to give her in their divorce settlement. Ross overheard the two women discussing Blake's night of passion with Alan-Michael and changed his mind about marrying Blake. Blake and Ross made up after she told him her version of what happened that night with Alan-Michael. Later, Ross finally proposed.

Harley and Mallet went to Washington, D.C., to return his guide dog and remember her father at the Vietnam Memorial. Harley was upset when she couldn't find Buzz' name on the wall. She was stunned to learn that Frank Achilles Cooper had returned to the States in 1977. As Harley tried to deal with the fact that her father had abandoned the family, Nadine lied and said that she had been told her husband was dead. Learning Nadine was married to Billy Lewis, Buzz headed for Springfield. Nadine was horrified to see him, especially when he found out she had faked her pregnancy, and he blackmailed her. When Frank and Harley saw Nadine with Buzz, she lied again and said that he was a long-lost cousin named Rex Manzini. Roger offered Buzz money to spy on the Lewises. Buzz learned that H.B. had been arrested in his early wildcatting years, and Roger had Gilly expose this fact as H.B. was accepting the Governors Award. H.B. gave up the award in shame.

Not recognizing Buzz, Harley asked him to help her search for her father. Worried, Mallet told Frank that his father was alive. Harley discovered that her father had had plastic surgery in California, and his medical records led her to his girlfriend Randi's trailer, where Mallet and Frank found her. Randi denied knowing Buzz, but Mallet didn't believe her after finding matches from the Springfield Inn. The maitre d' at the inn identified Randi and said she had been there with a Rex Manzini. Mallet tricked Randi into coming to Springfield. Buzz and Jenna began flirting despite his relationship with Randi and her relationship with Roger. Jenna hid Buzz

ON LOCATION

Harley and Mallet traveled to Washington, D.C., to pay tribute to her father at the Vietnam Memorial. Harley was concerned when she couldn't find his name, and she soon learned that Frank Achilles Cooper was alive and in the States.

from Mallet, but when Buzz asked her to marry him and skip town, Jenna declined.

At Frank and Eleni's wedding, Frank surprised Eleni by bringing her yaya (grandmother) and family over from Greece. Mallet caught Buzz spying on the nuptials and forced him to tell Harley his true identity. Afterward, both Harley and Frank wanted nothing to do with Buzz. Eleni gave birth to a daughter, Marina, on the day she married Frank. Marina was later diagnosed with a hearing problem that could be corrected only by an expensive operation. Because Frank had asked Eleni to give back the money she'd gotten in her divorce from Alan-Michael, they couldn't afford the procedure. After being laid off and learning insurance wouldn't cover the operation, Frank contacted his former chop-shop partner, Jonesy, about doing a robbery. Buzz stopped Frank from going through with it and

protected him when Jonesy tried to kill him for backing out. Then he blackmailed Jenna for the money to pay for the surgery.

Torn over whether to let Buzz or Frank walk her down the aisle, Harley decided to elope with Mallet, but Mallet said no. At this point Josh returned to Springfield to get Harley, but he backed off when he learned about her and Mallet. Harley and Mallet postponed the ceremony so Mallet could pay for Julie's wedding to Dylan. Wanting to lend a financial hand, Buzz went to Santa Fe and took money out of a trust fund he'd set up for his other daughter, Lucy. When Nadine saw a picture of Lucy in Buzz' wallet, he lied and told her she was the daughter of an old Army buddy. Lucy came to Springfield after learning Buzz had her money. The first person she met was Alan-Michael, who picked her up hitchhiking.

Harley was shocked to find that her friends and family had arranged a surprise wedding for her and Mallet. Touched by the role Buzz had played in all this, Harley let him give her away. Lucy interrupted the reception and confronted Buzz, who admitted he had wanted to keep his two families apart. Buzz gifted Harley and Mallet with a trip to the Florida Keys for their honeymoon. While there, Mallet got a job offer, and the couple decided to relocate.

Lucy turned to Alan-Michael for a place to stay. He took her in but told her she must keep quiet about their friendship. Lucy started working for Jenna at WSPR. Frank helped Buzz find Lucy and patch things up. Buzz told Nadine about Lucy's mother, Sylvie, and how she had left him with Lucy. Soon after, Nadine asked Buzz to marry her, but he wanted to be the one to do the asking. He was about to do so when a run-in with Jenna changed his mind. Although Nadine was

upset, she got her hopes up when Buzz learned Jenna was carrying Roger's baby. Lucy thought she had a future with Alan-Michael when they shared a kiss, but he told her he had to focus on Spaulding. When they got snowed in together at the cabin, Lucy boldly told him he was going to marry her someday.

Vanessa turned to Billy in the aftermath of Maureen's death, and Nadine saw them in each other's arms. Nadine waited until after Maureen's funeral to tell Bridget about her aunt Mo's death, and an angry Bridget threatened to go public with their pregnancy scam. Bridget went to David and told him everything, then went into labor. David delivered the baby. Scared of raising her son on her own, Bridget gave the baby to Nadine, with the provision that she name him Peter, after Hart's grandfather. Nadine quickly called Billy with the news that he had another son, then sent Bridget back to Ed's. Soon after, Bridget was stunned to find

Despite his relationship with Randi, Buzz was attracted to Jenna from the moment he laid eyes on her.

Hart on her doorstep. She fought the urge to tell him about little Peter, but she did tell David that Hart was Peter's dad. Nadine was upset when she deduced this, too, realizing Roger was the baby's grandfather. A suspicious Vanessa tracked down Nadine's doctor and learned that the Nadine Cooper who'd been his patient was a young girl.

When Bridget tried to seduce Hart again, he rejected her. Mortified, she snatched Peter and made plans to leave town. After questioning Bridget about the missing child, Vanessa realized Bridget was his mother. Vanessa forced Nadine to confess. A furious Billy kicked Nadine out, then proposed to Vanessa. Billy and Vanessa convinced Bridget that they could give Peter a much better home than she could. As Nadine reluctantly signed the divorce papers, Bridget signed over Peter to Billy and Vanessa, who soon remarried.

Bridget dealt with the pain of losing Peter by going back to her wild ways. David came to her rescue when she almost became a victim of date rape. Bridget got upset when she saw Hart kissing Julie. Julie, however, accepted Dylan's proposal. Hart got drunk after learning of Julie's engagement and kissed Bridget. Julie began having doubts about fitting in with the Lewises and went to see Hart. They had sex, but afterward Julie realized Dylan was the man she wanted. Unfortunately, Bridget learned about Julie and Hart's night together and interrupted Julie and Dylan's wedding with the bombshell.

A woman named Tangie Hill followed Josh to Springfield. She had had a fling with him in Italy. Roger recognized Tangie from his own past. Ross discovered $25,000 cash in a bag he thought was Blake's. Before Ross could confront Blake about it, Tangie took the bag and buried the money on the beach. Then she went

The Lewises gathered around to welcome their newest addition, Peter, unaware that Nadine was falsely passing off Bridget's baby as hers and Billy's.

Tangie and Bill almost perished when a thug named Ray burned down the lighthouse to smoke out Tangie and the money she'd stolen from him.

to Josh's and they made love. Little Bill stumbled on the money and used it to buy expensive perfume for Michelle. Josh vowed to stand by Tangie after she revealed she was running from a murderer whose crime she had witnessed. Ray, the mobster who was after Tangie, followed her to the lighthouse to get back the $25,000 she had taken, and set the place on fire with her and Bill inside. Luckily, Josh saved them.

When Dylan learned Julie and Hart had slept together in the house he had built for himself and Julie, he burned the place down, but his family protected him from being arrested. Seeking revenge, Dylan bought the Jessup farm when Hart was unable to pay the taxes. In the meantime, Julie got a job at the diner. Vanessa deduced that Hart could be Peter's father. Dylan learned the truth about Peter's paternity and convinced Bridget to tell Vanessa. Roger vowed to make Dylan pay for what he'd done to Hart. He sabotaged Lewis Construction, forcing Dylan to declare bankruptcy. Seeing how vindictive Roger could be, Bridget decided to leave

Peter with Billy and Vanessa. Vanessa tried to keep Billy from learning that Peter was Roger's grandson, but Billy heard the news, and the stress led him to start drinking again. The secret of Peter's parentage also took its toll on David. He and Kat were just getting their relationship off the ground when he missed a date with her to help deliver Peter. Kat broke up with him, but David soon won her back.

Gilly took advantage of Holly's vulnerable state to get more control at WSPR. Roger kept her in line by threatening to tell Hamp that she had once been arrested for prostitution. Hamp's distress about Gilly's career, coupled with his dislike for David, put a strain on their marriage. Hamp finally asked Gilly to choose between her career and her marriage, and he moved out when she chose the former. Gilly soon realized how important her marriage was to her, and she quit WSPR. Roger forced her to come back by threatening to reveal that David had once been convicted of murder.

David found himself mired in the ugly race relations on Fifth Street. After finding Stavros beaten on the floor of the diner and witnessing Vinny Morrison threatening Kat and taunting her with racial slurs, David got into a vicious fight with Vinny that ended with Vinny falling on his knife and dying. Fearful he would be arrested because of his criminal record, David fled. Kat went on the run with him, and Hamp filed kidnapping charges against David. David confessed to Kat that he'd been convicted six years ago for accidentally killing a man named Davenport. Gilly later said that she had actually killed Davenport, who was running the escort service for which she worked, and David had taken the rap to protect his sister. Macauley West, the arresting officer in the case, came back to Springfield after Nick questioned him about Gilly's confession. Nick was suspicious of Macauley's interest in the case. He also didn't like Macauley's interest in Mindy, especially when she seemed to return his affections. Mindy found a picture of Macauley with a mysterious woman, and Nick and Harley started searching for her. Mallet finally caught up with David and Kat. Nick and Harley discovered that Davenport's murderer was really the woman in the picture, Norrie Ryan, sister of Police Chief Ryan and Macauley's wife at the time. Ross cleared David of Vinny's murder.

Hamp tried to reconcile with Gilly, but she was unable to forgive him for the way he'd treated David. Along with quitting her marriage, Gilly also quit WSPR after Roger learned she'd been working with Alan-Michael to try to get Spaulding back from Jenna and Roger. Roger fired Holly from WSPR for refusing to air an interview with Jenna about her battle for Spaulding. Holly retaliated by offering her shares of WSPR to Jenna, then joined forces with Nick, Fletcher and Alan-Michael at the *Journal*.

In turn, Roger joined forces with Jenna to steal Spaulding. He told Jenna that Henry had claimed to be her father to keep her from finding out her real father was an inventor who had been cheated out of his life work by Brandon Spaulding. Roger encouraged her to sue the Spauldings. Ross upset Blake when he decided to represent Spaulding against Jenna. Alan-Michael found a document that proved the Spauldings hadn't cheated Jenna's father but lost it when he saw Frank in a passionate embrace with Eleni. After Jenna won the lawsuit, Henry encouraged her to learn all she could about running Spaulding. Roger was chagrined, but Jenna was the least of his problems. Blake continued to

be torn between her devotion to her father and her love for Ross, and Hart told Roger he wanted nothing to do with him after learning from Davis that Roger had stolen the Jessup farm. Roger gave Jenna a heartfelt speech about his feelings for her and Jenna accepted his proposal. The two threw an ostentatious party to announce the news. Hart tried to break them up by telling Roger that he'd seen Jenna and Buzz having a romantic dinner at Laurel Falls. Jenna lied that Hart was just trying to hurt her because she'd refused to sleep with him, and Roger disowned his son. When Hart learned the farm was being auctioned off, Roger refused to help him get the money to save it. Jenna bid on the property but lost out to Dylan. Hart left town again.

Jenna and Roger wed in a macabre church on the outskirts of Springfield with only Leo Flynn and the WSPR cameras in attendance. It didn't take long for their marriage to show its cracks due to their continued interest in other people. Buzz told Jenna that she and Roger probably had Spaulding illegally. Roger bribed Bess Lowell, Brandon's former secretary, who had a copy of the document Alan-Michael had lost, to keep quiet about the evidence. Bess had a stroke and was put in a nursing home. Eleni met her when Eleni's catering business was hired for the nursing home. She had no idea how important Bess was to Alan-Michael. Bess heard Eleni referred to as Mrs. Spaulding, and she got Eleni to bring Alan-Michael to her. Before he arrived, Bess hid the document in Marina's stuffed lamb. Bess asked Eleni to hide her from Alan-Michael. Roger hired a henchwoman named George to follow Eleni and uncover Bess' whereabouts after Bess told him and Alan-Michael that she would auction the document to the highest bidder. George took Eleni hostage, even though Eleni swore she knew nothing about the Spaulding document. Not wanting Eleni to get hurt, Bess went to the police and told them where she had hidden the document. But when Frank found the stuffed lamb, the paper wasn't inside. Not knowing this, George demanded the lamb as ransom for Eleni. Alan-Michael figured out George was hiding Eleni in an old spa and went there, with Lucy hot on his trail. When Jenna learned Roger was responsible for Eleni's kidnapping, she offered to help Buzz find her. George locked Alan-Michael and Eleni in a steam room and left them to die. Frank and Buzz rescued them just in time, but George got her hands on Lucy. Alan-Michael and Buzz rescued her, which led to Lucy and Alan-Michael's first kiss. Alan-Michael learned the

It was a wild celebration when Roger and Jenna threw a party to announce their engagement.

Spaulding document was missing and appealed to Bess to testify about what was in it. Bess agreed to do so in exchange for protection from Roger, but then she turned around and told Roger she would disappear if he made her a better deal.

Alan-Michael realized he needed Alex's expertise to get back Spaulding. Nick learned Alex's yacht had been shipwrecked and Alex was listed as missing. Fletcher finally tracked down Alex in Singapore and just missed catching her at the airport as she headed back to Springfield. Alex was shocked when she slipped back into her bed at the mansion and found Jenna and Roger in it! Alex stormed out, but not before vowing to get back her family home and company.

Roger's treatment of Eleni prompted Jenna to ask him for a divorce. Roger informed Jenna he would never let her go after he learned she was pregnant with his child. Jenna got more bad news when Buzz found the document that proved she wasn't entitled to Spaulding and passed it on to Alex. The Spauldings were given back all their assets, leaving Jenna penniless.

Alex was delighted when Nick decided to change his name to Spaulding, but she was crushed when he asked Mindy to be his wife. Just before their engagement party, Bess set up a secret meeting with Roger, but he never showed. During the party, Lucy found a pool of blood in the country club potting shed. Tests showed it belonged to Roger, who was nowhere to be found. Alex became the prime suspect when her bracelet was found in the shed and Mindy said she'd seen blood on Alex's dress. Jenna almost had a miscarriage after hearing of Roger's disappearance and was taken to the hospital. Just then, a visitor showed up at Holly's—it was Roger!

1994

After Josh rescued Tangie and Bill from the lighthouse fire, he told Tangie he loved her. Tangie revealed her painful past: Her parents had sold her at age fifteen to a Mr. Knight. What Tangie didn't reveal, though, was that Roger was Mr. Knight. Vanessa was frantic over Bill's brush with death and worried about Billy's strange behavior. She didn't know that he had started drinking again.

Meanwhile, Holly was caring for a wounded Roger at the Jessup farm. Eve spied her stealing medication at Cedars and followed her back to the farm, where Roger convinced Eve to remove the bullet. Roger then switched the bullet with one he had taken from Billy's gun and gave it to Holly for safekeeping. Roger was arrested for fraud for his part in helping Jenna get Spaulding. His ordeal brought him closer to Holly, and the duo renewed their romance. Roger told the police that Billy was the one who'd shot him. Nick found Billy's gun in a golf bag and told only Mindy that he had it. After his arrest, Billy asked Ross to defend him, but Ross was unwilling to jeopardize his relationship with Blake. Mindy told the family that Nick had Billy's gun, and they decided to turn it in. They were confident that it wouldn't match the bullet Eve had extracted from Roger. When it did match, Nick and Vanessa suspected Roger had framed Billy to get custody of Peter.

Tangie told Roger she would expose their past unless he dropped the charges against Billy. Roger retorted

Things got wild at Ross' bachelor party, but the festivities were nothing compared to the way the party ended: Ross was arrested when the FBI found the money Pauly planted in his home.

that her parents had been spies and that he had saved her life by taking her in. Meanwhile, Nick and Eve found the real bullet. Roger agreed to drop the charges against Billy, but only if Alex dropped the fraud charges against him. Roger went free, but Billy stayed in jail when he said that he really had shot Roger. He was sentenced to nine years.

Jenna miscarried after Roger vowed that he would take their child away from her when it was born. Although devastated by her loss, Jenna was happy to be free of Roger. She challenged Nadine for Buzz, and it wasn't long before she won him. Buzz tricked Alex into giving him money to help Jenna open an antique business, unaware that Jenna was planning to pilfer antiques from Alex. When Alex caught her, Buzz stopped her from pressing charges by returning the money and having Jenna return what she'd stolen. Jenna got a job at Dirty Dottie's Pawn Shop, but being a salesclerk wasn't up her alley, and she decided to start her own business again. Jenna found the perfect product by stealing the recipe for Eleni's homemade hand lotion and, much to Buzz's chagrin, she convinced Alan-Michael to invest in her new company.

At Dirty Dottie's, Jenna had had a run-in with a nasty customer named Pauly, who was looking for a silver box that now belonged to Eleni. Pauly took an interest in Nadine, who helped him land a job with Mindy. Buzz learned Pauly was a bank robber whom Ross had sent to jail years ago. Detective Cutter told him the money Pauly had stolen was never recovered. Buzz decided to help Pauly get the silver box, hoping to get a cut of the money.

Roger had offered Jenna $100,000 in the divorce settlement if she stayed away from Buzz, but she didn't, so he gave her only $10,000. Jenna sent Buzz the money anonymously, thinking he would feel better if he had money to give her for her company. Instead, Buzz gave it to Lucy to replace the money he'd taken from her trust fund. Buzz got the box from Eleni and gave it to Pauly, but not before taking the key hidden inside. Cutter followed Pauly to the airport locker where the money was hidden. They were both shocked when they opened the locker and found it empty, unaware that Buzz had taken the cash. Pauly caught on to Buzz and got his share of the money. Nadine realized Pauly was trouble and turned him down when he presented her with a large engagement ring. Blaming Ross and Buzz for his problems, Pauly set up Buzz to take the fall for the theft and implicated Ross by planting some of the stolen money in Ross' home.

Buzz and Jenna planned to elope with the ultimatum that if one of them didn't show, the relationship was over. To protect Buzz, Nadine flushed the stolen money down the toilet. The act ended up flooding the firehouse just as Cutter arrived to question Buzz. Buzz fled, thus missing his rendezvous with Jenna. While on the run, Buzz got ill and turned to Nadine for help. Nadine found the engagement ring meant for Jenna and hid it. Jenna learned the real reason Buzz hadn't showed up. Afraid of hurting each other, Jenna and Buzz both denied they were at the rendezvous.

Cutter and the FBI discovered the stolen money inside Ross' house and arrested the groom-to-be at his riotous bachelor party at the country club. Blake vowed to get him out and tricked Pauly into confessing on tape. Pauly took Blake and Nadine hostage when he found the tape, but Buzz rescued them. Pauly and Buzz were arrested for robbery. Buzz was fined $140,000 and ordered to do community service. He was remanded into Nadine's custody. Jenna offered him a fake passport to leave town, but Buzz couldn't desert his family again. She then tried to sell Alan-Michael her shares of the lotion business, but he refused to pay up when he learned Jenna had stolen the recipe from Eleni. Eleni put up her catering business as collateral for a loan to pay Buzz' fine.

Ross and Blake's wedding, held on the steps of the courthouse, was full of surprises. Jenna had a confrontation with Buzz that led to the destruction of the wedding cake; Alex ended up in the reflecting pool during a fight with Mindy; and Holly shocked Blake and Roger by arranging for Blake's grandfather, Adam Thorpe, to attend.

Buzz and Jenna called it quits, and Jenna learned she was pregnant soon after. Buzz agreed to Nadine's idea of raising the money to pay back Eleni by competing on a game show called "Soulmates," which tested how well married couples knew each other. After Buzz and Nadine won the first round, Jenna tipped off the show that they were no longer married. Buzz and Nadine promptly announced that they had recently remarried. They later admitted their remarriage was a scam. Nadine started to get friendly with Carroll, who worked for Lewis Construction, but was still hung up on Buzz. Jenna saw a videotape that Nadine had doctored to make it look like Buzz loved Nadine. Devastated, Jenna decided to tell Buzz about the baby anyway. But when she finally caught up with Buzz, he and Nadine were getting remarried in a chapel. Jenna had no idea they were only marrying to stay eligible for the game show. She decided to move on without him.

After winning the "Soulmates" championship, Buzz and Nadine impulsively made love. Nadine's bliss was shattered, though, when she saw an obviously pregnant Jenna. A guilty Nadine confessed to Buzz that she'd doctored the videotape, and Buzz stormed out before she could tell him about Jenna's baby. He raced back to Springfield and caught up with Jenna at the airport. He tried to get her to stay, but she told him it was too late and left without letting him know he was going to be a father. Nadine divorced him.

With Billy in jail, Bridget asked Ross what her rights were regarding Peter. When Ross accidentally revealed to Ed that Peter was Bridget's son, Ed confronted Vanessa and Bridget and felt badly when Bridget said she'd been afraid to confide in him because he was so judgmental. Bridget was surprised when Ed offered his support if she sought custody of Peter. She told Vanessa she wanted Peter back but had no luck finding a lawyer. Ross agreed to take her case after having a painful blow-up with Vanessa over Dinah coming to town. Roger offered to help by tracking down Hart. Josh learned where Hart was and told Roger he'd give him the address if Roger promised to leave Peter with Vanessa. Instead, Roger made a deal with Tangie, saying he would help her find her parents if she got Hart's address for him. When Tangie told Josh about Roger's request, Josh gave Roger the address, but not before warning Hart. When Roger and Bridget went to Vancouver to find Hart, he was already gone. Roger located Tangie's mother, and Mrs. Hill confirmed Roger's story that he'd saved Tangie by taking her in as his daughter. A grateful Tangie was unable to say anything bad about Roger at the custody hearing. The judge denied Roger's petition to overturn Peter's adoption but gave Roger visitation rights. Bridget then sued for custody. Vanessa hired lawyer Sid Dickerson, whose first move was to convince her to divorce Billy. Outside of court, Sid

Buzz caught Jenna at the airport as she was about to leave town, but he couldn't convince her to stay. She left without telling Buzz he was going to be a father.

ISSUES: ADOPTION

Bridget had second thoughts about giving up Peter and fought Vanessa for custody. Dylan and Ed sided with Bridget, while Roger tried to use the situation to get more access to his grandson.

pursued Gilly, on whom he'd had a crush when they were in high school together.

When Dylan donated bone marrow to save the life of his birth daughter, Susan Lemay (aka Daisy), and Susan's adoptive parents denied his request to see her, a hurt Dylan sympathized with Bridget. He told Vanessa that Peter belonged with Bridget, and Vanessa threw him out. Dylan moved into the boardinghouse, which brought him and Bridget closer. At the trial, Dylan read a letter from Billy in which Billy said he had always intended to let Bridget be a part of Peter's life. Dylan also admitted in court that he loved Bridget. When Sid started grilling Bridget on the stand, Vanessa remembered her own pain of giving up Dinah and demanded that Sid stop. She spoke to Bridget alone, and the two women worked out a deal to share custody of Peter, who was renamed Peter Lewis Reardon.

Jealous that Bridget was happy with her ex-fiancé, Julie tried to wreck Bridget and Dylan's relationship. She sent Bridget a fake telegram from Hart to meet him at the farm, then told Dylan. After Dylan confronted Bridget, she reassured Dylan that he was the man she loved, and they made love for the first time. Ed surprised Bridget by giving her the boardinghouse as a birthday present. Julie made trouble for Frank and Eleni as well when she got it in her head that Frank liked her after he threw Dylan out of the diner for upsetting her. When Eleni planned a surprise birthday party for Frank, Frank didn't show because a conniving Julie made him think Eleni had forgotten all about his special day. Frank felt horrible when he came home from a night of bowling with Julie to find Eleni still waiting for him.

Growing more and more obsessed with Frank, Julie accused Eleni of ignoring her family in favor of her catering business. Hoping to boost Julie's self-esteem, Frank nominated her for Spring Fiesta Queen, not knowing Buzz had nominated Lucy. Lucy was hurt when Frank broke the tie by voting for Julie. Julie was convinced that this meant Frank loved her, and Frank remained clueless

Julie's obsession with Frank grew after he cast the deciding vote to make her queen at the Spring Fiesta on Fifth Street. His sister Lucy was disappointed when he didn't vote for her.

about her crush until he found a drawer filled with mementos of him in Julie's room. Julie planned to seduce Frank at a secluded spot in the park but was attacked. Frank rescued her, and Julie played on his sympathy. Julie arranged a fake catering job for Eleni in Chicago, but her plans were foiled when Eleni returned early from her wild-goose chase. When Eleni was named Businesswoman of the Year, Frank, feeling inferior, got drunk and passed out, and a naked Julie climbed into his bed. Eleni walked in and threw them both out. Eleni turned to Alan-Michael yet again. Frank moved into a motel and booted Julie out when she tried to join him. Julie moved into the boardinghouse.

Eleni refused to give Frank another chance, even after he told her that nothing had happened between him and Julie. Frank wrote "I love you" on the wall of their house. He then wrote Eleni a letter of apology, but Alan-Michael found it and pocketed it. Frank was devastated when Eleni didn't respond. A lovesick Alan-Michael tricked Eleni into taking a business trip alone with him. The ex-spouses kissed but were interrupted by the news that Frank had broken his leg. Not knowing Frank was faking it, Eleni rushed home, but she still refused to reconcile. All that changed when Eleni finally found Frank's letter. They reunited and renewed their wedding vows. Mallet sent Julie a one-way ticket to join him in Florida when he learned of her trouble-making, but she cashed it in and used the money to go to Vancouver to look for Hart.

Fletcher distracted Alex from Nick and Mindy's impending wedding by whisking her away to a romantic island. Upon their return, Nick turned over his share of the *Journal*

to Fletcher, since it would be a conflict of interest for him to have both the paper and WSPR, which Alex had given him. Alex then gave the Spaulding mansion to Nick as an engagement gift. Alan-Michael pushed Alex to make him president of Spaulding. She agreed but changed her mind when she learned of his plan to go behind her back and buy WSPR from Nick and give it to Gilly. Seeing Alan-Michael's anger at Alex, Bess gave him the $2 million she received for helping to recover Spaulding. Alan-Michael was determined to start a business of his own. Lucy was thrilled when Alan-Michael took her to New York. She wanted to make love to him, but he put her off after learning she was a virgin. Lucy tried to make him jealous by telling him she had a hot date for her birthday, unaware Alan-Michael was helping Buzz plan a surprise party for her.

When Alex went to confront her son about the WSPR affair, she was stunned to find him at the Lewises marrying Mindy! Vanessa kicked Alex out after Alex blasted Nick, and Nick and Mindy wed

ON LOCATION AT SHELTER ISLAND

A troubled Vanessa went to her favorite childhood vacation spot to think. There she met and fell in love with a young man named Matt, unaware that he was Bridget's brother.

despite the interruption. Worried that Alan-Michael might team up with Alan upon Alan's release from jail, Alex decided to forgive her nephew and offered him the Spaulding presidency. At the time Alan-Michael was preoccupied with Eleni and turned Alex down. But once Eleni went back to Frank, he told Alex he would take the presidency after all. Having just discovered Alan-Michael was working with Jenna, Alex again changed her mind, and also threatened to sue him for trying to steal Spaulding investors for Jenna's business. Nick later warned Alex that someone was trying to steal her position as CEO of Spaulding. Roger tried to find out who was behind the threat, hoping to join forces with them to regain control of Spaulding.

Brokenhearted over divorcing Billy, Vanessa decided to get away for a while and went to her childhood vacation spot. There she met a mysterious young man named Matt, who rescued her when her rowdy poker game with some locals took a dangerous turn. Matt stowed away on her sailboat. She opened up to him about Billy and her past. When their sailboat capsized during a storm, they swam to a nearby desert island and made love in a cave. Josh arrived the next morning with a rescue helicopter, and Vanessa left without Matt, but not before thanking him for bringing her back to life. Matt wasn't ready to give up on his "Contessa" so easily, however. He hitched a ride on a truck driven by Carroll and headed to Springfield. At the Lewis warehouse, the truck was hijacked. After witnessing the hijacking, Matt fled and went to the boardinghouse, where a surprised Bridget revealed that Matt was her big brother! Meanwhile, Dylan, in need of money to save his failing business, sold the Jessup farm to Roger.

Bridget planned a dinner party to introduce Vanessa to Matt, but they already knew each other. When Matt wanted to resume their relationship, Vanessa was worried that it would affect her custody arrangement with Bridget. A hurt Matt thought she was ashamed of him. Not knowing of Matt and Vanessa's connection, Dylan hired him to do some remodeling at Vanessa's. Thrown together, Matt and Vanessa were unable to resist each other. Frank learned Matt was wanted for car theft, leading Dylan to suspect he might have had something to do with the Lewis hijacking. Matt explained that he had been set up, but he still looked guilty when Carroll recognized him as the hitchhiker he'd picked up the night the truck was stolen. The final nail in Matt's coffin was a scrimshaw key chain found

at the crime site. Not wanting anyone to know Vanessa had given him the key chain, Matt destroyed the receipt for it. Because he wouldn't explain why he destroyed this evidence, everyone believed he was guilty. Matt left town to prove his innocence.

Kat decided to join her mother on a summer trip to Europe, even though David had planned for them to spend that time together. While she was gone, David bought her an engagement ring. When Kat finally came back, she broke David's heart by telling him she'd fallen for someone else. Soon after, a strange girl flew into David's arms, begging for help. Unaware that this girl, Gabriella, was involved with the hijackers, David hid her in the boardinghouse. When Matt and Bridget saw her, they assumed she was David's new girlfriend, and Bridget let her have Kat's old room. David learned the truth when he kissed Gabriella and saw she had a dragon tattoo like the one Matt had said he'd seen on one of the hijackers. Matt was cleared and returned to Springfield, but Gabriella disappeared. Vanessa and Matt reunited.

They weren't the only happy couple in town. Ed proposed to Eve, who readily accepted. Michelle was upset but she gave them her blessing. The couple's engagement party ended badly when Ed got the wrong glass during a toast and accidentally drank champagne. He started having nightmares about his alcoholism and was forced to confide in Eve when Dylan was struck by a hit-and-run driver. Cutter told Ed that the driver had been drunk and that a bottle of scotch had been found at the accident site. Ed recalled buying scotch that night as a gift for a colleague. Eve covered for Ed, but Ed later found glass shards and alcohol-soaked clothes in the garage, along with a receipt from a mechanic that showed Eve had gotten his car repaired the day after the accident. Ed wanted to turn himself in, but Ross dissuaded him.

Sadly, Dylan was blinded in the accident. He had a dangerous operation to try to restore his sight, but it failed. Eve told the Lewises that he could regain some of his sight over time. Ed confessed to Bridget and Dylan that he might have been responsible for the accident. Cutter arrested Ed after discovering Eve had had Ed's car repaired. Dylan wanted to drop the charges against Ed, but Cutter refused to do so. After Ed was denied bail, Eve and Michelle were forced to spend an uncomfortable Thanksgiving together. Bridget forgave Ed and offered to mortgage the boardinghouse for his bail, but bail was denied.

David knew Gabriella was involved with the criminals who were responsible for the Lewis hijacking, but that didn't stop him from falling in love with her.

Gabriella was horrified when she learned her uncle Carlos had hit Dylan and set Ed up to take the rap. When Gabriella tried to go to the police, Carlos held her at gunpoint. David rescued her, and Carlos and his cohorts were arrested. Gabriella was jailed, too, for her part in the hijacking, and David learned she was going to be deported. He realized he was in love with Gabriella and married her so that she could stay in the country.

Vanessa knew she was in love with Matt but couldn't go public with their relationship. Josh saw her hugging Matt and knew something was up. Matt decided to leave town, but Vanessa begged him not to go and asked for Josh's help. When he refused, she accused him of trying to deny her happiness because he was so distraught over losing Reva.

Dylan's blindness made him feel helpless, and he secretly applied to an institution for the blind. He told only Mindy when he was accepted. Thinking all was well, Bridget threw a New Year's party for Dylan, who sneaked out in the middle of the celebration and left town.

Alan-Michael wanted to get back at Spaulding and decided to ask his father, Alan, for help. Alex had pre-dicted this and tried to talk to Alan, but he refused her visit. Alan-Michael learned his father had been granted an early release for saving a guard's life. He took out a personal ad in the paper asking his father for forgiveness and proved his loyalty by keeping the news of Alan's release to himself. Because of this, Roger had no clue that Mr. Tashiwa, the person he'd discovered was trying to take over Spaulding, was really Alan. Disguised as Tashiwa, Alan arranged a meeting at WSPR, where he asked for Roger's help in his quest for Spaulding. Roger claimed he could deliver Alex. When Holly caught Roger in Ross' office copying files, she was furious that he would put his relationship with Blake in jeopardy. Roger agreed to stop working with Tashiwa.

Alan got Jenna to tell him that Roger had quit because of Holly. Alan then sent Holly and Roger a dinner invitation that they thought was from Alex. They showed up at the mansion, where Alan had arranged an elaborate feast, then left to have a jailhouse dinner with Alex. After battling with Alan about Spaulding, Alex returned to the mansion and found Holly and Roger. She had them arrested for breaking and entering. Holly got Alex to drop the charges by threatening to tell Nick and Fletcher that Alex had faked an illness to get Nick more involved at Spaulding. Both men found out the news anyway. Nick was understanding, but a furious Fletcher broke off his relationship with Alex.

Tangie hit it off with Alan, whom she met while bartending at the Roadhouse, but she had no idea who he really was. Against Tangie's wishes, Blake tried to find out the identity of Tangie's mystery suitor. Alan thought Tangie was the one investigating him and broke up with her. Looking for his dad, Alan-Michael was lured into a shack by a man posing as Alan. The shack exploded, and Alan-Michael was mistakenly presumed dead. Thinking Alan had tried to kill him, Alan-Michael went into hiding. Harry, the culprit behind the explosion, attacked Tangie when he found her alone on the beach. Alan-Michael came to her rescue, and Tangie agreed to keep his whereabouts a secret. The two shared a tender kiss.

Roger began to suspect that Tashiwa was Alan and tricked him into a meeting. For the first time in five years, these two old foes faced each other. Alan promised to get Roger back in at Spaulding. Of course, Roger and Alan didn't trust each other, and Roger was determined to get something on Alan so he could have some control over their partnership. Roger stole a vial from Alan's briefcase and learned it was medication for a rare blood disease. Alan had a doctor tell Roger that Alan was dying. Alan's lie almost came true when he agreed to a meeting with Alan-Michael and Tangie. Believing Alan-Michael was dead, Alan thought it was really Harry summoning him and he armed himself with a gun, determined to make Harry pay for murdering his son. Harry took Tangie hostage. She escaped and warned Alan-Michael that his father was not the one who had tried to kill him, but when Alan pulled his gun on Alan-Michael, thinking he was Harry, Alan-Michael shot him. Roger talked Eve—who didn't know Alan—into admitting Alan to the hospital as a John Doe by lying that Alan was a government witness. Alan claimed he'd been shot by Harry.

Alan revealed that Alex, Vanessa and Blake had control of his assets and that he was determined to get them back. He then wanted his son to take over the Spaulding presidency. Meanwhile, Alex was planning to make Nick president. Alan had his henchwoman,

Susan, drug Nick while he was in the Bahamas on business. Susan then made a video of herself and Nick in what appeared to be a very compromising position. The next day Nick awoke to find a fake newspaper saying that Susan had been killed. The police pinned the crime on him, but Alex sent Buzz to sneak Nick out of the country before he could face the charges. Alex thought the matter was behind them until Alan showed up at the board meeting, video in hand. Nick was voted in as president anyway.

Blake was next on Alan's list. After Roger was unable to convince her to sign over her share of Alan's assets, Alan arranged to get to her through Ross. He framed Ross by having a Ross look-alike named Howie withdraw money from a Spaulding account. Next, Jenna gave Vanessa a locket from Alan, unaware that Alan had planted a bug inside. Alan was delighted when he got Vanessa and Matt on tape talking about their illicit affair. He now had something on all three women.

Nick saw Susan alive in Springfield and realized he'd been set up. Jenna helped Vanessa steal the incriminating tape of her and Matt. Alex turned to Roger to help her defeat Alan and he told her she should let Alan have what he wanted, since he was dying. Alex was stunned and wanted to help her brother. She got Blake's share of the assets, but Vanessa was not so easily swayed. Alex convinced Nick to help her sabotage Lewis Oil so that Vanessa would be forced to sign everything over in order to save the company. Mindy learned of this and walked out on Nick. Alex encouraged Nick to give up Spaulding and work on his marriage.

Alan told Alex he was responsible for all the attention Roger had been paying her, and Alex vowed revenge. One night, as Holly and Roger were planning a romantic evening, Alex lured Roger into her bed. Roger walked out before anything happened, but Holly saw him leaving. A vindictive Alex told Holly that she and Roger had been carrying on for months. Holly ran into Fletcher at the *Journal* and the two had sex on top of her desk. Meanwhile, Roger learned he'd been set up by both Alex and Alan. At Ed's Christmas party, Roger tried to convince Holly that Alex had lied. Holly wouldn't hear of it. Blake tried to comfort her father, but as usual, he was too consumed by anger and revenge to listen.

1995

ISSUES: LIVING WILLS

Eve wanted to put together a living will. Unable to face the pain of losing her, Ed resisted her efforts. When it became apparent that she would not recover, Ed was forced to make the painful decision to pull the plug.

After Eve fainted during her wedding to Ed, tests indicated she was suffering from a rare and possibly fatal disorder. Ed asked Rick to come back and take on Eve's case. After a five-year absence, father and son were reunited. Rick operated on Eve, but her condition didn't change. Eve was determined to fight and started taking an experimental drug. It didn't work, and she lapsed into a coma. Ed made the painful decision to pull the plug on her respirator. Lillian helped Rick cover up the crime. Rick confided in Mindy about Eve's death, and she took a business trip to Paris to avoid being questioned about it. After the funeral, Ed and Michelle went to Europe, and Michelle decided to stay on. Ed barely recognized her when she returned to Springfield a few months later, looking far more mature than the little girl he'd left behind.

Josh was seriously injured while rescuing Marina from a fire on Fifth Street. Despite the initial animosity between them, he and nurse Annie Dutton grew closer. Vanessa was shocked when Josh quit Lewis Oil. He wanted to do something more worthwhile and decided to work with Lewis Construction to rebuild Fifth

Josh became a hero when he valiantly saved Lucy and baby Marina from the devastating Fifth Street fire.

Street. Josh and Annie's relationship was just starting to take off when Josh became haunted by Reva's presence. First he smelled her perfume in the house, then he found a picture of her in his wallet that he thought he had taken out years ago. A romantic rendezvous with Annie was spoiled when Josh saw a vision of Reva just as he was about to make love to Annie. Josh went to Cross Creek, where he found Reva's ghost waiting. The two fondly remembered their past, but when Josh told her about Annie, Reva insisted that Josh would never find another woman like her. Annie arrived, and Josh convinced her that Reva's ghost was really there. When Reva made Josh choose between her and Annie, he chose Annie, and Reva agreed to let him go. Despite this promise, Reva began appearing in front of Annie. Josh ordered Reva out of their lives. Reva again agreed to go but reappeared when Marah's appendix burst. After Marah recovered, she told Josh and Annie that she had had a near-death experience in which Reva told her to go back to them.

Annie feared her past was coming back to haunt her when she got a mysterious call about a man named Jake. Rick urged Annie to come clean with Josh about her past, including the fact that she and Rick had once been married! Rick later told Ed about their marriage and how Annie had cheated on him. Ed discovered another of Annie's secrets when she showed up at his AA

meeting. Josh learned he would have to have Reva declared legally dead in order to remarry, an idea Marah did not take well. As Josh was trying to get Reva declared dead, she awoke very much alive in a small, Amish-like community called Goshen. She remembered nothing of her past and went by the name of Rebecca. When his car ran out of gas near Goshen, Buzz met Rebecca. Not able to get her out of his mind, Buzz went to visit her again. At the mention of Springfield, Rebecca/Reva had a memory flash. Later she had nightmares about drowning.

Hawk returned to Springfield to fight Josh's plan to have Reva declared legally dead. He also milked Rick for information on Annie. Both she and Rick were stunned to find out their divorce had never been finalized. Annie got another surprise when Josh presented a marriage license and the deed to the house adjoining an antique carousel. She tried to get Rick to go to the Caribbean for a quickie divorce, but he refused. Apologizing to Rick for the way she had treated him, she promised to tell Josh everything, but Hawk beat her to the punch after finding Annie and Rick's wedding photo. Josh was livid! Annie insisted on telling Josh all the sordid details of her past, including her alcoholism and her affair with Jake, and she gave Josh back his ring.

Rebecca/Reva ran into Alan—literally—after she accidentally hit him with her carriage when his car stalled in Goshen. Alan was seriously injured, and Reva took him in. When Reva called Alan's family, Hawk answered the phone. Reva only got to say hello before Alex interrupted, but Hawk recognized her voice. He rushed to the courthouse to stop Josh from having Reva declared dead, but he couldn't convince the judge that Reva was alive. Back in Goshen, Reva was stunned when Alan awoke and called her by her true name. The local doctor warned Alan about Reva's fragile emotional state, but that didn't stop Alan from telling Reva that they had once been married. Reva sketched a picture of Josh and asked if his name was Bud. Alan said it was but told her that Bud was someone who had hurt her very badly. Reva doubted his story when she had a brief, happy memory of her wedding to Josh. Alan's love for Reva grew as he watched her care for Abigail Blume, the deaf daughter of the people who had taken Reva in. Buzz showed up in Goshen again and told Reva about Alan's villainous ways, but Alan was able to explain away Buzz's claims, and he and Reva grew closer. However, she slapped him when he kissed her, declaring that she was Rebecca, not Reva.

When Rick and Annie came to Goshen with the trauma team, Alan made sure they didn't see Reva. Abigail was immediately drawn to Rick. Rick promised not to reveal where Alan was but later spilled the beans to Alex. Alex was anxious to find Alan so she could have him declared incompetent and get her hands on the Spaulding stocks he'd signed over to Amanda. She and Hawk went to Goshen. Reva recognized her father but did not reveal herself. When Alan asked Reva to make love, she seemed willing, but when he got into bed he found a dog there instead. Alan kissed her again when he saw her at the swimming hole, but when Reva pushed him away he stormed off. Suddenly Reva got a cramp and started to drown. Alan came back and rescued her, but not before the experience triggered Reva's memory. She felt ashamed when she remembered her title as "the

slut of Springfield" and could no longer face her saintly neighbors. Alan suggested they start a new life in Europe. Reva was about to agree until she remembered Marah and Shayne. A reluctant Alan agreed to take her

Reva turned up alive in the saintly community of Goshen, where Alan found her after she accidentally ran him over with her horse and buggy.

back to Springfield. They brought Abigail with them so she could be treated for her headaches at Cedars.

As Reva was headed home, Josh was trying to move on with his life. Annie went to Mexico with Rick to finalize their divorce, and Rick told her he still had feelings for her. Josh showed up and declared his love for Annie. She accepted his proposal, and Rick returned to Springfield alone. He wasn't alone for long, though. Abigail's affection for him grew when he successfully treated her headaches. Rick played hero after Abigail got trapped in a burning building. He appealed to her mother to let her stay in Springfield and study sign language, and Mrs. Blume agreed when Ed said that Abigail could stay with them.

In the meantime, Alan was trying to get Reva to leave town. He took her to the playground to observe Marah and Shayne, and she broke down when she heard Shayne call Annie mommy. Alex hired Hawk to find out what Alan was up to, and Hawk thought he spotted Reva, but only from behind. Alan tried to tell

Reva how happy Josh was with Annie. Reva didn't decide to leave town until she had a painful encounter with Marah. When she saw Reva, Marah told her to go back to heaven because she had a new mommy. Reva went to see her children one last time and ran into Hawk, who had a heart attack when he finally saw his long-lost daughter face-to-face. Reva used her gift of healing and helped him make a miraculous recovery. Annie thought Hawk was hallucinating when he insisted he'd seen Reva. Alex believed his story after seeing Reva on a tape from the surveillance camera at the diner. Alex got to Josh's right after he'd married Annie. Josh rushed to the airport, where Reva was about to leave for Europe with Alan. He and Reva had

DASTARDLY DEEDS AND BEYOND

Intent on exacting revenge, Brent faked his death and came back as a woman named Marian, fooling everyone in town. Nadine and Cutter got too close for Brent/Marian's comfort, and both paid dearly with their lives. But it was Lucy whom Marian was after, and she started out by pretending to be Lucy's friend.

an emotional confrontation. Marah arrived soon after, and Reva explained that she wasn't a ghost.

Ross told Josh he would have to have his marriage to Annie annulled or risk facing bigamy charges. Reva was crushed when she brought the kids Christmas gifts and Marah told her things were better when she was dead. Reva went to Alan, who told her he loved her. Josh went so far as to get a restraining order to prevent Reva from seeing Marah and Shayne. Annie insisted she didn't feel threatened by Reva, but Rick knew better.

Alan came through and got Alan-Michael the Spaulding presidency by tricking Alex into approving him for the job. Still, Alan-Michael was hesitant about accepting the position until Alex and Alan guaranteed him autonomy by agreeing to share the chairman of the board position. Lucy agreed to be Alan-Michael's secretary. She confided in Bridget that she thought it was time she lost her virginity. Alan-Michael was not pleased when Lucy starting dating Brent Lawrence, a new employee, and Lucy was equally jealous when she saw Alan-Michael and Dinah having a warm reunion. Alan-Michael issued a memo about employee fraternizing that had all of Spaulding abuzz about Lucy and Brent. He later bailed Lucy and Brent out when they were arrested for skinny-dipping in the country club pool.

When the innocent Lucy had second thoughts about sleeping with Brent, he raped her. A traumatized Lucy ran back to the boardinghouse, but when Buzz and Bridget questioned her, she denied that anything was wrong. Alan-Michael finally decided to declare his feelings for her, but she wasn't ready to handle it. Bridget saw bruises on Lucy and told Frank that she might have been raped. Frank vowed to make Brent pay, even though Lucy denied that Brent had hurt her. Alan-Michael fired Brent but Alan convinced him to rehire him to avoid a lawsuit. Alan had reason to keep Brent at Spaulding, since Brent had agreed to work with him to get back the presidency from Alan-Michael. Unfortunately, Alan had no idea just how dangerous Brent could be. Lucy warned Mindy about him when she saw Brent flirting with her at the Roadhouse. Brent followed Lucy back to the boardinghouse, and Alan-Michael overheard her angrily confront him about raping her. Alan-Michael ran Brent out of town and took Lucy to the Spaulding yacht to look after her. Meanwhile, Brent bought a gun.

With Alan-Michael's encouragement, Lucy told her family about the rape and decided to press charges, but the police let Brent go because of lack of evidence. Alan-Michael wanted to fire Brent again, but Brent's lawyer threatened a lawsuit. Brent swore to Alan that Alan-Michael would be destroyed, and Alan had no idea just how deep Brent's hatred ran. He had Brent tamper with financial reports to make Alan-Michael look bad, and the Spaulding board asked Alan-Michael to step down as president. Lucy told Alan-Michael that she was sure someone had set him up.

Alan-Michael got Brent on tape confessing to doctoring the Spaulding books, but Cutter couldn't arrest him because Alan-Michael had obtained the information illegally. Alan-Michael did use the tape to get the Spaulding board to give him back the presidency from Alan. Buzz and Frank tormented Brent and got him to admit to raping Lucy, then ordered him to leave town. Instead, Brent went to Tangie's and forced her at gunpoint to write his side of the story for the *Journal*, where she was now working as a reporter. Lucy was furious at Tangie's betrayal until she learned the truth. Alan-Michael's support of Lucy drew them closer, but their happiness was threatened when Brent held Lucy at gunpoint on the docks. Alan-Michael fought Brent for the gun, and Brent was shot. By the time Alan-Michael and Lucy got back with the police, Brent was gone.

It turned out the injured Brent was being cared for in a hotel by his sister, Cassie. Brent called in to an interview show Gilly was doing with Tangie and Dinah about women and violence. Lucy agreed to appear on the show, hoping to lure Brent out of hiding. After the program, Alan asked Tangie to stay with him to keep her safe from Brent, and the two made love. Alex threatened to tell Tangie that Alan had been conspiring with Brent, so Alan bribed Brent to disappear. The police got to Brent's room just after Alan and Brent left, and Tangie found a button on the floor that she recognized as Alan's. She confronted Alan about working with Brent, then turned him in to Cutter. Alan-Michael learned about Alan's duplicity from Brent, who told Alan-Michael the whole story before he apparently died. Alan hired Sid to defend him. Alan asked Tangie to run away with him, and when she refused, he ordered Sid to show her no mercy when she was on the stand. After the judge ruled there was insufficient evidence to convict Alan, Tangie left town.

Lucy considered leaving Alan-Michael after realizing Brent could have infected her with HIV during the rape. Another danger also threatened Lucy: Brent hadn't died and, disguised as a woman named Marian Crane, he got hired at Spaulding and set out to get revenge on everyone who'd hurt him. Brent tried to get a room at the boardinghouse to get closer to Lucy. When there wasn't one, he sabotaged the construction site where David was working. Josh, Matt and David were all hurt but recovered. Next, pretending to be a rape victim, Brent sat in on Lucy's rape counseling session. He stole the keys to the Spaulding files, hoping to get something he could use to hurt Lucy. Lucy continued to put off Alan-Michael, who had no idea of her HIV fears.

Brent stepped up his stalking of Lucy. As Marian, he tried again to get a room at the boardinghouse when Matt moved out and was furious when Bridget gave it to Marcus Williams, Dinah's friend from Paris, instead. He was further riled after hearing Lucy accept Alan-Michael's proposal. Brent stormed off and encountered a would-be rapist, whom he killed. Lucy and Alan-Michael saw a woman running from the crime scene but didn't realize it was Marian. Brent hacked into the Cedars computer and changed the results of Lucy's HIV test from negative to positive. Lucy accepted the false news bravely and told Alan-Michael, who vowed to remain by her side.

Nadine went to Marian's looking for Lucy and stumbled upon a secret closet, which revealed Marian was actually Brent. When Marian caught her snooping, Nadine, who had had dreams in which a person was murdered, suddenly realized she was the murder victim. Marian killed Nadine and dumped her body into the river. Frank spotted Marian and noticed that she matched the description of the woman who'd murdered the rapist. Unfortunately, Nadine's absence wasn't noticed, for she had been on her way out of town when she was killed.

Lucy's second HIV test came back negative. Upset about the discrepancy, Lucy took a third test. Brent tried to switch her sample with HIV-positive blood. Startled when Reva ducked into the lab while hiding from Josh, Brent accidentally dropped the positive

Marcus Williams, Dinah's friend from Paris, seen here on sax with Hamp, soon became embroiled in the Brent/Marian saga when he was accused of killing Cutter.

sample. He freaked out when he saw the blood on his shoe and began acting more irrational. He burned the mementos of his misdeeds and started to hear his mother's voice berating him. Brent's sister, Cassie, saw his state of mind and threatened to tell Lucy and Alan-Michael that he was alive. They almost learned it themselves when Lucy accidentally hit Marian with her car. Marian was taken to Cedars, where Rick realized she was really a man, but knowing nothing about Brent, he agreed to keep his secret. Susan Bates, the young woman Nick McHenry was seeing, thought Marian wasn't what she seemed and warned Lucy about her.

The evidence started to pile up against Marian/Brent. Hoping to get Marian to confess to killing the rapist in self-defense, Cutter asked her out. Marian didn't reveal anything, but Cutter wouldn't give up. At Marian's one evening, he noticed a bloodstain on the floor and got confirmation that Marian's hair matched a strand found in the murdered rapist's hand. When Marian caught on, she stabbed Cutter in the chest and left him to die on a deserted street. Marcus found Cutter and pulled the knife out just as the police arrived. Marcus ran but was caught at the airport thanks to a tip from Roger. It didn't help when Roger revealed Marcus had been arrested for assault in Europe. Dinah summoned Marcus' father, Griffin Williams, who came to his son's defense.

Lucy and Alan-Michael learned that she was truly HIV negative and that her first test had been altered by a computer hacker. Nick and Susan tried to convince Lucy that Marian was the one who did it. Marian decided to get rid of Lucy once and for all, but when she tried to attack her in the shower she found Susan there instead. Marian knocked Susan unconscious, and Nick found her. At the hospital, Alex interrupted just as Marian was about to unplug Susan's respirator.

Susan wasn't the only threat to Marian's secret. Marian thought she'd gotten rid of Nadine for good, but her body resurfaced down at the docks. Unaware of this, Marian continued pursuing Lucy. Pretending to get drunk at the Spaulding Christmas party, Marian got Lucy to drive her home. Marian prepared to make her move...

1996

It was New Year's Eve, and Springfield society was celebrating at a grand masquerade ball. While the festivities were in full swing, Susan awoke from her coma and told Frank it was Marian who had attacked her. She also accepted Nick's proposal. Unfortunately, the psychotic Brent/Marian eluded the police and made his way toward the ball. Taking advantage of the costumed event, he got close enough to Lucy to kidnap her and bring her to the abandoned lighthouse.

Finally, Alan-Michael began to put the pieces together and realized Marian was Brent. Lucy herself was stunned when Brent ripped off his Marian dis-guise. Brent told Lucy that he'd killed Nadine, and Frank learned the sad news when he recognized the wedding band found on the body he'd pulled from the river. He broke the news of her death to Buzz, who joined in the frantic search for Lucy. Brent lured Alan-Michael to the lighthouse, locked him and Lucy up and set a bomb. As Brent watched surreptitiously on a surveillance camera, Alan-Michael and Lucy pledged their love. Brent sent Alan a ransom vote via E-mail demanding $10 million for Alan-Michael and Lucy. When Alan arrived with the money and the police, Alan-Michael and Lucy managed to overpower

DASTARDLY DEEDS

Brent shed his Marian disguise and revealed himself to a terrified Lucy when he held her captive in the burned-out lighthouse.

Brent. In the struggle, Brent and the money fell from the top of the lighthouse. Frank managed to pull Brent to safety, but the money was lost. After Brent was arrested, he shocked everyone by insisting he was Marian, not Brent, and was carted off to a psychiatric hospital.

Nick decided to write off Spaulding and left on an extended honeymoon with Susan. Alan-Michael and Lucy started making wedding plans as well, and he and Amanda decided to surprise Lucy by holding the nuptials at Universal Studios in Orlando, Florida. Alex planned a surprise of her own after getting a call from Phillip, whom she asked to attend the wedding. Rick was thrilled to see his old pal, and Phillip told him that someone in his family had paid Gary Swanson to set Phillip up for Neil Everest's murder six years earlier. Unfortunately, the only evidence Phillip had was a document signed by "A. Spaulding." Lucy and Alan-Michael were married on top of the marquee at Universal's Pantages Theater. At the reception, Phillip made his presence known to his less-than-enthusiastic family. Alex told Phillip about Amanda's past as the Malibu Madam and blurted out the news to Alan. A devastated Amanda tried to justify her actions, but Alan wouldn't listen.

While honeymooning on their yacht, Alan-Michael and Lucy got caught in a dangerous storm. Alan went to rescue them, but by the time he got there the newlyweds had already been saved by a stranger known simply as Zachary. This stranger later turned up in Springfield, and Lucy learned that he'd come to restore Ed's lighthouse.

Phillip started snooping around to find out who had set him up. The Spaulding board forced Alan-Michael to hire Phillip to boost the company's image after Alan-Michael publicly exposed Amanda's past as a madam. Phillip soon ruled out Alexandra as "A. Spaulding" when Ross told him how she'd risked her own freedom to try to help Phillip. He then put Amanda at the top of the list when he learned she'd known Neil in California. Amanda swore she hadn't set Phillip up and shifted the blame to Alan by revealing that he'd once shared a cell with Neil. She found proof that Alan was, indeed, "A. Spaulding," but she pinned the crime on Alan-Michael to get back at him for exposing her past. When Alan considered dropping the Fifth Street redevelopment plans for Phillip's sake, Amanda threatened to expose him. Alan ignored her and confessed to Phillip. Fed up with his family's scheming, Phillip decid-

ed to leave town. Alan begged him not to go and collapsed due to injuries he'd suffered while rescuing Shayne from the demolition of a building on Fifth Street. Phillip decided to stay in town until his father recovered and moved in with Rick. Later, Phillip got an unpleasant shock when Lillian delivered divorce papers from Beth.

It was a full house at the Bauers when Rick and Michelle's great-aunt Meta came to visit. Meta was stunned when she met Zachary; he was a dead ringer for a man named Zachary whom she'd known as a child. Zachary felt an immediate connection with Michelle after he saved her from drowning and was haunted by her resemblance to Mary, a woman from his past whom Meta had also known. When Meta demanded answers from Zachary, he put her off. He also ignored a fisherman friend of his, who warned Zachary not to lose sight of his mission, which seemed to be more than just restoring the lighthouse.

Gilly's mother, Vivian, had a mission of her own after she found out Gilly was interested in Griffin. She warned Griffin to stay away from her daughter. Griffin took a job at the university, hoping to patch up his relationship with his son, Marcus. Vivian confessed to Holly that Griffin was Gilly's father. Holly urged Vivian to tell Griffin, but she slept with him instead. Griffin tried to tell Charles, Vivian's husband, about their affair, but Vivian lied and said that Griffin had made a pass at her. Gilly discovered Vivian had been spying for Alan. Griffin accused her of sleeping with him to get information on the Fifth Street Coalition and ended their relationship. When Vivian caught Gilly and Griffin together, she revealed the truth about Gilly's parentage. Gilly ran off, and Griffin wouldn't listen to Vivian's explanation of her secrecy. Charles told Vivian their marriage was over.

Griffin was shot during a rally to rebuild support for the Fifth Street Coalition, and Alan became the prime suspect after Griffin murmured Alan's name after being shot. Holly and Fletcher suspected someone else may have been involved instead. Fletcher found a rifle in Vivian's trunk, and she was arrested when ballistics tests showed it was the weapon used to shoot Griffin. Griffin, however, insisted Vivian wasn't the one who'd shot him. Fletcher wondered how Griffin could be so sure. It turned out that Griffin had orchestrated the whole thing. Griffin confessed, saying he wanted the shooting to overshadow the tabloid stories about himself and Gilly.

Vivian was cleared, but Marcus refused to have anything to do with his father.

Fletcher and Holly learned their daughter, Meg, who had Down syndrome, had a heart defect that would require immediate surgery. Overwhelmed with anxiety and fear, Holly couldn't bring herself to see her child. Oddly, a confrontation with Roger gave her the strength. Meg's surgery was successful, and her proud parents were soon able to bring her home.

Blake was fuming after seeing Amanda try to kiss

TROUBLED TRIANGLES

When Gilly took an interest in upstanding civil rights activist Griffin Williams, her mother, Vivian, vehemently objected. Gilly couldn't understand why, until Vivian revealed that Griffin was Gilly's father!

Ross, but her attempts to fight Amanda off only made her look bad. Ross upset Blake further when he suggested they stop their baby-making attempts for a while. Ross went to the Bauer cabin to think, and Blake followed. She was devastated when she saw Ross and Amanda kissing.

Although Abigail caught his eye, Rick was still hung up on Annie. When Annie rejected his declaration of love, Rick went to a bar, where he ran into a distraught Blake. Rick gallantly offered to see her home after she had had too much to drink, and their mutual comforting turned passionate. Back at the Bauer cabin, Matt told Ross about Amanda's escort service in California—in fact, Matt had been one of her escorts. Seeing Amanda's true colors, Ross hurried home to Blake and didn't suspect anything when he found Rick in the bathroom. He and Blake made up and made love.

Matt shared his sordid past with a devastated Vanessa. Not long after, Quint called with the news that Henry had died. Quint and Nola's son, A.J., who was now living with Nola, hoped his parents would reunite when Quint came to Springfield for the funeral, but his hopes were dashed when Quint showed up with his mistress on his arm. A hurt Nola asked Quint for a divorce.

The loss of her beloved father brought Vanessa and Matt closer, and she decided not to expose Amanda publicly in order to protect his reputation. Amanda burned all evidence of her and Matt's past, but Alex found a scrap of paper in the fireplace with the name Mandy Harper on it. She hired Hawk to investigate, and he located a woman named Misty who'd once worked for the Malibu Madam. Misty spilled the beans to Alex, who threatened to expose Amanda if she accepted Alan-Michael's offer of a vice presidential position at Spaulding. Ross was keeping quiet about Amanda for Vanes-

sa's sake, and Blake was mum about her night with Rick, but a guilty Rick came clean with Ed about his one-night stand with Blake. Abigail was now working for Alan and had just returned from New York, where

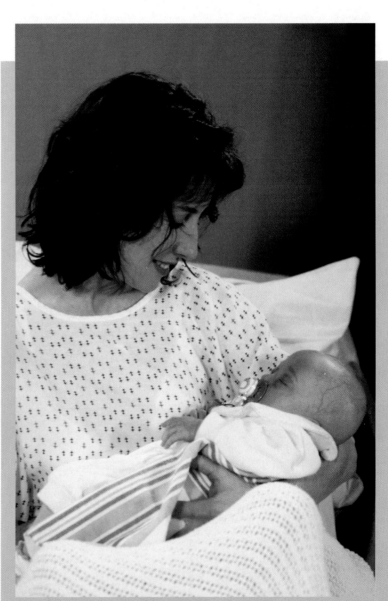

ISSUES: DOWN SYNDROME

Fletcher and Holly accepted daughter Meg's Down syndrome but were worried that society might not. Their joy in her birth was threatened when they learned Meg was suffering from a serious heart condition. Fortunately, Meg survived the surgery, and her proud parents brought her home in triumph.

Alan had sent her for a makeover and speech training. Rick was impressed by her stylish new image and asked her how she felt about him. Abigail replied that she didn't love him.

A.J., who was now calling himself J, came to Abigail's defense when she was teased about her newly cultured voice, and this made him more attractive to Michelle. Rick kicked J out when he caught J and Michelle kissing, and Nola warned her son not to mess with Michelle. J was disappointed when he learned Henry had left only $100,000 to his grandchildren and the bulk of the money to Hart. He turned to Michelle, and their night of fun ended in a motel. Nola and Ed thought the worst when they found J and Michelle the next morning, but J had been the perfect gentleman when Michelle felt she wasn't ready for sex.

Blake wasn't ready for the news that she was pregnant, since it meant either Rick or Ross was the father. When Blake learned she was carrying twins, she took a test using the alias Fern LePlante and discovered that her twins were indeed half-brothers.

Blake wanted to tell Ross the truth, but instead she lied and said she and Rick had only kissed. When Ross agreed to forgive and forget, Blake asked Annie to help her get rid of all evidence of the twins' paternity. Blake got Rick off her back by tampering with the results to make it appear that Ross had fathered both sons, not realizing she'd also made it look like the twins were identical. Rick was dealt another blow when Ed decided to accept a fellowship in Kenya to continue Eve's research. He was comforted by Abigail, who quit working for Alan and got a job at the hospital after she learned that Alan was trying to hurt Reva.

Quint returned to Springfield to work on a dig, and J took a summer job working for his dad. He was ecstatic when Quint dumped his mistress and asked Nola for forgiveness, but Nola was reluctant. Undaunted, Quinton took a job teaching at the university and tried to convince Nola to work with him.

After suffering from dizzy spells, Vanessa learned she had a degenerate brain disease. Nola saw Vanessa just after she'd gotten the news and learned the

Roger's disguise didn't fool Zachary, who was able to keep Roger away from Vanessa (far left, dressed as a nun), who was on her way to Switzerland for treatment while the rest of Springfield mourned her untimely "death."

Alone, in labor and stranded at the Bauer cabin, Blake feared for her life until Ross and Rick tracked her down. But having Rick deliver her twins was not an ideal situation for Blake, because one of the boys was Rick's.

whole sad story. Nola was supportive of her former rival but disagreed with Vanessa's decision not to tell anyone about her illness. Nola told Zachary about Vanessa. Vanessa was furious that Nola had revealed her secret but found herself strangely comforted by Zachary. After making arrangements for her children's future and begging Matt to reconcile his troubled relationship with Bill, Vanessa contemplated suicide. Fate almost made the decision for her when she crashed her car after suffering an episode of blindness while driving. Zachary came to her rescue.

Vanessa decided the accident was the perfect opportunity to free her family from the burden her illness would soon cause. She asked Zachary to help her fake her death and gave him her wedding ring to place inside her burning car. Matt refused to believe Vanessa was dead. Zachary arranged for Vanessa to stay in a convent/hospital in Switzerland where research was being done on her disease, and Roger spotted Vanessa, dressed as a nun, at the airport as she was leaving. Zachary managed to keep Roger away from her, and Roger's claim that Vanessa was alive went unheeded.

Rick confided in Phillip about his night with Blake. Blake was horrified when gossip started spreading around Cedars about a woman who was expecting twins that had two different fathers. Amanda went to Ross with her suspicion that the woman was Blake. Annie blurted out to Rick that he was the father of one of Blake's babies. After an emotional confrontation with Blake, Rick agreed to keep quiet. Blake went into labor at the Bauer cabin, and Rick was forced to deliver little Jason and Kevin. Ross questioned the fact that his supposedly identical twin sons did not look identical, but he accepted Rick's medical explanation. Holly, however, got her daughter to confess. Phillip also guessed the truth. Knowing firsthand what it was like to be lied to about one's paternity, he pushed Rick to come clean. When Rick and Abigail went to Goshen to visit her parents, the Blumes shunned Abigail for not following their ways, and Rick felt the pain of a parent denying a child.

Reva tried to humiliate Josh after he rejected her at a New Year's Eve charity ball. She ended the night in Alan's bed. Annie confronted Reva about Josh, leading Reva to file charges against Josh for bigamy. Josh convinced Reva that they could work things out without going to court. He was angered to learn of Alan and Reva's night together, and Reva vowed not to give him a divorce until she got custody of the kids. Alan moved out when Reva's lawyer said her living situation was as bad as Josh's. In court, Annie's past cost her and Josh the kids. The judge ruled Annie had to move out after hearing testimony from a widow whose husband was killed when Annie and her friend Jake were driving drunk.

Josh went to Cross Creek to think, not knowing Hawk had sent Reva there. They tenderly admitted their love for each other. Josh told her that his place was with Annie, though, and he fled when Reva kissed him. Upset by all the parental confusion, Marah ran away to Reva's, saying she wanted to live with her, but Reva realized Marah really wanted Annie to be her mother. Reva promised Marah that she would make it possible for Marah, Shayne, Annie and Josh to be a family. She married Buzz to make Josh think she'd lied about loving him, and she gave Josh custody of Marah

and Shayne. Reva watched as Josh and Annie made their marriage legal. After seeing a grateful Marah with Reva, Annie suspected that Reva had given up Josh for the sake of her children. Annie started suffering from migraines and went to a doctor for a prescription.

Alan vowed to destroy Buzz for taking Reva from him. He started a company named Advantage Systems and proceeded to buy up property on Fifth Street. Having been forced by Alex to turn down a vice presidency at Spaulding, Amanda teamed up with Alan. Phillip overheard that Alan was behind Advantage Systems and exposed him at Alan-Michael and Lucy's wedding, but Alan denied everything. Buzz and Reva got the evidence they needed when they got into an accident while following someone from Advantage. Alan, who was also in the car, was forced to reveal himself to save Reva's life.

Alan bought the diner and threatened to tear it down unless Buzz paid the mortgage on it. Buzz and Reva were unable to get a loan and feared they would lose the diner. They thought they had found a way out of their dilemma when Hart told them about Amanda's past. Alan defiantly told them to go ahead when they threatened to go public, but Alan-Michael beat them to the punch. Devastated by her father and brother's betrayal, Amanda was soon targeted by the IRS for tax evasion. To pay her huge tax bill, Amanda pitted Phillip and Alan-Michael against each other in a bidding war for her Spaulding stock. Phillip came out the winner. The battles with Alan brought Buzz and Reva closer, and they finally consummated their marriage.

When Shayne accidentally got caught in the demolition of the building on Fifth Street, Josh and Reva instinctively turned to each other, but she lashed out at him when things got too close for comfort. Rick blasted Annie after witnessing her constant pill-popping. He told Josh, and when Josh confronted Annie she threw the pills in the trash. Once Josh was gone, she fished them out.

Not one to give up his vengeful ways, Alan tormented Annie about Josh and Reva's deep feelings for each other, pushing Annie to become more dependent on pills. Annie stole Rick's prescription pad when she went out of town to attend a nurses' convention. Rick consulted with Josh, who agreed to an intervention. During the emotional confrontation, Annie told Josh that Reva really loved him and had only married Buzz for the sake of her children. Reva admitted this was true, but she and Josh realized it would be better for everyone if they stayed apart.

Annie's downward spiral continued. Phillip found her in a bar and took her to the Bauer cabin to detox. After a few painful days, Annie returned home free of drugs and alcohol, only to find Josh and Reva sharing a close moment with the children. She decided that the best way to keep Josh away from Reva would be to get pregnant, so she cut a slit in her diaphragm and seduced him. They were interrupted by the news that Reva's mother, Sarah, was ill in Italy, and Josh left with Buzz and Reva.

In Italy, Sarah made a deathbed confession to Reva: She'd gotten pregnant from an affair and had given the child up for adoption. Her dying wish was that Reva track down her lost sibling. Before she died, Sarah encouraged Josh not to give up on Reva. Annie finally got Josh back into bed, but Josh couldn't get Reva out of his mind. When he found Annie's slashed diaphragm, he went to Cross Creek, not knowing Reva had gone there to grieve for Sarah. They kissed and would have made love, but Annie arrived before things could go any further. Josh was stunned

In carrying out his redevelopment plan, Alan had a building demolished on Fifth Street, unaware that little Shayne was inside. Shayne survived, and the near tragedy brought Reva and Josh closer together.

when she joyfully announced that she was pregnant, unaware that it was a lie. Determined to make the pregnancy a reality, Annie blackmailed a former classmate named Fran to artificially inseminate her. Reva tried to stay away from Josh after hearing about the baby. She told Buzz about Sarah's deathbed confession and asked him to help her find her lost sibling. That wasn't the only baby secret Buzz had to deal with, though: Jenna Bradshaw was headed back to Springfield with Buzz's son Coop in tow.

Bridget admitted to Nola that she still had feelings for Hart, but he continued pursuing Dinah. Hart made Dinah doubt Roger by planting suspicions about Roger's involvement in Marcus' troubles. Holly gave Dinah proof that Roger had set Marcus up for theft

and that Roger was still hung up on Holly. Hart found a vulnerable Dinah at the farm and they made love. Later, Hart told Roger that he'd slept with Dinah. Dinah filed for divorce from Roger, who scrambled to cover up the fact that he'd been stealing from her trust fund. Dinah went to Hart, only to learn that he had been using her to get back at Roger. Hart went to Alan for help in bringing down the nefarious Mr. Thorpe. He also let Bridget know he wanted to play a bigger role in Peter's life. David was not happy to hear this, as he had just declared his love for Bridget. When Bridget rejected David, he asked Griffin to get him a job away from Springfield.

At Henry's funeral, Roger and Hart faced off over Dinah, who was determined to get her money back

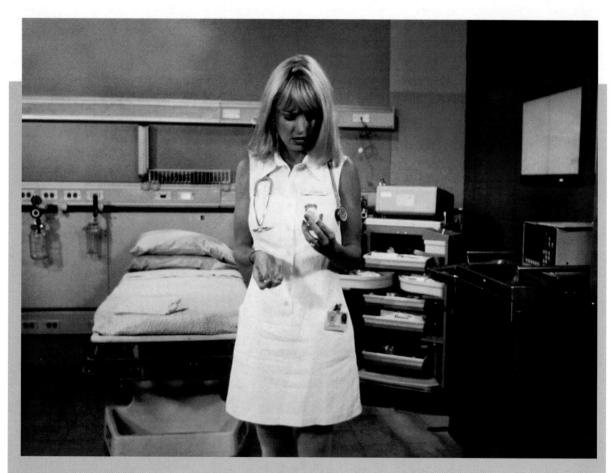

Issues: Addiction

A recovering alcoholic, Annie turned to prescription drugs when it seemed that Josh was turning to Reva. It wasn't long before she was hooked and would need serious detox to recover.

from Roger. She had read a letter from Henry in which he expressed his hopes that Dinah would use her trust fund for a good cause. Roger faked a heart attack so that he wouldn't have to reveal what he'd done with the money, but Hart told her that Roger had it stashed in a secret account in the Cayman Islands. Dinah pulled a gun on Roger, and Hart stopped her before she could pull the trigger. The two hatched a dangerous plan: Dinah would go back to Roger, and she and Hart would then make him think he was crazy and seize control of his assets.

Marcus wrote Dinah off after she went back to Roger and began focusing his attention on a mysterious girl named Dahlia, the daughter of Frank's high school friend Tina. Hoping to break free from her life as a hooker, Tina agreed to help her boyfriend rob the Spaulding mansion and was caught by Frank. Before going to prison, Tina asked Frank to take Dahlia in. She then lied to her daughter that she was leaving town to take a job. Marcus saw Frank taking Tina to prison and uttered the truth to Dahlia during a confrontation with Frank about Marcus and Dahlia's blossoming relationship. After a stunned Hart learned that Henry had left the bulk of his fortune to him, he offered the money to Dinah to replace her stolen inheritance. Dinah was touched but turned him down.

Roger tried to take Dinah to bed, but she lied and said she didn't want to risk his having another heart attack. Matt saw Dinah secretly observing Hart with Peter and confronted her. She told him that she and Hart had a plan and asked Matt to trust her. When Roger almost caught Dinah and Hart conspiring at the farm, Dinah reluctantly had sex with him to distract him. After Roger left, Dinah set fire to the bed. Hart saved her in time. A desperate Roger started poisoning Dinah with a psychoactive drug called Lonatrat. When Roger caught Hart and Dinah in an embrace, he caused such a commotion that he was arrested. Officer Nell Cleary confiscated the Lonatrat. Dinah almost jumped off the roof while under the drug's influence. Hart saved her again, and they realized Roger was drugging her. Hart stole the Lonatrat and replaced it with water but shot down Dinah's suggestion that they use the drug on Roger. Even without being drugged, Roger began to question his sanity, thanks to Dinah and Hart's clever tricks.

In a violent confrontation at Laurel Falls, Roger shot Hart. Roger thought he had killed his son, but the shooting was all part of Dinah and Hart's plan. Roger

buried Hart and was shocked to later see him alive and well at WSPR. Roger rushed to Hart's grave, only to be stopped by Quint, who was setting up a dig site there. Roger returned later and was caught with a coffin by Frank and Nell, who had gotten a letter from Hart admitting his fear of his father. Roger assaulted Frank and was arrested. Hart and Dinah made love and just missed being caught by Frank. Roger freaked when Hart visited him in jail dressed as a policeman. Leo Flynn questioned Roger's mental state when Roger insisted that he'd killed Hart but was now seeing him everywhere. Dinah allowed Frank and Nell to search the penthouse and made sure they found the Lonatrat. When Frank confronted Roger with it, Roger insisted it was water and drank the whole vial. He was taken to the hospital, where he tried to strangle Dinah. Hart caused his father further distress when he dressed up as a doctor and visited his room. Blake spotted him, but Hart got her to play along. Roger and Leo made plans for Roger to leave the country, but before he could go, Hart revealed himself to Roger at the Fifth Street Fair. Roger insisted it couldn't be Hart because he'd killed him, and he was hospitalized once more.

At a competency hearing, Roger tried to defend himself but came unraveled in the face of damaging testimony by Dinah, Hart and especially Blake. Dinah was given control of his assets when Roger was committed, and she and Hart flew to the Cayman Islands to get her money. Soon after their return Roger escaped from the institution. Posing as an exterminator, he broke into Hart's room and stole a picture of Hart and Dinah in the Caymans. Bridget found the photo and switched it with one of Peter before Roger could show it to the judge and prove he'd been set up. Hart was grateful, but Dinah was convinced Bridget had tipped off Roger about them. Amanda caught Roger stealing Alex's jewels to fund his escape but let him get away. Roger was soon caught, and despite Hart's reluctance, Dinah let the doctor schedule shock therapy for Roger. Hart tried to stop the procedure and Dinah finally changed her mind, but it was too late. After the shock therapy, Roger seemed to be a completely changed man, although no one believed his nice-guy act.

Despite her fear of Roger, Dinah accepted Hart's proposal. When a spiteful Bridget heard about the engagement, she made sure Frank found the lovers together. He arrested them for setting up Roger, but Roger convinced the judge to let them go. Roger was

As part of their plot to drive him crazy, Hart and Dinah made Roger believe he'd killed his own son.

also set free and conned Hart into letting him stay at the farm. Roger earned Hart's trust when he staged an accident for Dinah, then came to her rescue. Roger brought Dinah's ex-lover, Jean-Luc, to town, and seeing Dinah with him and her other Eurotrash friends made Hart realize just how different they were.

Roger next turned his attention toward Amanda. She scoffed at his suggestion that he could help her get the power she wanted at Spaulding. After he secured an important land deal for her, however, she named him vice president of Advantage Systems. Alan's anger over Roger's presence in his company prompted him to take action. When Amanda ignored Alan's warnings about Roger, he had her arrested for tax evasion on Christmas Day.

1997

Ross and Phillip proposed a toast to the 60th anniversary of Cedars Hospital

The residents of Springfield worked together to get the lighthouse up and running in order to save a sinking ship.

ROSS' TOAST

"One might say that Cedars Hospital is the heart and soul of this community. But I wonder how many of you realize that its roots were planted someplace else—in a little town called Five Points, where it was known simply as the Charity Hospital. The people who started it moved away, but they didn't want to lose their dream of an institution where people of any economic level, race or religion could go for help. Cedars Hospital was the offspring. It was established in Selby Flats. Our Cedars Hospital is the legacy of that hospital. Someday, maybe, Springfield will leave its own legacy in some other town. But for now, it's ours. It's us. You and me, our mothers and fathers, our sons and daughters...I look around at the torn tuxedos, ripped shirts and ruined dresses and say, Well done, friends. Tonight's efforts out at the lighthouse are a perfect example of what a community is...people reaching out to one another, strangers, friends, sometimes even sworn enemies." [Roger was part of the rescue team.]

FAMILY ALBUMS
THE BAUERS

We first met the Bauers in 1948, when Mama Bauer was being treated by Dr. Mary Leland, who happened to be Meta Bauer's roommate, although at the time Mary had no idea Meta was a Bauer, as she was living under the assumed name of Jan Carter. This was how Mary described Mama Bauer and the family: "She's of the old school and yet so understanding, so tolerant of what we call these young people of today. It's a most interesting family—a father, Papa, a mother, Mama, Gertrude (Trudy) and Bill (Willie). Papa's blustering, dominating—he's German—but oh so vulnerable if appealed to in the right way. If he has any fault at all, it's a theory...that the head of the house was Papa, and his children must be made well aware of that. Oh, I've seen these two young people chafe at the bit, and I've watched Mama pour oil to smooth the way towards a better understanding between her son and daughter and her husband." Mama died in 1949, and Papa Bauer went to live with newlyweds Bert and Bill. Meta (pictured above with Bill, Bert and Papa) had run away from home to escape Papa's Old World strictness and returned to the fold only after a tragic marriage led to the death of her child. Younger daughter Trudy married and moved away to New York City.

Bill Bauer was Bertha Miller's high school sweetheart. Whereas Bill was easygoing and content to work as a grocery store clerk, Bert was more ambitious, and this proved to be a source of constant conflict during their early years together. If she didn't get what she asked for, Bert simply did as she pleased. The couple was nearly penniless when Bert childishly treated herself to a mink stole on credit. She also nagged and nagged until Bill borrowed money to buy a new home. While the mink stole hung in an empty closet, the financial strain on Bill became increasingly intense. Soon after, their first son, Michael, was born. Bill and Bert later had another son, Billy, now known as Ed. Ed Bryce, who played Bill Bauer, described Mike as "the reasonable one, the rational one." Now that she was a mother, Bert did some growing up of her own, and Bill found financial success in public relations. But his social drinking led to alcoholism and a mistress. A mature Bert, following the wise counsel of her beloved Papa Bauer, helped Bill conquer the disease. Says Bryce, "He had his weaknesses—alcohol and women—and one line he used over and over was 'Don't shut me out, Bert [I need you too much].' In an effort not to wallow in self-pity, he changed the line to 'Don't shut me out, Bert [You're going to need me, girl].' He had great patience with her." As for Bert, she no longer needed to feed her selfish personal desires and wanted the best for her husband and sons instead. Sadly, just when it seemed things would work out, Bill reportedly perished in a plane crash on his way to see a client.

With Bill gone, Bert took sole responsibility for her two sons, of whom she was very proud.

Although troubled by the bouts of alcoholism that tormented his father, Ed Bauer was well on his way to a successful medical career at Cedars.

In 1977, Bill Bauer resurfaced in Springfield. He had been living a double life with a mistress in Canada and had come to town to visit his daughter from that union, Hillary, a nursing student who had an emergency appendectomy at Cedars.

Mike, who never seemed to pick the right woman, had a short, unhappy marriage to Julie Conrad, but the union produced the first Bauer grandchild, appropriately named Hope (below). Don Stewart (Mike) describes the Bauers as "based in reality and continuity. Mike is the pillar of the community. He was a single father well before his time, and he was quite good at it." Says Robin Mattson, who played the first grown-up Hope, "I always describe her as pure as the driven snow! I think she did some shocking thing like pose for an art class in her bathing suit, and it was a big moral decision for her. She was the daughter you'd like to have. That was Hope. All-American, devoted to her family." Adds Elvera Roussel, who played Hope for several years, "She loved her family very much. They were everything to her. The Bauers themselves were the best neighbors. You could always go to Charita for a cup of coffee and a cookie and some advice and a shoulder to cry on. If somebody was in trouble, Charita would be ready to lend a hand. You just knew that."

In 1983 Ed married Maureen Reardon. It was a Bauer marriage in every sense of the word, filled with conflict, compromise and a commitment to work things out, and of course, it was filled with love.

The Bauer family grew when Ed married Leslie Jackson and had a son, Frederick (right), named after Papa Bauer. Ambitious and driven, Ed was not cut out to be a husband. Eventually he and Leslie divorced, and she married his brother, Mike.

Unable to have children, Maureen raised Michelle (Ed's child with Claire Ramsey) as if she were her own. To Michelle, Maureen was the only mother she had ever known. As Rebecca Budig (Michelle) points out, "Claire gave Ed custody of Michelle, and Maureen raised her. She was her mom. She's really proud to be a part of the Bauer family."

Frederick, now called Rick, grew up to be a doctor like his dad. Michael O'Leary (Rick) describes him as "the all-American guy, the guy next door" and as a doctor known for his gracious bedside manner. For a while distant cousin Johnny Bauer (at left in photo) joined the clan.

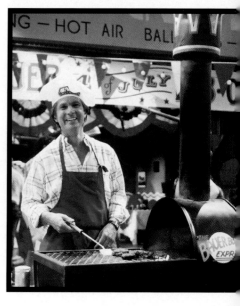

The annual Fourth of July Bauer barbecue was a very special family tradition.

After discovering Ed's unfortunate affair with Lillian Raines, a distraught Maureen died tragically when, in an attempt to get away and think things over, her car veered off the road. A devastated and chastened Ed donated her organs so that others might live. "Lucky is the person who gets Maureen's heart," he realized all too late. Like his brother before him, Ed was now a single parent to Michelle, who desperately missed her mother. It would not be an easy row to hoe.

In 1996 Ed Bauer relinquished his post as chief of staff at Cedars and went to Africa to do medical research...leaving Rick to look after a very grown-up Michelle. Says Michael O'Leary (Rick), "He's not quite ready to be the elder Bauer. Being a big brother is a tremendous responsibility." Rick does have a tendency to be overprotective. Rebecca Budig (Michelle) observes, "She doesn't treat him like her father. She just kind of disregards him. But she loves her brother a lot, and I think she likes having him around, although she talks like she doesn't."

Michelle, pictured above with her good friend Bill Lewis, remembered when her mother was alive. "Mother would get up before dawn to make this special barbecue sauce. It was made up by my grandmother. The house was full of all these wonderful smells. She [Bert] died when I was a baby, but I've heard stories about her all my life. Everybody loved her. Every year we made her recipes for the barbecue—potato salad, cole slaw, pies, cakes and bread pudding. Daddy's job was the hamburgers. Everybody had a job. When I was very little, my job was to keep my cat, Whiskers, out of the hamburgers.... At the end, we all watched the fireworks.... After a while we didn't even send out invitations. People came to the Bauer barbecue like they came to church on Easter Sunday. That one day of the year, everyone got along. Nobody argued or fussed, and Mother, she had this way of bringing out the best in everybody."

Soon after Ed left for Africa, Aunt Meta, Bill Bauer's older sister, paid a surprise visit to Springfield. She simply put down her suitcase and announced, "I'm Meta Bauer and I've come to take over this household." Says daytime legend Mary Stuart, who plays Meta, "I think she's in Springfield because she wants to be part of the family, and nothing is more fulfilling to a very mature lady than to be part of a family. She's had a troubled life. This is the first time she's really been happy. And now she has a chance to give back some of what she's learned."

A TRIBUTE TO CHARITA BAUER

When Charita Bauer died, "Guiding Light" paid this exceptional tribute to an exceptional woman when Jerry Ver Dorn spoke these words on air: "The continuing story of 'Guiding Light' is dedicated to the memory of Charita Bauer, whose portrayal of Bert Bauer has illuminated our lives for over 35 years. The spirit of Charita Bauer, her strength, her courage, her grand good humor, her passion for life and her humanity have touched all of us. She has graced our lives at 'Guiding Light' and will be with us always."

SOME REMEMBRANCES FROM THOSE WHO'S LIVES SHE TOUCHED:

Michael Zaslow (Roger Thorpe) "She wrote the book, she was the best. The grandest, the best, and she was so much fun to work with and very subtle as an actress....And always had the glint of humor behind what she did....I was so grateful to know her. They broke the mold with Charita. She was the 'Guiding Light'—no ifs ands or buts. She was the quintessential actress/star. She had such a big heart that even when her body started betraying her, her heart never left. We all felt that way about her."

Locke Wallace (Stage Manager) "She was the matriarch, the person that everybody looked up to for guidance...a very bright lady and a very, very talented artist, the leader who set standards for the young people that would come on the show. She would take them under her wing."

Ed Bryce (Bill Bauer) "She was a great lady. She did the story of the amputation. She also did the Pap smear test. I think they're two major things that she did in this world of ours. She was bright and cheerful and I don't ever remember her being sick or down."

Betty Rea (Casting Director) " I loved her dearly. We were very, very good friends. She was a remarkable woman. She didn't want to do the amputation story at first. She thought it wasn't pleasant for people. And then the people in the hospital where she had to have rehab said, 'Do you realize how many people you could help by doing this story?' And once she realized that she did it. The first day she was back at the studio she was very scared. It was very hard going back and doing that. And a lot of these stagehands would come over and say 'What's wrong, Charita?' She said, 'I don't remember a line.' And I looked at her and said, 'Why should you be any different?' She burst out laughing. Everybody adored her. I was very lucky to have known her."

Robert Newman (Joshua Lewis) "She had a tremendous amount of class. Very ballsy woman. Always said what was on her mind. And a tremendous confidence about who she was and what she did. There was so much brutal honesty in what she would say and so much simplicity in how she would deliver her words."

Bob Anton (Wardrobe Designer) "I had the great privilege of working and becoming close friends with Charita, who was certainly the most special person. She was just the brightest, funniest, absolutely wicked sense of humor...very loving and she loved 'Guiding Light' This thing that she went on radio for just a couple of months became her world and when they did a memorial for her and said that 'Guiding Light' will always be dedicated to the memory of Charita Bauer, you know she's still alive there."

Mary Stuart (Meta Bauer) "I adored Charita...and it's nice because I kind of feel like I'm keeping Charita alive. She was just a wonderful actress. And she loved the show. She loved acting. And it showed. She was just so good."

IN LOVING MEMORY, CHARITA BAUER 1923–1985

THE SPAULDINGS

In 1980 the Bauer and Spaulding families were united when innocent Hope Bauer married manipulative millionaire Alan Spaulding. Don't let this happy family portrait (from left to right: Phillip, Alan-Michael, Hope, Alan and Amanda) fool you, though. "Hope was never taken in by the Spaulding wealth," notes Elvera Roussel (Hope). "That's probably why the marriage didn't last."

NO._____

ALAN SPAULDING
SPAULDING TOWERS
1225 CEDAR BOULEVARD
SPRINGFIELD, U.S.A.

PAY TO THE
ORDER OF _____ 19___

CITY TRUST AND SAVINGS BANK
MAIN BRANCH
100 SPRINGFIELD AVENUE
SPRINGFIELD, U.S.A. $_____

_____ DOLLARS

⑆327⑈691⑆ 718 31311

The Spauldings are all about money and the power it can wield. Their corporate slogan might be "Families working for families," but the only family they're working for is their own.

Alan and Alan-Michael (below): Says Ron Raines (Alan) of his character's son, "There's something about Alan-Michael that makes him much more like his mother. She made a big impression on him long before I ever got to. There's a resentment Alan has toward his son's mother, and everything's tied in psychologically to that." After all, Alan-Michael has Bauer blood in him, and it was the Spaulding value system that prompted his mother to take him from the family when he was very young. But Phillip was Alan's son from the beginning...

Alan and Phillip (above): Although Phillip is adopted and Alan-Michael is blood, Phillip has always had the distinction of being the favored son. As Grant Aleksander (Phillip) puts it, "When Alan does something to hurt him, Phillip turns around and does something that's calculated to hurt Alan just as much, because Phillip knows that Alan wants his love more than anybody else in the family. In equal amounts, Phillip loves and hates this man, and it's very difficult for him to forge a solid relationship with him. Every time Phillip gets sucked into having a 'normal' relationship with Alan, he ends up being sorry." On describing Phillip, Aleksander says, "The first word that comes to mind is complicated. He has a big heart, but he's extremely insecure. Coming from a mixed-up background and a turbulent childhood, he wears his heart on his sleeve. He reacts in volatile ways a lot of the time. I've always thought of him as our little daytime Hamlet, because he has a hard time being happy. He can't get out of his own way."

Alan and His Sons: Ron Raines (Alan) feels that "Alan is his own worst enemy. He loves these kids as much as he's capable of loving them, but he's so damaged, thanks to Brandon." And Alan himself admits, "I did to my sons what Brandon did to Alex and me. I swore I never would, and I did."

Alan and Alexandra (below): As children, Alexandra and Alan had to protect each other from their overbearing father, Brandon Spaulding. "The kids had to stick together to survive," Ron Raines says. "And obviously our father was very sadistic. We've got some real dark qualities in our personalities because of the psychological pain that was inflicted on us: putting me in a dark closet, that kind of sick punishment. When kids grow up with that kind of stuff, they bond on another level. That's what Alex and Alan have, and they don't even know it. One minute they want to wring each other's necks, and the next minute they just adore each other." Adds Beverlee McKinsey, the first Alexandra, "She was just as powerful and devious as Alan, but they worshiped each other."

PHILLIP SPAULDING STEALS SHOW

Son Named CEO

Spaulding Enterprises The Next Generation

SPRINGFIELD MIRROR FINAL 35 cents

Family Scandal:
SPAULDING TAKE OVER
YOUNGER BROTHER BARES ALL

Alexandra Spaulding Returns To Head Company

ALEXANDRA SPAULDING

It was not sisterly love that brought Alexandra back to the fold after 20 years, but revenge, as Beverlee McKinsey explains: "When Brandon disowned her for going away with musician Eric Luvonaczek (pictured above)," with whom she had a child, "Alan took his father's side. It was the one thing Alex could not forgive him for. If the family hadn't kicked her out, she wouldn't have had to go to Europe, and she wouldn't have given up her baby. She blamed Alan for the loss of her child." Alex soon discovered some of Alan's underhanded dealings and blackmailed him into signing over his company shares to her. Alan fled to South America, and Alex became the head of Spaulding Enterprises...for the time being.

Unity was not a good word to describe the family when it came to business, for there wasn't a time when they weren't all vying for the presidency of Spaulding Enterprises, and they wouldn't hesitate to knife each other in the back to get it.

Spaulding's Iron Lady Overwhelms Competition

Ia

With Alan in prison and Nick gone, Alexandra ruled alone. Says Marj Dusay, who played Alexandra, "She has a great lust for power and for this company. The only area her father gave her any credit in was business."

That is, all of them except Lujack, Alexandra's long-lost son, who hated the very idea of being a Spaulding and opted for a career as a rock singer instead.

Years later, after Lujack tragically died, his twin brother, Nick, a reporter by profession, came to town. Vincent Irizarry (Lujack/Nick) remarks, "Nick did succumb and worked at Spaulding for a period of time, but he was doing that more for his mother. Then he lost his whole focus of what he was doing there. Little by little, other things seeped in, including greed and the desire for power." Nick eventually left Spaulding and went to work at the *Springfield Journal*.

By this time, Alan-Michael wanted the presidency of Spaulding for himself and was constantly hounding his aunt Alex for the prized position.

The fight for Spaulding intensified when Alan was released from prison and regained his social status in the community.

The Spauldings circa 1995: In 1995 Amanda returned to Springfield after a scandalous stint in Los Angeles as the Malibu Madam, and forced herself on the family. As Toby Poser (Amanda) puts it, "She thought she could make enough money and literally go back home and live the life she wanted as this 'princess.' She feels it's her birthright." Poser describes Amanda as "very conniving, slick and manipulating, but that's all because of her vast feeling of loneliness and her incredible desire to be loved by her family." Amanda aches to be accepted by her father and is constantly taunting Alan. According to Poser, "Amanda has keen business smarts, and she knows how to make a deal. She's very good at getting what she wants," and right now what she wants is to be a part of Spaulding. She got her father's attention by announcing her engagement to Roger Thorpe and making him vice president of the company!

Dinner at the Spaulding Mansion: Of Alan and Alex, Marj Dusay says, "We are the matriarch and patriarch of the Spaulding family. And no matter what, we're locked into each other. It's all for the family, which, of course, means it's for ourselves. Because we still see 'Spaulding' up there in neon lights, we will continue to sin."

In 1996 Alan-Michael married Lucy Cooper, and Phillip left his beloved Beth behind to settle a family vendetta. Says Grant Aleksander, "I think Phillip has finally realized that good, bad or indifferent, a Spaulding is who he is. He does things he's not proud of, and then he says, 'You have to look at the way I was raised. I'm a Spaulding.'" Phillip soon expressed his feelings about the family to Alan: "You know the way Spauldings manage people: find a weakness and use it to our advantage, wheel and deal and win at all costs— these are the lessons we learn as Spauldings. Somewhere along the line it stops being about business and turns into something ugly, and you know what, Dad? It starts at the top. We all learn it from you."

Who will be the next president of Spaulding? Stay tuned...

THE CHAMBERLAINS

Henry Chamberlain came to Springfield as a business associate and friend of Alan Spaulding, and stayed on to become a member of the Spaulding board.

With Henry came his beautiful daughter, Vanessa, a one-time lover of Ross Marler's, who wanted him back. Says Maeve Kinkead (Vanessa), "Henry adored Vanessa and was proud of her. He spoiled and indulged her. But he didn't give her any sense of security, and all her brattiness came from that. She was terribly funny, very artificial, and she caused trouble. She was a provocateur." According to Kinkead, Bill Roerick, who played Henry, molded the father-daughter relationship with love and caring, just as a father would.

The dashing Henry Chamberlain was quite the man-about-town, and for a while he squired Bea Reardon (below) to various Spaulding galas and affairs.

Quinton and Nola went off on archaeological digs, Vanessa and Billy Lewis had a son, little Bill, and Vanessa had her father to herself once more.

It meant everything to Vanessa to be a Chamberlain and to be a part of the family. "Vanessa entered a room, took center stage and told everybody how to behave," Maeve Kinkead remarks. "And then over the years, the privilege of wealth became more of a responsibility, and she became a truly loyal character, but still a capitalist." When it was revealed that she had a half brother, born of her father's affair with Stephanie Ryan, Vanessa was anything but pleased. Sean Ryan, aka Quinton McCord, was not a welcome addition to the family, and when he married Nola Reardon, "Vanessa's nose was really out of joint," Kinkead says. "It was so patently impossible! Please!"

A wonderful grandfather, Henry welcomed Dinah, Vanessa's daughter with Ross, with open arms.

Henry also had great fun teaching little Billy exactly what made a winning hand at poker.

A bitter Jenna threatened to ruin the family, and for a while, with the help of Roger Thorpe, she succeeded.

And then came Jenna. Years ago, Henry's friend Brandon Spaulding stole a patent from Jenna's inventor father, leaving him penniless and unable to claim his daughter. Jenna turned to a life of crime and became a jewel thief, while Spaulding proceeded to make big bucks off her father's invention. Henry tried to track down Jenna's real father, but he was already dead. He also tried in vain to find her mother.

Jewel Thief Plays Victim as Henry Chamberlain Collapses

City Council Approves Mayor's Decision

By trying to protect the Spaulding family and empire and prevent Jenna from suing for what was rightfully hers, Henry got himself into an impossible situation. Desperate, he lied and told Jenna she was his daughter. The hardened jewel thief turned immediately soft and vulnerable. Henry saw how upsetting this was to Vanessa—she was not about to share him! In time, though, Vanessa and Jenna formed a friendship, and Henry, who had developed a fondness for Jenna, remembered her in his will.

In the end, this was a father-daughter story. Says Maeve Kinkead, "Vanessa is now a grown woman who's made it, who's changed from a person who could never love or help anybody to someone who's very realistic about herself and what she can contribute to the world. She made a journey from spoiled rich girl to somebody who has a lot of heart and soul. Bill Roerick [Henry] saw her and Henry through their journey. That relationship was a very important part of the show, and Bill was a crucial part of it. He had the kind of moral voice that's not a trumpeting, false, small voice, but a presence. We lost that."

Vanessa Remembers Henry as Maeve Remembers Bill

Vanessa was not able to speak at her father's funeral, for she was shutting out her emotions and being strong for Henry's family and friends. But when she returned home and found a letter from him that had arrived that very day, her emotions burst to the surface and overwhelmed her. The letter read:

"Vanessa,

The bright sun of California woke me this morning, and my first thoughts were of you. You will forgive me, darling, won't you, if I wax a bit poetical? Here I am, an old man, far away from you, who can't help but count his blessings. What a wonderful life I have. A better family no man could wish for. Marvelous friends, and more love than anyone has a right to call upon. If only my stocks and bonds could guarantee me all the time I want with the ones I love.

"It makes me laugh to remember you as a teenager, wrinkling your nose in disgust when I would tell you money is only as good as the uses to which it's put. But now I think you share my feelings. Funny, I have traveled the world over and seen its glories, but no journey gives me more pleasure than the thought of coming home. And nothing tickles my fancy more than the tapioca pudding you make for me, and if you think this is a hint, you're right!

"You were such a tiny one, the terrible day that your mother died. I remember wondering how in the world I was going to do right by you. Somehow, my darling, through God's grace, we have done right by each other. And now, I have the supreme joy of knowing that you have found real happiness of your own. You've found a man who loves you for what you are—a woman capable of strength and endearing weakness. Knowing that you and Matt will share a lifetime gives me great peace.

"Darling one, you know this, but I must say it again. I treasure your love. In the darkest times it has strengthened me. It has made my life immeasurably, truly rich. You are my pride and my joy."

Vanessa put down the letter and cried out, "Daddy, I can't go on without you!"

In Loving Memory, William Roerick, 1912–1995

THE LEWISES

They were oil barons hailing from Tulsa, Oklahoma, and they had piles of money. No Spaulding snobbery here, though—the Lewises were a down-home bunch, and they knew how to have a good time! (Top row, left to right: Billy, Vanessa, Trish, Reva, Josh. Bottom row: Mindy, H.B.)

Like his friend and future father-in-law, Henry Chamberlain, patriarch H.B. was quite the charming gadabout. He was more than intrigued by the glamorous Alexandra Spaulding. Notes Beverlee McKinsey (Alexandra), "They had a wonderful time." H.B. would later marry the fiery Reva Shayne.

Trish was the first Lewis to come to town. At the time, she was married to Holly's brother, Andy Norris. Along came Josh, pictured here in his most unfavorite outfit—actor Robert Newman always complained whenever he had to wear a suit! Says Newman about Josh, "At his core, he is brutally honest, and I mean that in both good and bad ways. I think that sometimes to a fault he tries so hard to find the truth." Josh worked for Alan Spaulding as a liaison between Spaulding and Lewis Oil.

The Lewis Brothers—Josh and Billy. "Josh has always been sort of the black sheep," Robert Newman explains. He really doesn't go for the family thing. Not that he doesn't love his family...I think Josh is more about what it's like to be a human being." As for his relationship with big brother Billy, whom he always thought of as the favorite son, "He hates and loves him at the same time. Josh has always been very upfront and honest with him, especially when Billy's been drinking. Billy's the crazy one, the I'm-going-to-do-whatever-I-want kind of guy, the wildcatter. Josh is the more reserved brother."

When Dylan, Billy's child with Reva, arrived in town, Billy proudly made him head of Lewis Construction.

Daughter Mindy had been rooting for Billy and Vanessa to get together, and she was happy when they finally did. According to Jordan Clarke (seen here with Mindy, Vanessa, Trish and little Bill), who plays Billy, "He's a fun-loving guy, a real family man. He's hard-nosed and yet he's a softie. He's a bad good guy. I mean, he's a good guy, he's just a little headstrong."

(Right) Billy on his and Vanessa's second wedding day, with good friend Hampton Speakes and four generations of Lewis men (H.B., Billy, Dylan, little Bill and Peter). Jordan Clarke says, "Being a part of the Lewis family, that's what it's all about."

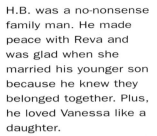

H.B. was a no-nonsense family man. He made peace with Reva and was glad when she married his younger son because he knew they belonged together. Plus, he loved Vanessa like a daughter.

It took a while for Billy to get used to baby Peter (Bridget's child with Hart, whom Nadine tried to pass off as hers and Billy's), until Vanessa learned the truth, adopted the boy and made him part of the Lewis family.

And oh, did he spoil his grandchildren! For Mindy's eighteenth birthday, H.B. rented out the country club and bought her a fur coat, which she refused to take off all night!

It wouldn't be Christmas unless Marah, Shayne and little Bill gathered round to hear H.B. read their favorite Christmas tale. About his "dad," Robert Newman (Josh) says, "There's something about Josh and H.B.—it's an honesty thing. I think H.B. knows Josh better than he knows himself, and he calls him on it."

Although Reva had been married to both Billy and H.B., her marriage in 1989 to her soul mate, Josh, brought the Lewis and Shayne clans together. (From left to right: Sarah and Hawk Shayne, H.B., Reva, Marah, Josh, Mindy, Rusty, Billy).

A TRIBUTE TO LARRY GATES

ROBERT NEWMAN (JOSHUA LEWIS) REMEMBERS LARRY GATES:
"A few weeks before he died, Larry and I sat together in his small room overlooking his beautiful property in Cornwall, Connecticut. We talked of acting and life, which we both agreed often overlap. He said this to me of acting: 'Never forget that true acting is simply the telling of a story, and storytelling is the root of all theater. Watch a very small child tell a story to another very small child. You'll never see better acting than that. Tell the story, Robert, the rest of it will take care of itself.' His approach to life was equally simple. He just enjoyed the hell out of it. I'm sure I can speak for the entire 'Guiding Light' family in response: 'We'll miss you, Larry. We enjoyed the hell out of you, too.'"

**IN LOVING MEMORY, LARRY GATES
1915–1996**

A TRIBUTE TO VINCE WILLIAMS

Vince Williams played Hampton Speakes, Billy Lewis' football buddy and a close friend of the Lewis family since childhood. He was "very excited to be the first black contract actor on daytime's oldest soap." Says Jordan Clarke (Billy Lewis), "When that character auditioned, I auditioned everybody, and Vince walked in...it was a scene where we were talking about the past and how I had thrown him this touchdown pass, and he picked up a box of Kleenex and tucked it under his arm. And he had that big goofy face and he starts running in slow motion, and I said I love this guy. I love him...When I was in Africa, I bought a medallion of a Nigerian God—it looked just like Vince! He was really touched and he told me it was the patron saint of children." Williams left a son, Heru Hampdyn Behm-Leon Williams IV—a combination of African folklore and family names—and another son only eight months old. Williams was a talented musician, who used music as a means to bond with his boys. Family and friends will miss the music, but mostly they'll miss the man.

**IN LOVING MEMORY, VINCE WILLIAMS
1958–1997**

THE REARDONS

(Below) Tony Reardon, Maureen and Nola's brother, at his bar, Company, with former New York City Ballet great Edward Villella. Tony was dating one of Villella's dancers and Villella wanted her back. One day a house literally fell off a truck and crashed into Bea's boardinghouse. Tony used his smarts and ingenuity to turn the misplaced house into a bar/restaurant, and thus Company was born. Actor Gregory Beecroft (Tony) remarks, "He was poor and rather uneducated, but he was intelligent and motivated. He could have done anything." Company became a favorite Springfield hangout. Tony eventually married Annabelle Sims and moved to Boston, but the restaurant remains.

The Reardon Women: Bea, Maureen and Nola

Bea Reardon's husband had disappeared years ago, leaving Bea to head the Reardon clan. Bea ran a boardinghouse on Seventh Street. Maureen was the sensible, down-to-earth daughter who would marry into the stable Bauer family, while impetuous, high-spirited Nola would marry a Chamberlain— well, half a Chamberlain—and go off on archaeological digs. Says Ellen Dolan (who played the first Maureen) of the family, "They were typical Irish...I love you, I hate you, I love you. The Bauers were more centered." Lisa Brown (Nola) adds, "They were working-class, real people," and when Nola was younger, she wanted none of that. "She was from the wrong side of the tracks, and she had dreams of becoming so much more than that."

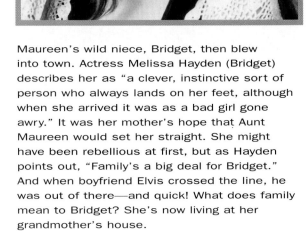

Jim Reardon came to town under the alias of John Stephens and was unmasked at Cedars by Maureen. Along with Dr. Claire Ramsey (pictured here), Jim was researching a strange virus known as the "Dreaming Death," and he didn't stay in Springfield very long.

The next Reardon to arrive was youngest daughter Chelsea. She came to announce her engagement to a race car driver, got into an accident and fell in love with Johnny Bauer (below), host of WSPR's "One on One." By this time, Bea was gone and Maureen, or "Mo," was now the matriarch of the family. Says Kassie DePavia (Chelsea), "The Reardons were a great bunch, a very wholesome, very down-to-earth family. They made it a point to be together every Christmas, every Thanksgiving, every family celebration. It was lovely to be a part of that." An obsessed fan came between Chelsea and Johnny, and Chelsea eventually left for London with manager Jackson Freemont to pursue a singing career.

Maureen's wild niece, Bridget, then blew into town. Actress Melissa Hayden (Bridget) describes her as "a clever, instinctive sort of person who always lands on her feet, although when she arrived it was as a bad girl gone awry." It was her mother's hope that Aunt Maureen would set her straight. She might have been rebellious at first, but as Hayden points out, "Family's a big deal for Bridget." And when boyfriend Elvis crossed the line, he was out of there—and quick! What does family mean to Bridget? She's now living at her grandmother's house.

Obsessed with Roger Thorpe's son, Hart Jessup, Bridget had his child out of wedlock. She was a young mother when her uncle Ed gave her Company for a birthday present. Bridget rose to the occasion and would have made her aunt Maureen, who had been killed in a car accident, very proud.

In 1996, disillusioned with her marriage to the philandering Quint, Nola returned to Springfield to help run the boardinghouse and manage Company. Says Lisa Brown (Nola), "When you're young, all you want to do is get away from home and anything that reminds you of home. And then you go out in the world and do whatever it is that you do, whether it's pursuing a career or getting married. It's a life process. There needs to be a working through of relationships, and that's what Nola's done. With Nola leaving Quint and being a Reardon again, what that means for her now is coming back to her family." Her son, J, came with her.

And as for the youngest Reardon, Peter, Bridget likes to call him "the short man." Well, this "short man" has quite a family lineage. He's a Reardon and a Thorpe by birth and a Lewis by adoption. That means he has two mothers, Bridget and Vanessa, and his grandfather is the infamous Roger Thorpe. One might say that Peter has a very interesting future in store.

Nola with Matt at his wedding to Vanessa. By the time Nola settled back in at Springfield, her nephew Matt had arrived to see his sister Bridget but had stayed on to marry Vanessa. "Matt had left home fairly young," explains Kurt McKinney (Matt). "His parents had a sour marriage, and his father played around. They came from a pretty good-sized Irish Catholic family, and he and Bridget found themselves having to take care of their younger brothers and sisters. They were miserable and started getting into trouble, so Matt decided to bail." Bridget was not overjoyed to see him. Adds Melissa Hayden, "He left early and left her with the burden, and she was furious at him." They have since found a common ground. Of Matt and Nola's relationship, McKinney says, "Nola's smotherly. She goes a little over the top sometimes and forgets that Matt's a grown man. She wants to run everyone's life. She's very nosy, but she cares."

THE COOPERS

The first of the Coopers to make himself known in Springfield, Frank Cooper was a mechanic who ran a chop shop. Says actor Frank Dicopolous (Frank), "The character is Greek, and I'm 100 percent Greek. The character was a mechanic, and I was a mechanic. Talk about art imitating life!" The family started out as just a brother and a sister, but Frank was much more than a brother to Harley. "To this day I don't think there was a greater brother-sister team," Dicopolous notes. "His mother and father abandoned him when he was a kid, and he raised Harley all by himself. Mom wanted to pursue a career as movie queen/model/actress extraordinaire in California. Dad went off to Vietnam." As for the chop shop, "Frank didn't want Harley to grow up the way he did. He wanted her to have better. He wanted her to go to school. And he wanted to make enough money to get her the hell out of Springfield, even if it meant breaking the law." Says Beth Ehlers (Harley), "She might be a dolt with everybody else, but the second she got with Frank, she turned into a nine-year-old. She could tell him anything. When she got pregnant, he was the one who helped her keep it hidden and helped put the baby up for adoption."

DA and Springfield's Finest Expose Corruption in the Ranks

DET. A. C. MALLET, D. A. ROSS MARLER, CADET HARLEY COOPER

Harley went on to become a cop, as did Frank. She had married and divorced Alan-Michael Spaulding and fell in love with detective A.C. Mallet, while Frank met and married Eleni Andros.

When "Pops" Cooper died and left Frank his diner, Wheels and Meals, it would become the focal point of the family. No matter what was going on in their lives, they always felt at home in the diner. What Company was for the Reardons, Wheels and Meals was for the Coopers. Here, Harley, Dylan Lewis (Harley's first love and the father of her adopted baby girl) and Frank hang out at the diner.

Eleni was a wonderful cook and would later go on to run a successful catering company. Frank wasn't pleased when she added Greek dishes to the diner's menu, but the customers loved them. Eventually Frank and Eleni married, not because Uncle Stavros had arranged it, but because they fell in love. Says Jennifer Roszell (the present Eleni) of the family, "I imagine the audience can relate a lot to the Coopers because of the challenges they face every day. They're the everyman family. They're a team, and they all have a great sense of humor. They may not always agree with each other, but when they yell and fight it's because they love each other and they think the other person is doing something stupid. They are passionate."

The Cooper clan expanded when Nadine returned, followed by Buzz, and Uncle Stavros brought Eleni Andros over from Greece as a prospective bride for his nephew Frankie. Dicopolous says, "Frank's dad was his hero, 'cause he was a war hero. To have him come back after all those years, and then to find out he was the biggest loser, just shattered Frank's world. And he was furious with Nadine. He never had a chance to enjoy that special relationship between mother and son." In time, Frank came to forgive Nadine. "They became very good friends, very close. He began to understand what she went through and was still going through." According to Beth Ehlers, "Harley never knew her. Nadine walked out on Harley at such a young age that her daughter had no memory of her." As Jean Carol (Nadine) describes her, "Nadine was quite an interesting piece of work, a misfit with a heart of gold, who started out as a self-centered, manipulative gold digger but eventually found a purpose in life with her family."

(Below) The Coopers circa 1994. Harley married Mallet in 1993 and moved to Florida. Then Lucy, Buzz's daughter from another marriage, came to town. Nadine and Buzz never did remarry, but by this time, everyone was getting along just fine. "They're all crazy," declares Sonia Satra (Lucy). "They're a regular family."

From girl talk: Gilly, Lucy and Eleni share a little gossip and chow down...

It's holiday time, as Buzz and Stavros put up the Christmas decorations.

Buzz serves Thanksgiving dinner. Jean Carol (Nadine) sums it all up: "We're everyday people. Normal people. People that people identify and are familiar with. Everybody's been in a diner, for heaven's sake—although not everybody's been in a mansion!"

...to serious talk: Dylan and Hart, who usually fell for the same woman, engage in deep conversation with Eleni and Frank.

REVA'S ROMANCES

Red-hot Reva! According to Kim Zimmer, who personifies the irrepressible, irresistible Reva Shayne Lewis Lewis almost Sampson Spaulding Lewis Cooper, "They wanted a redhead, someone a little more fiery than they thought I was." Well, Kim didn't need red hair to play Reva, and she more than made the role her own. "The character of Reva is so unusual. She's able to make an audience laugh and cry at the same time. She's such an open book, her emotions are so raw, and she tells it like it is—no sneaking around, nothing done on the sly, and if you don't like it, tough, 'cause this is what she wants out of life, and she's going for it full-tilt boogie and no-holds-barred!" And what does Reva want most? Romance!

For someone who was born on the wrong side of the tracks, Reva sure cornered the market on knowhow. She's the kind of woman who makes men go wild—and there have been more than a few. But first, last and always, there was Josh.

The connection between the Lewises and the Shaynes began in Reva's childhood, when mama Sarah Shayne was the Lewis housekeeper. The Lewis boys were closer back then, but Reva was so full of life and humor and a yearning to love and be loved that her youthful friendship with one of the brothers led to their first kiss and soon turned into love. Who was the man who would become her soul mate and her heart? Joshua Lewis.

They were friends...

...and they were lovers (right). But that was just the beginning. Says Zimmer, "Josh and Reva have a true love/hate relationship. They love each other so much it hurts. Their relationship is so honest and so raw that there's no other man Reva would ever think of being with. The other men who did come into her life were important and she loved them, but they were dalliances, sidetracks."

When Josh left Reva to go to college, a hurt and angry Reva married older brother Billy (below). Zimmer explains, "She was so mad that the only way she could think of to ultimately get back at Josh was not to find some other boy from school, but to get his brother!"

Just as Josh and Reva were about to get back together, a deep, dark secret from the past tore them apart, and Reva and H.B.(left) suddenly found each other. "It was special," Zimmer says. "Harlan was the father figure in her life. She could always go to him whenever one of his sons had hurt her. Harlan gave her unconditional love. They thought their relationship might have a future because they were so much alike. H.B. and Reva had a zest for life that was unstoppable. He opened up the floodgates for her. And then when she got pregnant purely by accident, there was nothing Reva wanted more in life than to give H.B. a child. And H.B., of course, was both shocked and thrilled. When Reva lost the baby, that led to the downfall of their relationship."

Alan Spaulding (above) was responsible for Reva's arrival in Springfield. Her divorce from Billy supposedly still pending, Alan brought her to town to break up Billy and Vanessa. It was all part of a business deal. At one point, when Reva was in a coma, Alan actually married her. According to Zimmer, "She should have plotted Alan's murder. But she did care a great deal for him, and in her heart she knew he needed not so much to love her, but to possess her. He could give her the high life and all the things she craves. Reva was totally seduced by the power Alan Spaulding wields."

It was that Alan Spaulding–type power that attracted Reva to newcomer Kyle Sampson (above) in 1985. Kyle was able to seduce her away from H.B. As Zimmer puts it, "He was an incredibly powerful man who was also, unlike Alan at the time, incredibly passionate. He made no secret of his desire to have this woman. He came into her life at a time when he believed he was a Lewis. So, in a way, Reva got another Lewis man."

When Reva announced she was pregnant with H.B.'s child, Josh left Springfield for the Lewis oil fields of Venezuela. There he met and married a beauty known as Sonni/Solita, but the union was troubled and the passion between Reva and Josh remained untamed (left).

In 1989 Reva and Josh were finally married at Cross Creek, where they had first made love as teenagers. They already had a daughter, Marah. On their wedding day, Josh spoke these tender words to the woman he was destined to marry: "From this moment on, we are going to be the family that we were always meant to be. The family that we always were. Always Reva." And Reva answered, "Always Bud." However, they did not live happily ever after...

A year after they were married, Reva gave birth to a son, Shayne. Suffering from severe postpartum depression, she drove off a bridge into the murky waters of the Florida Keys. Her last words were "I'm coming, Bud!" Unable to accept her death, Josh spent the next five years of his life searching for his one true love. Ironically, it was Alan Spaulding who found Reva in Goshen, five years after she disappeared. She was amnesiac until Alan saved her from drowning and her memory returned (below). Alan wanted Reva for himself and didn't want her to return to Springfield, but she did anyway.

Just as ironically, Josh was not pleased to see Reva risen from the dead (above). He had spent five long years searching for her. Now he was building a new life with nurse Annie Dutton (right in photo), whom the kids adored, and he was angry that Reva never let him know she was alive. When Reva arrived on Alan Spaulding's arm at the New Year's Eve masquerade ball in 1995, sparks flew in all directions. Annie realized the story of Reva and Josh was going to continue...one way or another.

Men weren't the only thing Reva was passionate about. "Reva without children is like a year without sunshine," Zimmer points out. "Her weakness for her children comes from her intense desire to give them a stable family environment, and that's something she felt she couldn't offer them when she returned to Springfield." The children loved Annie. To them, she was now their mommy. Reva made the painful, excruciating sacrifice of giving up both Marah and Shayne. Then she married Buzz Cooper, who described her as "the woman who makes my life heaven and hell."

Reva did love Buzz to death, although she couldn't say the same about life at the diner. Says Zimmer, "It's been really good for Reva to have this breathing space with Buzz, to have the unconditional love of a good man. Buzz is the perfect replacement. He puts up with a lot from her, not to mention the fact that they're very virile together. He's opened her eyes to another kind of power, the power of family and love and devotion to a cause. He is the king of Fifth Street. But I don't know how long Reva's going to be satisfied with that. I think she's going to start getting a little antsy." And she did.

Honest to a fault, Reva couldn't stay with one man while she loved another, and that man was, of course, her true love, her love for "always," Josh.

Reva on Reva: "The audience loves to hate her. She's so bad, but she really isn't out to destroy anyone. She's just out to have a good time! She's a good ol' gal. I get to be romantic, I get to be bitchy and I get to be funny. Who could ask for more?"

Reva (Kim Zimmer) talks about the Lewis men, and the Lewis men talk back:

REVA ON BILLY:

"Billy was a wild horse. And Billy was the best in bed. He and Reva made mad, passionate, wild love. It was pure sex.

BILLY (JORDAN CLARKE):

"The Reva snake bit the Billy boy! Kim's exciting. It's exciting for us to work with her. Billy and Reva and Josh and H.B., we're like a family. Billy and Reva really love each other, and when Reva goes into that high-flying mode, she taps into the same part in Billy."

REVA ON H.B.:

"H.B.'s love was unconditional. It was a love that came out of need. It was special." H.B. (Larry Gates): "Kim Zimmer—love her. She's a free spirit if I ever saw one. She's tough and vulnerable. It remains a privilege to work with her."

REVA ON JOSH:

"Josh and Reva's love was a love that comes from the soul. It was so deep that it was impenetrable. It was a love no one else could touch. And it took passion to a higher level. They made great love, and it was not just sex. It was love. It was making love."

JOSH (ROBERT NEWMAN):

"Reva's my one and only. The woman that just never could get away. I think they're joined at the hip. They just can't live without each other, and because of that, Josh can never be 100 percent with anybody else."

ROGER THORPE

How can one describe Roger Thorpe, villain extraordinaire? His portrayer and the guardian of his character, Michael Zaslow, puts it this way: "He's got tremendous piss, vinegar and energy, and he's very smart. He knows how to study other people and events, but he really doesn't have a window into himself. He's tremendously passionate and sensitive to a fault, and he's driven, but he has no self-recognition and no self-love. He thinks he's operating in his best self-interest, but he's not.

He's his own worst enemy in a lot of ways. He keeps shooting himself in the foot." Says Robert Milli (Roger's father, Adam) of the father-son relationship, "Adam was straight-laced. He was the antithesis of Roger. He always gave Roger the benefit of the doubt, though, until Roger went too far. After that, Roger was like an indigestible food to Adam." Lenore Kasdorf (Roger's former lover Rita Stapleton) adds, "At the end of the world there will be roaches and Roger."

ROGER AND HOLLY/ LOVE AND HATE

It was Holly's father, Stanley Norris, who introduced his young, impressionable daughter to the slick, ambitious Roger Thorpe. Little did he know that Holly's looks and naivete appealed to Roger. Holly was smitten from the start. Dating Roger had an edge of danger that she would continue to find attractive, no matter who she was involved with. Says actress Maureen Garrett (Holly), "It's the most interesting relationship I've ever played, because here you have a woman facing her nemesis." Then there's the power of first love. Zaslow explains, "They were lovers as children, and that sort of love can die, but it didn't in their case and they became soul mates." But Roger also had eyes for Holly's sister-in-law, Janet Norris, leaving Holly to turn to the respectable Ed Bauer for comfort and support. Roger and Holly were married to other people, he to Peggy Fletcher and she to Ed, when they conceived a child, Christina. Roger really believed he was a good husband to Peggy, but Peggy couldn't live with the lie of his illegitimate child.

Roger's obsession with Christina would affect many other lives as well. "He's aware of the love of his children," Zaslow points out, "but he's very much motivated by the fact that they are his flesh and blood. They share the bloodline. They're almost like possessions." Holly and Roger divorced their respective mates and eventually married each other. It wasn't long before the marriage, which at first sizzled with

passion, turned abusive, and Roger raped Holly. Says Zaslow, "Roger thought that a woman, a wife, can't say no to her husband. He was tremendously jealous of what he perceived as her attraction to Ed. Ed was so much more educated and appealing than Roger was. Roger is tremendously insecure. That's what drives him. He reacted violently and raped Holly. It was an act of violence and aggression, not an act of sex." In a brave and unprecedented move, Holly pressed charges and Roger was found to be at fault. Released on bail, he continued to threaten Holly and Ed, and when he started beating up on Ed, Holly took a gun and shot him not once, but three times. Being Roger, he survived and lived to plot his revenge.

Roger found Holly and Chrissy hiding in Santo Domingo. When she refused to let him see his daughter, Roger dragged Holly at gunpoint through the jungle, the Bauer brothers on his tail. Ed and Roger grappled on the edge of a cliff. Shots rang out, Roger slipped and an injured Ed valiantly tried to pull him to safety. It was too late. Roger fell to his death...on April Fool's Day. After the ordeal, Holly took Christina to Switzerland to start life anew.

It was ten years later—15 in soap opera time— when Roger amazingly resurfaced. A master of disguise, he was first seen lurking on a deserted island, calling himself Adam Malick and hiding behind a mask (left). He had been rescued and then employed by "the Agency," and the skills he learned would serve him well. It was on the island that Roger met his daughter again, now known as Blake, when she and fiancé Phillip Spaulding were searching for Phillip's aunt Alexandra, who was missing in a plane crash. The unwitting Blake and the mystical Adam formed a bond, but little did she know he was the father she idolized and the man her mother loathed.

THORPE ALIVE

But for Roger, says Zaslow, "Spaulding Enterprises will always be the big brass ring."

Roger made his usual dramatic entrance and shook up Springfield just as Phillip and Blake were about to say their vows. Roger and archenemy Alan Spaulding, who was trying to stop the wedding, engaged in a brutal fight. In the struggle, Phillip was shot, and to Holly's horror, Roger's true identity was revealed.

Although they had other mates, it was inevitable that Holly's and Roger's lives would become inexorably intertwined once again. Says Garrett, "We fight so well together." For a time they jointly owned Springfield's TV station, WSPR, and whenever they were in the same room, the sparks flew!

But it would continue to be a Clash of the Titans between Alan and Roger—seen here at an unusually civil moment at a Fifth Street Fair—for control of the company.

OTHER WOMEN/OTHER MEN

Although still obsessed with Holly, Roger got closer to his business goal when he married the powerful Alexandra Spaulding (above). "As always, it was a complex motivation," Zaslow notes. "He started out wanting to manipulate and get himself in there. She was vulnerable and a woman of a certain age, and all that appealed to him. It wasn't passionate love, though he empathized with her and cared about her, but control of Spaulding was the driving force." Says Marj Dusay (the second Alexandra), "I think there are times she found him fascinating. She was vulnerable enough to want to believe she could handle him. You always think you can manage people like Roger, but you can't. I think she was hurt by him and pulled in by him. Why did she do it? She thought he would 'powerize' her somehow."

Holly took up with straight-arrow Ross Marler but, says Jerry Ver Dorn, who plays Ross, "She was obsessed with Roger and still is. That's what broke us up in the end." Ross' affair with Holly's daughter, Blake, was the ultimate betrayal.

An attempt to ward off a midlife crisis with younger Mindy Lewis ended both Roger's marriage to Alex and his involvement in Spaulding... for now.

Suffering from migraines, Holly turned to Dr. Daniel St. John for solace and relief. St. John turned out to be a murderer who, in an effort to get Holly to say "I do," held a gun to her head in a deserted mountain cabin and summoned a minister to conduct the ceremony. Roger was part of the rescue team who saved Holly.

Indeed, whoever Holly decided to date, it seemed that Roger was always nearby.

It had to happen. Holly had gone to her mountain cliff house with Michelle for a vacation and was pursued by Roger's bitter, vindictive lawyer, Davis, who held her captive. Roger appeared and fought with Davis. In an ironic twist, Roger saved the life of the man he perceived as his rival for Holly's love, Ed Bauer, in much the same way Ed had tried but failed to save Roger in Santo Domingo. A frightened Holly asked Roger if he would spend the night. For the first time since the rape, Holly and Roger made love. Says Garrett of the rape and Holly's forgiveness, "It was so complex. She was very young and had no idea how to deal with a rage-aholic, which is what Roger was. It was way beyond her. So she withdrew, and then his anger surfaced. Years later, when they came to terms with it, she came to a point of forgiveness and understanding." But Holly still couldn't quite get past the rape—not yet. "We know something now that we didn't know then about kindness and forgiveness and maybe even love," Roger told her. Holly responded, "Some things are unforgivable. Some doors are shut and can't be reopened. Stay or go, but understand that." "How could I have destroyed what I loved best," Roger wondered, "and even made the loveliness of it so ugly to you?"

As in times past, Roger blamed Ed for Holly's rejection of him. He barged in on Ed's Christmas party to beg her to reconsider his proposal. She refused.

On the rebound and in an attempt to gain control of Spaulding once again, Roger married Jenna Bradshaw, whose father had supposedly been cheated out of the ownership of Spaulding, which would have made Jenna his rightful heir. Jenna and Roger were outcasts in Springfield society, and no one came to the wedding. Roger knew but didn't tell her that her father had signed over his rights to the company years ago. When she found out, Jenna sued him for divorce.

It seemed as if things would come full circle for Holly and Roger when she took him in and nursed him back to health after he was shot by Billy Lewis. She was the only one he could turn to. Holly and Roger surprised and shocked the residents of Springfield when they became engaged. But Roger's duplicity and fierce desire to control the Spaulding empire caused them to separate yet again. Roger tied the knot (some said noose) with Dinah Marler. Said Dinah's father, Ross, "Roger will be on Dinah's trust fund like mold in a summer camp shower stall." He was right. Roger did it for the money, and Dinah did it to spite her parents. Dinah ended up in love and in bed—with Roger's son Hart.

Meanwhile, Holly married Fletcher Reade, with Roger as an uninvited guest. "She has reached a plateau of sorts and has a marriage with a normal man," Garrett says. "But she could still get drawn into the dark side. She hears Roger and something pricks up inside. Something in her still can't let go. Somewhere inside her a coil is tightly winding, winding, winding. When is it going to unspool? I don't know." Notes Jay Hammer (Fletcher), "Our show is called 'Guiding Light.' To have light, you also have to have dark, and the thing about Roger is that, ironically, he's the engine, the fulcrum, the cog, the wheel that spins that light. We learn about other people and other relationships because of what Roger has done. His dastardly deeds, the lies, the stealing, the attempted murders are driving the whole town. He's showing people what they don't want to be. In his desperate scramble for his satisfaction, his happiness and his need to be fulfilled, he's a moral lesson in and of himself."

With his marriage to Dinah in tatters, Roger turned to spirited Spaulding daughter Amanda. As Zaslow puts it, "She's a mighty, mighty attractive woman, and very smart. It's a way into Spaulding, which he hasn't lost sight of."

Of Roger's relationship with little Peter, Melissa Hayden (Bridget) reports, "With the baby and visitations, he's always been great. He's an amazing grandfather. He's wonderful with the baby."

THE FAMILY

His love for his children has always been Roger's Achilles' heel. Says Zaslow, "They're his bloodline, they're extensions of himself, so it's still all about him." Adds Elizabeth Keifer (Blake), "Blake loves her father, but she's also never really had her father's love. That's the core of Blake's problem. She puts up with a lot from Roger because she still thinks she's going to have a real father one day. She's always lived with this fantasy. She forgives her father because that's who he is, and he loves her so much. Then she turns around and it's like the rug's been pulled out from underneath her."

There was a son, but it was not the ideal father-son relationship. Hart Jessup was the product of an affair Roger had when he was working for the Agency. Hart knew his father only through his mother's letters, and she had painted him as a hero. When Hart learned his father had swindled his grandfather out of his family farm, he left town, vowing never to speak to him again. A one-night stand with Bridget produced a son, and when Hart returned, he took up with his father's new wife, Dinah Marler Thorpe.

Whatever scheme Roger is cooking up next, you can be sure it will be full of intrigue and romance...and one way or another, that romance is bound to involve Holly. Says "Guiding Light" head writer James Harmon Brown, "Theirs is a lifelong battle. It'll always be there." Zaslow continues, "We should be a part of each other's lives." According to Garrett, "There's so much danger and passion and fire in the relationship. Her defining story is Roger—that's where her molten core lies. It's all there, the love, the hate, the pain, the passion. She's his heart, and he's her mate...her soul mate."

LOVE STORIES

LESLIE AND MIKE BAUER

He was her father's protégé when ambitious Ed Bauer met and married Leslie Jackson. But Ed couldn't deal with being a husband and potential dad—it interfered with his career. As a result, he turned to drink and abuse and had a brief affair, while Leslie turned to Ed's brother, Mike, for comfort and support. Leslie eventually went back to a repentant Ed, and Mike soon learned she was carrying his brother's child. He then fell for the devious charms of Charlotte Waring, and the two were wed.

Hurt, vulnerable and fed up with her marriage, Leslie took her young son, Rick, and rebelliously married older millionaire jet-setter Stanley Norris over the objections of her family and friends. The marriage ended disastrously with Norris' death. When Leslie was accused of his murder, Mike took her case and defended her in court.

During the Norris murder trial, Mike and Leslie fought their reawakened feelings for each other. When Leslie was acquitted, Mike left Charlotte, and in the spring of 1973 they were married. What did Leslie see in Michael? According to Irna Phillips, "She finds a gentleness, a compassion, a sweetness in Michael that were never part of his brother's makeup. Compassion, gentleness, sweetness equaled what to Ed? Weakness. Breathes there a man who doesn't have to ultimately realize that gentleness, compassion and sweetness are an essential part of masculinity?"

Sadly, their happiness was short-lived. Leslie was accidentally killed by a man who had waged a vendetta against Mike. At her funeral, the Rev. Evans urged her bereft family and friends to "help us keep Leslie alive in our hearts, where we keep our happiest memories." It would be a long time before Michael Bauer found love again.

Raised in a boardinghouse on Seventh Street, Nola Reardon dreamed of getting out of her lower-class neighborhood. Her quest led her to the doorstep of archaeologist Quinton McCord, who had come to town with a secret agenda and the desire to escape from a past that had caused much heartbreak. Says Michael Tylo, who played Quint, "At first Nola thought he was weird, and he thought she was flaky." Nola took a job as Quinton's live-in assistant and embarked on an exciting and dangerous adventure. Quint's ex-lover, Helena, showed up determined to win Quinton back, and his archnemesis Silas Crocker kidnapped Nola not once, but twice.

In St. Croix, while searching for a lost city known as the Temple of Gold, Nola almost drowned. Quinton came to the rescue, and they shared their first kiss. Only then did she stop addressing him as "Mr. McCord" and begin calling him Quint. The rescue cost Quint the Temple of Gold, but it marked the start of a beautiful romance. There would be other obstacles to overcome: Quinton took in a mysterious woman known as Rebecca, aka Mona, a figure from his past. Then the truth came to light that he was Henry Chamberlain's long-lost son. Through it all, Nola and Quint's love grew. Facing death in a cave-in with the evil Silas, Quinton penned this letter to his love:

"Dear Nola: The time has finally come to face the fact that I may never see you again. Beautiful, enchanting Nola. I've thought of you constantly during these past few days. Now at last I am finally beginning to understand what is truly precious during a man's short life.... You are my greatest gift.... I know now that I was wrong to turn my back on the present, for you have shown me how exhilarating it can be.... Thank you for teaching me to love.... Dearest Nola, I do love you. I've always loved you." This time, it was Nola who saved Quint's life.

Quint and Nola were engaged on May 3, 1982, and Henry threw an elaborate antebellum ball to celebrate their engagement. Except for Nola and Vanessa showing up in the same dress, everything went smoothly. The match of sister-in-laws was not made in heaven, but everything else was.

THE WEDDING:

Their wedding was not without its share of wackiness and adventure. Nola's mom, Bea, insisted on making the dress despite the fact that she couldn't sew. When she realized she was unable to do it, former hooker Lola Fontaine, who was now bartending at Company, had to finish the job with former colleagues Trixie and Mabel. If that wasn't enough, the church where Quinton and Nola were to be married burned down the week before the wedding. And on the big day, Nola's family accidentally left her behind, and she ended up hitching a ride on a fire engine! With Pachelbel's "Canon" playing in the background, Quinton and Nola were finally wed on June 24, 1983. After the ceremony, Quint surprised Nola with a romantic ride in a hot-air balloon—a ride to happily ever after.

THE HONEYMOON:

For their honeymoon, the newlyweds chose Ireland, and it was filled with mystery and romance. No sooner had they arrived than the owner of the inn were they where staying began to spin the legend of two young people who fell in love at the same inn a hundred years ago. Nola, who adored romantic stories, was enthralled. The families of the young lovers had prevented them from taking their vows in the local church. The young man was killed shortly afterward in a war, and the young woman died of grief. Since then, the bells of the church had not rung. The innkeeper convinced Nola that she and Quinton might be descendants of the two lovers, whose names were Nora Reardon and John Chamberlain, and suggested they might be able to free the lovers' restless spirits by taking their wedding vows in that very church. The skeptical Quinton began to think there was more to this legend than met the eye...

NOLA'S MOVIE REEL

A young woman with an overactive imagination and a love of old movies, Nola often had fantasies derived from her own desires and dreams, says actress Lisa Brown, who plays Nola. They were always sparked by real-life situations that Nola was trying to come to terms with.

Now Voyager: After Quinton fueled Nola's romantic ideas by taking her to San Francisco, Nola envisioned herself in the Bette Davis role (after the character's glamorous transformation), with Quinton in the Paul Henreid role.

Casablanca: Enjoying the attention she got from both Quinton and Kelly while recovering from Kelly Louise's birth, Nola imagined herself in Ilsa's place, having to choose between two captivating men.

Shipmates Forever: After Quinton consoled her following a bitter run-in with Kelly, Nola put him, Kelly (pictured here) and many other residents of Springfield into the nautical musical, in which Nola won over Kelly with her skillful dancing.

Camelot: Nola dreamed that she had been condemned by King Quinton and his wizard, Renfield, for lying that Rebecca had faked being mute.

As Guinevere, Nola faced certain death.

In the nick of time, Quinton was transformed into Lancelot and whisked his fair lady away to safety.

The Wizard of Oz: Nola sought an audience with the Wizard for advice on what to name her newborn son.

While back in Springfield:
Nola and Quint had narrowed it down to three names for the baby: Thomas Henry (after Quinton's father, Henry, and Nola's father, Tom), Quinton Jr. and Anthony James (after Nola's two brothers). Viewers of "Guiding Light" were invited to dial a special 900 number to cast their vote. The calls came pouring in. "Anthony James" was the winner. Dubbed "A.J." as a child, he likes to be called "J" now that he's a teenager.

Postscript: As it has a habit of doing, reality set in. Quint had an affair, and Nola returned to Springfield. But he is the love of her life, and she is his, and he soon followed. According to Lisa Brown, "The good news is that they can always find one another again."

THE FOUR MUSKETEERS AND THE LOVE STORY OF PHILLIP AND BETH

Mindy went to the prom with Phillip, and Beth was escorted by Rick, but when Phillip and Beth were crowned king and queen of the senior class, they knew they were in love. According to Judi Evans, who played Beth, "It was young love, the way we all want love to be, with some harsh realities mixed in."

Their exciting adventures as a quartet earned them the nickname "The Four Musketeers." Phillip Spaulding and Rick Bauer became lifelong friends at Lincoln Prep and transferred to Springfield High for their senior year. When Melinda Sue "Mindy" Lewis came to town to join her daddy, oilman Billy Lewis, she quickly set her sights on Phillip. To get his attention, Mindy pretended she had been thrown from her horse and injured. At the hospital, Mindy's roommate was a shy girl named Beth Raines. Both Phillip and Rick were charmed by the lovely Beth.

Devastated by the revelation of the true identity of his father and forbidden to see Beth by her twisted stepfather, Bradley, Phillip let himself be seduced by Mindy. And that was only the first obstacle that lay in the path of Phillip and Beth's burgeoning love. In a jealous fit, Bradley raped his stepdaughter, and a traumatized Beth pushed Phillip away. It would take a long time for Beth to reveal her painful secret, but as Judi Evans points out, "You never felt sorry for her and you always cheered her on, because everything she went through always made her stronger." To escape Bradley, Phillip and Beth ran away to New York. They were joined by Rick and Mindy, who began to fall for each other on this Christmastime adventure. With Bradley safely in jail, Phillip and Beth planned to marry, but on their wedding day, Beth overheard Billy confront his spoiled princess of a daughter, Mindy, who was pregnant with Phillip's child. Beth called off the wedding and Phillip married Mindy. Says Grant Aleksander (Phillip), "Mindy fell in love with who Phillip was and what he represented to her, but she never knew Phillip's heart. Because they were going to have a child, Phillip was very protective of Mindy, like a younger sister—no one dared mess with her."

When Mindy lost the baby and they divorced, Phillip yearned to reunite with his true love, but Beth had become involved with Lujack, the gangleader with a heart of gold, who turned out to be Alexandra Spaulding's long-lost son. Says Judi Evans, "When Beth's life changed, her love changed. Lujack made her feel less sheltered. He didn't take care of her the way Phillip did, but she was able to take care of him in a way. They were equals, and they helped each other." According to Vincent Irizarry (Lujack), "Even though he was the leader of a street gang, he was an honorable person, he was somebody you could count on if you were a friend. He had a strong code of honor and would literally fight to the death in support of you." Was Beth the love of Lujack's life? "Without a doubt," Irizarry confirms. "It's one of those relationships in which you realize your greatest potential, and I feel Lujack found that with Beth." Phillip's jealousy led to an explosion that blinded Beth, and he was subsequently blackmailed into marriage by Alexandra's stepdaughter, the devious but delightful India Von Halkein. Beth regained her sight, and Lujack began pursuing a music career. Sadly, when the making of his first music video turned deadly, Lujack was critically injured in an explosion and tragically died in Beth's arms. Free from India, Phillip set out to win Beth's forgiveness and her heart, but their happiness was short-lived. An art smuggling scam led to Beth's kidnapping, and when it was discovered that the boat she'd been in had sunk, Beth was presumed dead. Phillip eventually married Blake Thorpe, daughter of the nefarious Roger Thorpe. He was, of course, unaware that Beth was alive, but mute and suffering from amnesia.

Despite the forces conspiring to keep them apart, Phillip and Beth found each other once again. As Grant Aleksander puts it, "Phillip and Beth were a first and a true love, and I think she will always have the largest part of his heart." Beth accepted Phillip's proposal. Then she learned she was pregnant and mistakenly thought the child was Neil's. Later, Neil was killed in an explosion and Phillip was framed for murder. With Rick's help, he faked his own death to escape prosecution.

(Below) Phillip and Beth's wedding day: Valentine's Day 1991. By then, Beth had given birth to their daughter, Lizzie.

Beth was being cared for by an architect named Neil Everest (above), who brought her along when he took a job in Springfield. Blake had Phillip committed after he kept insisting he'd seen Beth, even though she knew it was true. Blake wasn't about to give up her claim on the Spaulding name, so she joined forces with Neil, who was equally determined to hold on to Beth.

(Left) Three generations of Raines women.

Postscript: Phillip, Beth and Lizzie went to Arizona to do community service for their part in the fraud surrounding Phillip's supposed death, while Rick went off to Chicago to do his. Today, Rick is back in Springfield and so is Phillip, but without his beloved Beth. A Spaulding vendetta caused them to split, but there are many who hope the separation will be short-lived.

FRANK AND ELENI COOPER
AN OLD WORLD LOVE STORY WITH
NEW WORLD TOUCHES

Uncle Stavros thought it was time his nephew, Frankie, took a wife, and so he brought Eleni Andros to the United States. It was not love at first sight for Frank and Eleni. They battled over her passage money, and she worked at the diner to pay it off. Eleni took to calling him "The Big Frank" because he was always ordering her around— and that was the beginning of their romance. But Frank waited to profess his love as he painstakingly built a house for him and Eleni. Enter Alan-Michael Spaulding. Truly taken with Eleni, Alan-Michael made his move. When Alexandra summoned Frank to Paris to do some detective work, Alan-Michael suggested Eleni follow in the Spaulding jet, but when she arrived she found a hooker in Frank's bed, planted by Alan-Michael. Heartbroken, Eleni learned she couldn't re-enter the States because she was an illegal alien! A gallant Alan-Michael offered to marry her right there in the customs office and make her his "legal" wife. Meanwhile, Frank had returned to put the finishing touches on their dream house. Says actor Frank Dicopoulos (Frank), "He'd built that house from the ground up, built the whole thing just for her, putting in everything she loved and wanted." When Eleni told Frank what she'd done, he smashed the house to bits.

Although the glamorous life was the antithesis of who Eleni was, she did come to love Alan-Michael. According to actress Melina Kanakaredes (former Eleni), "Eleni was genuinely drawn to that side of Alan-Michael. I think most Greek women have that tendency to want to mother. Frank had that sweet, I-can't-do-anything-myself, I-need-you kind of quality, and Alan-Michael had it even more because his life had been so bad."

Eleni and Alan-Michael were married again in a traditional Greek ceremony in her native Crete, with her family in attendance. When Alan-Michael's machinations were revealed—the hooker, the hasty customs house marriage and the fake birth-control pills he'd substituted— Eleni, unable to live with the duplicity, left him and went back to decent, honest, loving Frank. She didn't know it at the time, but she was pregnant with Frank's child. They made plans to marry. It was what Uncle Stavros had wanted, but it was a long time coming.

The wedding on Fifth Street was a fun-filled block party filled with family and friends, tradition and love. Eleni bartered baklava for bouquets of flowers, an anonymous Buzz (Frank's long-lost father) provided 500 steak dinners and, as a wedding gift, Mindy designed the dress for the eight-and-a-half-month pregnant bride. From his office window, a sad Alan-Michael watched.

When the lights unexpectedly went out, Frank said his vows from the heart: "I get suspicious of people who make promises. If they're saying what they're going to do instead of doing it, I wonder how much it can mean. So I can only say that what I am to you tonight, I always will be. I don't know any other way to be than in love with you, than to honor you. I don't know if I'll be a good father—I think I will—but I know I'll be the proudest father any child could ever have. And I know you will always have a safe home with me. If floods come to wash it away every night, every morning I'll build you a new one. It still seems like I should be promising you something harder to do."

Eleni answered with equal emotion: "You are so patient and kind. There is nothing that you cannot ask of me. I would fight a mountain lion for you, Frankie. And all these people here who love you, they would do the same. Frank, I will be your loyal wife and loving friend to your friends. I will teach our children the gentleness and goodness you have shown me. I will love you with all my strength and I will defend you from discouragement and harm. When you are sick I will make you well, and when you are sad I will make you laugh at my crazy heart. Our home will be clean and warm and honest and welcoming. I will make it a castle for you, my king of Fifth Street. To work hard but be generous, to forgive—these are the things I promise you. And when we are old, Frankie, and our hair is white and our children grown up and our promises are all kept, my love for you will still burn like a star inside me, the way it does tonight."

It was not smooth sailing for Frank and Eleni Cooper. His pride was hurt when her catering business took off, and his stubborn chauvinism frustrated her. But in 1994 they expressed their love and their faith in the future when they renewed their vows.

Frank is a caring man, a family man. When he put his life on the line and became a cop, Eleni wasn't happy, but she knew he had done it to make his family feel more secure. "It means a great deal to him to take care of those he loves," explains Frank Dicopoulos. "He's changed his life, he's made something of himself, and he's proud of it." According to actress Jennifer Roszell (Eleni), "Eleni cares so passionately about family, and I think that's one of her biggest strengths. She's got tremendous moral fiber. She's compassionate and extremely, fiercely protective of family and people she cares about."

Being traditional, Eleni was more nervous about her baby being born illegitimate than she was about saying "I do." Happily, the baby waited until after the reception to be born.

RICK BAUER AND ABIGAIL BLUME

He had been a loser in love, mainly to his best buddy, Phillip. First there was Beth, then there was Meredith Reade. But when the discovery of Reva led Rick Bauer to Goshen, where he met the innocent Abigail Blume, it was the start of a relationship like no other.

A childhood illness had left Abigail deaf, and Rick convinced her to come to Springfield for treatment to restore her hearing partially. Once there, Abigail realized there was more to life than what she'd experienced in Goshen, and she found herself falling in love with Rick. Amy Eckland (Abigail) describes her as "innocently wise and honest and passionate inside." Michael O'Leary (Rick) adds, "She's going to be his teacher. She's going to teach Rick values and morals and insights. She has a tremendous amount of wisdom, and Rick was drawn to that." For her move to Springfield, Abigail paid the painful price of being disowned by her family back in Goshen. Says Eckland, "She's deeply hurt and devastated, but she can't argue with her parents. She's hoping the day will come when they will be more forgiving of her."

Is Rick the love of Abigail's life? "Absolutely, desperately," replies Eckland. "I see him as handsome and warm, funny and safe, and he takes care of people. He's always attuned to other people and what their feelings are. That's Rick." Says O'Leary, "Abigail is intelligent and funny and moral and beautiful," but most important, "they were friends first, and she's his soul mate."

WEDDING ALBUMS

For some couples, their vows are truly "till death do us part." For others, it takes them two trips to the altar to get it right. There are some who make it to the church but not beyond, and there are others who say vows several different times before they finally settle down. But one thing is certain: Romance is rampant in Springfield, and "for better or for worse," couples keep saying "I do."

HOPE BAUER AND ALAN SPAULDING

He had been her father's enemy for years, and if they hadn't been stranded on a desert island together, their relationship would not have progressed past that of employee and boss. For starters, Hope was a "good girl" and Alan was married. But when Alan was sick and delirious on that desert island, Hope nursed him back to health, and in turn he took care of her. "When Alan whittled a comb and gave it to Hope as a gift, she saw the beast turn into a man and she responded," explains actress Elvera Roussel (Hope). Thinking they were going to die, Alan and Hope made love for the first time. The next day, they were rescued. Says Roussel, "Hope didn't walk out on her family. She always tried to bring everybody together." Despite their vastly different backgrounds and value systems, Hope and Alan were married in 1980 in a simple ceremony at the home of her grandmother, Bert, and a reluctant Mike Bauer gave his daughter away. Alan would go on to have many affairs, but for Hope, he was and always will be the great love of her life.

YOUNG LOVE

MORGAN RICHARDS AND KELLY NELSON

Eighteen-year-old Morgan Richards and Cedars resident Kelly Nelson chose magical Laurel Falls for their hastily arranged wedding in 1984. The bride wore a tiara of fresh flowers, and the school choir was rounded up to sing their special song, "You Needed Me." It had been a stormy on-again, off-again relationship from square one. Morgan's mother, Jennifer, and Kelly's godfather, Ed Bauer, were worried, and not without good reason. But as John Wesley Shipp (Kelly) puts it, their love had "an aching kind of innocence, and then an innocence lost. The first young love is pure and innocent...and nothing ever quite feels like that again, and nothing is as painful. Everybody, no matter how young or old, can embrace that kind of love."

MINDY LEWIS AND KURT CORDAY

In a wedding to rival that of Charles and Diana's, spoiled Mindy Lewis married the man of her dreams, handsome, hardworking Kurt Corday, in the fall of 1985 on ex-husband Phillip's country estate. The family had fallen on hard times, so Mindy financed her dream day with the missing $10 million in ransom money from the kidnapping of Kyle Sampson, which she had happened upon at the bar Company. Kyle had ruined her father's business, so it was "finders keepers," Mindy rationalized. The original church was booked, the gowns got mixed up and all hell broke loose at the reception when, in the culmination of the Infinity saga, Billy was brainwashed into shooting Kyle, the perpetrator David Preston was shot by his lover Suzette Saxon, and Mindy was arrested because the $10 million she used was stolen. It was a most unusual wedding day, to say the least!

CHELSEA REARDON AND JOHNNY BAUER

According to Kassie DePavia (Chelsea), "Chelsea Reardon was spunky, hardheaded and a perennial loser in love." After a broken engagement to Phillip Spaulding—the Spaulding family never accepted her—Chelsea turned to Johnny Bauer, host of "One on One," and in 1990 the two planned to wed. But a demented fan of Johnny's started terrorizing Chelsea at WSPR. First Chelsea found a headless bridal doll, then her wedding dress was slashed. The nervous bride unknowingly drank a cup of mocha that had been poisoned by the crazed fan. Chelsea collapsed at the altar before she could say "I do." "It was the beginning of the end," says DePavia. Johnny went back to former girlfriend Roxie Shayne, and after recovering, Chelsea went to London with Jackson Freemont to pursue her singing career. DePavia points out, "I was on the show for four years and four months, and I think I'm the only soap opera character that never married or got pregnant."

GILLY GRANT AND HAMPTON SPEAKES

It was a rocky road for ex-football star Hampton Speakes and WSPR station manager Gilly Grant as secrets from the past and Hamp's jealous daughter, Kat, conspired to break them up. Amelia Marshall (Gilly) sums it all up: "Gilly was a '90's woman, and sometimes her efforts to prove herself made her overlook the important things in life, namely family and children and love. It was her first marriage, and she couldn't quite find a balance. But there was something so special about Gilly and Hamp. He was her first big love." Their 1992 wedding was a star-studded affair. Hamp's football buddies Gale Sayers (Chicago Bears), Harry Carson and Bart Oates (New York Giants) came to cheer them on, and the groom, a talented musician himself, surprised his bride with guest Roberta Flack, who sang a special song to fit the occasion.

FIRST THERE WAS ALAN-MICHAEL SPAULDING...

Harley was dating Cameron Stewart and Alan-Michael was dating Dinah Marler, but at a school dance, Alan-Michael kissed Harley on a dare, and the couples soon switched partners. Their marriage, however, was strictly business: He wanted to collect his trust fund and needed a wife; she was from the wrong side of the tracks and wanted to marry money. They drafted a prenuptial agreement on a napkin before they said "I do." Says Beth Ehlers (Harley), "I hid the prenuptial agreement inside a doll, and we had to go to the garbage dump to find it. There we were, knee-deep in garbage, looking for this doll!" The marriage didn't last, but there remained an attraction and a mutual warmth between them, and today they are the best of friends.

HARLEY AND MALLET

Harley was a rookie—a bundle of contradictions—and he was a cop. Beth Ehlers notes, "She was very independent on the outside, while on the inside she was a pile of mush. But she was a rock, and the audience loved her strength." Mallet "was very internalized," Ehlers adds. "The one person he could open up to was this big-mouthed little thing who thought she stood a lot taller than five foot four!" To him she was always "Cooper" and would remain so even after they fell in love. According to Ehlers, "People grow and change. Harley needed to go through what she went through in order to appreciate this man coming into her life." They tried eloping (left), but it didn't feel right. "Harley would be perfectly happy getting married in a white sarong on an island somewhere. But that would break Frank's heart, and Mallet wanted something better for his bride."

(Right) Surprise birthdays are fairly common, but surprise *weddings?* Harley was summoned to the courtroom by Buzz, supposedly to make a graduation speech to the police academy. She was surprised to find Mallet there and the room decorated with balloons. Senator Collier, who had convinced Harley to join the force, was on hand to officiate, and Eleni supplied the dress, courtesy of Mindy. A good time was had by all, but one thing was missing. If you look closely, you can't see Harley's feet. Someone forgot to bring a pair of shoes, and she was wearing clunky oxfords under her beautiful dress—but no matter. Says Ehlers, "She found her prince, and they went off into the sunset." That was in 1993. Harley and Mallet honeymooned in Florida. They liked it and they stayed.

The year 1993 was a big one for weddings in Springfield, and almost every bride went to Melinda Lewis Designs to be fitted for her gown. This year's crop of young lovers walked the runway with their beaus. From left to right: David Marshall and Katherine Speakes; A.C. Mallet and Harley Cooper; Dylan Lewis and Julie Camaletti; and the star of the evening, designer Mindy Lewis.

DYLAN LEWIS AND JULIE CAMALETTI

Julie Camaletti was not as lucky in love as her brother, A.C. Mallet, was. Julie was actually in love with Hart when she agreed to marry Dylan. If she stayed with Hart, she reasoned, she'd continue to give in to her baser impulses, which she was brought up to believe didn't fit the image of who she was supposed to be. Marrying Dylan seemed to be the "right" thing to do. As for Dylan, he was ready—ready to marry the woman he loved, ready to have a house and a family, and Julie didn't have the emotional strength to say no. Enter Bridget

Reardon, who was wildly jealous of the comely Julie. After finding out that Julie had slept with Hart on the eve of her marriage to Dylan, Bridget rushed to the church, and stopped the wedding cold with her revelation before the bride and groom could say "I do." Dylan never forgave Julie. He and Bridget began to date and eventually became lovers, but that was after Bridget slept with Julie's other ex-boyfriend, Hart, and had his child.

MARRIED ONCE/MARRIED TWICE, AND THEN SHE MET MATT

VANESSA AND BILLY

It was a classic case of opposites attract when Vanessa Chamberlain married high-living oilman Billy Lewis in 1984. Says actress Maeve Kinkead, "She was upper-class, she was old money and she was highly educated, sophisticated and elegant. And he was her big, bad Billy." In spite of their differences, their relationship was a passionate one, very much like that of Scarlett O'Hara and Rhett Butler. The search for daughter Dinah with former lover Ross Marler put too much strain on the marriage, though, and they eventually divorced. In 1993, they tried again.

Henry Chamberlain may have walked his beloved daughter down the aisle, but he didn't give his blessing. Explains Kinkead, "He thinks it's in Billy's nature to be thoughtless and impetuous. Vanessa thinks it doesn't matter, he's the person she loves. It may not be what she should want, but it's what she does want. She's a one-man woman, and that man is Billy."

The day was a triumph for bride and groom, as this was not their first attempt to remarry. Last time, the groom not only didn't show but ended up drunk in Vegas and came back married to Nadine Cooper. Little Billy was ecstatic when his parents tied the knot. Unfortunately, they were not to live happily ever after.

VANESSA AND MATT

After Billy went back to the bottle, shot Roger and was sent to prison, a heartbroken Vanessa filed for divorce. She seemed to be facing a life of emotional barrenness...and then she met Matt Reardon. "It was a joy for her, feeling connected to some wonderful life force again," Kinkead remarks. According to Kurt McKinney (Matt), "It wasn't supposed to happen and it wasn't supposed to last. Matt came from a working-class family, but these two people still had so much in common. Matt didn't have to be this upper-crust type to fulfill the needs of this woman. And he didn't need someone from his own class and his age to fulfill what he needed in a romantic relationship. What they had was stronger than all that." Indeed, their wedding was the antithesis of the elegant country club affair that used to be de rigueur for Vanessa. For starters, little Billy picked up his mother's dress, left it on top of the car, then ran over it by mistake. The dress Vanessa ended up saying "I do" in came from Nola's closet, a gift from a sultan. The groom's outfit

came from Nola's coffers as well, after the tuxedo he ordered turned out to be a too-light shade of powder blue. As for the reception, Nola slaved over an exotic dish, only for the bride and her guests to succumb to food poisoning the morning after. The honeymoon was canceled, but no one could deny the deep love that Vanessa had for Matt, and he for her. The bridegroom was a happy man that day. Says Kurt McKinney, "You meet certain people in your life that you have a feeling about, a chemistry with. Matt was really just searching his own soul and finding himself, and in the process he found the love of his life. Fate brought them together." When Vanessa became ill, she didn't want to burden her loved ones and her family. So she faked her death in a car crash and disappeared, leaving only her wedding bands behind. "There's something that tells Matt she's still on this earth somewhere," McKinney points out. "He feels it. He believes it. And it's going to take more than a handful of rings to make him believe she's really gone."

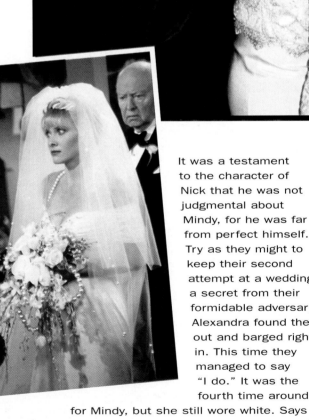

TWO TRIES AND
THEY STILL
COULDN'T
GET IT RIGHT

MINDY LEWIS AND NICK MCHENRY
It was love at first sight when Mindy Lewis spotted Nick McHenry in a New York bar and thought that he was Lujack resurrected. Indeed, she discovered he was the son Alexandra Spaulding never knew she had, and Alexandra was no friend of Mindy's. Nevertheless, they fell in love and planned to marry. Mindy's fervor in protecting Nick from the truth about his parentage led to their wedding-day disaster. Confronted by Alexandra and unable to face Nick with the awful truth that she knew Alexandra was his biological mother, Mindy abandoned a bewildered Nick at the altar and headed off for parts unknown.

It was a testament to the character of Nick that he was not judgmental about Mindy, for he was far from perfect himself. Try as they might to keep their second attempt at a wedding a secret from their formidable adversary, Alexandra found them out and barged right in. This time they managed to say "I do." It was the fourth time around for Mindy, but she still wore white. Says then—executive producer Jill Farren Phelps, "When you're young and you've made some mistakes, and you've finally met the man you're going to spend the rest of your life with, you're entitled to get married in a white dress." The wedding was a success, but the marriage was not. Life in the Spaulding mansion and an attempt to adopt a child proved too much for the couple, and eventually they parted ways.

NADINE COOPER'S WACKY WEDDINGS

NADINE COOPER AND BILLY LEWIS

Ambitious and impulsive, Nadine Cooper wanted to marry money, and she did. On the night that Billy Lewis was supposed to marry Vanessa, he got drunk, took Nadine to Vegas and tied the knot with her! Says Jean Carol (Nadine), "When Billy wanted to marry her a second time to show Springfield that he really loved her, that was a biggie for Nadine." Desperate to hold on to her man, Nadine pretended to be pregnant (with the help of lots of padding) and tried to pass Bridget's baby off as hers and Billy's. The plan backfired when Vanessa guessed the truth.

NADINE COOPER AND BUZZ COOPER

She was the first love of his life, as he was hers. They were teenagers when they married, and they had two children, Frank and Harley. But she deserted the family for the glamour of Hollywood, and he went to Vietnam. Vulnerable and lonely after her fiasco with Billy, Nadine offered to work as a waitress at the diner, and a mutual affection grew again between them. They had no plans to remarry—until they became contestants on the TV game show "Soulmates" to try to win back the money Eleni had put up for Buzz's bail. The show went something like this: *Him:* "Recently divorced Greek-American, forties, father of three (possibly four), successful diner owner, seeks a slim, attractive waitress type (I love blondes), for companionship and maybe more. You should be down to earth and able to roll with the punches whenever I do something crazy, like come back from the dead. Sense of humor a must, color photo a plus." *Her:* "Sunny divorcée with a zest for life, looking for romance with a stable, loving teddy bear who knows exactly what he wants and doesn't play games. I'm a natural blonde, mid-thirties, smart but not academic, into bowling, golden oldies, and red '57 Chevys with leather backseats. I do wear a fur coat sometimes, but it's a fake. I hope you're not! Let's get to know each other one step at a time." They made the perfect couple and they won! But in order to collect the prizes and the money, they needed to prove that they were husband and wife. A quick trip to Vegas did the trick.

BLAKE THORPE AND ROSS MARLER

She came to town as Alan Spaulding's lover, then married his son Phillip and moved on to Alan-Michael, but that was a lifetime ago for Blake Thorpe. Says Liz Keifer (Blake) of the Spaulding men, "Alan makes Blake angry, and Phillip, well, she just wants him to be erased. She and Alan-Michael did find a connection, as they were attracted to the power in each other." Then she discovered Ross. Keifer describes Ross as Blake's "first real love. It was her first soulful, unselfish, healing love, as opposed to that drama queen stuff." It didn't start out that way. Ross was her mother's boyfriend, and Blake slept with him for sport and for revenge. Says Keifer, "It's great to pull the tiger out of a button-down stuffed shirt! Ross and Blake complement each other. He brought out her trust, and she brought out his passion and sexuality. And she allowed him to throw caution to the wind. They helped each other become better human beings."

"Blake's a pip," notes Jerry Ver Dorn (Ross). "Ross is at the point in his life when he could have gone sour or good, and suddenly he found a whole bunch of good. He's very lucky to have Blake come into his life and shake things up." So far this couple has survived Amanda's manipulations and the arrival of evil stepchild Dinah. Then there's the fact that Ross is technically Roger Thorpe's son-in-law, and the two men hate each other's guts. Will they survive the fact that one of their newborn twins has a different father? Says Ver Dorn, "They'll fight like hell to stay together." Adds Keifer, "I call him the perfect dance partner, and as far as I'm concerned, Ross and Blake can survive anything."

A ROMANCE OF HOPE

NICK MCHENRY AND SUSAN BATES

Nick had finally put his marriage to Mindy Lewis behind him when Susan Bates arrived at the *Springfield Journal* looking for work. Nick dismissed her, and Susan assumed it was because she was HIV-positive. After Nick found out about her condition, he apologized profusely and asked her out on a date. Susan didn't want pity, she wanted a job, but Nick persisted and they fell in love. When Susan nearly died at the hands of psycho Brent Lawrence, Nick realized how precious she was to him, and he proposed. They were married at the Spaulding mansion and honeymooned in Europe. Says Vincent Irizarry (Nick), "I would have to say that the love of his life is

Susan. They have a commitment to one another and a love that seems to surpass the earthly constrictions of their lives. They're sharing each other despite her suffering. The selflessness that they are giving each other, that's what love is about."

A ROMANCE OF YOUTH

ALAN-MICHAEL SPAULDING AND LUCY COOPER

It was love at first sight for her, but not for him. While Lucy had a major crush on Alan-Michael, he was still carrying a torch for his ex-wife Eleni. Eventually they dated, but the fact that she was a virgin scared him off. He turned to Tangie Hill, while Lucy dated Spaulding co-worker Brent Lawrence, which was a horrible mistake. Brent raped Lucy and then, masquerading as a woman named Marian, terrorized her for months. The nightmare escalated when Brent/Marian held Lucy and Alan-Michael hostage in the lighthouse. When the twosome discovered a bomb, they declared their love for one another, thinking their lives were over. After that experience, this young couple was ready for some FUN! She wanted the wedding of her dreams but couldn't quite decide exactly what that was, so Alan-Michael took matters into his own hands and decided to surprise his bride. It was a proud moment for dad Buzz Cooper when he marched his daughter down the red carpet to the Pantages theater, where she rode a cherry picker up to the marquee to say her vows. Will they live happily ever after? Says Sonia Satra, "Working through all the trauma together certainly made them stronger." Michael Dietz (Alan-Michael) adds, "She has so much energy and enthusiasm, and she showed him a different way of living. Unfortunately, the family sometimes gets in the way, but she's the most important thing in his life." Wouldn't it be wonderful if every couple who walked down the aisle and said "I do" was headed for a lifetime of happily ever after?

Alan-Michael knew Lucy loved the movies, so he put her, along with their friends and family, on the Spaulding jet and headed for—where else?—Universal Studios in Orlando, Florida.

Prodigal son Phillip chose the occasion to return to the fold. Dressed as Frankenstein, he checked out members of the Spaulding clan before he made his presence known. The family, of course, had no idea he was among them.

HAPPY ANNIVERSARY

In 1937 the Rev. John Ruthledge arrived in Five Points, U.S.A., and placed his reading lamp—which came to be known as the Friendship Lamp—in his window as a sign for all who needed guidance to seek his help. Eventually the locale was moved to Springfield, and the lamp was replaced by a lighthouse. The citizens knew that if they brought their problems to "the light," they would find a ray of hope. In honor of the 60th anniversary of the longest running show in broadcast history, the lighthouse was restored so that the families of Springfield would not have to face the future without their "Guiding Light."

On June 26, 1977, with Charita Bauer (Bert) taking center stage at New York's elegant St. Moritz Hotel, "Guiding Light" celebrated its 25th anniversary as a television serial and its 40th year in broadcasting. That same year the show expanded to an hour, dropped "The" from its title, and welcomed the Spauldings to Springfield.

The cast of "Guiding Light," 1982. The show won the Emmy for Best Drama that year, and...

After 15 years on the radio, "The Guiding Light" moved to television. Above, some of the younger members of the cast celebrate 15 years on television, bringing the grand total to 30 years on the air! The year was 1966, and young Peggy Scott (Fran Myers, third from left) was dating Johnny Fletcher (Don Scardino, fourth from left) against her parents' wishes.

...in celebration of its 30th year on television and 45th year on the air, cast and crew partied at New York's Empire State Building.

(Above) "Guiding Light" celebrated the taping of its 10,000th episode on September 18, 1986. In honor of the occasion, the show threw a pancake breakfast, and as you can see, a good time was had by all.

The cast in 1987, the year "Guiding Light" reached a milestone of 50 years on the air!

(Right) Past and present casts celebrated the show's 50th anniversary with an elegant black-tie affair at the New York State Theater at Lincoln Center. They were joined on this special occasion by Arthur Peterson (first row, second from left), who originated the role of the Rev. Ruthledge in 1937.

The cast posed for the picture at left in 1989. That was the year Reva and Billy learned Dylan was their son, and millionaire Alan Spaulding was jailed for shooting the infamous Roger Thorpe.

(Right) The cast celebrated the taping of the 12,000th episode by singing "Oh, What a Beautiful Morning" on "CBS This Morning," then headed to the Turtle Bay Cafe, where the festivities continued.

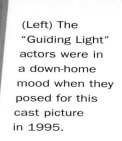

(Left) The "Guiding Light" actors were in a down-home mood when they posed for this cast picture in 1995.

On January 16, 1997, cast and crew re-created a 1937 radio episode of "The Guiding Light," complete with commercials. The performance was held at New York's Museum of Television and Radio and broadcast nationally. In an ironic twist, Michael Zaslow, who plays Springfield's resident villain, Roger Thorpe, portrayed the good Rev. Ruthledge. As an added touch, the cast was outfitted in vintage 1937 attire. It was a wonderful trip down memory lane and a fitting tribute to the longest running show in broadcast history! Happy Anniversary! What more can you say about a show that has lasted for 60 years and is still going strong? A lot...

**MARY ALICE
DWYER-DOBBIN**

LUCY JOHNSON

KIM ZIMMER

MARY ALICE DWYER-DOBBIN: EXECUTIVE-IN-CHARGE OF PRODUCTION, PROCTER & GAMBLE

"It's an exciting time to celebrate the 60th anniversary of 'Guiding Light.' As technology has taken us from radio to television to cyberspace, one constant has remained: our fans' loyal devotion to this long-running serial. Generations of viewers have watched the show because they became hooked on good stories and appealing characters. And Procter & Gamble is committed to using that rich history to keep viewers happily entertained and to reach out for a new generation of soap enthusiasts. In creating the show in the '30s, Irna Phillips was thinking ahead and knew that people would be looking for a message of hope and could find it listening to 'Guiding Light.' We salute the countless people who have worked on the show all these years. They, too, have had the foresight to take risks to keep the show fresh and current with the times. We're proud of 'Guiding Light' as we honor its past, present and future."

LUCY JOHNSON: SENIOR VICE PRESIDENT DAYTIME/CHILDREN'S PROGRAMMING AND SPECIAL PROJECTS, CBS

"'Guiding Light' is built on a 'strong foundation,' that of the 'family unit.' One of the keys to its long-lasting success is that the show stays creatively mindful of those roots. It is a centered show with a strong character base that pays off its history. It might shift emphasis through the years, but it stays true to its foundation and its roots." Ms. Johnson feels that we are on the brink of a new era and there's a positive new life to the show. The future is, of course, unknown, but the show has "been re-energized...revived. 'Guiding Light' honors its past while it stays contemporary and that combination makes the show enduring."

JAY HAMMER (FLETCHER READE)

"What these stories provide is a validation—because our viewers know where we are coming from, they know what has happened to us and they have felt those things with us and have shared those things with us...and sharing, that's the first thing we try to teach our children, how to share, how to cooperate, how to socially integrate themselves."

WENDY FISHMAN: DIRECTOR OF DAYTIME PROGRAMS NEW YORK, CBS

"The fact that it's lasted this many years is just incredible! That makes it very unique. One of the things that has contributed to its success is that 'Guiding Light' is always taking chances. They always try to be on the cutting edge...They always try something new, and they always take a risk in trying to break new ground. And they have an incredible cast, they have for as long as it's been on the air. The story lines are engaging—it's like the old 'Guiding Light.' I think the future is very bright.

KIM ZIMMER (REVA SHAYNE COOPER)

"That it has survived all of the modern technology and the desire to compete with the bizarreness of television now…and have the sense of family and tradition which this show demands, which is something that I hope we never lose because it is so full of tradition. And you have people that are still here that can hold on to that tradition. So I'm hoping that we don't let the fans down in the course of the next 50 years, that we can give them that sense of being able to turn on the television and feel like they're relating to something they know…and 'Follow the light.'"

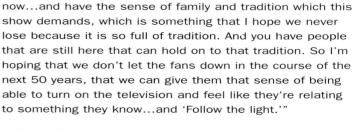

ELVERA ROUSSEL (HOPE BAUER SPAULDING)
"They were not doing exploitative story lines, they were doing honest story lines about real human emotions and real family values being in contrast with people's fighting the badness in them. It was a defining of good and evil. It was very good at defining the struggle against evil. Like Roger always being the representation of evil and the Bauers always being the representation of good. And the Spauldings coming in and being another representation of evil. And how the good tried to help the evil."

SHARON LEAL (DAHLIA CREED)
"There is such integrity behind the show. I think that's what really makes us stand out, there's a lot of heart…and it's nice to be a part of that."

ROY STEINBERG: PRODUCER
"I think more than any of the other shows, 'Guiding Light' deals with tradition, family and hope. It started with the Rev. Ruthledge putting that light in the window. And I think it's still the show that deals with a kind of spirituality of families being there for each other, especially today when families are more splintered and people are all over the country and all over the world sometimes. It's a fictionalized embodiment of what the family could be."

MAEVE KINKEAD (VANESSA CHAMBERLAIN REARDON)
"We have a tradition of top-notch acting—Bill Roerick, Larry Gates…and because we're one of the longest running shows, we have that richness that's been there….We just get richer and richer."

THE LATE LARRY GATES (H.B. LEWIS)
"Has the best cast, bar none, and that goes for nighttime too. It's a simple story of a family and if they keep it that way, it will go on forever. The best story of people caring about one another that there is on TV. Wouldn't trade the experience. Being involved in long story, a good story where things happen. Working with wonderful actors. It's been a joy, a sheer pleasure, and I feel deeply privileged to be a part of it."

JERRY VER DORN (ROSS MARLER)
"It's a very realistic, tender kind of show with great depth to it. And it's always been blessed with a house full of good actors. It's a show that has a real identity to it. It centers in and around family. And the originators of the show realized how explosive and powerful dealing with family and small towns can be. To my mind it should be on the cover of *Time*. What in show business lasts 60 months?"

ELVERA ROUSSEL

SHARON LEAL

MAEVE KINKEAD

LARRY GATES

A Tour Behind the Scenes of "Guiding Light"

RADIO DAYS

True to the humanitarian spirit of "Guiding Light," behind the scenes 1947 found cast members Mary Lansing (Julie Collins), Hugh Studebaker (Dr. Charles Matthews), Laurette Filbrandt (Trudy Bauer) and announcer Herb Allen participating in a Knit for Needy Children drive.

For four years from 1952 to 1956, members of the cast of "Guiding Light" raced from the studio at Liederkranz Hall, where they performed "live on TV" in the morning, to the station five blocks away, where they performed the same show for radio audiences. Below Bert and Bill Bauer discuss family problems on one of the first TV sets—the Bauer kitchen.

THE TRANSITION TO TELEVISION

A Day in the Life of "Guiding Light"

EPISODE #12560

TAPE: DECEMBER 6, 1996

AIR: DECEMBER 26, 1996

Bruce Barry is our director for A Day in the Life of "Guiding Light." Bruce's first job was in the third sub-basement of CBS in the videotape library. It was as associate director that he got his first shot at directing: The director, who had never missed a day in 26 years, had a heart attack. Once Bruce got his first taste of directing actors in a professional situation, "That's where I got bit!" Today, Bruce is in charge of training prospective new directors at "Guiding Light." "It's been really rewarding for me. They observe when I block scripts.... I look at their paperwork and I feel like a teacher, grading it, making corrections, making comments on their shots and their blocking, giving hints about what pitfalls to watch out for. I've had a tremendous amount of people who have gone on to become very good directors, and I'm proud to have been there at the beginning when they were showing an interest in it." For Bruce, the key to an episode's success "is all about the thread of the scene and the focus of the show. If you don't grab them with a story, then it's all for naught."

Bruce Barry directing one of Roger's "death" scenes in the 1980s.

Bruce's preparation begins when he receives the edited script and establishes a theme for the episode. Then he organizes the details—props, technical requirements and special effects requirements. He prepares notes and works out the camera blocking, camera shots, lighting plot, actor movements and, of course, actor motivation. The workday starts at 7 a.m., and the schedule goes like this: dry rehearsal, camera block (dress rehearsal), tape.

The schedule doesn't allow for a lot of rehearsal time, so Bruce chooses the scenes he feels need the most work and "dries them twice."

Here Bruce confers with Justin Deas (Buzz Cooper) on the script. "We have a wonderful company of people," says Bruce.

Kim and Kim—Kim Zimmer (Reva) and Kimberly Brown (Marah), who play mother and daughter—share a warm offstage moment. Kimberly says, "When I first met her, I was like, 'Oh wow! This is neat. This is the Kim Zimmer they've all been talking about!' We're great friends now, we kid around backstage, laugh.... She's very funny, and we have a great relationship."

THE MAGIC OF THE MAKEUP
AND HAIR ROOM

After dry rehearsal, it's off to makeup and hair. Makeup artist Paul Gebbia works on Cynthia Watros (nurse Annie Lewis) while...

Linda Williams, head of hair design, gets Kim Zimmer (Reva) ready for the country club Christmas party. "The actors are in your chair at 6:45 a.m. waiting for a haircut, and I tell them, 'Can you really trust me at this hour with a scissors?'" she jokes. During dress rehearsal, Linda goes onto the set to touch up the actors right before they tape. "I feel this is our most important time because it's what goes on the air. You can do a wonderful job in the chair, but by the time they get to the set, they're all messed up."

...makeup artist Joe Cola works his magic on Sharon Leal (Dahlia Creed). Joe started his career at the Metropolitan Opera and came to "Guiding Light" in 1979. On an average day, he makes up 15 to 20 people. Joe explains, "We do major touch-ups after the dry rehearsal, because it doesn't matter how pretty they are in the makeup room, they've got to look pretty when that camera starts rolling. So you have to maintain their looks for the rest of the day." For Joe, scars, burns, bruises and breaks are the most fun: "The Mallet burn, the whip scars on Sonni/Solita's back...that's when you really get to be creative." Joe has worked on every soap in New York City, and he chose to work on "Guiding Light" because of the people. "They're nicer," he points out. "They know who they are. They're more genuine. It's a classy daytime serial."

Hairdresser Ralph Stanzione gets Jennifer Roszell (Eleni) ready for the same affair.

WARDROBE AND PROPS

THEN: Robert Anton became wardrobe designer in the early eighties. "We had just introduced the characters of Vanessa Chamberlain and that great little tramp from the wrong side of the tracks, Nola Reardon," he recalls. "All the hour shows were becoming much more spectacular in terms of production. Prior to that, clothes were borrowed from stores or manufacturers, worn once or twice and then returned." Audiences would see the same dress move from show to show. It was Robert's idea to create an individual wardrobe for each character that dramatically supported both the character and the story. One of his favorite costumes was the one designed for the Antebellum Ball, where both Vanessa and Nola showed up in the same dress. "The characters wouldn't go out together and buy the same dress, so I had to look at them and ask myself, what is so famous that they would both individually come to the same conclusion?" What Robert saw was "a little spark of Scarlett O'Hara in both of them."

Wardrobe assistants Rose Cuervo, Michael Difonzo and Raul Ferreira make sure everything is steamed, pressed, sewn and ready to wear.

NOW: (above) Costume designer Suzanne Schwarzer and assistant designer Alyson Hui ready the day's clothes. New to "Guiding Light," Suzanne is trying to push the show "into a very *Vogue,* very *Harper's Bazaar,* very chic" direction and regain some of that lost movie star glamour.

And you thought a television studio was glamorous? This is the wardrobe room, complete with washing machine, dryer and boxes of bras, teddies, tights and other necessary items.

Up on the fifth floor, the Spaulding Christmas tree waits in the wings.

Right around the corner in the prop room, set designers Barry Axtell, Shelley Barclay and Jane Patterson ready Dinah's Christmas present to Hart: a show saddle wrapped in red. Although his title is set designer, Barry is really a set decorator. He reads all the advance scripts and makes a "mental note of what's to come...if we're going to blow anything up, or anything that will send up a red flag as far as props go." Barry and his staff have to keep tabs on more than 300,000 items (if you count pens and silverware) housed in the studio or at the warehouse. Some of the treasures found on those shelves include:

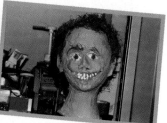

Signs for the Springfield Cab Co....

...and Fire Department.

A treasure chest of Andoran gold that figured in a hidden treasure storyline.

One of Roger Thorpe's many clever disguises. He used this one to escape from a mental institution.

Police mug shot #94556, from Alan Spaulding's last arrest.

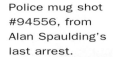

Among the chimes and clocks hangs the sign for the Springfield lighthouse, built in 1887.

The Cedars hospital cart is ready for its rounds. These blood samples figured prominently in the Brent/Marian storyline, when Brent switched the samples so that Lucy would believe that she'd contracted AIDS.

SCENERY

Art director Rick Dennis is responsible for the design of all the scenery on the show. According to Rick, "What's important is not only the way the scenery looks, but how it works with the storyline. So we have to make sure all the sets that are written into scenes by the writers will fit into the studio every day. Then we plan the layout and make sure each of those sets is up on a particular day." After that's done, Rick works with the set designers on decor and purchases furniture, drapes and so forth: "It's just like doing a home."

Rick works closely with scenic designers Maureen Going (above) and Kennon Rothchild and head of props Ron Lebrecht.

Head carpenter Manny Sanchez makes sure that sets are built to function as planned; that is, doors open and close and then fold into flats when the day's work is done.

The production office is run by production coordinators Wally White, David Kreizman and Natasha Katzive. Says Wally, "It's the Grand Central Station of Springfield. Everything comes in and goes out of here." The coordinators keep things running in the office between the producers, directors and actors—a very complex task that requires excellent coordination. Each one is assigned to a director and follows through on everything that happens with that director's script. According to Natasha, "There is no typical day. The only thing that's typical is that it's always crazy and there are always a hundred things to do."

The Spaulding Library, "undressed."

Temp Megan Secord and Lisa Randolph, who is in charge of the Viewer Feedback Line, fill in next month's calendar.

Producer Roy Steinberg (left) joined the staff of "Guiding Light" in 1990. Roy loves producing because he helps to "put it all together." He must deal with everything from a set not working, to coordinating the taping of a car chase. "Having spent my life in the theater, producing 'Guiding Light' is like opening night every day."

The Cooper Diner, "dressed" for Christmas.

A nine-year veteran of "Guiding Light," Cathy Maher Smith shares producing responsibilities with Roy Steinberg and Robert Kochman. "Working for Procter & Gamble has been a great experience for me both professionally and personally. I met my husband while I was on 'Edge of Night,' got married when I was on 'Search for Tomorrow,' and had both my kids while on 'Guiding Light.' I'm lucky it's such a great place for a working mom."

Associate producer Francine Versalie (above) has been with "Guiding Light" for 10 years. One of Francine's main responsibilities is continuity and the day-to-day tracking of production elements. She works closely with the show's executive producer in the control room, as well as with writers, directors and the producers. Francine reads all the advance show outlines to get a five-week jump on any special production needs and coordinates with department heads to make those needs a reality.

Casting director Glenn Daniels and assistant casting director Melanie Haseltine (right) are responsible for "discovering" everyone who appears in front of the "Guiding Light" cameras. Glenn comes from the world of film, and to him, the show is "like a movie that never ends. It's constant and always changing, and you're always several weeks ahead of yourself." Melanie casts under fives (those with under five lines) and extras on a daily basis, and works on contract roles with Glenn.

Alexandra Johnson (above) was an intern on "Guiding Light" while she was still in school. She is now an associate producer in charge of scheduling and script preparation. Alex also works with consultants—from medical, legal and law enforcement areas, as well as with computer experts—when story requires it. "All of this makes it an exciting job that's always changing. I don't think I could do a nine-to-five desk job. I think I'd be bored out of my mind."

Assistant to the writers Jill Lorie Hurst looks over scripts with writer Nancy Williams Watt. Jill is basically a liaison between the writers and production. Everything relating to the script— notes, changes and so forth—crosses her desk. For Jill, one thing she enjoys is "getting to work with different levels of writers. It's fascinating to watch when it really, really works, when a breakdown becomes a wonderful script and a beautiful show."

Production administrator Linda Mysel (left) deals with business affairs, including unions, vendors and billing. "I'm like the Little Dutch Boy with my finger in the dike!" she muses. A lot of what she does is translate, "because accounting doesn't always understand production and vice versa. In show business, what you have to do is connect the 'show' part with the 'business' part."

Matron Maria Dedvukaj (left) takes good care of her actors. "If they need help, they always come to Mother, and if they want to talk, I'm always here to listen—it can be a very pressured atmosphere," she explains. Maria also takes care of the crew. "They always come to me and I give them a little rubdown, try to make them feel comfortable and feel like they're wanted." Maria says "Guiding Light" people are the best— no prima donnas here. "They're warm. They're caring. They worry about you. They care if you have a problem. That's why working with them is like working with a family."

As Phillip and Rick on "Guiding Light," they've been good friends since high school days, but they're friends in real life as well, although there is a bit of "The Odd Couple" about them. When asked for permission to photograph their dressing room, Grant Aleksander (Phillip) said he'd have to ask Mikey, otherwise known as Michael O'Leary (Rick), to clean up the room.

Taking a break between scenes, Kim Zimmer heads for her dressing room on six.

On screen they're Blake and Ross, wife and husband, but on the Internet they're known as "Bloss." Off-screen they're great pals. Liz Keifer pays Jerry Ver Dorn a visit in his dressing room and heads right for the phone.

INSIDE THE CONTROL BOOTH—
READY TO TAPE

Since taking over in November 1996, Executive Producer Paul Rauch is in the control room for the taping of every show, his hands-on input ensuring that the show will fit his goals.

A 22-year veteran of "Guiding Light," Senior Producer Robert Kochman spends much of his time with Executive Producer Paul Rauch in the control room. While Paul concentrates on actors and directors, Robert is his right-hand man. Respected and admired, the actors often come to Robert with problems, and he plays diplomat. Robert has been a line producer for 15 years, and, as such, he must pay attention to music, sound effects and all the elements necessary to produce a good show. As Robert says, "It's like being the third eye."

Associate director Matt Lagle accompanies the director all day long. In the control room, he's the director's right-hand person, readying the shots and making notes for the edit. After the studio day is over, Matt oversees the editing of the show.

Production assistants Rose Mooy and Ilene K. Frankel time the show and take notes for the directors. It is their responsibility to make sure the show fits into its 60-minute time slot, including commercials. They estimate how long each scene is, then add the scenes up and assist in making cuts.

Audio mixer Butch Inglese works with the TD.

Technical director (TD) Bob Eastman is in charge of the technicians on the show, those who handle the cameras, audio, utilities and tape. In the control room, he's the guy on the left-hand side of the director, sitting at the switcher.

(Above) Music director Robyn Cutler and music assistant Jon Hopkins report to supervising music director Barbara Miller-Gidaly. Barbara and Robyn select all the music for each episode.

In a little booth that resembles a treehouse, Tim Pankewicz (right, holding picture of sound effects head Joe Gallant) makes sure doorbells and phones ring, thunder roars and the sound of heavy rain can be heard.

DOWN ON THE SET

(Left) Work on the set begins with the reading of the cart. That's when director Bruce Barry meets with the producer, stage manager and set decorator to make sure all the props for the day are in order, such as... James Rainbow's floral arrangements (above). How many champagne glasses, candles and files will be needed in a scene? Once the director gets to see what everything looks like, that's when they do things like "kill the coffee table."

(Right) Lighting director Tony Girolami sets the scene.

Every Christmas, "Guiding Light" gathers cast and crew and their families.

After actor Jerry ver Dorn greets viewers with: "From our family to yours, all of us at 'Guiding Light' wish you the happiest of holidays," everyone waves and says "Merry Christmas" on screen while the show's credits roll. Writers' assistant Jill Lorie Hurst says, "I still get a lump in my throat when I watch the Christmas crawl.... And everybody's family, of course, loves it. The first time my name ran on television, my grandmother ran out into the hallway. She was in a senior citizens complex and she said, 'I have to go tell someone!'"

Back on the set, set designer Barry Axtell and his prop crew, Ron Lebrecht and Jane Paterson, dress the Georgian Room at the country club for Billy Lewis' Christmas bash. In this particular week, there were four Christmas parties at the country club, and they each had to have a different look!

Kimberly Brown does a camera check.

(Left) Kim Zimmer, senior producer Bob Kochman, Kimberly Brown, director Bruce Barry and Sasha Martin (Marina Cooper) sample the Christmas dinner.

(Above) Stage manager Ann Vettel instructs the extras.

(Right) Bruce Barry gives his actors final notes.

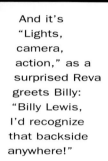

And it's "Lights, camera, action," as a surprised Reva greets Billy: "Billy Lewis, I'd recognize that backside anywhere!"

(Below) Meta Bauer (Mary Stuart), newly returned to Springfield, takes a moment to savor the scene.

In the spirit of the holidays, the families of Springfield come together as Bruce directs the Bauers and the Marlers in serenading the country club revelers with carols. The script reads: "It's a warm, wonderful and upbeat moment as we pan the faces of the assembled as they all sing 'Joy to the World.'"

It's a wrap! Merry Christmas to all, and to all a good night!

THE PEOPLE BEHIND "GUIDING LIGHT"

EXECUTIVE PRODUCERS

THEN...

THE RADIO YEARS
David Lesan, Joe Ainley, Carl Waster
THE TELEVISION YEARS
Lucy Ferri Rittenberg 1952–1976
Allen Potter 1976–1983
Gail Kobe 1983–1987
Joe Willmore 1987–1989
Robert Calhoun 1989–1991
Jill Farren Phelps 1991-1995
Michael Laibson 1995–1996

...AND NOW

Executive producer Paul Rauch took over the helm of "Guiding Light" in November of 1996. Rauch has also served as executive producer of "Another World," "One Life to Live" and "Santa Barbara," and as CBS vice president, East Coast, for various primetime, daytime and children's series. He worked with the legendary Irna Phillips, who created "Guiding Light," with Agnes Nixon when she was the show's head writer, and he was the Procter & Gamble supervisor who took the show from 15 minutes to half an hour and the first producer to produce an hourlong daytime show. What does Rauch want to accomplish at "Guiding Light"? "I want the production to look classy. I want to make the studio look like the biggest studio that any soap opera has anywhere in soapdom. I want terrific reviews. I want this show to look big, romantic and lush. I want people to talk about this show, to love the story, the characters, the conflict, the passion, the way they tell the story. That's what I want for this show."

THE STORYTELLERS

IRNA PHILLIPS

Created by the legendary Irna Phillips in 1937 as a 15-minute radio show, "Guiding Light" had a strong religious foundation. Indeed, the lead character was the Rev. Ruthledge, and his sermons were turned into a best-selling book. It was Irna's desire to depict the melting pot that was and is America, and her vision still shines brightly on today's "Guiding Light."

AGNES NIXON

me earn my stripes! Talk about challenges!" Agnes would put her own very special stamp on the show. And she did everything—long term, outlines, scripts, all while raising four children. A firm believer that education can be entertainment, if packaged properly, Nixon fought hard for the landmark Pap smear story after a dear friend died of cancer. Because uterine cancer was 100% curable if caught in time she wanted to do the story. At first the networks and executives were afraid that it would scare people away. Her reply, "I don't think so if you give it to a beloved character and they're hooked on other stories... And I think that was the first socially relevant issue integrated into a major story of a soap opera." It was... Played by "great talent" Charita Bauer, "Guiding Light's" beloved Bert, the response showed what an impact powerful daytime storytelling can have. During her tenure (1958 to 1966) on "Guiding Light" Agnes Nixon kept the show at the top of the ratings. She then moved on to "Another World," before creating her own shows "One Life to Live" and, of course, "All My Children" for ABC.

In 1958 Irna Phillips turned the head writing duties of "Guiding Light" over to Agnes Nixon, who would become a legend in her own right. Nixon had started as an associate writer in 1953. About working with Irna, she says, "It was a dream job—three days out of Northwestern. I couldn't believe my luck. She certainly taught me a lot, but the big thing was she gave me a break at the time. She saved me from going into the burial garment business with my father." One week before Irna left the show, she killed off the very popular character of Kathy Holden. "That was Irna's gift to me. She was going to make

In 1997 former "Guiding Light" scriptwriters Barbara Esensten and James Harmon Brown prepare to take over the helm. Says Esensten, "We're really excited, especially this year, in the show's 60th year. There is no other show on television, prime time or daytime, that can hand you so much delicious material. One wonderful thing about 'Guiding Light' is those families are still there, going back to the very beginning.... And the romance...Whether you're doing a business-oriented story or a mystery or a murder, at the core of it always has to be romance, what's at stake for the lovers. That's what we care about on 'Guiding Light.'" Brown concurs, "One of the great things about this show is that it has such great history. The stories that involved the history of the show and the families of the show are always the richest because there is so much background and there is so much emotion based on who these people are and where they come from. So we plan to go ahead to the past. It's a special show and we feel we're being a small part of it's future history...because of what it has meant to daytime TV and the quality it has maintained over 60 years."

Michael Conforti/Actor Turned Writer who has been a script writer, breakdown writer and head writer, first played reporter Wally Bacon. About scripts: "It is thrilling to watch these great actors say your words. I will always remember the first day I had a script air when Michael Zaslow said my words and he liked them. I could tell he enjoyed it. And I'll never forget it. It was as big a rush, as big a thrill, as any stage experience as an actor I ever had." On what makes a good story: "It's coming up with a compelling story that will involve the audience and excite the writers and, of course, excite you who are writing and excite your bosses. Get the audience to say, 'Wait a minute. what happens next?' Those are the questions you ask yourself... 'What happens next? And then what happens?' And if you're writing the story well, and you're pitching in the meeting and you come to the end of it, and they look at you and they go, 'And then what happens?'—You know you've done your job well"

Nancy Williams Watt: Nancy started on "Guiding Light" as a writers assistant. Having already written for "Search for Tomorrow," Nancy took the assistant's job against the advice of many friends. However, after a few months she was writing breakdowns, scripts, then editing and has been drafted as co-head writer twice. However, Nancy truly prefers editing and script writing. "My major strengths as a daytime writer are my love and understanding of character and emotional scenes which engage the audience." Nancy feels that "Guiding Light" is special because of the relationships, "not just the ones on screen, but the people who play the characters...here is the reason this show is passed on from generation to generation."

Ask anyone familiar with "Guiding Light" what makes the show unique, and they'll answer, "Betty Rea and her eye for first-class actors." Betty may see as many as 200 to 300 actors for a particular role! "Eventually you get to the point where everybody you're interested in goes on tape," she explains. After that, a group decision is made by the executive producer, the writers, CBS and Procter & Gamble. "That's a lot of people that have to agree," Betty says. "But every now and then, someone will come in with that certain spark." Some of Betty's "Guiding Light" luminaries have gone on to TV and movie

CASTING CONSULTANT BETTY REA

stardom, including Sherry Stringfield, Jimmy Smits, Ian Ziering and Kevin Bacon. The casting of Michael Zaslow as Roger Thorpe is a prime example of Betty's uncanny sense of what will work. "For the part of Roger, who was to be an undergraduate, the show saw every blond boy in New York. Somebody sent Michael to me and I went to the executive producer, Lucy Rittenberg, and said, 'We just found Roger. This is his picture.' She said, 'You're crazy!' I said, 'But you always knew I was crazy.' To which Lucy replied, 'I know it, but this is going too far, Betty. He's dark and he's older.' I said, 'Yup...I think we should bring up to the writers that the character should be darker and older. He's got the arrogance and everything they're looking for. They expected these little blond boys to have it, but they didn't.'" And that was the beginning of Michael Zaslow's reign as Roger Thorpe. In a profession not known for awards—there is no Emmy for casting—Betty has won several, most notably *Soap Opera Digest*'s 1994 Special Editor's Award.

Stage manager Locke Wallace came to "Guiding Light" in the spring of 1968 as a "vacation relief" when the show was only 15 minutes long. "It was a real nice, short job," he recalls. "I was home for dinner every night. There was a small cast, there were no TelePrompTers. The ladies did their own hair. Most of them did their own makeup. As for the music, it was not this orchestral music, it was an organ player."

It was a very simple show at the time, and as Locke explains, when the actors blanked out on their lines, "I was always right near them, and I knew just how loud to whisper so that the boom wouldn't pick it up, and I would give them a key word to get them back on the speech. In 1977, when the show went to an hour, it became an entirely new animal. Everything was shot out of order and it became a 12-hour workday.

He's also known as Dr. Locke, and he's on staff at Cedars. It was as Doc Locke that Locke attended Beth's wedding and the Cedars Anniversary Ball. He also testified for Rick Bauer at a hearing once, saying, "Gentlemen, let me

LOCKE WALLACE

tell you, one of the most important things for me is a doctor who can think on his feet. And when it comes to thinking on his feet, Dr. Rick Bauer is absolutely marvelous." Locke has done remotes all over the globe— Hilton Head, South Carolina; Florida; St. Croix; and the Canary Islands, where they shot on a steep mountain "where the astronauts trained." Does he have a favorite episode? "I think the scenes that make these shows work, day in, day out, are the bread-and-butter scenes, the family scenes in

which the mother talks to the son, the sister talks to the brother or the lover talks to his lover, and they're tight and they're well acted and they have a human interest and they have relationships that hit home." As stage manager, Locke is sensitive to actors' needs, being an actor himself. "For an actor to operate at his or her optimum, he or she has to be able to concentrate and relax. I try to keep all distractions down, no moving during dress rehearsal, no noise.... Those distractions can just throw you, and it's not fair to an artist to do that. The actor is important—that performance, those words, those pictures. That's the tone I try to set."

Director JoAnne Sedwick began her "Guiding Light" career in 1979 as a production secretary and backup PA. When she came on the show, Lucille Wexler had just sent Ben out the attic door. Says JoAnne, "The first thing I remember is seeing Ben lying on the sofa and I thought, Why is he looking so funny?" JoAnne has the unique experience of directing her own mother, Margaret, who plays a doctor and has been delivering "Guiding Light" babies since Jackie was pregnant with Alan Spaulding's child. JoAnne says that directing her mom is not any different than any other actor, "except I won't forget her name."

MICHAEL O'LEARY (DR. RICK BAUER)

Michael was an usher at CBS on "The Price Is Right" when he heard about an audition for "Guiding Light." They already had a Rick (Phil MacGregor)—what they needed was someone to read with the actors in audition scenes. "So I did it and went back home" which was California. A few days later, while his mother was watching her favorite soap, "Guiding Light," Michael got the call. "I said to my mother, 'They want me to go back to New York to be on 'Guiding Light.' To play that role right there. I'm going to be on your soap opera and I'm going to be in that part. And she goes, 'Shh! Not now Michael please...Phillip's going to tell Rick to take a leap here, it's a very important part...just go in the backyard and clean up the deck area.' Finally she got it and she got very excited and started to cry."

TINA SLOAN (LILLIAN RAINES)

"They wanted a strong woman to play a weak woman. And Lillian was, as the mother of an incest victim... you know they close their eyes and they're very weak, but they were afraid if she was too weak, it wouldn't have any power. They said I'd just do it for six months and I thought oh what fun!— it's a very difficult story." Sixteen years later, Lillian is still an important part of Cedars Hospital and the Springfield Community.

TINA SLOAN

FRANK DICOPOULOS (FRANK COOPER)

Frank auditioned for the role of Will Jeffries. "I was probably the sickest I've ever been in my life. I had the worst cold you could ever possibly imagine. I could hear myself talking in my head. It was a scene in a cafeteria...somebody walks in with a tray, Kristi Ferrell (Roxie Shayne) is already seated, and you ask her, 'Is this seat taken?' And she says, 'No it's not.' And then you're supposed to pull out the chair, sit down and start your scene. I walked right up, pulled out the chair, sat down, started eating and then looked up and said, 'Oh! I'm sorry. Is this seat taken?' It got a great reaction. Everybody else was so serious coming into this and I was just, that's Frank."

FRANK DICOPOULOS

FRANK BEATY (BRENT LAWRENCE/MARIAN CRANE)

He had no idea what he was getting into. Frank came on as this nice, "maybe too nice guy...a Spaulding executive who immediately had eyes for Lucy...Then I'll never forget this as long as I live. The executive producer brought me into his office and sat me down, and all the while, I had been sort of wondering where my story line was going to go...and it looked like I was going to meet my end and that was fine. I had a good run. He said, 'We want to first of all thank you for a great job...everything is going well and we appreciate it. We have a story in mind that we want to throw at you,' and my first thought, was, Good, they want to keep me around. Then he started telling me the story about this older woman who moves into town, gets a job at

Spaulding, becomes friends with Lucy. I'm like okay, fine, that's great, but where do I come in? I'm expecting this woman to be my crazy mother. Then he finally says, 'She goes home to her apartment one night and pulls off her wig and her face and it's you.' And I'm like, what! This has to be a joke...I've finally gotten comfortable on this show and doing my work and now I'm going to be a woman!" Frank got a month off to prepare, part of which was spent at Miss Veronica Vera's School for Boys who want to be Girls, where he learned how to put on pantyhose, work with a waist cincher, fake breasts, wig, full makeup, and donned a tutu for his dance lessons. He then spent over two hours a day in the makeup chair. Talk about acting challenges! He did a magnificent job.

WENDY MONIZ (DINAH CHAMBERLAIN THORPE)

"I had gone to the audition and it went well and I had a callback. I knew the screen test was coming, and I needed something to wear. I'd been in the city about a year and a half...feeling very cocky in New York, so I don't have to cross the street at the light...and I was sort of rushing and I crossed the street and it was a red light. I wasn't paying attention. Cars were rolling up to stop at the light and this cab stopped right on my foot! Actually ran over it twice because he had to back up to get off it. I looked down and saw white (her sock) and I thought it was bone and I went into shock. Everybody's gathering around and the poor cab driver came out and just felt terrible. Here I am in the middle of Fifth Avenue and all of these people are looking at me and I'm like, you know my foot was probably broken for all I knew, and all I could think about was I blew my screen test for 'Guiding Light' and I'm mumbling about it. And these people are looking around, going, 'This girl's crazy.' She just got her foot run over and she's worried about missing her soap opera!" Happily, Wendy didn't break her foot, but tragedy struck 'Guiding Light,' when Leonard Stabb was in a serious hang gliding accident and the part of Dinah was put on hold. Three years went by, and they brought back the character and "I had to go back and start from the beginning." This time Wendy waited for the red light.

ON THE SET

First days on the set can be nerve-wracking. On Beth Ehlers' (Harley Davidson Cooper) first day, her character gave birth. Kassie de Pavia's (Chelsea Reardon) was in a car crash. Some other tales...

CYNTHIA WATROS (ANNIE LEWIS)

Before she was Annie Lewis, Cynthia was a waitress for a day, playing opposite Kurt McKinney. Says Watros of the experience, "It was terrifying. It was my first time on a soap and soaps go extremely fast. So all of a sudden I hear five, four, three, two, one, and we had to start

WENDY MONIZ

CYNTHIA WATROS

kissing. And this is after I saw body makeup being applied on Kurt's body and I thought, Oh my God! I don't know how to do this. So we just get on the bed. We introduced each other, while I have to kiss him…Just before, I'm like, 'Hi, I'm Cynthia.' 'Hi, I'm Kurt. How are you?'"

GRANT ALEKSANDER (PHILLIP SPAULDING): ON GETTING THE PART

"I was very lucky. It all happened very quickly and I was thrilled. That was one of the best Christmases, 'cause I got hired right before Christmas. It was just heaven! I was tending bar, making 70 bucks a night and all of a sudden I'm making all this money to be an actor and it was like, God's in his heaven and all is right with the world!" **First day on the set:** "Harry Eggart was directing. All I had to do was walk into a darkened Spaulding mansion, into the living room which was covered in sheets, closed for the winter and look around and say, 'Hello, anybody home? Dad? Hope?' Take a big pause. Look down stage and sit. And then say, 'Welcome home Phillip.' Tough work day. Came home with my backpack from Lincoln Prep, where I'd been kicked out of school."

ROBERT NEWMAN (JOSH LEWIS)

ROBERT NEWMAN

Ten days after he arrived in New York, Robert Newman was offered a three-year contract to play Josh. "I had six days to go home and pack up my life in L.A. and move to New York. My first call was at 7 a.m. on a Monday morning. I was staying at the Times Square Motor Hotel and I walked down to the old studios at 26th street at about 6:30 and the guard wouldn't let me in because he didn't know me from Adam and he didn't know what I was doing there. Finally someone came along and I got in. And I remember thinking, *I'm going to walk in there and they're going to say, oh no, we made a big mistake. We didn't want that guy! We wanted the good one!* But they welcomed me with open arms, and everybody was great."

JUDI EVANS (BETH RAINES)

Judi says of her first day, "I was wheeled in on a gurney and I couldn't stop giggling…all bruised and bloodied and I kept giggling because it tickled…it was fun, like being on a ride. They're saying you can't giggle, you're unconscious. I said sorry."

LISA BROWN

LISA BROWN (NOLA REARDON CHAMBERLAIN)

Lisa originally auditioned for the role of Morgan and had Nola created for her by then head writer Douglas Marland. Her first day on the set, "I was delivering a tray to Kelly (dressed only in a towel)—it was breakfast—and I remember being so scared that the things on the tray, the silverware, and the cups were shaking. I thought, *Oh, my gosh, can't they hear it clamoring and clanking?* And I remember being in my apartment, and I had rehearsed with a tray and of

RON RAINES

course, you don't shake in your own living room. But I can remember being so scared that the tray was shaking."

RON RAINES (ALAN SPAULDING)

"I remember when I first got on the show, you start talking to people and they tell you what a pivotal character you are—you know everyone, and everyone knows you. Of course you don't know any of these people and you come in, and you get this, Everybody hates me! Everybody, right! So that was a little shock! Because I've always played these nice guy characters." Although the Spauldings resemble the "Addams Family," on the set they genuinely enjoy each other. "We're all kind of quirky in our funny ways which is good, because all these characters are so wacky!"

FRAN MYERS (PEGGY FLETCHER) AND ROGER NEWMAN (KEN NORRIS)

They met on the set of "Guiding Light" and then married in an "off screen" love story. Says Fran, "We had no story connection. We worked together only a couple of times, passing in the halls of the hospital. I remember being afraid I would laugh...but he's also very professional so I knew I wouldn't. I think that little meeting in the hall, was the one scene that we had." He played Holly's older brother, and she married Roger Thorpe. Says Roger, "Roger Thorpe attacked Janet (his on-screen wife) once and we had a fight." Says Fran, "He was a jealous fool." Both Newman's had been child actors and after they left "Guiding Light", they went to California to try their luck. Family responsibilities led them into writing. For awhile they worked together on "Another World" and "One Life to Live." Today Roger's a scribe for "Guiding Light" and Fran writes for "Days of Our Lives."

JOHN WESLEY SHIPP (KELLY NELSON)

John played a good guy, Ed Bauer's nephew and a resident at Cedars, but when it came to wardrobe..."It was so funny, the first day they had the costume designer in...they were going over the 'look.' It was Bobby Anton, who worked a lot with Doug Marland, and in his raspy voice he was saying this character's look is this and that character's look is that...of course, with John Wesley Shipp it's not so much a question of how to dress him, as how to undress him!" John recently did a movie for HBO which had a nude scene, prompting his grandmother to ask, "Are you ever going to do anything and keep your clothes on?" Says Shipp, "I'm sure they'll eventually say, John keep your shirt on."

JOHN WESLEY SHIPP

SHOOTING STARS
THEIR LIGHT FIRST SHINED BRIGHTLY IN SPRINGFIELD

Guiding Light" boasts an impressive list of acting graduates. Mercedes McCambridge was the angelic voice of Mary Ruthledge on the radio from 1937 to 1939, although most people remember her as the voice of the Devil, who possessed Linda Blair in 1973's *The Exorcist*. In between, McCambridge won an Oscar in 1950 for *All the King's Men*. Sandy Dennis played Alice Holden in 1956, then went on to receive an Academy Award for *Who's Afraid of Virginia Woolf?* Glenn Walken was young Mike Bauer from 1954 to 1956, and brother Christopher Walken filled in when Glenn was unavailable. Award-winning stage and film actor Barnard Hughes played Dr. Bruce Banning, Meta's last and loving husband, from 1961 to 1966, and Maureen O'Sullivan (Mia Farrow's mom), who earned fame for playing Jane in the *Tarzan* films of the 1930s and 1940s, left her loincloth far behind when she portrayed town historian Emma Witherspoon in 1984. After a brief stint in Springfield as Clara Jones, Anna Maria Horsford joined the hit sitcom "Amen" in 1986, while Joseph Campanella, who played Joe Turino, moved on to films. Jimmy Smits, the star of "L.A. Law" and "NYPD Blue," worked as an extra on an island remote. Talented stage and screen actress Blythe Danner also graced the show.

One of today's brightest stars, Kevin Bacon (above), played troubled teen Tim Werner from 1980 to 1981. Says stage manager Locke Wallace of the talented young actor, "Kevin was great. He was always on the set one scene before. He'd be getting the feel of the set, looking at his script and his lines. What a sweet guy and a thorough professional. I admire him very much and I respect him for his professionalism." Playing a young alcoholic on "Guiding Light" prepared Bacon for his breakthrough role as Fenwick in Barry Levinson's 1982 film *Diner*. He later found stardom in *Footloose, Murder in the First, Apollo 13* and *Sleepers*. Bacon made his directorial debut in 1996 with a Showtime film, *Losing Chase*, starring his wife, Kyra Sedgwick.

The roles of Dr. Jim Frazier and his wife, nurse Martha, provided jobs for four very talented actors at the beginning of their careers. James Earl Jones played Jim until Billy Dee Williams

(right) took over, and Cicely Tyson (right) originated the role of Martha. She was followed in the part by Ruby Dee. Jones is an accomplished Tony Award–winning stage and film actor who provided the voice of Darth Vader in the *Star Wars* trilogy. Williams had a featured role in two installments of that trilogy, *The Empire Strikes Back* and *Return of the Jedi*. His other film credits include *Lady Sings the Blues*, and *Brian's Song*. Tyson spent less than a year in Springfield before moving on to such notable films as *Sounder* and *The Autobiography of Miss Jane Pittman*. She also had a starring part in the landmark TV miniseries *Roots*. A star of TV, film and the theater, Dee appeared in *A Raisin in the Sun* and Spike Lee's *Do the Right Thing*.

From 1977 to 1981 JoBeth Williams (right) played reporter and homewrecker Brandy Shellooe. Williams made her feature film debut in *Kramer vs. Kramer*, went on to star in *The Big Chill* and was nominated for an Emmy for her roles in the miniseries *Baby M.* and the TV movie *Adam*. Recently she starred as lawyer Reggie Love in "The Client."

Keir Dullea played Dr. Mark Jarrett, a brilliant neurosurgeon who dabbled in art forgery with India Von Halkein. Keir's first feature was *The Hoodlum Priest*. He went on to play David in *David and Lisa* before flying high in Stanley Kubrick's classic *2001: A Space Odyssey*. Coincidentally, Keir had worked with two of "Guiding Light"'s grand old gentlemen, Larry Gates and Bill Roerick, before he joined the cast, and remembers "being impressed by the high caliber of all the GL actors."

SOME WHO LEFT DAYTIME FOR PRIMETIME

An Emmy nominee for her role as Josh Lewis' disturbed wife, Sonni/Solita Carrera, Michele Forbes left her character behind and headed into a recurring role as Ensign Ro on "Star Trek: The Next Generation." She also starred in the films *Kalifornia* and *Swimming with Sharks* before joining TV's "Homicide: Life on the Street" as medical examiner Julianna Cox.

Although his character, Cameron Stewart, was headed for college when actor Ian Ziering left the show, Ziering went back to high school when he took on the role of Steve Sanders in the popular series "Beverly Hills, 90210."

While she was in Springfield, Paige Turco's Dinah Morgan Marler was torn between Cameron Stewart and Alan-Michael Spaulding. Paige traded them in for a quartet of oversized turtles in the feature films *Teenage Mutant Ninja Turtles II* and its sequel. She was a regular on the TV series "American Gothic" before joining the force on "NYPD Blue."

Putting "Guiding Light" behind her after three years as sexy troublemaker Blake Thorpe, Sherry Stringfield quickly moved to primetime as Laura Kelly on "NYPD Blue" and went on to create the role of Dr. Susan Lewis on television's megahit "ER." Sherry has since left "ER" and is now enjoying private life.

Nia Long had already won acclaim for her role in the film *Boyz N the Hood* when she joined "Guiding Light" as Hampton Speakes' daughter, Kat. Long moved out of Springfield to play Will Smith's fiancée on "The Fresh Prince of Bel Air" and later gave birth on an episode of "ER." Film credits include *Made in America*, in which she co-starred as Ted Danson and Whoopi Goldberg's daughter.

"Guiding Light" was Melina Kanakaredes' first job out of college. She describes her character, Eleni, as "having a core of honesty, and yet she was fiery. She had her spiciness." While she was still on "Guiding Light," Melina did a stint on "NYPD Blue" as Jimmy Smits' reporter girlfriend. She also starred in the primetime series "New York News" before nabbing her first film role in the action-packed Geena Davis thriller *The Long Kiss Goodnight*.

GUEST STARS WHO CAME THROUGH SPRINGFIELD

Teresa Wright took on the role of Grace Cummings, Vanessa's aunt, and Jan Sterling played Miss Foss, a maid.

Seventy-two-year-old screen legend Joan Bennett arrived in Springfield in 1982 for a personal appearance as herself (below). When the elegant actress was in need of a hairdresser, she called Gracie Middleton's beauty shop. Gracie (Lori Shelle) came to Bennett's lavish Springfield Towers suite to save the day, but not before she alerted her movie-mad friend, Nola Reardon (Lisa Brown), that a genuine movie star was in town.

(Below) Six guest stars took part in the selection of the Sampson Girl. Television talk show host Dick Cavett and actor James Coco are pictured here with contestants Jessie Matthews (Rebecca Staab), Mindy Lewis (Krista Tesreau), Beth Raines (Judi Evans) and Roxie Shayne (Kristi Ferrell). Rounding out the panel were Dorothy Loudon, Chita Rivera, Leslie Uggams and Tammy Grimes. Says Cavett of the experience, "I remember wanting to ad lib a line that the contest was rigged and see if they could improvise around it." Mindy was unanimously voted the winner, and one of her prizes was an appearance on Dick Cavett's show.

Cavett's wife, Carrie Nye, played delicious villain Susan Piper. "I have never enjoyed anything so much in my life!" exclaims Nye. "I had the best wardrobe—all those high-heeled shoes and that silk charmeuse, those fabulous slinky clothes and hats and yachts and wonderful nightgowns. I had a lover, a ninja, and I would do karate kicks in Chanel shoes." The last we saw of Susan, "Her high-heeled shoes were floating to the top of a quicksand pit, so they have the option of bringing me back." Springfield residents, beware!

(Above) The *Journal*'s ace reporter, Fletcher Reade, was spotted escorting gossip columnist Cindy Adams to a Springfield affair. Hmm...one wonders what appeared in their columns the following day.

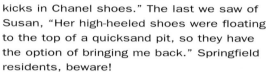

In 1993 Joe Lando, who now stars as Sully in the hit series "Dr. Quinn, Medicine Woman," spent his summer hiatus playing McCauley West on "Guiding Light." West, seen here with Gilly Grant (Amelia Marshall), was an ex-cop turned defense lawyer who became embroiled in a mystery surrounding Gilly's brother, David.

On a more serious note, Mackenzie Phillips, who has struggled with drug problems herself, took on the role of Rachel Sullivan, a substance abuse counselor who helped organize an intervention when Annie became addicted to prescription drugs. At the end of the episode, a hotline number was put up on the screen.

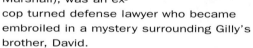

LET ME ENTERTAIN YOU/ WIRED FOR SOUND

It was the brainchild of then head writer Doug Marland to feature musical guests at Springfield's popular disco, Wired for Sound. All the guests would have a direct impact on the story and interact with Springfield regulars, including budding singer/songwriter Floyd Parker (Tom Nielsen), Floyd's manager Josh Lewis (Robert Newman) and disco manager Tony Reardon (Gregory Beecroft).

One of the first to perform was superstar Neil Sedaka (below). It wasn't soap addiction that prompted Sedaka to appear on the show. He did it to please longtime family housekeeper Mary Moses, a fan of "Guiding Light" for 15 years. Neil even managed to get 60-year-old Mary (standing to his left) a bit part in the post-performance party scene at the Spaulding mansion.

The gang—Kelly Nelson (John Wesley Shipp), Maureen Bauer (Ellen Dolan), Josh Lewis (Robert Newman), Hillary Bauer (Marsha Clark), Tony Reardon (Gregory Beecroft), Lesley Ann Monroe (Carolyn Clarke), Ed Bauer (Peter Simon) and Floyd Parker (Tom Nielsen)—gathers around Ashford & Simpson as they prepare to perform.

Wired for Sound also played host to Judy Collins. Best known for her ballads, Judy was joined by Springfield's own Floyd Parker on sax. The song was Judy's "It's Going to Be One of Those Nights." No doubt it was.

(Right) Jennifer Holliday, a sensation in her first Broadway musical, *Dreamgirls*, played an actress/singer who wanted to get into show biz.

(Below) The B-52's get ready to literally do a number on Floyd (Tom Nielsen).

"GUIDING LIGHT" GOES PRIMETIME

In 1983 "Guiding Light" went primetime in *The Cradle Will Fall*, a TV movie based on the best-selling novel by Mary Higgins Clark. The suspense drama starred James Farentino as Dr. Edgar Highley, a respected Springfield physician, Lauren Hutton as Kathy DeMaio, an assistant district attorney working with Ross Marler (Jerry Ver Dorn), and Ben Murphy as medical examiner Richard Carrol, who was in love with Kathy. Besides Ver Dorn, other Springfield residents who appeared in the drama were Charita Bauer (Bert), Carolyn Clarke (Lesley Ann Monroe), Joe Ponazecki (Det. Larry Wyatt), Elvera Roussel (Hope Spaulding) and Peter Simon (as Cedars' own Dr. Ed Bauer).

FANFARE

THE FANS TALK ABOUT THEIR SHOW

"Guiding Light" fans are known for their intense loyalty and involvement: They decided Meta's fate when she shot Ted White, they chose the name of Quint and Nola's baby, and the first week the Viewer Feedback line was installed, 9,000 of them called in to express their opinions about the show. To many viewers, "Guiding Light" isn't just a soap, it's an heirloom, one that is passed along from generation to generation like fine china. "I was weaned on GL. I'm the second of three generations of GL fans," says Jean Drouliard of Modesto, California. Jean Satzer of Oakland, California, recalls, "When I got home from school my mother would have a snack waiting for me, and we would watch GL together." Such second- and third-generation fans are not unusual for this show, which even has fourth-generation viewers. "My great-grandmother started listening to it on the radio, and it's been a tradition ever since," says Kate of Baltimore, who has passed the tradition on to her own child. "My two-year-old will hear the theme music and say 'Guiding Light' even before the announcer does. She likes to dance to it, and she knows 'Roger bad.'"

Online services have become a forum for GL fans, who sing the show's praises and vent their frustrations in cyberspace. Jean Drouliard uses AOL to promote Save Our Afternoon Program (SOAP), an organization started in 1992 by Eleanor Keeling to fight her Sacramento, California, affiliate's decision to pull GL from its schedule. Such loyalty to a soap is not unique, but the reasons GL's fans have for watching the show certainly are. Joy Lamb loves GL "because it still invests time in true romance and fantasy. Other soaps seem

to have forgotten the elements that have made soaps a success, but GL is still shining after all these years." History is important to Megan FitzPatrick of Bensalem, Pennsylvania. "It's what makes GL the best soap on TV," she says. "'Guiding Light' has been a part of my family for all of its 60 years. One of my favorite memories is watching with my grandmothers all through my childhood. I can remember gossiping with my mom's mom about all the happenings on GL."

The element that attracts Christine Brantley is the comedy. "GL has never lost its sense of humor," says the Wilmington, North Carolina, fan. "They also have a way of keeping family values alive while trying to survive among other shows that don't."

Jenni Holmes of St. Louis remembers "playing sick before the days of VCRs, just so I could see Mindy's wedding to Kurt Corday. I was sick for days!"

Val Wirth of Jacksonville, Florida, was drawn to GL because "it has always been a sweeter, more sentimental show than most." Cinda Brown of Newport News, Virginia, admits it's the sad parts of the show that stick in her mind. "I'll always remember Jerry Ver Dorn announcing Charita Bauer's death. Or Roger chasing Rita through the funhouse." But she has happy memories, too. "Nola's fantasies, the Four Musketeers at the prom, Josh and Reva's wedding, the blackout. Oh, and I really remember that moment when Sherry Stringfield's Blake decided she was going to take Holly's man, Ross, away from her and said, "You took my man, Mother. I think I'll take yours."

For many viewers, the excitement of meeting in person the GL actors they love is as memorable as their favorite storylines. "I can remember meeting Grant Aleksander in a mall in the early 1980s, and it was such a thrill," says Janet Laiacona. "I couldn't wait for my niece to open that picture of us Christmas morning." Jenni Holmes met Krista Tesreau (a former Mindy) at a fan luncheon in St. Louis. "She was really sweet. I had received mail from her in response to my fan letters, but I was ecstatic when I met her and impressed by the way she made her fans feel special." Adds Ms. Gourley of Green Cove Springs, Florida, "I have met only one actor from the show, Frank Grillo. My daughters and I had corresponded with him through AOL and jumped at the chance to meet him. We were able to talk with him, get a picture of us with him, get his autograph and even get a kiss on the cheek! That has to be my top GL memory."

On location at Universal Studios in Orlando, Florida, fans lined up to watch Lucy Cooper (Sonia Satra) and Alan-Michael Spaulding (Rick Hearst) tie the knot.

In the summer of 1957, as an episode of "The Guiding Light" drew to a close, the announcer said, "Tomorrow is Papa Bauer's 65th birthday. It might be a good idea to congratulate him personally."

He went on to give a mailing address. For Theo Goetz, who portrayed the kindly if

opinionated Papa Bauer, that simple announcement opened the floodgates. Within a period of weeks, 49,000 pieces of correspondence flooded CBS. The letters contained everything from handkerchiefs to 50-cent pieces and long, congratulatory messages signed by entire families. This avalanche of mail was the response of 10 million viewers to the warmth and love generated by this dignified gentleman, a man who had become a part of their lives.

Handsome Rick Hearst was a favorite with the Florida fans.

To give true meaning to the phrase "You're never too young or too old," Brett Cooper, who plays Reva's son Shayne, enjoys his share of mail. This particular letter from Jean Bellerby and her best friends, Karin Stieger and Linda Roberts, stated in part, "We are all real big fans of yours and we love watching you on 'Guiding Light.' We were all wondering if you have a fan club and if so can you please send us all information? Also can you send us each an autographed photo of your very sexy self?"

MELINA KANAKAREDES

MELINA KANAKAREDES (ELENI COOPER)

While in Italy filming a movie, Melina was with some friends for a weekend at their summer house outside of Rome. It was two in the morning and they're driving along, four girls in a car with a dog: "They have little barricades up on the streets at certain hours and the police are checking everybody and of course they pull us over. They want passports. I only have a driver's license, the driver doesn't even have her wallet. He's pulling me out of the car and the girl who's driving is saying that he's going to take us in, that we're supposed to have our visas with us. She told him we were actresses, he didn't care. He's ready to take us in and the other girl says 'Sentieri.' That's what 'Guiding Light' is called in Italy. And it's two years behind so I was still on over there. He shines his flashlight for the first time on my face and he goes, 'Eleni!' He runs up, this beast of a man starts kissing me! He wanted me to autograph his ticket book, for his wife Francesca. And he's like, 'I won't take you in now, but you be careful Melina…you take picture?' And there I have a picture now with a policeman."

MILLETTE ALEXANDER (SARA MCINTYRE) GETS A CALL FROM A FAMOUS FAN

"I was having my hair done and getting my makeup on and running over my lines and somebody yelled down the hall, 'Millette, there's a phone call for you.' I said, 'Find out who it is, I'll call them back, I'm busy, I can't come right now.' There was some silence. Then they said, 'You'd better come now!' 'I can't come now. Who is it? I'll call them back!' And they said, 'It's Joan Crawford!' I said, 'Don't be ridiculous. Find out who it is and tell them I'll call them back!' And so, I forget who it was, he came into the room and said, 'Millette, it's Joan Crawford! Get up out of the seat and go and talk to her.' So I did and it was she, and evidently at that point her daughter was on one of the shows and had to take a leave of absence and, she (Joan) was going to take over for her, so she wanted some hints on who did my hair, who did my makeup and how the whole thing worked. It was just one of these quirky things that come up."

GRANT ALEKSANDER

GRANT ALEKSANDER (PHILLIP SPAULDING)

"When you're the young leading man you get your share of panties, and naked pictures, and locks of hair and teeth. I've gotten everything in the mail…it's unbelievable. I had one woman in Canada that desperately wanted to know when we were going to see my bare or stocking feet on the show. And she sent me along pieces of paper to trace my feet on to send back to her, and I wrote back and said, 'If you should ever be unfortunate enough to actually see my feet, you would change your mind in a New York minute. The ugliest feet in daytime!'"

MICHAEL O'LEARY (RICK BAUER)

In contrast, when Phillip's pal Rick went to Lucy and Alan-Michael's wedding he went alone and there was a scene of him dancing alone in the street. "I really did it as a joke and then I got this letter. It was so sad. It said please find someone to be with."

MICHAEL O'LEARY

THE ENVELOPE, PLEASE...

© N.A.T..A.S.

"Guiding Light" has received many well-deserved awards during its 60-year history, and nothing can quite match the excitement of talented nominees, hearts racing, palms sweating, as they await the magic words: "The envelope, please." To the winners and everyone else who has contributed to the show—because in the end, this is a team effort—congratulations!

The Emmy—given by the National Academy of Television Arts and Sciences for excellence in daytime drama

1995–1996

OUTSTANDING SUPPORTING ACTOR IN A DRAMA SERIES
Jerry Ver Dorn (Ross Marler)
Says Ver Dorn of winning an Emmy, "It was very gratifying, particularly because it gave me a chance to say something about Bill Roerick [who had passed away in 1995]. He was a very special part of the show for a long time. I just wanted to thank him publicly and I'm glad I had that opportunity, and I think I spoke for a lot of cast members because a lot of them were pleased that I did what I did."

OUTSTANDING YOUNGER ACTOR IN A DRAMA SERIES
Kevin Mambo (Marcus Williams)
A newcomer to the show, Kevin made a major impression his first day on the set. "I had to

run around and fight with cops in a hallway, act with Michael Zaslow, be naked with Wendy Moniz and go swimming at the pool."

OUTSTANDING MUSIC DIRECTION AND COMPOSITION FOR A DRAMA SERIES
Allan Bellink, Wes Boatman, Ron Cohen, Robyn Cutler, Barry DeVorzon, Ed Dzubak, Jonathan Firstenberg, David Grant, Richard Hazard, John Henry, Daniel Lawrence,

Michael Licari, Rick Rhodes, John E. Young

OUTSTANDING ACHIEVEMENT IN MAKEUP FOR A DRAMA SERIES
Joseph Cola, Helen M. Gallagher, Paul J. Gebbia, Josephine Ross

OUTSTANDING LIVE AND DIRECT-TO-TAPE SOUND MIXING FOR A DRAMA SERIES
Thomas K. Bornkamp, Edward Dolan, John B. Fitzpatrick, Joseph N. Gallant Jr., Jon F. Hopkins, Butch Inglese, Timothy Pankewicz, Robert Drew Primrose, Richard E. Sens Jr., Eric Shuttleworth, Anthony Valentino, William J. Van Den Noort

OUTSTANDING LIGHTING DIRECTION FOR A DRAMA SERIES
Tony Girolami, Brian W. McRae

"Guiding Light" had a record 11 nominees this year. They were: (Front row) Melissa Hayden (Younger Actress), Justin Deas (Supporting Actor), Melina Kanakaredes (Younger Actress), Fiona Hutchinson (Lead Actress), Bryan Buffinton (Younger Actor), Maureen Garrett (Supporting Actress), Hilary Edson (Supporting Actress), Monti Sharp (Younger Actor). (Back row) Michael Zaslow (Lead Actor), Peter Simon (Lead Actor), Jerry ver Dorn (Supporting Actor).

OUTSTANDING SUPPORTING ACTOR IN A DRAMA SERIES
Jerry Ver Dorn (Ross Marler)

On being a supporting actor, Ver Dorn says, "I was essentially Uncle Ross, helping other people's storylines, which I find to be gratifying. I like supporting roles. I find it very challenging. The worst thing that could happen would be if I were on every day."

OUTSTANDING LEAD ACTOR IN A DRAMA SERIES
Justin Deas (Buzz Cooper)

OUTSTANDING ACHIEVEMENT IN MAKEUP FOR A DRAMA SERIES
Paul J. Gebbia, Suzanne Saccavino, Carlos Yeaggy, Joseph Cola, Helen Gallagher

OUTSTANDING ACHIEVEMENT IN LIGHTING DIRECTION FOR A DRAMA SERIES
Brian W. McRae, William D. Roberts

OUTSTANDING LEAD ACTOR IN A DRAMA SERIES
Michael Zaslow (Roger Thorpe)

When Michael Zaslow was nominated and failed to win an Emmy in 1992, he received a consolation note from his daughter, Marika. "I know how much it means to win," she wrote, "but there's always a next time." More important, she added, "You're best at being a daddy." There were no consolation notes in 1994, only heartfelt congratulations when an elated Zaslow won his well-deserved award.

OUTSTANDING SUPPORTING ACTOR IN A DRAMA SERIES
Justin Deas (Buzz Cooper)

OUTSTANDING YOUNGER ACTRESS IN A DRAMA SERIES
Melissa Hayden (Bridget Reardon)

"I definitely poured my heart and soul into the year," Hayden says. "It was a big year for me workwise, a lot of really intense, emotional stuff. And then it came time for the awards ceremony, and I flew my brother in so he could be my date. We got dressed up and made a big deal of it. We're like, This is so much fun just to be here! I realized how lucky I am and what an enviable position I'm in."

OUTSTANDING DRAMA SERIES DIRECTING TEAM
Bruce S. Barry, Lisa Connor, Matthew Lagle, Brian Mertes, John O'Connell, Irene Pace, Scott Riggs, Jo Anne Sedwick

OUTSTANDING ACHIEVEMENT IN MUSIC DIRECTION AND COMPOSITION FOR A DRAMA SERIES
Wes Boatman, Barry DeVorzon, A.J. Gundell, Richard Hazard, John Henry, Larry Hold, Michael Licari, Dominic Messinger, Barbara Miller-Gidaly

1992–1993

OUTSTANDING SUPPORTING ACTRESS IN A DRAMA SERIES
Ellen Parker (Maureen Bauer)
Beloved Maureen Bauer died in a car crash the year talented Ellen Parker won her Emmy. She is still sorely missed by the residents of Springfield and her fans.

OUTSTANDING YOUNGER ACTOR IN A DRAMA SERIES
Monti Sharp (David Grant)

OUTSTANDING DRAMA SERIES WRITING TEAM
Lorraine Broderick, James Harmon Brown, Michael Conforti, Nancy Curlee, Stephen Demorest, Bill Elverman, Barbara Esensten, Trent Jones, Gail N. Lawrence, Sally Mandel, Patrick Mulcahey, Roger Newman, Dorothy Ann Purser, James E. Reilly, Pete T. Rich, Peggy Shcibi, Courtney Simon, Wisner Washam, Nancy Williams Watt

OUTSTANDING ACHIEVEMENT IN MULTIPLE CAMERA EDITING FOR A DRAMA SERIES
Thomas K. Bornkamp, Brian D. Rosner, Richard E. Sens Jr.

1991–1992

OUTSTANDING SUPPORTING ACTRESS IN A DRAMA SERIES
Maeve Kinkead (Vanessa Chamberlain)
Recalls Kinkead of Emmy night, "I loved it because I got to recite my poem. My biggest memory was how nice it felt to be totally relaxed and not hysterical or beside myself in any way, but just able to get up there, say thank you, read my poem and make people laugh!"

OUTSTANDING ORIGINAL SONG
"I Knew That I'd Fall" by A.J. Gundell

OUTSTANDING ACHIEVEMENT IN MUSIC DIRECTION AND COMPOSITION FOR A DRAMA SERIES
Wes Boatman, Barry DeVorzon, A.J. Gundell, Richard Hazard, John Henry, Theodore Irwin, Michael Licari, Barbara Miller-Gidaly

OUTSTANDING ACHIEVEMENT IN GRAPHICS AND TITLE DESIGN
Wayne Fitzgerald

1990–1991

OUTSTANDING YOUNGER ACTOR IN A DRAMA SERIES
Rick Hearst (Alan-Michael Spaulding)
As the youngest member of the powerful Spaulding family, this talented actor held his own—not an easy feat.

OUTSTANDING ORIGINAL SONG
"Love Like This" by A.J. Gundell

OUTSTANDING ACHIEVEMENT IN MUSIC DIRECTION AND COMPOSITION FOR A DRAMA SERIES
Barry DeVorzon, A.J. Gundell, Richard Hazard, John Henry, Theodore Irwin, James Elliot Lawrence, Barbara Miller-Gidaly, Rob Monsey

1989–1990

OUTSTANDING LEAD ACTRESS IN A DRAMA SERIES
Kim Zimmer (Reva Shayne)
Three-time Emmy winner Kim Zimmer has this to say about her multiple Emmys: "For my ego, it's been wonderful. My kids love it because they know that each one belongs to one of them! Each time I won one, it was even more special than the last one. The first time it was a shock because I was such a dark horse. The second time, I had just had a baby and that made it extra special. And the third time I won, I was leaving the show, so that was kind of bittersweet."

OUTSTANDING DRAMA SERIES WRITING TEAM

Peter Brash, Richard Culliton, Nancy Curlee, Stephen Demorest, Garrett Foster, Trent Jones, Gail N. Lawrence, Pamela K. Long, Pete T. Rich, Jeff Ryder, Melissa Salmons, Patty Gideon Sloan, Nancy Williams

1986–1987

OUTSTANDING LEAD ACTRESS IN A DRAMA SERIES
Kim Zimmer (Reva Shayne)

OUTSTANDING ACHIEVEMENT IN MAKEUP FOR A DRAMA SERIES

Joseph Cola, Suzanne Saccavino

OUTSTANDING ACHIEVEMENT IN HAIRSTYLING FOR A DRAMA SERIES

Ralph Stanzione, Linda Williams

1985–1986

OUTSTANDING DRAMA SERIES WRITING TEAM

Nancy Curlee, Stephen Demorest, Victoria Gialanella, Mary Pat Gleason, Pamela K. Long, Trent Jones, John Kuntz, Gail N. Lawrence, Megan McTavish, Pete T. Rich, Jeff Ryder, Addie Walsh, Christopher Whitesell

OUTSTANDING ACHIEVEMENT IN HAIRSTYLING FOR A DRAMA SERIES

Ralph Stanzione, Linda Williams

OUTSTANDING ACHIEVEMENT IN COSTUME DESIGN FOR A DRAMA SERIES

Nanzi Adzima, David Dangle, Bud Santora

1984–1985

SPECIAL RECOGNITION AWARD FOR 34 YEARS OF SERVICE
Charita Bauer (Bert Bauer)

OUTSTANDING LEAD ACTRESS IN A DRAMA SERIES
Kim Zimmer (Reva Shayne)

Zimmer relates her hair-raising experience that night: "I'd done something really funky with my hair—I spiked it because I never thought I'd win. I brought my family in from Michigan—my mom and dad, my sister and her husband—and that's what made it so special for me. When I came out of the hair room and I'd done this thing to my hair, my mother was like, *Oh my God*! And then I won! And it made *Time* and *Newsweek*!"

OUTSTANDING SUPPORTING ACTOR IN A DRAMA SERIES
Larry Gates (H.B. Lewis)

Said the late Larry Gates on winning this award, "I was surprised and very flattered and very happy for the show. The important thing is not recognition, it's achievement."

OUTSTANDING DIRECTION FOR A DRAMA SERIES

John T. Whitesell, Bruce Barry, Matthew Diamond, Irene M. Pace, Robert D. Kochman, Joanne Rivituso, Jo Anne Sedwick

OUTSTANDING ACHIEVEMENT BY A DRAMA SERIES DESIGN TEAM

David Dangle, Richard C. Hankins, Paul W. Hickey, Ralph Holmes, Ron Kelson, Wesley Laws, Harry Miller, Ron Placzek, Jene Youtt

1983–1984

OUTSTANDING SUPPORTING ACTRESS IN A DRAMA SERIES
Judi Evans (Beth Raines)

"I'd been on the show nine months when I got nominated," says Evans. "I was so young and so dumb, I didn't know what an Emmy was! But I was truly excited. It made me think, *Wow, maybe I did pick the right profession*. I finally made a right choice in my life. And it was thrilling. I was shocked. I couldn't speak. The presenter shook me and said you have to say something. And I was crying. I didn't know what to say. So I just said, okay, thanks. It was like a whirlwind. Afterward I felt I had to grow up and prove I was an actress, that it wasn't just pure luck."

OUTSTANDING ACHIEVEMENT IN DESIGN EXCELLENCE FOR A DAYTIME DRAMA SERIES

Costume Designers: Robert Anton, David Dangle Art Directors: Richard C. Hankins,

Harry Miller. Set Directors: Paul W. Hickey, Wesley Laws. Lighting Directors: Ralph Holmes, Lincoln Stulidk. Makeup: Joseph Cola, Suzanne Saccavino. Hair Designers: Linda Williams, Alba Samperisi. Music Supervisor: Barbara Miller

1982–1983

OUTSTANDING ACHIEVEMENT IN ANY AREA OF CREATIVE TECHNICAL CRAFTS

LIGHTING DIRECTION
Lighting Director: Nicolas Hutak

1981–1982

—A BANNER YEAR FOR "GUIDING LIGHT"!

OUTSTANDING DAYTIME DRAMA SERIES
Executive Producer: Allen M. Potter. Producers: Leslie Kwartin, Joseph Willmore

OUTSTANDING WRITING FOR A DAYTIME DRAMA SERIES
Douglas Marland, Nancy Franklin, Patrick Mulcahey, Gene Palumbo, Frank Salisbury

OUTSTANDING ACHIEVEMENT IN ANY AREA OF CREATIVE TECHNICAL CRAFTS

TECHNICAL DIRECTION/ ELECTRONIC CAMERAWORK
Technical Directors: Frank Florio, Malachy G. Wienges

1980–1981

OUTSTANDING WRITING FOR A DAYTIME DRAMA SERIES
Douglas Marland, Robert Dwyer, Nancy Franklin, Harding Lemay

1979–1980

OUTSTANDING DAYTIME DRAMA SERIES
Executive Producer: Allen M. Potter. Producers: Leslie Kwartin, Joseph Willmore

Five-time Emmy nominee Bryan Buffinton (Bill Lewis Jr.) meets the press and has this to say about not winning: "I'm appreciative that I'm recognized for the stuff I do. And when I got my first Emmy nomination, I was proud. I was ten and to be nominated that young, you're so nervous. Now I'm at the point where it's just an honor to be nominated. If you're nominated, I think it's just as good as winning."

SOAP OPERA DIGEST SOAP OPERA AWARDS

This is a fan award, and there's nothing quite like a soap opera fan! Fans

choose their favorites based on nominations made by the editors of *Soap Opera Digest.*

1994

OUTSTANDING SUPPORTING ACTOR
Justin Deas (Buzz Cooper)

OUTSTANDING YOUNGER LEADING ACTRESS
Melissa Hayden (Bridget Reardon)

1993

In 1993 Betty Rea, casting director extraordinaire, was chosen to receive *Soap Opera Digest*'s coveted Editor's Award for Outstanding Contribution to Daytime Drama. Said "Guiding Light"'s then executive producer, Jill Farren Phelps, "Betty Rea is our own national treasure, so it is high time that she be honored in a public way."

Three of Betty's acting finds, Michael Zaslow, Monti Sharp and Sherry Stringfield, presented her with the prestigious award.

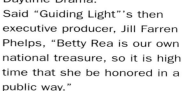

OUTSTANDING MALE NEWCOMER
Monti Sharp (David Grant)

HOTTEST MALE STAR
Mark Derwin (A.C. Mallet)

1992

OUTSTANDING VILLAIN
Michael Zaslow (Roger Thorpe)

1991

OUTSTANDING SUPPORTING ACTOR
Jordan Clarke (Billy Lewis)

MOST EXCITING FEMALE NEWCOMER
Kimberley Simms (Mindy Lewis)

1990

OUTSTANDING FEMALE NEWCOMER
Jean Carol (Nadine Cooper)

1988

OUTSTANDING ACTRESS
Kim Zimmer (Reva Shayne)
An ecstatic Kim Zimmer accepts her award.

SOAP OPERA WEEKLY HALL OF FAME AWARDS

These awards celebrate those who have made outstanding contributions to daytime television. Nominees are chosen by *Soap Opera Weekly*'s editors and the winners selected by a committee of industry professionals and past inductees.

1994
Former head writer Douglas Marland and creator Irna Phillips were inducted in the first annual ceremony.

1995
Mary Stuart, who played Jo during the entire run of "Search for Tomorrow," is now Meta Bauer on "Guiding Light."

1996
"Guiding Light"

OTHER PRESTIGIOUS AWARDS

1996
"Guiding Light" receives a Media Access Award for Abigail's story. The Media Access Award honors programs, companies and individuals who have accurately portrayed people with disabilities and provided employment opportunities to disabled professionals.

The Down syndrome Congress National Award for Television goes to "Guiding Light" for the story of Holly and Fletcher and their daughter, Meg.

The American Federation of Television and Radio Artists (AFTRA) honors 60 years of "Guiding Light"—60 years of giving actors employment.

1994
Soap Opera Update MVP Awards—"Guiding Light" wins Best of the Best show award.

1992
Head writer Nancy Curlee and her team win the 1991 Writers Guild of America Award for Best Daytime Series.

1981
Afternoon TV magazine bestows awards on "Guiding Light" in four categories: Best Show: Allen Potter, executive producer. Best Writing: Doug Marland, head writer. Best Actress: Lisa Brown (Nola Reardon) Best Single Performance: Jane Elliot (Carrie Todd), for Carrie's confession

AND LAST BUT NOT LEAST...SPRINGFIELD DAY

Seventeen Springfields throughout the United States honored "Guiding Light" by declaring June 30, 1992, the show's 40th television anniversary, Springfield Day. Keys to the city were presented at WSPR.

THE GUIDING LIGHT

CAST LIST

CHARACTER	ACTOR	YEAR

RADIO CAST LIST

CHARACTER	ACTOR	YEAR
Rev. Tom Bannion	Frank Behrens	1938–39
Bill Bauer	Lyle Sudrow	1948–52
"Mama" Bauer	Gloria Brandt	1948–49
"Mama" Bauer	Adelaide Klein	1949
Meta Bauer	Gloria Blondell	1948
Meta Bauer White	Dorothy Lovett	1948–49
Meta Bauer White Roberts	Jone Allison	1949–52
Fredrick "Papa" Bauer	Theodore von Eltz	1948–49
Fredrick "Papa" Bauer	Theo Goetz	1949–52
Trudy Bauer	Laurette Fillbrandt	1948
Trudy Bauer	Charlotte Holland	1949–51
Ross Boling	Karl Weber	1950–51
Ray Brandon	Donald Briggs	1946–47; 50–51
Ray Brandon	Willard Waterman	1947–49
Ray Brandon	Staats Cotsworth	1949–50
Rev. Bill Brown	Jerry Walters	1945–46
Frank Collins	Willis Bouchey	1947
Julie Collins	Mary Lansing	1946–47
Roger Collins	Sam Edwards	1946
Celeste Cunningham	Carolyn McKay	1937–41
Charles Cunningham	Willis Bouchey	1937–41
Edward Cunningham	Reese Taylor	1942
Edward Cunningham	Ken Griffin	1942–43
Helen Cunningham	Lesley Woods	1939–41
Court Davis	Duke Watson	1946
Ellen, the housekeeper	Henrietta Tedro	1937–41
Jack Felzer	Paul Barnes	1940
Ethel Foster	Sundra Love	1939
Clifford Foster	Bret Morrison	1939
Mrs. Gaylord	Helen Buell	1944–46
Dr. Richard Gaylord	John Barclay	1944–46
Phyllis Gordon	Sharon Grainger	1944–46
Peggy Gaylord	Jane Webb	1944–46
Edward Greenman	Reese Taylor	1942
Edward Greenman	Ken Griffin	1942–43
Joan Greenman	Cheer Brentson	1942
Joan Greenman	Beverly Ruby	1942–43
Norma Greenman	Eloise Kummer	1942–43
Ronnie Greenman	Norma Jean Ross	1942
Mrs. Hanson	Alma Platts	1945
Ned Holden	Ed Prentiss	1937–47
Ned Holden	John Hodiak	1941
Ned Holden	Ned LeFevre	1944
Rev. Dr. Paul Keeler	Bernard Lenrow	1949–50
Rev. Dr. Paul Keeler	Bill Smith	1950–52
Jacob Kransky	Seymour Young	1937–42
Mrs. Kransky	Mignon Schreiber	1937–43
Rose Kransky	Ruth Bailey	1937–42
Rose Kransky	Louise Fitch	1942
Rose Kransky	Charlotte Manson	1942–43
Dwight Lamont	Maurice Copeland	1945–46
Fredrika Lang	Peggy Fuller	1937–39
Fredrika Lang	Muriel Brenner	1939–40
Nina Lawrence Chadwick	Lois Zarley	1943–46
Nina Lawrence Chadwick	Barbara Luddy	1946
Tim Lawrence	Les Mitchell	1943
Tim Lawrence	Rye Billsbury	1943–46
Mary Leland	Anne Seymour	1948–51
Dr. Jonathan MacNeill	Sidney Breese	1943–46
Peter Manno	Michael Romano	1937; 44–46
Iris March	Betty Arnold	1939–42
Claire Marshall Lawrence	Eloise Kummer	1943–46
Claire Marshall Lawrence	Sharon Grainger	1946
Lucille Marshall	Constance Crowder	1945–46
Laura Martin	Gail Henshaw	1940–41
Dr. Charles Matthews	Hugh Studebaker	1947–49

CHARACTER	ACTOR	YEAR
Bertha Miller Bauer	Ann Shepard	1949–50
Bertha Miller Bauer	Charita Bauer	1950–52
Eileen O'Brien	Lucy Tedrow	1939
Abigail Peck	Henrietta Tedrow	1945–46
Torchy Reynolds Holden	Gladys Heen	1939–42
Torchy Reynolds Holden	Dorothy Reynolds	1942
Joe Roberts	Larry Haines	1950–51
Joe Roberts	Herb Nelson	1951–52
Joey Roberts	Tarry Green	1950–52
Kathy Roberts	Susan Douglas	1950–52
Mary Ruthledge Holden	Mercedes McCambridge	1937–39
Mary Ruthledge Holden	Sarajane Wells	1939–44
Mary Ruthledge Holden	Vivian Fridell	1942
Rev. Dr. John Ruthledge	Arthur Peterson	1937–46
Ellis Smith	Raymond Edward Johnson	1937–39
Ellis Smith	Sam Wanamaker	1939–40
Ellis Smith	Phil Dakin	1940
Ellis Smith	Marvin Miller	1940–42
Ellis Smith	Karl Weber	1942
Nancy Stewart	Laurette Fillbrandt	1942
Rev. Frank Tuttle	Phillip Lord	1945
Marjorie Vance	Jean Mowry	1945
Ted White	Arnold Moss	1948–49
Ted White	Bert Cowlan	1949–50
Ted White	James Monks	1950
Charlotte Wilson Brandon	Gertrude Warner	1947
Charlotte Wilson Brandon	Betty Lou Gerson	1947–48
Charlotte Wilson Brandon	Lesley Woods	1949–51
Spike Wilson	Frank Dane	1937–38

TELEVISION CAST LIST

CHARACTER	ACTOR	YEAR
Agnes	Libby Lyman	1995
Alex	Tom Klunis	1974
Paulie Amato	Michael Madeiros	1982
Warren Andrews	Warren Burton	1983–87
Ari Andros Spaulding Cooper	John Syragakisari	1992–94
Eleni Andros Spaulding Cooper	Melina Kanakaredes	1991–94
Eleni Andros Cooper	Jennifer Roszell	1994–present
Eleni Andros Cooper	Wendy Kaplan	1994–95
Jory Andros	James M. Gregory	1992–94
Ya Ya Andros	Irma St. Paul	1992–94
Ted Austin	Roger Rathburn	1988
Wally Bacon	Jack Armstrong	1985
Wally Bacon	Michael Conforti	1986
Clarence Bailey	Philip Bosco	1979
Clarence Bailey	Lawrence Weber	1982–85; 87–90
Dr. Baird	Peter Cappell	1953–55
Diane Ballard	Sofia Landon	1977–81
Victoria Ballenger Jackson	Carol Teitel	1973–74
Dr. Bruce Banning	Les Damon	1956–60
Dr. Bruce Banning	Barnard Hughes	1961–66
Dr. Bruce Banning	Sydney Walker	1970–71
Dr. Bruce Banning	William Roerick	1974
Susan Bates Spaulding	Nancy Bell	1995–96
Jeffrey Battles	Brian Chandler	1990–91
Bertha "Bert" Miller Bauer	Charita Bauer	1952–84
Bill Bauer	Lyle Sudrow	1952–59
Bill Bauer	Ed Bryce	1959–63; 65–69; 77–78; 83
Bill Bauer	Eugene Smith	1964
Frederick "Freddie" Bauer	Albert Zungalo III	1970–71
Frederick "Freddie" Bauer	Gary Hannoch	1972–76
Frederick "Freddie" Bauer	Robbie Berridge	1976–78
Frederick "Rick" Bauer	Phil MacGregor	1982–83
Dr. Frederick "Rick" Bauer	Michael O'Leary	1983–91; 95–present
Hillary Kincaid Bauer	Linda McCullough	1977–78
Hillary Kincaid Bauer	Marsha Clark	1978–84
Hope Bauer	Jennifer Kirschner	1962–65

CHARACTER	ACTOR	YEAR
Hope Bauer	Paula Schwartz	1968
Hope Bauer	Elissa Leeds	1968–73
Hope Bauer	Tisch Raye	1975–76
Hope Bauer	Robin Mattson	1976–77
Hope Bauer	Katherine Justice	1977
Hope Bauer Spaulding	Elvera Roussel	1979–83
Jack Bauer	Alan North	1988
Johnny Bauer	James Goodwin	1986–90
Lacey Bauer	Geri Betzler	1987
Lainie Bauer	Terri Keane	1988
Meta Bauer White Roberts	Jone Allison	1952
Meta Bauer Roberts Banning	Ellen Demming	1953–74
Meta Bauer	Mary Stuart	1996–present
Michelle Bauer	Rachel Miner	1989–95
Michelle Bauer	Rebecca Budig	1995–present
Mike Bauer	Glenn (Christopher) Walken	1954–56
Mike Bauer	Michael Allen	1958 –62
Mike Bauer	Paul Prokopf	1962–63
Mike Bauer	Gary Pillar (Carpenter)	1963–66
Mike Bauer	Robert Pickering	1968
Mike Bauer	Don Stewart	1968–84
Papa Bauer	Theo Goetz	1952–72
Trudy Bauer	Helen Wagner	1952
Trudy Bauer Palmer	Lisa Howard	1957–58
William Edward "Billy" Bauer	Pat Collins	1958–61
Dr. William Edward "Ed" Bauer	Robert Gentry	1966–69
Dr. William Edward "Ed" Bauer	Mart Hulswit	1969–81
Dr. William Edward "Ed" Bauer	Peter Simon	1981–84; 86–96
Dr. William Edward "Ed" Bauer	Richard Van Vleet	1984–86
Muffy Baxter	Bradley Bliss	1984
Pat Beagle	Arthur E. Jones	1985–86
Anne Benedict Fletcher	Joan Gray	1956–62
Anne Benedict Fletcher	Elizabeth Hubbard	1962
Helene Benedict	Kay Campbell	1957–64
Henry Benedict	John Gibson	1959–62
Henry Benedict	John Boruff	1962–66
Henry Benedict	Lester Rawlins	1967
Henry Benedict	Paul McGrath	1967
Dr. Erik Bernhoff	Frederick Rolf	1980
Professor Blackburn	Robert Burr	1986
Dean Blackford	Gordon Rigsby	1977–79
Kate Blair	Peggy Price	1986
Neil Blake	Patrick Horgan	1979–80; 82
Abigail Blume	Amy Ecklund	1995–present
Charlotte Blume	Tandy Cronyn	1995–96
Max Blume	Peter Brouwer	1995–96
Blanche Bouvier	Jennifer Leak	1981
Alex Bowden	Ernest Graves	1960–66
Carter Bowden	Alan Austin	1980
Joe Bradley	Michael J. Stark	1980–81
Cooper Bradshaw	Michael Cugno	1996
Jenna Bradshaw	Fiona Hutchison	1992–94; 96–present
Sophia Breitner	Lizabeth Pritchett	1986
Bridget	Melissa Hayden	1991
Cat Brixton	Don Fisher	1986–87
Dr. John Brooks	Charles Baxter	1954
Jonathan Brooks	Damion Scheller	1984
Cindy Brown	Dursby Simpson	1968
Martin Bruner	Clement Fowler	1983
Dinah Buckley	Courtney Sherman	1970–71
Julie Camaletti	Jocelyn Seagrave	1991–94
Lt. Wally Campbell	Alexander Courtney	1969
Lt. Wally Campbell	Jack Ryland	1969
Cardinal Mallone	Michael Lombard	1986
Dr. Dick Carey	Paul Nesbit	1972
Dr. Dick Carey	Roger Morden	1972–73
Carol	Louise Stubbs	1965–66
Sonni/Solita Carrera Lewis	Michelle Forbes	1987–89
Welles Carrera	John Cunningham	1988
Rebecca Cartwright (Mona Enright)	Leslie O'Hara	1982–83
Anthony James "J" Chamberlain	George Pilgrim	1996
Anthony James "J" Chamberlain	Ethan Erickson	1996–present
Henry Chamberlain	William Roerick	1980–96
Quinton McCord Chamberlain/Sean Ryan	Michael Tylo	1981–85; 96
Vanessa Chamberlain Lewis Lewis Reardon	Maeve Kinkead	1980–87; 89–present
Vanessa Chamberlain	Anna Stuart	1980–81
Pam Chandler	Maureen Silliman	1974–76
Dr. Peter Chapman	Curt Dawson	1978–80
Max Chapman	Ben Hammer	1978
Claudine	Goli Samii	1996
Nell Cleary	Mary Peterson	1995–96
Mark Cody	James Harper	1989
Derek Colby	Harley Venton	1980–82
Judge Collier	Ellen Holly	1991–93
Philip Collins	Carson Woods	1960–61
Julie Conrad Bauer	Sandra Smith	1962–65
Linell Conway	Christina Pickles	1970–72
Marion Conway	Lois Holmes	1971
Marion Conway	Kate Harrington	1971–72
Frank Achilles "Buzz" Cooper, Sr.	Justin Deas	1993–present
Frank Cooper	Frank Dicopoulos	1987–present
Harley Davidson Cooper Spaulding (Camaletti);	Beth Ehlers	1987–93
Lucy Cooper Spaulding	Sonia Satra	1993–97
Marina Nadine Cooper	Alysia Zucker/Casey Rosenhaus	1993–96
Marina Nadine Cooper	Sasha Martin	1996–present
Nadine Cooper Lewis Cooper	Jean Carol	1988–1995
"Pops" Cooper	Vince O'Brien	1989–90
Kurt Corday	Mark Lewis	1985–86
Doris Crandall	Barbara Becker	1961–62
Camilla Crawford	Penelope Windust	1972
Dahlia Crede	Sharon Leal	1996–present
Tina Crede	Nikki Rene	1996
Dr. Ruth Creighton	Roni Dengel	1979
Silas Crocker	Benjamin Hendrickson	1981–83
Grace Cummings	Teresa Wright	1986
John Cutler	Jack Betts	1987
Lisa Cutler	Sherry Ramsey	1986
Patrick Cutter	Scott Hoxby	1993–95
Gina Daniels	Annabelle Gurwitch	1984–85
Dr. Louie Darnell	Eric Brooks	1983–86
Dr. Matt Davenport	James Carroll	1982–83
Davis	John deVries	1991
Wayne DeVargas	Peter Brouwer	1984
Darcy Dekker	Robin V. Johnson	1984
Sgt. DeMarco	Michael Mikler	1969
Suzanne Devereaux	Juliet Pritner	1991
Dr. Dey	Barbara Andrus	1992–93
Sid Dickerson	Kelly Neal	1994–95
Claudia Dillman	Grace Matthews	1968–69
Marty Dillman	Robert Lawson	1968
Marty Dillman	Christopher Wines	1968–69
Dimitra	Stephanie Tashman	1995
Dirty Dottie	Bobo Lewis	1994
Agatha Dobson	Elizabeth MacRae	1983
Donna	Tammy Lang	1993–95
Ken Draper	Michael John McGuiness	1995
Lisa Dravecky	Mady Kaplan	1990
Dr. Renee DuBois	Deborah May	1979–80
Emma Earnest	Agnes Young	1972–73
Dr. Harold Eberhart	Jordan Charney	1974
Eddie	Edward Vilella	1983
Betty Eiler	Madeleine Sherwood	1971–72
Charles Eiler	Graham Jarvis	1971–72
Elvis	Paul Kaup	1991
Emily	Elizabeth Swain	1980–82
Enright	Phillip LeStrange	1986–87
Mark Evans (Samuel Pasquin)	Mark Pinter	1981–83
Neil Everest	Patrick O'Connell	1989–90
Evie	Trisha M. Housier	1990
Dr. Greg Fairbanks	David Greenan	1979–80
Andy Ferris	Victor Slezak	1984–85
Nancy Ferris	J. Smith–Cameron	1984–85
Dr. Ingrid Fischer	Tania Elg	1980
The Fisherman	Robert Karricart	1996
Dr. Barry Flannery	Robert Phelps	1974
Billy Fletcher	James Long	1970–73
Billy Fletcher	Matthew Schlossberg	1973
Billy Fletcher	Shane Nickerson	1973–76
Billy Fletcher	Dai Stockton	1976
Fred Fletcher	John Gibson	1958
Jane Fletcher Hayes	Pamela King	1961–63
Jane Fletcher Hayes	Chase Crosley	1963–68

CHARACTER	ACTOR	YEAR
Johnny Fletcher	Sheldon Golomb	1962
Johnny Fletcher	Donald Melvin	1963–64
Johnny Fletcher	Daniel Fortas	1965
Johnny Fletcher	Don Scardino	1965–67
Dr. Johnny Fletcher	Erik Howell	1967–71
Dr. Paul Fletcher	Michael Kane	1956
Dr. Paul Fletcher	Bernard Grant	1956–70
Leo Flynn	Robert Lupone	1990; 92–96
Lola Fontaine	Megan McTavish	1983–84
Carlo Fontini	James Coco	1986
Miss Mildred Foss	Jan Sterling	1969–70
Whitney Foxton	Joseph Maher	1978
Dr. Jim Frazier	Billy Dee Williams	1966
Dr. Jim Frazier	James Earl Jones	1966
Martha Frazier	Cicely Tyson	1966
Martha Frazier	Ruby Dee	1967
Jackson Freemont	Michael Wilding, Jr.	1985–87
Fritz	Bill Britton	1982
Dr. Wilson Frost	Jack Betts	1973–74
Lee Gantry	Ray Fulmer	1969–71
George	Sherilyn Wolter	1993
Gerhardt	Stephen McHattie	1986–87
Lady Agnes Gilmore	Lori March	1987
Ginger	Alison Janney	1993–95
Sally Gleason	Patricia Barry	1984–87
Lucien Goff	Andreas Katsulas	1982
Grady	Eddie Mekka	1992–93
Georgene Granger	Delphi Harrington	1977
Malcolm Granger	Ed Seamons	1976
Dr. Charles Grant	David Wolos-Fonteno	1995–present
Dr. Charles Grant	Ron Foster	1991–1995
David Grant	Monti Sharp	1992–95
David Grant	Russell Curry	1995–96
Gilly Grant Speakes	Amelia Marshall	1989–96
Laura Grant	Katherine Anderson	1953
Laura Grant	Alice Yourman	1953–62
Dr. Richard "Dick" Grant	James Lipton	1952–62
Richard Grant	Ed Prentiss	1953
Ulysses Grant	Sam Schacht	1990
Vivian Grant	Petronia Paley	1992–present
Dr. Eve Guthrie Wyland Bauer	Hilary Edson	1992–95
Jim Haggerty	Nick Gregory	1992–93
Tom Halverson	Chris Sarandon	1969–70
Dr. Gavin Hamilton	Paul McGrath	1968
Dr. Mark Hamilton	Burton Cooper	1978–79
Richard Hanley, D.A.	Mandel Kramer	1953
Dr. Gwen Harding	Elizabeth Allen	1983
Pauly Hardman	Joe Marinelli	1994
Sid Harper	Philip Sterling	1952–54
Cain Harris (Harry Kane)	Jerry Lanning	1986
Lionel Harris	Jack White	1983–89
Harry	Mark Margolis	1994
Jack Haskell	Paul Larson	1966
Susanna "Susie" Hayden	Lori Putnam	1983
George Hayes	Philip Sterling	1962–68
Leona Herbert	Rosetta LeNoire	1972
Tangie Hill	Marcy Walker	1993–95
Wanda M. Hite	Carey Cromelin	1985–90
Mrs. Hoffman	Lilia Skala	1974
Jane Hogan	Mary Pat Gleason	1984–85
Alice Holden	Sandy Dennis	1956
Alice Holden	Diane Gentner	1956–58
Alice Holden	Lin Pierson	1958–60
Mark Holden	Whitfield Connor	1955–59
Robin Lang Holden	Zina Bethune	1956–58
Robin Lang Holden	Judy Robinson	1959–60
Robin Lang Holden	Abigail Kellogg	1960–61
Robin Lang Holden Bowen	Nancy Malone	1961–63
Robin Lang Holden Bowen Fletcher	Ellen Weston	1963–64
Robin Lang Holden Fletcher	Gillian Spencer	1964–67
Jenny Holmes	Mary Ellen Stuart	1987–88
Hutchins	Rodney Clark	1991
Leslie Jackson Bauer Norris	Lynne Adams	1966–71; 73–76
Leslie Jackson Norris	Kathryn Hays	1971
Leslie Jackson Norris Bauer	Barbara Rodell	1971–73
Dr. Stephen Jackson	Stefan Schnabel	1965–81

CHARACTER	ACTOR	YEAR
Karl Jannings	Richard Morse	1959–60
Ruth Jannings Holden	Irja Jensen	1958
Ruth Jannings Holden	Louise Platt	1958–59
Ruth Jannings Holden	Virginia Dwyer	1959–60
Dr. Mark Jarrett	Keir Dullea	1986
Jean-Luc	Emmanuel Xuereb	1996
Ann Jeffers	Maureen Mooney	1975–80
Spence Jeffers	John Ramsey	1976
Dr. Will Jeffries	Joseph Breen	1987–89
Jenkins	Roland Hunter	1989
Jenkins	Robert Krebs	1989
Wayne Jennings	Roger Baron	1981–82
Jessica	Laura Rhodes	1996
Hart Jessup	Jeff Phillips	1991–92
Hart Jessup	Leonard Staab	1993
Hart Jessup	Sean McDermott	1993
Hart Jessup	Marshall Hilliard	1996
Hart Jessup	Frank Grillo	1996–present
Nurse Jodie	Alice Oakes	1985–86
Nurse Janet Johnson	Ruth Warrick	1953–54
Nurse Janet Johnson	Lois Wheeler	1954–58
Clara Jones	Anna Maria Hosford	1979
Dana Jones	Katell Plevin	1989–90
Harry Jones	Mark Margalis	1994
Jory	Roger Howarth	1992
Joseph	Jack McLaughlin	1991
Keith	Jesse L. Martin	1992
Rev. Dr. Paul Keeler	Ed Begley	1952
Rev. Dr. Paul Keeler	Melville Ruick	1952–54
Dr. Jim Kelly	Paul Potter	1954–55
Ron Kennedy	Matthew Barry	1982
Khristos	David Lee Russek	1995
Jack Kiley	Tom Tammi	1992
Lady Kimball	Anita Dangler	1970
Simone Kincaid	Laryssa Lauret	1977–78
Judge Evan Kruger	Hansford Rowe	1969
Stavros Kouperakis	Eugene Troobnick	1991–1995
Kaz Kowolski	Phillip Sterling	1987
Scott Lacey	David Leary	1979
Dr. Paul LaCrosse	Jacques Roux	1979–80
Duke Lafferty	Gary Phillips	1980–81
Gloria LaRue Harper	Anne Burr	1952–54
Mrs. Laurey	Lois Wilson	1954–55
Mrs. Laurey	Virginia Payne	1956
Brent Lawrence/Marian Crane	Marc Wolf	1996
Brent Lawrence/Marian Crane	Frank Beatty	1995–96
Cassie Lawrence	Nina Landey	1995
Lila Lawrence	Barbara Stein	1995
Lazarus (Man from Amsterdam)	Stephen Sutherland	1987
Connie Lemay	Debra Cole	1989; 94
Susan Lemay	Brittany Slattery	1994
Detective Stuart Levy	Stuart Ward	1991–96
Nurse Annie Dutton Lewis	Cynthia Watros	1996–present
Dylan Shayne Lewis	Morgan Englund	1989–1994
Harlan Billy "H.B." Lewis	Larry Gates	1983–88; 96
Billy Lewis II	Jordan Clarke	1982–87; 89–94; 96
Billy Lewis II	Geoffrey Scott	1994
Billy Lewis III	Bryan Buffinton	1989–present
Joshua Lewis	Robert Newman	1981–85; 86–91; 93–present
Marah Shayne Lewis	Ashley Peldon	1989–91
Marah Shayne Lewis	Kimberly J. Brown	1995–present
Melinda Sue "Mindy" Lewis Spaulding Corday Jeffries	Krista Tesreau	1983–90
Melinda Sue "Mindy" Lewis Jeffries	Kimberley Simms	1990–92
Melinda Sue "Mindy" Lewis	Ann Hamilton	1993
Melinda Sue "Mindy" Lewis McHenry	Barbara Crampton	1993–95
Patricia "Trish" Lewis Norris	Rebecca Hollen	1980–85
Shayne Lewis	Brett Cooper	1993–present
Brian Lister	Richard Clarke	1982–83
Jamie Loomis	Alan Coates	1982
Gabriella Lopez	Veronica Cruz	1994–95
Bess Lowell	Elizabeth Lawrence	1993–94
Gunther Lugosi	George Kappaz	1982

CHARACTER	ACTOR	YEAR
Brandon "Lujack" Spaulding Luvonaczek		
	Vincent Irizarry	1983–85
Eric Luvonaczek	Ted Sorel	1992
Nick McHenry Spaulding Luvonaczek		
	Vincent Irizarry	1991–96
Simon Hall Luvonaczek	Shawn Thompson	1985–87
Dr. Eileen Lyndon	Cynthia Hayden	1987–89
John "Mac" McIntyre	Arnold Robertson	1953
MacGregor	Ken LaRon	1989
Anthony Camaletti "A.C." Mallet	Mark Derwin	1990–93
Flip Malone	Paul Carpinelli	1968–69
Dr. Bertrand Mandel	Fred J. Scollay	1974
Helena Manzini	Rose Alaio	1981–83
Giancarlo Marino	Joe Petruzzi	1991
Dinah Morgan Chamberlain Marler		
	Jennifer Gatti	1986–87
Dinah Morgan Chamberlain Marler	Paige Turco	1987–89
Dinah Morgan Chamberlain Marler Thorpe		
	Wendy Moniz	1995–present
Jason Frederick Marler	Samantha Stein	1996
Dr. Justin Marler	Tom O'Rourke	1976–83; 87
Dr. Justin Marler	Christopher Pennock	1990–91
Kevin Ross Marler	Brandon Unger	1996
Lainie Marler Bowden	Kathleen Kellaigh	1979–80
Ross Marler	Jerry verDorn	1979–present
Samantha Marler	Suzy Cote	1989–92
Edna Marsh	Zamah Cunningham	1958
Karen Martin	Trudi Wiggins	1971–72
Ellen Mason	Jeanne Arnold	1969–73
Grove Mason	Vince O'Brien	1969–70
Janet Mason Norris	Caroline McWilliams	1969–75
Mrs. Matson	Fran Bennett	1965–66
Calla Matthews	Lisby Larson	1985–86
Gordon Matthews	Ed Penn	1986
Jesse Matthews	Rebecca Staab	1985–86
Rose McLaren Shayne	Alexandra Neil	1987–89
Alex McDaniels	Keith Charles	1976
Ben McFarren	Stephen Yates	1976–82
Jerry McFarren	Peter Jensen	1976
Jerry McFarren	Mark Travis	1977
Dusty McGuire	Jamie Donnelly	1969–70
Nurse Marion McHenry	Marion Lauer	1968–72
Dr. Sara McIntyre	Patricia Roe	1967–68
Dr. Sara McIntyre	Jill Andre	1968
Dr. Sara McIntyre Werner Blackford Thorpe		
	Millette Alexander	1969–82
Josh McPhee	Ben Thomas	1979
Tyler Meade	Paul Collins	1969–70
Deborah Mehren	Olivia Cole	1969–71
Gil Mehren	David Pendleton	1970–71
Gil Mehren	James A. Preston	1971
Gordon Middleton	Marcus Smythe	1978–79
Gracie Middleton	Lori Shelle	1981–83
Elsie Miller Franklin	Ethel Remey	1956–57
Audrey Mills	Louise Troy	1974
Roy Mills	Josef Sommer	1974
Lesley Ann Monroe Andrews	Carolyn Ann Clark	1981–84
Carmen Monvales	Julie Carmen	1978
Carmen Monvales	Blanca Camacho	1978–80
Dr. Gonzalo Moreno	Gonzalo Madurga	1978
Sylvia Moreno	Feiga Martinez	1979
Vinnie Morrison	Kevin McClatchy	1993
Andrew Murray, D.A.	Dana Elcar	1962
Musette	Nadine Kay	1992
Rebecca Nash	Christopher Norris	1992
Dr. Frank Nelson	Keith Charles	1981
Dr. Kelly Nelson	John Wesley Shipp	1980–84
Dr. Peter Nelson	Gene Rupert	1963–64
Ira Newton	Sorrell Booke	1969
Ira Newton	Larry Gates	1972
Nick	Rex Everhart	1983–84; 89–90; 95
Andrew Norris	Barney McFadden	1975
Andrew Norris	Ted LePlat	1980–81
Barbara Norris Thorpe	Augusta Dabney	1970
Barbara Norris Thorpe	Barbara Berjer	1971–81; 89; 95–96
Holly Norris	Lynn Deerfield	1970–76
Holly Norris Bauer Thorpe Lindsey Reade		
	Maureen Garrett	1976–80; 88–present
Ken Norris	Roger Newman	1970–75
Stanley Norris	Michael Higgins	1970
Stanley Norris	William Smithers	1971
Maggie O'Byme	Sheila Coonan	1980–81
Carroll O'Malley	Will Lyman	1994–95
Sir Clayton Olds	Myles Easton	1970
Father O'Shea	Bernie McInerny	1992–93
Mrs. Pappas	Shirl Berheim	1991
Mrs. Pappas	Florence Anglin	1993
Floyd Parker	Tom Nielsen	1979–85
Katie Parker	Denise Pence	1977–85
Dr. Parlier	Stanley Albers	1988–89
Darren Patterson	John Rockwell	1980
Kate Pearson	Jane Farnol	1970
Peggy	Suzanne Douglas	1986
Peter	Greg Wrangler	1986
Peter	Michael Botshens	1986
Dan Peters	Paul Ballantyne	1954
Dr. Peters	Laura Hughes	1995
Pharoah	Don Chastain	1989
Phaser	James Lynch	1988–89
Ivy Pierce (Brenda Lowry)	Deborah May	1982–83
Susan Piper	Carrie Nye	1984
Mrs. Popoff	Rosemarie Dana	1991; 93
David Preston	John Martinuzzi	1984–85
Pretty Boy	David Rod Coury	1984
Ruth Price	Beatrice Winde	1990
Rita Putnam	Anne Shaler	1972
Beth Raines	Judi Evans	1983–86
Beth Raines Bauer Spaulding	Beth Chamberlin	1989–91
Bradley Raines	James Rebhorn	1983–85; 89
Nurse Lillian Raines	Tina Sloan	1983–present
Dr. Claire Ramsey Jarrett	Susan Pratt	1983–86
Randi	Kathy Tragasee	1993
Rashid	Andre Ware	1996
Ben Stoddard Sampson Reade	Gregory Burke	1989–96
Ben Stoddard Sampson Reade	Brian McElroy	1991
Fletcher Reade	Jay Hammer	1984–present
Meg Reade	Jacqueline Falchier	1996
Dr. Meredith Reade Bauer	Nicolette Goulet	1987–89
Bea Reardon	Lee Lawson	1981–87; 90
Bridget Reardon	Melissa Hayden	1991–present
Chelsea Reardon	Kassie Wesley	1986–91
Dr. Jim Reardon	Michael Woods	1983–85
Matt Reardon	Kurt McKinney	1994–present
Maureen Reardon Bauer	Ellen Dolan	1982–86
Maureen Reardon Bauer	Ellen Parker	1986–93
Nola Reardon Chamberlain	Lisa Brown	1980–85; 95–present
Peter Lewis Reardon	Joseph Phillips	1993–96
Sean Reardon	W. T. Martin	1995
Tony Reardon	Gregory Beecroft	1981–85
Peggy Regan	Patricia Wheel	1954
Mrs. Violet Renfield	Beulah Garrick	1981–83
Alicia Rhomer	Cynthia Dozier	1985
Dr. Carl Richards	Wayne Tippit	1974
Chad Richards	Everett McGill	1975–76
Jennifer Richards Evans (Jean Marie Stafford)		
	Geraldine Court	1980–83
Morgan Richards	Kristen Vigard	1980–81
Morgan Richards Nelson	Jennifer Cook	1981–83
Joe Roberts	Herb Nelson	1952–55
Joey Roberts	Tarry Green	1952–53
Joey Roberts	Richard Holland	1953
Kathy Roberts Lang Grant Holden		
	Susan Douglas	1952–58
Christie Rogers	Ariana Munker	1970–71
Rae Rooney	Allison Daugherty	1989–90
Rosie	Gretchen Koerner	1995
Chief Ryan	Richard Borg	1992–93
Norrie Ryan	Candace Evans	1993
Dr. Tim Ryan	Jordan Clarke	1974–76
Kyle Sampson	Larkin Malloy	1984–87
Lt. Jeff Saunders	David Little	1984–85
Suzette Saxon	Frances Fisher	1985
Amber Schine	DeLane Matthews	1986
Ben Scott	Bernard Kates	1965–68
Dr. Emmet Scott	Kenneth Harvey	1976
Dr. Emmet Scott	Frank Latimore	1976–79
Dr. Emmet Scott	Peter Turgeon	1982

CHARACTER	ACTOR	YEAR
Jackie Scott Marler Spaulding	Cindy Pickett	1976–80
Jackie Scott Marler	Carrie Mowery	1980–82
Maggie Scott	June Graham	1965–68
Nurse Peggy Scott Fletcher Dillman Thorpe		
	Fran Myers	1965–79
Dr. Margaret Sedwick	Margaret Gwenver	1979–96
Dick Sexton	Patrick James Clarke	1986
Raymond Shafer	Keith Aldrich	1977
Isabella Shankford	Victoria Boothby	1995
Sharina	Janet League	1984
Roz Sharp	Carolyn Byrd	1984
Baby Marah Shayne (principal)	Nicole Otto	1987
Baby Marah Shayne (backups)		
	Sarah & Rebecca Perch	1987
Hawk Shayne	Gil Rogers	1985–90; 95–present
Reva Shayne Lewis Lewis Spaulding Lewis Cooper		*Nov 3 2006*
	Kim Zimmer	1983–90; 95–present
Roxanne "Roxie" Shayne Corday	Kristi Ferrell	1984–88
Rusty Shayne	Terrell Anthony	1986–89; 96
Sarah Shayne	Audrey Peters	1987–91; 96
Brandy Shellooe	Sandy Faison	1977
Brandy Shellooe	JoBeth Williams	1977–81
Gladys Shields	Louise Troy	1978
Eli Sims	Stephen Joyce	1983
Annabelle Sims Reardon	Harley Jane Kozak	1983–85
Amy Sinclair	Joanne Linville	1959
Amy Sinclair	Connie Lembcke	1960
Gavin Sinclair	Jack Gilpin	1985
Gavin Sinclair	Bob Burris	1985
Smitty	Curt May	1990
Alan Spaulding	Christopher Bernau	1977–84; 86–88
Alan Spaulding	Daniel Pilon	1988–89
Alan Spaulding	Ron Raines	1994–present
Alan-Michael Spaulding	Carl Evans	1987–89
Alan-Michael Spaulding	Rick Hearst	1990–96
Alan-Michael Spaulding	Michael Dietz	1996–97
Alexandra Spaulding von Halkein Walls Thorpe		
	Beverlee McKinsey	1984–92
Alexandra Spaulding	Marj Dusay	1993–present
Amanda Wexler Spaulding Middleton McFarren		
	Kathleen Cullen	1978–83; 87
Amanda Wexler Spaulding	Toby Poser	1996–present
Brandon Spaulding	David Thomas	1979
Brandon Spaulding	John Wardwell	1983
Brandon Spaulding	Keith Charles	1984
Elizabeth Spaulding Marler	Lezlie Dalton	1977–81
Lizzie Spaulding	Hayden Pannettiere	1996
Phillip Spaulding	Jarrod Ross	1977–81
Phillip Spaulding	Grant Aleksander	
		1982–84; 87–91; 96–present
Phillip Spaulding	John Bolger	1985–86
Victoria Spaulding	Kim Hamilton	1984
Hampton Speakes	Vince Williams	1989–95
Katherine "Kat" Speakes	Nia Long	1991–94
Edith Spurrier	Clarice Blackburn	1988; 92
Dr. Daniel St. John	David Bishins	1990–92
Chet Stafford	Bill Herndon	1980–81
Logan Stafford	Richard Hamilton	1980–81
Nurse Stanhope	Donna Oddams	1969
Eve Stapleton McFarren	Janet Grey	1976–83
Rita Stapleton Bauer	Lenore Kasdorf	1975–81
Viola Stapleton	Sudie Bond	1975
Viola Stapleton	Kate Wilkinson	1975–81
Judy Stassen	Ruth Manning	1969
Lt. Pete Stassen	Karl Light	1969
Steve	Michael Hammond	1991
Cameron Stewart	Ian Ziering	1986–88
George Stewart	Joe Lambie	1987–88
Julia Stoddard	Meg Mundy	1986; 88
Maeve Stoddard Sampson Reade		
	Leslie Denniston	1985–88
Susan	Lia Yang	1994
Rachel Sullivan	Mackenzie Phillips	1996
Nick Sutton	W.T. Martin	1987–88
Gary Swanson	William Bell Sullivan	1989–90
Capt. Jim Swanson	Lee Richardson	1972
Det. Tagne	Daniel Ralph Byers	1990
Glenn Taggart	Lee Moore	1995
Tanya	Barbara Ring	1984

CHARACTER	ACTOR	YEAR
Tanya	Hilary Edson	1984
Johnny "Dub" Taylor	Maarko Maglich	1984–85
Lila Taylor Kelly	Nancy Wickwire	1954–55
Lila Taylor Kelly	Teri Keane	1957
Dr. Bart Thompson	Barry Thomson	1954
Adam Thorpe	Robert Gerringer	1972
Adam Thorpe	Robert Milli	1972–81; 89; 94
Christina Thorpe	Gina Foy	1975–78
Christina Thorpe	Cheryl Lynn Brown	1979–80
Christina Blake Lindsey Thorpe Spaulding		
	Elizabeth Dennehy	1988–89
Christina Blake Thorpe Spaulding		
	Sherry Stringfield	1989–92
Christina Blake Thorpe Marler	Elizabeth Keifer	1992–present
Roger Thorpe	Michael Zaslow	1971–80; 89–present
Carrie Todd MacKenzie Marler	Jane Elliot	1981–82
Tracy	Christine Langner	1991
Trevor	Norman Snow	1985; 91–92
Joe Turino	Joseph Campanella	1959–60
Clay Tynan	Giancarlo Esposito	1982–83
Helen Tynan	Micki Grant	1982–84
Christine Valere	Ariana Munker	1986–87
Paul Valere	Robin Ward	1987
Vaughn	Lee Moore	1989
Vera	Frances Foster	1985–92
David Vested	Peter D. Greene	1970–71
David Vested	Dan Hamilton	1971
Kit Vested	Nancy Addison	1970–74
Francesca Vizzini	Nadia Capone	1991
Marco Vizzini	Ed Setrakian	1991
Baron Leo von Halkein	George Guidall	1986
Dorie Smith von Halkein	Kimi Parks	1986–87
India von Halkein Spaulding	Mary Kay Adams	1984–87; 90
Marie Wallace Grant	Joyce Holden	1954
Marie Wallace Grant	Lynne Rogers	1955–62
Locke Walls	Jeremy Slate	1985
Charlotte Waring Fletcher Bauer/Tracy Delmar		
	Victoria Wyndham	1967–70
Charlotte Waring Bauer/Tracy Delmar		
	Melinda Fee	1970–73
Dr. Waterman	Maurice Copeland	1978
Linette Waterman	Eileen Dietz	1978
Maya Waterman	Sands Hall	1978
Jean Weatherill	Jennifer Harmon	1991
Jason Weber	Marc O'Daniels	1965–66
Matt Weiss	Jeff Gendelman	1990
Dr. Joe Wemer	Ben Hayes	1966–67
Dr. Joe Werner	Ed Zimmermann	1967–72
Dr. Joe Werner	Berkeley Harris	1972
Dr. Joe Werner	Anthony Call	1972–76
Tim "T.J." Werner	T.J. Hargrave	1974–76
Tim Werner	Kevin Bacon	1980–81
Tim Werner	Christopher Marcantel	1981
Tim Werner	Nigel Reed	1981–82
Macauley West	Joe Lando	1993
Lucille Wexler	Rita Lloyd	1978–80
Maggie Wexler	Margaret Impert	1969
Peter Wexler	Leon Russom	1969
Peter Wexler	Michael Durrell	1969–71
Charlotte Wheaton	Barbara Garrick	1985
Lawson Whitehall	Andrew Brock	1987–89
Lawson Whitehall	Andrew Gorman	1987–89
Griffin Williams	Geoffrey C. Ewing	1996–present
Marcus Williams	Kevin Mambo	1995–present
Martin "I.Q." Wilson	Jaison Walker	1984–86
Trudy Wilson	Amy Steel	1980–81
Det. Kirk Winters	James Horan	1981
Marian Winters	Katherine Meskill	1958
Emma Witherspoon	Maureen O'Sullivan	1984
Wyatt	Keith Christopher	1995–96
Lt. Carl Wyatt	Gerald S. O'Loughlin	1962
Lt. Larry Wyatt	Joe Ponazecki	
		1979–82; 87–88; 90–91; 94
Paul Wyland	Mark Deakins	1992
Anita Ybarra	Carla Pinza	1988–89
Esteban Ybarra	Gonzalo Madurga	1988
Zachary (Smith)	Brody Hutzler	1996–97
Zamana	Adolph Caesar	1994

THE GUIDING LIGHT

Executive Producer: Paul Rauch

Senior Producer: Robert D. Kochman

Producers: Roy Steinberg; Catherine Maher Smith

Writers: Barbara Esensten and James Harmon Brown with Michael Conforti, Nancy Williams Watt, Kathleen Kennedy, N. Gail Lawrence, Jeanne Glynn, Sharon Epstein, Roger Newman, Pete T. Rich, Loren Segan, Tita Bell

Senior Director: Bruce S. Barry

Directors: JoAnne Sedwick, Brian Mertes

Associate Producers: Francine Versalie, Alexandra Johnson

Art Director: Rick Dennis

Scenic Designers: Maureen Going, Kennon Rothchild

Set Designers: Barry Axtell, Shelley Barclay

Costume Designer: Suzanne Schwarzer

Assistant Costume Designer: Alyson Hui

Lighting Designers: Tony Girolami; Brian W. McRae, A.S.L.D.

Casting Director: Glenn Daniels

Assistant Casting Director: Melanie Haseltine

Associate Directors: John M. O'Connell, Matt Lagle, Karen Wilkens

Stage Managers: Locke Wallace, Ann Vettel, Adam Reist

Production Assistants: Ilene K. Frankel, Rosemary Mooy

Supervising Music Director: Barbara Miller-Gidaly

Music Director: Robyn Cutler

Production Coordinators: Natasha Katzive, David Kreizman, Wally White

Assistant to the Executive Producer: Jan Conklin

Assistant to the Writers: Jill Lorie Hurst

Production Manager: Ed Anderson

Unit Managers: John Keeler, John Baxley

Facility Manager: Kimberly Armstrong

Production Administrator: Linda Mysel

Technical Director: Robert F. Eastman

Audio: Butch Inglese

Video: Bill Vignari, Howard C. Rosenzweig

Videotape Editors: Tom Bornkamp, Richie Sens, Jr.

Chief Engineer: John P. Valentino

Camera: Jerry Gruen, Mark Schneider, Tom Stallone, Bob Del Russo

Boom Operators: Tony Valentino, Eric Worth

Sound Effects: Joseph Gallant

Music Mixers: Tim Pankewicz, John Fitzpatrick, Jon Hopkins

Utility: Doug Kent, Andy Capuano, Andrew Robinson

Make-up: Paul Gebbia, Joe Cola, Helen Gallagher

Hairdressers: Linda Williams, Carol (Cici) Campbell, Ralph Stanzione

Wardrobe: Rose Cuervo

Scenic Artists: Ralph Cava, James St. Clair, Mary Citarella, Thomas Southern

Special Effects: Anthony Parmelee

Title Design: Wayne Fitzgerald

Theme Music: Rob Mounsey

Executive in Charge of Production: Mary Alice Dwyer-Dobbin

Recorded at the New York Production Center, New York City

PHOTO CREDITS

All photographs and images are copyright © CBS, Inc., and are provided courtesy of CBS, Inc. Photographer credits, as available, are as follows:

Front Cover:
Zaslow/Kiefer/Garrett/ver Dorn—E.J. Carr
Aleksander/O'Leary—Greg Weiner
Charita Bauer—Mario Ruiz
Zimmer/Newman—Robert Milazzo
Kinkead/Moniz—Robin Platzer/Twin Images
Title Page: E.J. Carr
18: Bob Stahman
19: (lower right) Irv Haberman
20: Bill Warnecke
21: Bill Warnecke
22: Irv Haberman
24: Irv Haberman
26: Bill Warnecke
27: (upper right) Irv Haberman
27: (lower left) Bill Warnecke
28: (upper left) Lennie Lautenberger
(lower right) Irv Haberman
29: Emil Romano
30: Bill Warnecke
31: Irv Haberman
32: Irv Haberman
34: Emil Romano
35: Emil Romano
36: (upper left) Irv Haberman
(lower right) Emil Romano
37: Bill Warnecke
39: Bill Warnecke
40: Robert Milli
41: Irv Haberman
42: (lower left) Emil Romano
(upper right) Emil Romano
43: (upper left) Emil Romano
(lower right) Emil Romano
44: Robert Milli
45: Irv Haberman
46: Robert Milli
47: Irv Haberman
50: (upper left) Robert Milli
(lower right) Bill Warnecke
52: (upper left) Anne F. Lewis
54: (lower left) Bob Greene
55: (lower left) Emil Romano
58: Bob Greene
61: Irv Haberman
64: (upper right) S. Karin Epstein
66: (bottom right) Wagner International/CBS Archives
67: Emil Romano
69: Courtesy of *Soap Opera Weekly*
86: (lower left) Andrew Popper/courtesy of *Soap Opera Weekly*
(upper right) Andrew Popper/courtesy of *Soap Opera Weekly*
88: Irv Haberman
89: Ira Lewis
94: (lower right) Mario Ruiz
97: (upper left) Mario Ruiz
(lower right) Mario Ruiz
98: (upper left) Mario Ruiz
(lower right) Mario Ruiz
100: (lower left) Mario Ruiz
(upper right) Mario Ruiz
102: Mario Ruiz
105: (upper left) Mike Fuller
(right) Mario Ruiz
106: (lower left) Mike Fuller

107: (upper left) Mario Ruiz
125: E.J. Carr
131: Nora Feller
140: Robin Platzer/Twin Images/courtesy of *Soap Opera Weekly*
141: Mark Weiss/courtesy of *Soap Opera Weekly*
150: Danny Sanchez
151: E.J. Carr
161: E.J. Carr/courtesy of *Soap Opera Weekly*
163: Victoria Arlak
165: E.J. Carr
167: Jerry Wachter/courtesy of *Soap Opera Weekly*
170: Victoria Arlak
172: E.J. Carr
174: Victoria Arlak
176: E.J. Carr
177: Robert Milazzo/courtesy of *Soap Opera Weekly*
178: Robin Platzer/Twin Images
179: Barry Morgenstein
181: Victoria Arlak
183: Dana Belcher
184: Robert Milazzo
185: E.J. Carr
186: Barry Morgenstein
188: Barry Morgenstein
192: Robert Milazzo
193: E.J. Carr
194: E.J. Carr
195: Dana Belcher
197: Dana Belcher (both pictures)
198: Barry Morgenstein
200: Barry Morgenstein
201: (top) E.J. Carr
(bottom) Dana Belcher
202: (upper left) Bill Warnecke
204: (lower right) Victoria Arlak
206: (upper left) E.J. Carr
(upper right) E.J. Carr
(middle right) Barry Morgenstein
(bottom left) Barry Morgenstein
211: (bottom left) Victoria Arlak
211: (upper right) Victoria Arlak
(middle right) Victoria Arlak
212: (top left) Victoria Arlak
212: (middle left) Barry Morgenstein
(bottom left) Robert Milazzo
214: (upper right) E.J. Carr
216: (upper right) E.J. Carr
217: (top) Krista Tesreau private collection
(lower right) Victoria Arlak
219: (lower left) Robin Platzer/Twin Images
(lower right) Robert Milazzo
222: (upper left) Mario Ruiz
223: (upper right) Victoria Arlak
(lower right) Victoria Arlak
225: (upper right) E.J. Carr
(bottom right) E.J. Carr
226: (top) E.J. Carr
(middle right) Barry Morgenstein
(bottom right) E.J. Carr
227: Robin Platzer/Twin Images
229: (lower left) Raeanne Rubenstein
230: (lower left) E.J. Carr
(upper right) E.J. Carr

231: (top) Barry Morgenstein
(lower right) Danny Sanchez
233: E.J. Carr
234: (top) Wagner International/CBS archives
(middle left) S. Karin Epstein
(middle right) S. Karin Epstein
235: (upper right) Barry Morgenstein
(lower right) Robin Platzer/Twin Images
236: (top) Robin Platzer/Twin Images
(lower left) Donna Svennevik
237: (middle left) Victoria Arlak
(middle right) E.J. Carr
238: (top left) Barry Morgenstein
(bottom left) Barry Morgenstein
239: (upper left) E.J. Carr
(upper right) Victoria Arlak
(middle right) E.J. Carr
240: (upper left) Irv Haberman
241: (top left) Raeanne Rubenstein
(upper right) Andrew Popper
242: (bottom left) Ira Lewis
(bottom middle) Ira Lewis
(bottom right) Courtesy of *Soap Opera Weekly*
243: (top right) Courtesy of *Soap Opera Weekly*
244: (bottom left) Mario Ruiz
245: (bottom left) Mario Ruiz
247: (top center) E.J. Carr
(bottom left) E.J. Carr
248: (top left) Robin Platzer/Twin Images
(lower left) Robin Platzer/Twin Images
(lower right) Giorgio Palmisano
249: (upper right) Barry Morgenstein
(lower left) Barry Morgenstein
(middle right) Greg Weiner
251: (lower left) Mark Weiss
252: (upper left) Victoria Arlak
253: (upper left) Victoria Arlak
(middle right) Victoria Arlak
254: (top right) Victoria Arlak
(middle right) Victoria Arlak
255: (top) Victoria Arlak
(middle bottom) Barry Morgenstein
256: (top right) Robin Platzer/Twin Images
(lower left) Robin Platzer/Twin Images
258: (upper left) Robert Milazzo/courtesy of *Soap Opera Weekly*
(bottom right) E.J. Carr
259: (upper right) E.J. Carr
(middle) E.J. Carr
(lower left) E.J. Carr
(middle bottom) E.J. Carr
261: (upper right) Georg Lantosh
262: (upper left) Nora Feller
(upper right) Robin Platzer/Twin Images
(middle left) E.J. Carr
263: (third from top) Giorgio Palmisano
264: (second from top) Greg Weiner
(third from top) Barry Morgenstein

p266–276: E.J. Carr, except:
268: (top) courtesy of *Soap Opera Weekly*
269: (top row right/and second from right) Natasha Katzive
277: (top right) E.J. Carr
(bottom left) Gregory Cherin
(bottom left) E.J. Carr
281: (top) E.J. Carr
282: (top) E.J. Carr
(bottom) Greg Weiner
283: (top) E.J. Carr
(bottom) Robert Milazzo
284: (top) E.J. Carr
286: (bottom left) Scott Watters
(second from top/right) E.J. Carr
(bottom right) E.J. Carr
287: (top right) Jim Antonucci
(middle right) Victoria Arlak
(bottom right) Barry Morgenstein
289: Camera One/courtesy N.A.T.A.S.
290: (top right) E.J. Carr
(middle right) E.J. Carr
(bottom right) Ken Offricht
291: (top) E.J. Carr
(middle) Greg Weiner
(bottom) Greg Weiner
292: (top left) Emmy © The National Academy of Television Arts and Sciences
(middle bottom) John Paschal/Celebrity Photo Agency
293: (top left) Steve Trupp/Celebrity Photo Agency
(bottom left) Darleen Rubin/courtesy N.A.T.A.S.
(top right) Robert Milazzo
(middle) Robin Platzer/Twin Images
(right/second from top) Robin Platzer/Twin Images
294: (top left) Robin Platzer/Twin Images
(second from top/left) Robin Platzer/Twin Images
(bottom left) Victoria Arlak
(top right) Robin Platzer/Twin Images
(bottom right) Kimberly Butler
295: (top left) Robin Platzer/Twin Images
296: (middle) Larry Lettera/courtesy of N.A.T.A.S.
(top right) Sean Hahn
(second from top/right) Barry Morgenstein
297: (top middle) E.J. Carr
(bottom right) Robin Platzer/Twin Images

Back Cover:
Dicopoulos/Ehlers: CBS
Moniz/Grillo/Kinkead/McKinney: Greg Weiner/Barry Morgenstein
Hutchison/Deas: Greg Weiner
Gates/Zimmer: CBS
Leal/Buffinton/Erickson/Budig/Mambo: Greg Weiner/Bob Cass
Hearst/Satra/Raines/Dusay/Poser/Aleksander: Robert Milazzo/Barry Morgenstein
Garrett/Zaslow: S. Karin Epstein

Author Photo: Jim Mackiewicz